*Black Educational Choice*

# Black Educational Choice

## Assessing the Private and Public Alternatives to Traditional K–12 Public Schools

Diana T. Slaughter-Defoe, Howard C. Stevenson,
Edith G. Arrington, and Deborah J. Johnson, Editors

*Foreword by James A. Banks*

PRAEGER

AN IMPRINT OF ABC-CLIO, LLC
Santa Barbara, California • Denver, Colorado • Oxford, England

Copyright 2012 by ABC-CLIO, LLC

All rights reserved. No part of this publication may be reproduced, stored in a retrieval system, or transmitted, in any form or by any means, electronic, mechanical, photocopying, recording, or otherwise, except for the inclusion of brief quotations in a review, without prior permission in writing from the publisher.

**Library of Congress Cataloging-in-Publication Data**

Black educational choice : assessing the private and public alternatives to traditional K–12 public schools / Diana T. Slaughter-Defoe ... et al., editors.
    p. cm.
Includes bibliographical references and index.
ISBN 978–0–313–39383–9 (hardback) — ISBN 978–0–313–39384–6 (ebook)
1. African Americans—Education. 2. Alternative schools—United States. 3. Alternative education—United States. 4. Educational change—United States. 5. School choice—United States. 6. Academic achievement—United States. I. Slaughter-Defoe, Diana T.
LC2717.B56 2011
379.1′110896073—dc23       2011037272

ISBN: 978–0–313–39383–9
EISBN: 978–0–313–39384–6

16  15  14  13  12    1  2  3  4  5

This book is also available on the World Wide Web as an eBook.
Visit www.abc-clio.com for details.

Praeger
An Imprint of ABC-CLIO, LLC

ABC-CLIO, LLC
130 Cremona Drive, P.O. Box 1911
Santa Barbara, California 93116-1911

This book is printed on acid-free paper ∞

Manufactured in the United States of America

*To America's First Family—President and Mrs. Obama and their daughters and to all other African American children and their parents nationwide.*

# Contents

# Tables and Figures

# Foreword

## James A. Banks

The United States faces a national crisis because students in other nations such as South Korea, Finland, Japan, and the United Kingdom are outperforming them in math and science achievement. This is compelling evidence that the United States will be unable to meet its scientific and technical needs in the present and future unless it makes a national commitment to improve schools for the nation's most vulnerable and neglected students, such as Latino and African American youth (Darling-Hammond, 2010).

The future of the United States will be significantly shaped by the educational, social, and economic status of African American and Latino youth. These groups are the "canaries in the cold mine" in the United States because the United States' destiny is intricately tied to theirs. The scores of Asian and White students are above the Organization for Economic Cooperation and Development (OECD) average in each subject area. However, when the scores of African American and Hispanic students are added, the U.S. national average drops to the bottom of the rankings (Darling-Hammond, 2010). As students of color and English Language Learners (ELLs) become an increasingly large percent of the U.S. student population, the nation's educational destiny will become more tightly connected to the academic status and achievement of these students, most of whom are structurally excluded and marginalized within our society and schools. Their status and destiny are harbingers of the future of the United States. Thus, it is imperative that the nation creates equitable schools and narrows the significant gap in educational achievement between U.S. students and those in other developed nations.

As the grim statistics in this timely and important book indicate, the achievement gap between African Americans and Asian and White mainstream groups is wide and intractable. Schools continue to fail African American students abysmally, and—especially for African American males—schooling too often results in a "school-to-prison pipeline." African American parents and communities are painfully aware of the ways in which too many of their children are receiving a substandard education and are often marginalized even in high-achieving, predominantly White middle-class schools. That is why they are seeking alternatives to regular public schools in unprecedented numbers. The percentage of African American students attending alternative public or nonpublic schools increased from 23 percent in 1993 to 32 percent in 2003 and 2007.

However, as the incisive and well-researched chapters in this book indicate, the quality and range of alternative schools are diverse and complex, and African American parents and students will not necessarily find "superman" and academic utopias in them. This book provides empirical evidence —from both quantitative and qualitative studies—of the effects of alternative private and public schools from the perspectives of students, teachers, and parents. Alternative schools, the authors of the chapters in this book conclude, have both strengths and weaknesses. The rich theoretical and empirical insights in this book will help all of the stakeholders in the education of African American youth to make thoughtful and informed decisions about private and public alternatives to traditional K–12 public schools. I hope it will also help readers to deepen their commitment to traditional public schools and to understand why it is not possible for alternative schools to reach beyond the grasp of the social, economic, and political context in which they are embedded, and that we need excellent traditional public schools within a democratic society in order to construct equitable alternative schools and choices for the nation's most vulnerable citizens. Excellent traditional K–12 public schools as well as excellent public and private alternative schools are also needed to prepare all citizens to function effectively in a democratic and just society (Banks, 2007). Educational researchers, practitioners, and policy makers should be indebted to Professor Diana T. Slaughter-Defoe and her colleagues, Professors Howard Stevenson and Deborah Johnson and Dr. Edith Arrington, for creating this informative, engaging, and needed book. I hope it will attain the wide readership it deserves.

## REFERENCES

Banks, J. A. (2007). *Educating citizens in a multicultural society* (2nd ed.). New York: Teachers College Press.

Darling-Hammond, L. (2010). *The flat world and education: How America's commitment to equity will determine our future*. New York: Teachers College Press.

# Preface and Acknowledgments

Originally, editors intended to simply update the 1988 volume, *Visible Now: Blacks in private schools*, edited by Slaughter-Defoe was Slaughter then! and Johnson. However, when we (Slaughter-Defoe, Stevenson, Arrington) began our research for the volume and discussed, over the summer and fall 2009, what we were finding, we became cognizant that our earlier perspective had to broaden to consider: (a) newer, non-traditional settings in which significant numbers of Black elementary and secondary students are being educated today (e.g., charter schools); (b) in-depth knowledge, partly resulting from both theoretical and methodological advances, now available about Black students' cross-racial experiences in both these school settings; and (c) the implications for parental empowerment and family engagement, as well as (d) Black students' adaptive and optimal personal-social development as well as academic achievement.

In this volume, we present the voices of the students, as well as the voices of parents and administrators. We have interdisciplinary and inter-ethnic, together with interracial, perspectives on the contemporary issues confronting Black students and their parents. And finally, thanks to the rigor of graduate selection and training, we have the engagement of many more graduate student perspectives in several chapters.

Today, Black families, and families generally, are exploring school choices for their children, inclusive of the benefits and challenges of their educational options or choices. *Black Educational Choice* presents research on non-traditional African American school choices and the stories of the children's experiences with race across schools from interdisciplinary perspectives. The factors identified through research reported in this volume are important to consider first in making the choices, and second, in following up with selected schools once the choices have been made. Factors transcend school type and even mission. They include, for example, parental involvement and empowerment, school racial composition, and opportunities for esteem-building and enhancement within school settings.

The book is organized around a series of 20 chapters in 4 parts. After an introductory chapter, four parts are introduced with educational research and thematic content presented in each part. Each part is reflective of prevalent educational choices, including related benefits and challenges, experienced by African American families who made a non-traditional alternative school choice.

In the Graduate School of Education at the University of Pennsylvania, two persons assisted us in bringing this volume to fruition: Savannah Shange and Krystal Anderson. Savannah shared with Krystal an extraordinary commitment, reliability, dependability, and contributing spirit throughout our work.

Savannah is a Fontaine Fellow pursuing a joint doctoral degree in Africana Studies and Education at the University of Pennsylvania. From the project's inception, she brought her background in independent schools, her fluid and honed writing gifts, and her experience with processes associated with book publishing to the team. Formerly an advisee of both Drs. Slaughter-Defoe and Stevenson, she presently matriculates in our Education, Culture, and Society Program.

Krystal was a graduate student in our Reading, Writing, and Literacy Program, who completed her degree in spring 2011. She served as a part-time administrative assistant to this project throughout the editorial process, beginning almost immediately after we received the ABC-CLIO contract. Krystal's careful, thoughtful, and orderly approach to this project made it possible to keep track of the efforts and contributions of 32 authors to 20 chapters across many challenging phases in a project that extended over several months.

These individuals, as well as editors and contributors to this volume, share a passion for racial justice, challenging educators, researchers, policymakers, and parent leaders to adapt to current diversification of educational choice among African American families.

Throughout the process, our team has felt encouraged and supported by ABC-CLIO because of the always timely and wise counsel of both senior editors, first Robert Hutchinson, and later, as we entered the editorial process, Valentina Tursini. Thanks to the nurturance and care of our editors we essentially had a trouble- and hassle-free editorial process. We thank you both for being the consummate professionals you obviously are.

Diana T. Slaughter-Defoe
Howard C. Stevenson
Edith G. Arrington
Deborah J. Johnson

# Introduction: Towards Black Educational Choice

*Diana T. Slaughter-Defoe, Michael J. Myers II,*
*Howard C. Stevenson, Edith G. Arrington,*
*and Deborah J. Johnson*

At this time in African American history there is a profound and deep need for information that can inform the educational choices of persons who parent and teach African American children and youth, as well as for the youth themselves. A quarter century of emphasis on standards reform initiatives in public education has not produced unequivocal benefits to African American public school students. There is considerable dissatisfaction with the supposed benefits of educational policies associated with high stakes testing, and zero-tolerance policies that seem to encourage push-out and dropout student behaviors. Not surprisingly, families are increasingly seeking and participating in available alternatives to traditional schools, many of which include independent private, parochial, and charter schools. But what does available research tell us about the strengths and challenges of the alternatives being pursued? Chapters in this volume, written by educational researchers from diverse disciplinary perspectives, address the contemporary issues surrounding the school choices of families of African American school children. Contributors to this volume have carefully reviewed and conducted studies, both quantitative and qualitative, in desegregated private school settings, contemporary charter schools, or parochial schools. The consequences of the school choices of families, charged with the education of their biological or adoptive African American children, are examined from the perspectives and attitudes of the participating youth, their peers, their parents, and their school faculty.

## BACKGROUND

*Visible Now: Blacks in private schools*, edited in 1988 by two of the current editors, Slaughter and Johnson, focused on two broad questions: First, why were Black parents sending their children to private schools in the 1980s, and second, what were the experiences of the attending children? The book reported research on these broad topics through that time period, with contributors acknowledging an increase in the percentages of African American children attending non-public schools since even before the 1983 *Nation at Risk* report. The present volume continues to focus on the results of parental and family educational choice, but emphasizes research conducted since the 1990s, including follow-up research at some of the same private schools, as well as newer studies that address African American children's schooling experiences in both the school types originally depicted in *Visible Now* and other contemporary alternatives to neighborhood public schools.

Together, these educational choice patterns can be viewed as contemporary initiatives attempting to address identified problems and critiques of tax-free public and neighborhood schools that African American families prefer to avoid by choosing against them. The specific researches and reviews of research included in the chapters of this volume identify the strengths and challenges of the parental educational choice patterns. Families expect the newer K–12 initiatives to be improved and enhanced "pipelines" to higher education. However, how effective are these educational initiatives and related school choices for African Americans today? Today's African American families are choosing charter schools and other alternatives to traditional public schools more than ever. What have been the experiences of children and their families in these contexts? How are policymakers and educational administrators adapting to the increase and diversification of school choices by African Americans? We believe these venues have both strengths and challenges that chapter authors will describe and interpret. Using an overview of available research, this volume seeks to provide educators, other school support personnel, researchers, academicians, and parent leaders with the information and critical insights needed to teach, serve, and quite literally save African American children by evaluating the school choices currently pursued on their behalf.

The present volume is organized into four Parts that describe, interpret, and discuss research in each identified part: Part I: Portraits of Independent Schools and Black Children (Chapters 1 [Slaughter-Defoe], 2 [Brown], 3 [Shange and Slaughter-Defoe], 4 [Stevenson and Arrington], 5 [Arrington and Stevenson], 6 [Kuriloff, Soto, and Garver], and 7 [Johnson, Slaughter-Defoe, and Banerjee]); Part II: Understanding Parental Educational Choice for African American Children (Chapters 8 [Carlson], 9 [Wilson], and 10 [Rana et al.]); Part III: The Consequences of Choice: Educational Benefits to Children—To Communities? Special Focus on Charter Schools (Chapters 11 [Lundy-Wagner and Turner], 12 [Huerta, Fuller, Parker, and d'Entremont], 13 [Scott], 14 [Garcia and Stigler], and 15 [Franklin]). Part IV: Race and the

Contemporary Education of African American Children: Theoretical and Policy Issues (Chapters 16 [Cooper], 17 [Perez-Felkner, Hedberg, and Schneider], and 18 [Mandara , Moore, Richman, and Varner]). A concluding Chapter 19, by the Editors offers comments related to future theory, practice, and policy in reference to the development and learning of African American children.

This introduction has three goals. First, we offer some background to standards reform initiatives that cover the time period, 1989–2009, in which demographic increases in Black educational choices of alternatives to traditional public schools could be observed. Second, setting the tone and context of the volume from a demographic perspective, we briefly identify African American family patterns of school choice since the 1990s, outlining the percentages of Black children and youth participating in these types of school contexts over a similar time period, 1993 to 2007. Third, and finally, we briefly summarize current information about the Black–White academic achievement gap and focus on race- and gender-related trends that contribute to notions of the "school to prison pipeline" that we assume families seek to avoid by vigorously cultivating alternatives to neighborhood public schools.

## CONTEMPORARY HISTORICAL BACKGROUND TO STANDARDS REFORM: AN OVERVIEW

In 1983, the publication of *A Nation at Risk* (National Commission on Excellence in Education, 1983) in the United States placed the issue of educational reform at the top of the national policy agenda (Knight & Erlandson, 2003; Olson, 1998; Sanders & Horn, 1998; Holland, 2001; Education Consumers Foundation, 2008; Buddin & Zamarro, 2009). The report illustrated the lack of academic achievement among U.S. students when compared to international students. It also demonstrated the decrease in reading, science, and math scores and also the decreased scores of student performance on the Scholastic Achievement Test (SAT) exam. Issues of national security helped frame the report, and subsequently policymakers, by arguing that if a foreign country "had attempted to impose on America the mediocre educational performance . . . would [be perceived] as an act of war . . . We have, in effect, been committing an act of . . . unilateral educational disarmament" (p. 5). Recommendations were offered as to how the nation could increase the academic achievement of its pupils.

### From *A Nation at Risk* to No Child Left Behind (NCLB)

Following the release of the report, then-President George Bush, convened with the governors from all fifty states to explore the problems associated with the educational delivery system and to also create a plan for addressing stated problems. With assistance from both the White House and from experts within the field of education, the governors developed the National Education Goals 2000. These goals focused upon student citizenship; student readiness for school, school safety, graduation rates, economic productivity, and progress in the field of science. In 1991, President Bush and the federal government adopted a plan to implement these goals called America 2000. The Clinton administration later implemented the Goals 2000, which reinforced the afore-mentioned goals by implementing a more effective evaluation system (DeLacy, 1999; Hanushek & Raymond, 2005; Knight & Erlandson, 2003).

The Clinton administration continued to push the need for rigorous assessments and also passed the Improving America's Schools Act (IASA) of 1994. Under this Act, states were required to identify low-performing schools, to create assessment tools linked to the state standards for reading and math, and to track the performance of students on the state assessments. The IASA also required states to test students more frequently, with certain states assessing students at every grade level. Moreover, this Act required states to create three distinct categories of student achievement to demon-strate how its students were performing on the state's exam—below profi-cient, proficient, and advanced (Goertz & Duffy, 2003). The IASA established a foundation for the No Child Left Behind Act (NCLB).

During both the first Bush and Clinton administrations, individual states could freely determine how these goals would be attained (DeLacy, 1999; Hanushek & Raymond, 2005). Many states moved towards high-stakes testing to achieve their desired goals. In 1998, Jencks and Phillips published their edited volume on the Black–White achievement (test) gap. Within this context, fueled by the increasing attention to research about gaps in test scores between Black and White students, the No Child Left Behind Act of 2001 (NCLB) was passed. The emphasis on standards reform is occurring in an era of increasing linguistic and cultural diversity with student populations in U.S. classrooms. At the same time, the United States has increasingly relied upon standardized testing outcomes to evaluate student achievement in its schools. For example, Adequate Yearly Progress (AYP) is defined as a pre-determined percentage of students from each defined subgroup being required to score at the level deemed proficient in mathematics and language arts on each state's high-stakes test yearly (e.g., New York State's Regents Exam and Pennsylvania's PSSA exams) until 100 percent meet proficiency by 2013/2014 (NCLB Act, 2002). While the administration of President Obama has changed certain ele-ments of NCLB (e.g., all students are now required to be proficient by 2020), states are still responsible for ensuring all of their students make AYP as per student scores from each state's high-stakes exam (Causey-Bush, 2005).

### The Rise of Standards-Based Reform Initiatives

Standards aim to define what students, teachers, administrators, and states need to know and be able to do as it relates to their performance. These defined objectives intend to provide a clear understanding of instruction, assessment, and how states and programs can determine what practices are effective in achieving desired student outcomes. The two main elements of standards-based reform include the following: (a) linking the goals of the federal government to the implementation of state-level policy, and (b) linking classroom practices to state policy.

Standards-based reform seeks to increase student achievement by (a) creating and aligning ambitious standards with assessments, and by (b) holding states, districts, and schools accountable to increasing student achievement vis-à-vis rewards and sanctions. The operating assumption is that in doing so, these components will provide students with clear and high expectations and will provide schools with the autonomy to determine how to foster student achievement. Furthermore, when these components are paired with providing professional development for teachers in support of teaching to standards, and students have more time to learn, the theory holds that these concepts will all work towards motivating and preparing teachers to utilize instructional techniques that facilitate the academic success of all students (Darling-Hammond, 2000; David, Humphrey, & Young, 2001; Linn, 2000; Roscigno, Tomaskovic-Devey, & Crowley, 2006).

NCLB relies heavily upon high-stake tests to measure the efficacy of schools to produce desired student outcomes (Hanushek & Raymond, 2005; Knight & Erlandson, 2003). The federal government's passage of NCLB was in the spirit of what many states, including New York, were already doing with regards to accountability and the levying of sanctions to schools that do not meet necessary standards (e.g., graduation rates and student safety). Under NCLB however, the accountability systems have become more intrusive, comprehensive, and pervasive while also implementing harsher penalties for public schools that fail to meet NCLB mandates (Knight & Erlandson, 2003).

The policies that stem from standards-based reform focus upon increasing standardized testing, identifying "failing schools," and introducing competition to public education (Roscigno, Tomaskovic-Devey, & Crowley, 2006), while completely ignoring the embedded nature of inequality and how local disadvantages and advantages work towards producing and reproducing inequality. This oversight is extremely problematic considering that context does matter because it invariably shapes the child's socialization and relations with peers, teachers, and family members (Slaughter-Defoe, 1995)—all of which are indicators for future educational outcomes. If context did not matter, then the fact that one out of every 10 schools in the country graduates fewer than 60 percent of its students every year, and that these schools are disproportionately in large urban schools comprised of poor African American and Latino students, would be irrelevant (The Editorial Projects in Education Research Center, 2009). However, despite the attractiveness of this model, there is *no* conclusive evidence that standards-based initiatives and high-stakes testing, in and of themselves, are effectively closing the achievement gap (Advancement Project, 2010; Amrein & Berliner, 2003a, 2003b; Causey-Bush, 2005; Braun, Wang, Jenkins, & Weinbaum, 2006; Darling-Hammond, 2000; Elmore, 2003; Figlio, 2006; Gorlewski, 2008; Heubert, 2004; Linn, 2000; Michigan State Board of Education, 1992; Roscigno, Tomaskovic-Devey, & Crowley, 2006). Simply stated, standards and tests of those standards alone will neither improve schools nor create educational opportunities where they did not previously exist (Darling-Hammond, 2000; Roscigno, Tomaskovic-Devey, & Crowley, 2006).

An assumption of this volume is that many African American parents have intuitively surmised and adopted this premise and seek other, as yet uncritically evaluated from a research perspective, educational options for their children. Next, we present the demographic trends in African American student enrollments that parallel the initiatives undertaken during the emergence of the era of standards reform.

## AFRICAN AMERICAN FAMILY PATTERNS OF SCHOOL CHOICE: 1993–2007

According to a survey report (Grady & Bielick, 2010) issued by the National Center for Education Statistics (NCES) and estimating the patterns of school choice being exercised through student enrollments:

> School choice in American education has long been available to parents with sufficient resources to send their children to private schools or move to a particular school district. Choice within the public school system did not become readily available to parents until the 1960s, however, with the advent of alternatives such as magnets (Schneider, Teske, & Marschall, 2000). Since then, the range of school choice options has expanded to include interdistrict choice plans, intradistrict choice plans, charter schools, and vouchers to attend private schools. In addition, NCLB has a public school choice provision that requires that students enrolled in a Title I school that is identified for school improvement, corrective action, or restructuring have an opportunity to attend a public school that has not been so identified. See No Child Left Behind Act of 2001, Title I, Section 1116 (b)(E). Parents may also choose to home school their children.[1] Charter schools are public schools that provide free elementary or secondary education to students under a specific charter granted by the state legislature or other appropriate authority (Hoffman 2008). A magnet school is a school designed to attract students of different racial/ethnic backgrounds or to provide an academic or social focus on a particular theme (Hoffman 2008) . . . all types of school choice options are not available in all communities. (Grady & Bielick, 2010, p. 1)

The 2010 NCES survey report built upon two earlier surveys addressing trends in the use of school choice in distinguishing between whether youth attended their assigned neighborhood public school or instead chose, presumably with the help of their families, to enroll in alternative public (typically magnet or charter) or non-public (private religious or private sectarian) schools. In 1993, 23 percent of Black youth ages 5–17 attended one of these alternatives; this figure increased to 26 percent by 1996, 29 percent by 1999, and 32 percent in both 2003 and 2007 respectively. Between 1993 and 2007, the percentage of Black youth in public assigned schools declined from 77 to 69 percent. In 2007, Black youth made up 22 percent of the overall student enrollment in public/chosen schools (charter, magnet), 9 percent in private/religious schools, and 11 percent in private/non-sectarian schools. Describing the trends, the 2010 NCES survey report noted:

> From 1993 to 2007, the percentage of students enrolled in assigned public schools decreased from 80 percent to 73 percent. The trend away from attending assigned public schools was evident for White students; *Black students* [italics ours]; non-poor students; students whose parents' highest level of education was some college or graduate or professional education; students in two-parent households; and students from all regions (East, West, Midwest, South) of the country. The trend away from attending assigned public schools was not shared by all types of students. No measurable difference was found in the percentage enrollment in assigned public schools from 1993 to 2007 for the following students: Hispanic students, near-poor and poor students, students in one-parent households, and students whose parents' highest level of education was a high school diploma or GED or less. (Grady & Bielick, 2010, p. 8)

## ESCAPING THE SCHOOL TO PRISON PIPELINE BY EMBRACING SCHOOL CHOICE

For too many youth in large numbers of African American communities, males in particular, one consequence of not being empowered to exercise school choice is to embrace, by default, what has come to be known as the "school-to-prison pipeline." The concept originated in 2007 as the "cradle-to-prison pipeline" with a report from the Children's Defense Fund (CDF). CDF has historically reported on many childhood inequalities experienced by America's youth, especially youth in poverty, and inclusive of disparate educational opportunities:

> Poor urban schools have the highest numbers of teachers who are inexperienced or do not have degrees in the subjects they teach. Eighty-six percent of Black, 83 percent of Latino and 58 percent of White fourth graders cannot read at grade level ...
>
> Black students are more likely than any other students to be in special education programs for children with mental retardation or emotional disturbance. Black and American Indian children are almost twice as likely as White children to be retained in a grade ... Black, Latino, and American Indian children are more than twice as likely as White children to drop out of school. According to the U.S. Department of Education, only 59 percent of Black and 61 percent of Latino (youth) graduated from high school on time with a regular diploma in 2006. When Black children do graduate from high school, they have a greater chance of being unemployed, and a lower chance of going to college full-time than White high school graduates. Only 48,000 Black males earn a bachelor's degree each year, but an estimated 1 in 3 Black men ages 20–29 is under correctional supervision or control. Approximately 815,000 Black males were incarcerated serving sentences in state or federal prisons or local jails at mid-year 2007. (Cradle to Prison Pipeline Campaign, February 19, 2009)

The "school-to-prison pipeline" is created and sustained by various social and educational policies that work together to "push children out of school and hasten their entry into the juvenile, and eventually the criminal, justice system, where prison is the end of the road. Historical inequities, such as seg-regated education, concentrated poverty, and racial disparities in law enforce-ment all feed the pipeline" (National Association for the Advancement of Colored People Legal Defense and Educational Fund, n.d., p. 1).

Zero-tolerance policies from the Gun-Free Schools Act of 1994 became enforced more vigorously following the Columbine High School massacre in 1999. These policies have increased the disproportionate criminalizing of Black and Latino youth behavior through the increase of police presence on school grounds and the aggressive targeting of minor interpersonal conflicts as if they might become shooting incidents (Advancement Project, 2010). Given the urgent need for equitable education of African American youth, recent emphasis on standards reform and zero-tolerance may have contrib-uted to, or at the least inadvertently precipitated, the emergence of this "school-to-prison pipeline" (Advancement Project, 2010).

The failure of the standards reform movement to effect and sustain rapid changes in the Black–White achievement gap has contributed to the urgency of the overall context in which African American families are seeking and attempting to make the best available school choices for their children. Con-sequently, today there continue to be noticeable increases in African American student enrollments in private schools. Reports are that despite increased vulnerability to school closings, parochial schools continue to serve significant numbers of children of African American families. Since the 1980s, the charter school movement has emerged. The dramatic increase in African American student enrollment in these schools seems to have occurred simul-taneously with the relative demise of the Black Independent School move-ment. And, although we could not verify this perception, it seems that increasing numbers of African American families are presently home school-ing their children.[1] We sincerely hope that the information in this volume will help these many and varied caregivers and teachers of Black children and youth to make the very best possible educational choices for their children.

## NOTE

1. Home schooling is a special category of choice exercised presently by families of approximately 2.9 percent of all U.S. children ages 5 through 17. Less than 0.8 percent of these children are Black. About 77 percent of the home-schooled children are White, but 4 percent or fewer are Black. In 2007, home-schooled children tended to be the children of better-educated two-parent families in the South (46%) or West (26%), rather than the Midwest (16%) or Northeast (13%) regions of the country. The children lived in rural (34%) or suburban (33%) communities, rather than cities (22%) or small towns (11%).

## REFERENCES

Advancement Project. (2010, January). Test, punish, and push out: How zero toler-ance and high-stakes testing funnel youth into the school-to-prison pipeline. Retrieved May, 1, 2010 from http://www.advancementproject.org

Amrein, A., & Berliner, D. (2003a). The effects of high-stakes testing on student motivation: Do high-stakes teasing policies lead to increased student motivation to learn? And do these policies lead to increased learning? *Educational Leadership 60*(5), 32–38. Retrieved from ERIC database.

Amrein, A., & Berliner, D. (2003b). The testing divide: New research on the intended and unintended impact of high-stakes testing. *Peer Review, 5*(2), 31–32. Retrieved from ERIC database.

Bruan, H.I., Wang, A., Jenkins, F., & Weinbaum, E. (2006). The Black–White achievement gap: Do state policies matter? *Education Policy Analysis Archives 14* (8). Retrieved from ERIC database.

Buddin, R., & Zamarro, G. (2009). Teacher qualifications and student achievement in urban elementary schools. *Journal of Urban Economics, 66*(1), 103–115. Retrieved from EBSCO MegaFile database.

Causey-Bush, T. (2005). Keep your eye on Texas and California: A look at testing, school reform, No Child Left Behind, and implications for students of color. *The Journal of Negro Education, 74*(4), 332–343. Retrieved from JSTOR Database.

Children's Defense Fund (2007, October 10). *America's Cradle to Prison Pipeline Report*. Washington, DC: Author. Retrived March 7, 2011 from http://www.childrensdefense.org/child-research-data-publications/data/cradle-prison-pipeline-report-2007-full-highres.html

Darling-Hammond, L. (2000, Fall). New standards and old inequalities: School reform and the education of African American students. *The Journal of Negro Education 69*(4), 263–287. Retrieved from ERIC database.

David, J.L., Humphrey, D.C., & Young, V.M. (2001, August). *When theory hits reality: Standards-based reform in urban districts*. Retrieved online from http://policyweb.sri.com/cep/publications/pewfinal.pdf. Date last reviewed May 5, 2010.

DeLacy, M. (1999). *Summary and comments on the studies produced by the Tennessee Value-Added System (TVAAS)*. Retrieved online from www.tagdpx.org. Date last reviewed February, 17, 2010.The Editorial Projects in Education Research Center. (2009, April). Closing the graduation gap: Educational and economic conditions in America's Largest cities. *Cities in Crisis 2009*. Bethesda, MD: Editorial Projects in Education, Inc.

Education Commission of the States. (2008). *State Education Governance Models*. Retrieved online from www.ecs.org. Date last viewed February, 17, 2010.

Elmore, R.F. (2003). A plea for strong practice. *Educational Leadership*, 61, 6–10.

Figlio, F.N. (2006). Testing, crime and punishment. *Journal of Public Economics. 90*, 837–851. Retrieved from ERIC database.

Goertz, M.E., & Duffy, M. (2003). Mapping the landscape of high-stakes testing and accountability programs. *Theory Into Practice, 42*(1), 4–11. Retrieved from ERIC database.

Gorlewski, J. (2008). Research for the classroom. *English Journal, 98*(2), 94–97.

Grady, S., & Bielick, S. (2010). *Trends in the Use of School Choice: 1993 to 2007* (NCES 2010-004). National Center for Education Statistics, Institute of Education Sciences, U.S. Department of Education. Washington, DC.

Hanushek, E., & Raymond, M. (2005). Does school accountability lead to improved student performance? *Journal of Policy Analysis and Management, 24*(2), 292–327. Retrieved from ERIC database.

Heubert, J.P. (2004). High-stakes testing in a changing environment: Disparate impact, opportunity to learn, and current legal protections. In S. Fuhrman &

R. Elmore, (Eds.), *Redesigning accountability systems for education* (pp. 220–242). New York: Teachers College Press.

Hoffman, L. (2008). *Numbers and Types of Public Elementary and Secondary Schools From the Common Core of Data: School Year 2006–07* (NCES 2009-304). National Center for Education Statistics, Institute of Education Sciences, U.S. Department of Education. Washington, DC. Retrieved October 29, 2008, from http://nces.ed.gov/pubs2009/2009304.pdf

Holland, R. (2001, April 1). How to build a better teacher. *Policy Review (Hoover Institution),106*, p. 37. Retrieved from EBSCO MegaFile database.

Hong, W., & Youngs, P. (2008). Does high-stakes testing increase cultural capital among low-income and racial minority students?*Education Policy Analysis Archives, 16*(6), 1–21. Retrieved from ERIC database.

Jencks, C., & Phillips, M. (1998). *The Black-White test score gap*. Washington, DC: Brookings.

Knight, S.L., & Erlandson, D.A. (2003). Harnessing complexity: A framework for analyzing school reform. *Planning and Changing. 34*(3&4), 178–196. Retrieved from ERIC database.

Linn, R.L. (2000). Assessment and accountability. *Educational Researcher, 29*, 4–16. Retrieved from ERIC database.

Michigan State Board of Education, L. (1992). *Appropriate assessment of young children*. Retrieved from ERIC database.

National Association for the Advancement of Colored People Legal Defense and Educational Fund, Inc. (N.D.), *Dismantling the school-to-prison pipeline*. Retrieved online from http://www.naacpldf.org/content/pdf/pipeline/Dismantling_the_School_to_Prison_Pipeline.pdf. Date last reviewed April 29, 2010.

National Commission on Excellence in Education. (1983). *A nation at risk: The imperative for educational reform*. Retrieved online from www.ed.gov. Date last reviewed March 21, 2010.

Olson, L. (1998). A question of value. *Education Week, 17*(35). Retrieved from EBSCO MegaFile database.

Roscigno, V.J., Tomaskovic-Dewey, D., & Crowley, M. (2006). Education and the inequalities of place. *Social Forces, 84*(4), 2112–2137. Retrieved from ERIC database.

Sanders, W.L., & Horn, S.P. (1998). Research findings from the Tennessee Value-Added Assessment System (TVAAS) database: Implications for educational evaluation and research. *Journal of Personnel Evaluation in Education, 12*(3), 247–256. Retrieved from EBSCO MegaFile database.

Schneider, M., Teske, P., & Marschall, M. (2000). *Choosing schools: Consumer choice and the quality of American schools*. Princeton, NJ: Princeton University Press.

Sharp, E.B., & Joslyn, M.R. (2008, September). Culture, segregation and tolerance in urban America. *Social Science Quarterly 89*(3), 574–593. Retrieved from ERIC database.

Slaughter, D., & Johnson, D. (Eds.) (1988). *Visible Now: Blacks in private schools*. Westport, CT: Greenwood Press.

Slaughter-Defoe, D. (1995). Revisiting the concept of socialization: Caregiving and teaching in the 90's—A personal perspective. *American Psychologist, 50*(4), 276–86. Retrieved from ERIC database.

Slaughter-Defoe, D., & Carlson, K. (1996). Young African American and Latino children in high-poverty urban schools: How they perceive school climate. *Journal of Negro Education, 65*(1), 60–70.

# PART I

. . . . . . . . . . . . . . . . . . . . . . . . . . . . . . . . . . . . . . . . . .

# Portraits of Independent Schools
# and Black Children

Before 1980, three traditions of independent education significantly influenced African American education. The first tradition, religious-based education, particularly that provided by Catholic and Lutheran schools, was (and is) very influential. A forthcoming volume by Patricia Bauch, *Catholic schools in the public interest: Past, present, and future trends* (Greenwich, CT: Information Age) is illustrative. A second tradition is represented by the continuing efforts of African Americans themselves to erect and sustain schools for their children. The philosophical orientation, academic mission, and financial status of these schools vary, but they share an emphasis on the need for educational independence and self-reliance. (See Diana Slaughter and Deborah Johnson [1988] *Visible Now: Blacks in private schools*, and Carol Lee and Diana Slaughter-Defoe Historical influences on African American education in James and Cheryl Banks' *Handbook on multicultural education* [1995 ed.] for early discussions of this school type.)

A third tradition is the attendance of African Americans at private elite schools. This tradition gained momentum during the 1960s Civil Rights Movement. Administrators in established private schools, aware of the mandate for public school desegregation, showed an early interest in desegregating their schools. By 1969, reports were published describing the experiences of African American students in some private schools. By the late 1970s, legislation supported desegregation of private schools. Part I presents research conducted in some private independent elite schools with Black youth. Since this student population is thought to be particularly competitive for college admissions and thus, targeted for leadership roles both within African American communities and American society generally, the experiences of this small group of children are highly significant. The struggle of one small but prestigious independent school across a quarter century with issues of race and racial stratification opens Part I. Collectively, chapters in Part I portray the particular challenges to Black students, their parents, school faculties, and even their peers, in the schools. Nonetheless, the children have developed effective coping strategies that are supported by their parents.

# 1

. . . . . . . . . . . . . . . . . . . . . . . . . . . . . . . . . . . . . . . .

# Negotiating Race and Class in Anderson School: 1983–1994

## Diana T. Slaughter-Defoe

## INTRODUCTION

Why do Black parents choose to send their children to predominantly White private schools, and what are the experiences of their children in these schools? In the early 1980s, Slaughter and Schneider framed these questions for the first time in the history of educational research. Anderson School was one of four private schools studied intensively from the perspective of how it addressed the concepts of race and class as mirrored in school identity. In particular, parental educational goals, school administrative leadership style, teacher class-room practice, and family engagement were studied, particularly as these themes appeared to impact, and be impacted by, race and class.

In the 1980s, Anderson School was unusual, existing as an open-education, child-centered, multiracial (50% Black), small, private alternative educational institution in Chicago, Illinois. To date, administrative school leadership at Anderson has been White and female. This chapter focuses on how Anderson's overall school leadership, including directors, teachers, parent leaders, and parents addressed race and social class issues between 1983 and 1994. In this chapter, I focus on two time periods, 1983–84, and 1994. When I address the findings of the original 1983–84 ethnographic study, and the 1994 follow-up, I link them to U.S. culture and schools as educational institutions during that time period, 1983–94. I believe the study of racially desegregated private schools must of necessity consider the meaning of racial desegregation, social and economic equity, and integration as perceived and experienced by school participants because the concepts infuse and inform educational goals and practices toward Black children. I have always believed the concepts to be integral to Black educational history within the race- and class-stratified society of the United States. Here, I argue that the leadership at Anderson, in both 1983–84 and 1994, eventually took a similar race- and class-centric perspective, but the school's identity during that time period was first infused with assimilationist, and later pluralistic, perspectives on both race and class. The educational goals of Black and White parents whose children attended Anderson mirrored their cultural backgrounds and the school into which their families had been acculturated.

In the research, three alternatives were considered with reference to parental educational choice. First, the parents may have chosen the schools in accordance with their goals. Second, the schools may have chosen students whose families' educational goals coincided with their own. A corollary would be that the children of such parents would be more likely to be retained in the schools. A third position was favored: Parents and each school, from the inception of initial inquiries about admissions, engaged in a mutual, reciprocal interactive socialization process in which the school's philosophy was gradually adopted by families, partly because of perceived academic and social benefits to their children. The mission of Anderson as articulated by this leadership would be wholly or in large part shared by constituent families with children in the school. Nonetheless, given a race- and class-stratified society, how would the Black and White parents and the predominantly White administrative leadership manage the challenges posed? I argue that changes in the views of administrative leadership over time reflect the pressures created by the significant presence of two racial groups in the parent communities.

## METHOD

### Administrator Interviews

The questions pursued by the biracial interview team in the initial 2-hour 1983 interviews (Slaughter & Schneider, 1986) addressed: (a) the respondent's educational and occupational background inclusive of future personal educational plans, how the respondent came to be recruited as director or headmaster, and a description of current administrative responsibilities; (b) the respondent's educational goals for teachers and students, including an account of the school's history and traditions; (c) the respondent's perception of how parents, teachers, and students participate and interact in the life of the school, both formally and informally, and with special attention to ethnic and racial minority participation; and finally, (d) the respondent's perceived role in the organization and management of the school, particularly in establishing and implementing school policies.

During the fall 1994 follow-up, the interview was repeated since a new administrator had been hired. A former teacher, this new administrator's 1983 teacher interview was also available. I administered the administrator and teacher interviews in 1983, and the administrator interview in 1994. During the administrator interviews, Dr. Barbara Schneider collaborated with me in 1983, and Dr. Carol Stowe collaborated with me in 1994. Administrator interviews were taped, transcribed, and reviewed for corrections by myself. In addition, Stowe and I recorded a discussion of the taped 1994 interview, which was also transcribed. All documents were available to me for purposes of drafting this chapter.

### Parent Interviews

The primary purpose of the approximately 2.5-hour parent interview was to determine why the Black families at Anderson had chosen to send their children to private school. Since both Black and White parents were studied, it was possible to determine how the reasons of the Black parents were similar to, and different from, those of a comparably chosen group of White parents. The design of the semi-structured parent interview was partly open-ended in order to assess how parents perceived or construed their experiences. Examples of questions included: What did a better education mean to the parents; how had they arrived at such a concept; what specific experiences in their own schooling and overall lives contributed to the evolution of their views; and how did their choice of school for their child relate to their perceptions of their children's future needs and lives? The parent interview had six parts. Data reported here make use of responses to child home and school socialization queries (Parts IV and V), specifically, responses to specific questionnaire items addressing race, and demographic data (Part I). Demographic data and close-ended questions helped to identify consistent themes and issues for parents; also, extensive coding of parental educational goals was conducted (Parts II-III and VI are not relevant to data discussed in this chapter.)

Trained and supervised interviewers contacted Black and White parents. To identify White parental participants, teachers at Anderson were asked to select White children observed to be friendly to the attending Black children. White parents from this list were randomly selected. At Anderson, 37 Black parents and 15 White parents of children in grades K–7 were interviewed. Also, the director was asked to identify at least three "parent leaders" for special interviews regarding their perceptions of the school's organization and management. In 1983, no African American "parent leaders" were identified at Anderson. Interviewers and interviewees were racially matched, with parent interviews being completed the spring and summer (1983) prior to the year-long classroom observations in 1983–84.

### Observations

The focus of the classroom observations was on the experiences of Black children in Anderson classrooms, and the contribution of the mission and philosophy of the school, as articulated by administrators, parents, and teachers to those experiences. During the 10-month academic year, 1983–84, I spent a total of 40 school days observing in K–8 classrooms at Anderson. When observations began in the overall study, parent, administrator, teacher, and parent leader interviews were either completed (parent, administrator) or very near completion (teacher, parent leader). Observations followed a written protocol that was consistent with the written and face-to-face consultation of George and Louise Spindler (1982, 1983).

## RESULTS

### Sociocultural Context: Anderson School—A Chicago-Based Challenge to Race and Class in American Schools

#### Background to Anderson School

Anderson School was founded in 1962. From its inception, Anderson was characterized as a progressive, independent school whose mission incorporated racial and class diversity. This study of Anderson parents, teachers, classrooms, and administrative and parent leaders was conducted 21 years after its founding. During a time when schools and school districts resisted school desegregation, African American students were enrolled in significant numbers and percentages at Anderson. In 1965, Anderson received Head Start funds for its extensive Montessori program and served poor children from its community. Anderson's commitment to scholarships for some children began when the Head Start monies stopped in the 1970s.

#### Race and Class in American Education

Although American educational history has emphasized the importance of equal educational opportunity for all individual citizens, by 1980, just before this study of Anderson School began, individual scholars (e.g., Franklin, 1978; Cheng, Brizendine, & Oakes, 1979) openly questioned whether the individual rights of majority White students should prevail over the collective interests of other racial and ethnic groups. The critique was particularly poignant and applicable to African Americans who experienced an historically acknowledged racial and class-stratified society (de Tocqueville, 1835; Myrdal, 1944; Warner, Havighurst, & Loeb, 1944).

In 1944, for example, Gunnar Myrdal pointed to the essential dilemma of modern American democracy: the Negro problem. The strong American value for individual initiative and success in the society was contradicted by racial and class barriers to opportunity. Focusing on southern educational inequalities, Myrdal summarized:

> The whole southern Negro educational structure is in a pathological state. Lack of support, low standards, and extreme dependence on the Whites make Negro education inadequate to meet the aims of citizenship, character or vocational preparation. While illiteracy is being eliminated, this is only in a formal sense-since children who are taught to read and write and do arithmetic seldom make use of these abilities. (p. 951)

According to Ravitch (1983), 10 years later in 1954, the *Brown v. Board of Education* decision supported Myrdal's conclusion: Within a democratic society, schools could not be simultaneously racially segregated and equal.

### Race in Chicago

Northern cities could not boast of more liberal attitudes and practices toward Black education than their southern counterparts. Homel (1974), for example, reported that Blacks in Chicago constituted 1.9 percent of the total population when the city of Chicago was chartered in 1837, but that the charter limited access to public education to White students. Baron (1963) stated that an ordinance passed in 1863 required Black children to attend separate public schools from White children. However, Illinois contributed no funds to educate Black children, and it was not until 1874 that the state officially admitted Blacks to public schools, about 49 years after the first free schools were authorized by the Illinois state legislature. De facto segregation of schools continued even after the Chicago Black population increased substantially between World Wars I and II. Thus, in 1964, Philip M. Hauser, chair of the Advisory Panel on Integration of the Public Schools of Chicago, stated:

> I had hoped ... that I could comment favorably on the actions taken by the board of education in the Chicago public schools. Unfortunately this is not possible ... the Negro schools, despite their greater need, have teachers with less experience and less advanced training than White schools. (Hauser, 1964, pp. 44–46)

A University of Chicago professor and Hyde Park resident, Hauser contended that the elimination of de facto segregation was a moral and legal imperative if the city were to prosper and the United States was to continue to live up to its democratic creed, thus justifying its leadership of the free world.

Despite the obvious economic and social advantages of northern urban life, the Chicagoan Black community was undoubtedly resentful of the historic treatment experienced in relationship to the "free" public schools attended by its children and youth. Further, racially isolated or segregated schools were perceived to be associated with social and economic deprivations (e.g., family and school poverty, low academic standards, ineffective and incompetent teachers, and substandard physical facilities) that were linked to children's academic failures.

### Leadership Style and School Identity: Race at Anderson School in the Early 1980s

Prior to the 1970s, research on race and the development of African American children usually stressed the goal of no difference between Black and White people. When the Clarks found young African American children positively evaluated and preferred Black dolls less often, compared to the responses of White children to White dolls, their data were used to buttress the hypothesis of developing self-hatred on the part of African American children who were believed to strongly prefer to be White (Clark & Clark, 1939, 1940, 1947). Ultimately, racial desegregation in schools and classrooms was posited as the remedy for these feelings.

Although what has become known as the "assimilation" paradigm still prevailed (Slaughter & McWorter, 1985), by the mid-1980s, a series of important empirical study findings (Slaughter-Defoe, Johnson, & Spencer, 2009) cast doubt upon the presumed correlation between Black children's racial attitudes and preferences and their self-esteem, and particularly in reference to children's self-concept of academic ability. For example, Spencer's early 1980s research (summarized and extended in Spencer, 2006a, 2006b) demonstrated that children's esteem levels were not correlated with their levels of racial awareness, racial attitudes, or preferences. Furthermore, social status was implicated. Middle-income African American children were more likely to demonstrate favorable patterns of pro-Black bias in racial attitudes and preferences than lower-income African American children. In both income groups, between the ages of 3 and 9, reference group orientation primarily developed from a pro-White to a "no-preference" category. Predictably, measures of racial awareness, racial attitudes, and racial preferences were correlated with measures of social cognition (awareness of real world relations). However, measures of self-esteem and of these racial variables were not significantly correlated.

### 1984 Anderson Parental Perspectives on Racial Identity and Classroom Practice

Black and White parents at Anderson in the 1980s, as well as school administrators, knew little about such studies, and continued to believe that the valued perspective to affirm was no essential differences between Black and White children or their families. Members of both groups were to be perceived by those concerned with social justice as equally worthy of social and economic advantages, to be desirous of both ending racial segregation, and of progressing toward racial integration for the sake of their children and their children's children.

Contrasting the Black and White parents at Anderson in 1983, the director stated during an interview with myself and Dr. Barbara Schneider:

> The White parents who come here are people with options . . . and they are pretty confident and secure that their kids are going to make it . . . Our Black parents who come here haven't had those advantages. And, they are not so sure. They know what a struggle it was for them (and) there aren't very many Harvard graduates among them . . . by golly, they want to be sure that their kids . . . not only to the extent success can be assured, but they surely don't want anything to be a roadblock. And a school that doesn't teach reading well and

doesn't send the kids on to quality schools is not a school they want to see their kids in. And I don't blame them.

Later, when asked whether she believed Anderson is an ethnically and racially integrated school, the director responded:

Not as much as it should be... Our board is underrepresented by Blacks. Our faculty is underrepresented by Blacks... I feel the children group together sometimes by color. How much of this we could do something about and how much of this is inherent in the society right now, I am not sure... we do a better job than other schools. But that doesn't mean we should rest on our laurels.

Observations are that both the school administrator and the White parents had so bought into the "assimilation" paradigm that they viewed desegregation as an end goal, whereas Black parents perceived it as a strategy to relieve their children of the burdens of racial desegregation. The different conceptual paths could have led to different expectations or hopes of Anderson School for Black and White parents, though it is possible that most Black parents "tabled" any such expectations at the time for the perceived future academic gains for their children as a consequence of attending Anderson, and for the experience of genuine parental participation and involvement in school—a value strongly supported by Anderson from its inception.

### 1984 Anderson Faculty and Parent Leader Perceptions of Educational Goals

Anderson School could boast, due to its origins as a preschool, strong parental involvement, not simply from the perspective of participation, but also from the vantage point of parental governance. In 1983–84, Anderson proudly continued to pursue socioeconomic, cultural, and racial diversity among its students; 25 percent of the faculty shared the school's early history, reflecting varied perspectives.

Faculty and parent leaders were in unanimous agreement that an ethnically and racially integrated school is beneficial for all children and that Anderson should exploit the opportunity to expose its children to the contributions of different peoples to the United States and to the world. One White teacher whose child attended Anderson stated: "I thought it was very important for my child to have an early experience with an authority figure who is Black."

The director also had a view which elaborated benefits to White children. When asked what effect attending a more ethnically diverse school has on the quality of education, she commented:

To the extent that education means what your life is all about, your understandings, your awareness, your sympathy, an enormous amount... We brought up four children here (i.e., in the community in which the school was located)... we did so in spite of the high cost of private education and frequent loss of bicycles and pennies (so) we would not live in a lily-white suburb. And I just feel that preparing your children for the world to come, I don't mean heaven, I mean the place they are going to live in ... the only way you are going to have racial equality is if you have people who are going to live together. Work together. To find out the rotten people as well as the good. I think it is very easy for people living out ... to idealize the racial relations. They don't have to deal with naughty people as well as nice people every day. I want my children to particularize.

### 1984 Parent Leader Perspectives of Race at Anderson

The three parent leaders generally echoed these sentiments. With respect to certain aspects of curriculum, however, one felt: "(The) emphasis on Black is overdone ... (They) bend over backwards ... No exposure to White's culture, history ... (but we) would rather have (our child) there than in some rich, snotty suburb." A second leader felt the emphasis appropriate for supporting the Black child's esteem as a Black person because the general society is less prone to be supportive of them than for White children. However, the third parent leader preferred leaving discussion of Black and minority issues in school curriculum to others because: "I'm not a minority so I don't think about these things ... I have no objection to it being done in the school ... and it is being done at Anderson ... we don't object to Black history." Earlier in the interview this parent commented: "When choosing the school I was impressed with (the) social diversity of (the) school ... percentage of minority people (being) high. We try to maintain diversity by giving scholarships ... (Our school) Works like public schools should work in terms of integration."

The identified parent leaders at Anderson were White. From their comments, as well as those of the director, the parents clearly perceived themselves as having the economic option to live elsewhere in the suburbs than in the racially desegregated Chicago community in which they resided. In the 1980s, these options were not as readily available to the Black parents.

Ten of the 14 other White parents interviewed at Anderson were categorized as possessing *Humanistic* educational goals, as were 9 of the 22 Black parents interviewed. Of six key elements in the *Humanistic* response pattern, the first is that the parents want their children to learn in an environment that is pleasant, joyful, and relatively noncompetitive. They judged the goodness of a school according to whether children are both academically productive and happy within it, and they felt very competent to make such judgments. The second feature of a *Humanistic* response pattern is that the parents stressed the importance of teachers who create an atmosphere that fosters children's curiosity, creativity, and problem-solving skills as necessary components of the learning process. The parents expected parents and teachers to have open, close relationships, and frequent communications about each child's welfare and development. Small classes, individualized instruction, and the significance of the school to the child's personal-social development are stressed, as is the absence of excessive bureaucratic constraints.

### 1984 Black Parental Educational Perspectives at Anderson

However, significant numbers of Black parents at Anderson also endorsed *Authoritative* (27.3% versus 6.7% of the White parents) and especially, *Deliberate* (31.8% versus 20%) educational goals. Specifically, the first key element (of six) of *Authoritative* parents, as defined in the study was that the parent reached the decision to send their child to a school after a very systematic investigation of alternative options, primarily because they see themselves as being very responsible for the quality of their child's education, both inside and outside of school. Somewhat in contrast, the first key element (of five) of *Deliberate* parents, again as defined in the study, was that the parent believed good teachers to be absolutely essential for children to learn. Because the parents firmly believe that children cannot learn without good teachers, the hallmark of an excellent school is excellent teaching. In short, parents are not educators, teachers are. These parents emphasized that a good school provides training in interpersonal communication, organization, and generally, social skills. Success in school, and in life, requires exposure to such training that, in turn, builds self-confidence. The parents openly expressed dissatisfaction with the poor quality of education they experienced at similar ages and were determined to achieve a better education for their children.

Fundamentally, the *Deliberate* educational goal category endorses a teacher-centered approach to curriculum delivery, a perspective quite oppositional to the dominant philosophical bent of Anderson School in 1980. Therefore, data indicated that greater numbers of Black, than White, parents at Anderson were probably compromising receipt of preferred educational environments in the service of other goals and aims. I believe an important goal for the Black parents at Anderson was the opportunity for their children to experience an education with children perceived to be of other races, cultures, and social backgrounds, that is, the opportunity for the children to experience cultural pluralism in schools. Further, as noted earlier, anticipated future child academic benefits, and the immediate opportunity to engage themselves in school governance were also probably important attractions to Black families.

Importantly, White parents reported that diversity was not important to quality education, stressing that all children learned in school that there were no essential racial or cultural differences between Blacks and Whites.[1] In contrast, significantly more Black than White parents stressed the importance of the opportunities their children had to learn about other cultural and social traditions, and particularly as a result of peer contacts in school. Both groups of parents had favorable views of integrated schools, believing this would prepare children for living and coping in a racially integrated society, and to pragmatically adapt to American society as it is and would become. For the Black parents, integration had become a perceptible strategy for the social mobility of their children into the next generation, given the burdens they perceived themselves to have experienced as a result of racially segregated education.

However, during the 1980 observations, and as a result of sociometric status data collected from the children, I learned of things the Black parents could not know. Although their children were indeed succeeding in school (based on academics and esteem data), for example, their peer status and related relationships were determined almost solely by the within race rankings received. It seemed as if Black children were learning, even in the racially desegregated school they attended, that they had to lean upon one another for genuine acceptance and social status. Further, by 1986, Black scholars had rejected assumptions that Black children could not achieve academically because of the effects of socioeconomic status on their families (e.g., Slaughter, 1969, 1977; Clark, R., 1983) and schools (e.g., Clark, K., 1965; Edmonds, 1979, 1981), or because they attended predominantly Black schools (e.g., Sowell, 1977; Woodard, 1977; Sizemore, 1983, 1984).

### Leadership Style and School Identity: Race and Class at Anderson School in 1994

At the end of the 1983 interview, Anderson's director commented on the kind of teacher she liked. Since I believe that director played a very influential role in selecting her replacement, and given that one of her teachers ultimately succeeded her, the director's perspective is of interest. Slaughter and Schneider previously reported (vol. 1, p. 386):

> Describing the kind of teacher she likes, the director comments "... one who excites children, provides them with things to think about and learn, and at the same time, listens to them and learns from them. And tailors the learning experience to them ..." She seeks to hire: "... a non-judgmental, only secure people are non-judgmental. People who are fearful are judgmental. And people who are judgmental are rotten teachers. And rotten colleagues. Because they cannot listen to either their children or their colleagues ... the quality of being able to both give and take in dialogue with anybody. Although it would be tempting to say that there are good teachers who are not good colleagues, in the end I think there aren't many people (like that)."

The appointment of the new director[2] and the rising property values in the neighborhood in which Anderson was located, were two of the most pertinent social and cultural changes that occurred between 1983 and 1994. Both changes unexpectedly impacted the school's identity with regard to race and class issues.

The new director was present during the original study in the role of teacher and assistant director. Although she preferred teaching to administration, she stated that she moved into administrative roles so that she could afford to stay at the school and maintain her own daughter's enrollment there.[3] She described herself as a product of the 1960s, preferring dialogue and collaboration to hierarchy. She grew up feeling somewhat marginalized, citing her Jewish heritage, and considered that to be one reason she found critical pedagogical theory engaging. By midlife and mid-career, it would be appropriate to also describe her as a self-identified feminist, though in her early years she embraced more traditional conceptions of femininity and womanhood. Her long tenure in school administration meant that she had been key in hiring almost every staff member. She had helped to increase the numbers of teachers of color. Not surprisingly, she was able to turn that political support base into a profitable self-study group that focused on adapting and changing the Anderson School curriculum toward multicultural social and historical perspectives.

The new director's views of curriculum were present in an earlier conversation with me in 1983, when she was still actively engaged in classroom teaching. She started the first segment of what came to be a 5-hour interview by stating:

> I tend to pick books that are about poor Black kids and they (her Anderson Black students) probably can't relate to that because most of them are not poor . . . I happened to read *Roll of Thunder, Hear My Cry*, which is a wonderful book about Black sharecroppers in Mississippi during the depression . . . and I had a group of them read *Sounder* . . . then I had a parent conference with two Black parents and at that time we were reading a book about a girl who was living up on the North Shore, like in Lake Forest, and she is in 8th grade and having a nervous breakdown. (The) Black parents reported that their son was finally reading a book that the son could relate to. He could relate to her teenage thing more than he could relate to books about Black culture. (But) that doesn't stop me from teaching it . . . I think it is because they think it (i.e., the other two books) is saying something bad about them. They feel uncomfortable with it . . . I have never been able to figure out exactly what it is. They certainly don't identify with the characters.

Educated at a small, elite mid-western coed college, the director had been part of a generation of students who questioned authority and who were determined to cut their own path in U.S. society. At that time, rather than see herself as many others undoubtedly saw her (White and educated, privileged), she instead saw herself then as she felt (Jewish and marginalized; female and occupationally and socially constrained). Therefore, it was inevitable that she would initially position herself left of the students and families served by Anderson. Specifically, to her as a teacher, social and personal responsibility had to supplement the academics and knowledge provided; reflective and critical thinking skills had to address not only the texts of study, but also the student herself:

> I see one of my jobs as teaching these kids is how to manage in the city . . . some of the kids, and the Black kids in particular are so sheltered, unbelievably sheltered. Children who are literally terrified of being out in the world . . . one's father is a police (officer) . . . and she goes nowhere without some police officer picking her up and driving her where she is going.

However, her own words during the 1994 interview also suggested that presentation of the Slaughter and Schneider (1986) research findings ultimately inspired her to embark with her teaching faculty on an intensive self-study with the goal of examining their educational practice toward the ultimate aim of building multiculturalism into the design of the school curriculum. They wanted to be more than simply a high quality educational institution from the perspective of perceptual and constructivist traditions endorsed by Montessori, Dewey, and Piaget. In addition, they wanted to also evolve into a first-rate private alternative school endorsing multicultural principles and practices in anticipation of a changing and challenging twenty-first-century world.

In the mid-1990s through to the turn of this century, Anderson School was still on this path, but the school also confronted immediate challenges posed by declining participation of White families; increased demands of the Black families for more traditional education experiences (e.g., preparation for standardized test-taking in grades 7–8 so that children would qualify for admission to the best available high schools, and more structured curricula that were less subject to the preferences of the immediate teaching faculty); and the strong demands of Black parents, including active Black board members, for the presence of more faculty of color in the school. Mature faculty members have even confronted personal, uncomfortable, even painful, experiences associated with their own racial (and other "minority status") memberships.

## SUMMARY AND CONCLUSION

In 1983–84, Anderson was unusual as a child-centered, multiracial school. The 1983 director's comments also point to race and class tensions balanced daily by faculty, parents, and children committed to minimizing racial differences between Black and White school participants. This chapter has described how the various constituents achieved this balance, inclusive of related expectations for student racial identity development and school achievement. One implication was that expectations for the development of African American identity were considered primarily the responsibility of the home environment. Also, during this era, African American perspectives on what and how children learn were undervalued. For example, a teacher commented: "Black students' parents are conscious . . . that their child has to do very well to succeed. I have felt that there is a difference when talking to Black parents—a different value system."

This chapter also described how the school leadership, including parents and parent leaders, addressed race and social class issues on individual interview questions in 1983–84. Particular focus was on African American parents' educational goals and expectations for children as perceived by all school constituents, and as contrasted with those of White parents. In summary, sharing similar social status was not sufficient to override differential, historic sources of social capital and the impingement of race among Anderson's constituents.

I concluded that the educational implication was that during that era desegregation (integration) was an end-goal for middle- and upper-income White parents in Anderson School, but it was merely a strategy or tactic for obtaining improved educational quality for the predominantly middle-income Black parents. The Black parents relished the opportunities their children had for in-school peer group social and cultural diversity. Though opinions varied, typically Blacks had pursued desegregation to rid their families of the burdens of de facto segregation, and not necessarily to achieve racial integration.

The appointment of the new director, and the rising property values in the neighborhood in which Anderson was located were two sociocultural changes that occurred between 1983 and 1994. The new director, a visionary, could see where ideas and actions connect. A risk taker, she saw and valued what was at stake, and also saw that Anderson's fiscal security supported innovative initiatives that would sustain the school, inclusive of addressing the race and class issues differently. Therefore, she became a most effective change agent. Importantly, she nurtured change agents in the student body, the teaching staff, and to a modest extent, the parent body. She diligently worked on the school curriculum and structure with the goal of what others (e.g., James and Cheryl Banks, Enid Lee) would refer to as "empowering school culture and social structure." She challenged faculty to create curriculum for Black History Month that was not defined solely as Martin Luther King and slavery, and she did not stop there. Her next step was to challenge the very concept of Black History Month, and to ask why Black history was not part of history every month in the school.

Nonetheless, anticipating the future, she reported that one of her most intransigent battles had been that against standardized testing. No matter how persuasive she was with parents, especially Black parents, they argued for the immediate goal of children who test well, over the longer-term goal of resisting principles linked to racism and classism in the larger society. In managing this issue, as with other issues, she had taken a critical stance and had invited others to join her in the process of closely examining their educational practice.

I concluded that because the director was an educational change agent who thought globally and acted locally in her long tenure at Anderson, by 1994 she had created a school where children of multi-racial backgrounds succeeded academically. Anderson may not have achieved racial integration, but it was on the path to authentic cultural pluralism and multiracial tolerance within this essentially upper-middle class urban school community.[4]

## NOTES

1. Overall, the 1983–84 study (Slaughter & Schneider, 1986) found no significant racial differences in the numbers of mothers who reported attending peer racially

desegregated schools at the ages of the study children. No more than a third of the parents in each group had this experience (32% Black; 20% White). For Black families, experience with private schooling was new, and for both Black and White families, experience with peer desegregated schooling, public or private, was relatively new. This was true of Anderson parents as well.

The views of the liberal White parents at Anderson were typical of White persons who believed, like Gordon Allport (1954), in the importance of interracial contact as a vehicle for reducing racial prejudice and stereotyping. Many White supporters of school desegregation had adopted a more utopian perspective, linking school desegregation to racial integration. Jill St. John (1974), for example, concluded a review of desegregation studies by reporting that few Black social scientists appeared to be conducting school desegregation research: "Black social scientists are conspicuously absent among researchers who measure the effects of school desegregation. This is a loss, for their contribution might well involve asking more relevant questions about the desegregation process and about its effect on students' racial identification, militancy, and political self-consciousness." (p. 7). Probably, the thrust of the desegregation studies emphasized no color differences, and consequently, the paradigm itself may have had little interest to large numbers of Black social scientists.

2. She was appointed director in 1986. At the time of the 1983 interview, this director had taught at Anderson for seven years in the middle grades and had been teaching for a total of 14 years, seven of them in a very disappointing situation in a Chicago suburban school district. Thus, by 1994, she had worked at Anderson for nearly 18 years, and had been its director for eight of those years, beginning in 1986. During this time, she primarily lived as a single parent within a mile of the school, participating as an active member of its surrounding community, while raising her daughter who attended Anderson prior to high school.

3. By the time she was appointed director, she had served as the school's assistant director, with major responsibility for admissions, and for some classroom teaching. She reported that salary would definitely not be a reason to work at Anderson. Rather, the prospective teacher would have to have a commitment to Anderson's educational philosophy; she believed that many qualified Blacks could not afford to teach for such a reduced compensation, observing in 1983 that she took "an enormous salary cut" upon coming to Anderson from the suburban public school she freely and willingly left.

4. This Chapter 1, and the ensuing Chapter 2, both focus on how Anderson's school leadership, including teachers, parents and students addressed race and social class issues across the time period, 1983–2007. However, this chapter focuses primarily on faculty and parents, and Chapter 2 focuses primarily on faculty and students.

## REFERENCES

Allport, G. (1954). *The nature of prejudice*. Cambridge, MA: Addison-Wesley.

Banks, J., & Banks, C. McGhee (Eds.). (2007). *Multicultural education: Issues and perspectives* (6th ed.). New York: Wiley & Sons. (Originally published 1985).

Baron, H. (1963). History of Chicago school segregation to 1953. *Integrated Education*, *1*(1), 17–19, 30.

Cheng, C., Brizendine, E., & Oakes, J. (1979). What is "An Equal Chance" for minority children? *Journal of Negro Education*, *48*(3), 267–287.

Clark, K. (1965). *Dark ghetto*. New York: Harper & Row.

Clark, K., & Clark, M. (1947). Racial identification and preference in Negro children. In T. Newcomb, & E. Hartley (Eds.), *Readings in social psychology* (pp. 602–611). New York, NY: Holt.

Clark, K., & Clark, M. (1940). Skin color as a factor in racial identification of Negro preschool children. *Journal of Social Psychology, 11*, 159–169.

Clark, K., & Clark, M. (1939). The development of consciousness of self and the emergence of racial identification in Negro preschool children. *Journal of Social Psychology, 10*, 591–599.

Clark, R. (1983). *Family life and school achievement*. Chicago: University of Chicago Press.

De Tocqueville, A. (1966). *Democracy in America*. New York: Harper & Row. (Originally published 1835).

Edmonds, R. (1979). Effective schools for the urban poor. *Educational Leadership, 37* (1), 15–18, 20–24.

Edmonds, R. (1981). The last obstacle to equity in education: social class. *Theory into Practice, 20*(4), 269–272.

Franklin, V.P. (1978). American values, social goals, and the desegregated school: A historical perspective. In V. P. Franklin and J. Anderson (Eds.), *New perspectives on Black educational history* (pp. 193–212). Boston: G. K. Hall & Co.

Hauser, P. (1964). Dynamic inaction in Chicago's schools. *Integrated Education*, 1(11). 44–50.

Homel, M. (1974). Race and schools in nineteenth-century Chicago. *Integrated Education*, 12(4), 39–42.

Lee, E., Menkart, D., & Okazawa-Rey, M. (Eds). (1998). *Beyond Heroes and Holidays: A Practical Guide to K–12 Anti-Racist, Multicultural Education and Staff Development*. Washington, D.C.: Network of Educators on the Americas.

Myrdal, G. (1944). *An American dilemma: The Negro problem and modern democracy*. New York: Harper & Row.

Ravitch, D. (1983). *The troubled crusade: American education, 1945–1980*. New York: Basic Books.

Sizemore, B. (1983). *An abasing anomaly: The high achieving predominantly Black elementary school*. Funded by the National Institute of Education under Grant application No. 9-001721. (Pittsburgh, PA, University of Pittsburgh). See also: Point of View, 1984, Washington, D.C.: Congressional Black Caucus Foundation, Inc., pp. 4–5.

Sizemore, B. (2008). *Walking in circles: The Black struggle for school reform*. Chicago: Third World Press.

Slaughter, D. (1969). Maternal antecedents of the academic achievement behaviors of Afro-American Head Start children. *Educational Horizons, 48*, 24–28.

Slaughter, D. (1977). Relation of early parent, teacher socialization influences to achievement orientation and self-esteem in middle childhood among low income Black children. In J. Glidewell (Ed.), *The social context of learning and development* (pp. 101–131). New York: Gardner.

Slaughter, D., & McWorter, G. (1985). Social origins and early features of the scientific study of Black American children and families. In M. Spencer, G. Brookins & W. Allen (Eds.), *Beginnings: The social and affective development of minority status children* (pp. 5–18). New York, NY: Erlbaum.

Slaughter, D., & Schneider, B. (1986, April). *Newcomers: Blacks in Private Schools*. Final report to the National Institute of Education. Volumes 1 & 2. (Contract No.

NIE-G-82-0040). Northwestern University, Evanston, IL. (ERIC Document Reproduction Service Nos. ED 274 768 and ED 274 769).

Slaughter-Defoe, D., Johnson, D., & Spencer, M. (2009). Race and child development. In R. Shweder (Ed.), *The Child: An Encyclopedic Companion* (pp. 801–806). Chicago: University of Chicago Press.

Sowell, T. (1977). Choice in education and parental responsibility. In Institute for Contemporary Studies (Ed.), *Parents, teachers and children: Prospects for choice in American education* (pp. 165–184). San Francisco: Institute for Contemporary Studies.

Spencer, M. (2006a). Phenomenology and ecological systems theory: Development of diverse groups. In W. Damon, & R. Lerner (Eds.), *Handbook of child psychology* (6th ed., vol. 15, pp. 829–893). Hoboken, NJ: John Wiley & Sons Inc.

Spencer, M., Harpalani, V., Cassidy, E., Jacobs, C., Donde, S., & Goss, T., et al. (2006b). Understanding vulnerability and resilience from a normative developmental perspective: Implications for racially and ethnically diverse youth. In D. Cicchetti, & D. Cohen (Eds.), *Developmental psychopathology*, (2nd ed., vol. 1, pp. 627–672.) Hoboken, NJ: John Wiley & Sons, Inc.

Spindler, G. (Ed.) (1982). *Doing the ethnography of schooling: Educational anthropology in action.* New York: Holt, Rinehart & Winston.

Spindler, G., & Spindler, L. (1983). Anthropologists view American culture. *Annual Review of Anthropology*, 12, 49–78.

St. John, N. (1974). *School desegregation: Outcomes for children.* New York: Wiley.

Warner, W., Havighurst, R., & Loeb, M. (1944). *Who shall be educated?* New York: Harper.

Woodard, K. (1977). An examination of a Black liberation school: The Kawaida educational and development center. *Integrated Education*, 15(2), 37–41.

· · · · · · · · · · · · · · · · · · · · · · · · · · · · · · ·

# "It's About Race . . . No, It Isn't!" Negotiating Race and Social Class: Youth Identities at Anderson School in 2005

*Enora Brown*

## INTRODUCTION

By 2005, Anderson School had accomplished what few other independent schools dared or desired to pursue. For over 45 years, school personnel and families sustained the school's mission to serve an economically and racially diverse student population and to provide progressive education for all youth. This two-pronged mission-in-practice drew African American and Latino parents to Anderson to pursue a quality education and self-affirming growth experiences for their children in a desegregated setting, as public school options withered. It also provided a welcome context for me to conduct an ethnography to examine how the identities of 7th and 8th grade middle school youth were constructed within school culture through their experiences and relationships with peers, teachers, and parents. This inquiry addresses the nuanced dynamics of race and social class, which characterize life at Anderson, pervade the relational challenges among students, educators, and parents, and have implications for present and future visions and possibilities that youth have of themselves and others.[1]

Previous research shows that schools are "official" purveyors of socio-cultural knowledge, replete with experiences that convey meanings about youth and who they will become. School policies, pedagogical practices and social interactions among students, teachers, and parents reciprocally influence their intersubjective experiences, expectations, and relationships. The internal dynamics of race, social class, linguistic diversity, ethnicity, and gender may promote social hierarchies embodied in students' views of themselves in relation to others. Daily interchanges among students and teachers may bolster or devalue these social self-dimensions (Hall, 2000; Irvine, 1990;

Luttrell, 2003) through positive or negative self-ascriptions and differential treatment by youth and adults (Brantlinger, 1993; Valenzuela, 1999). Curricular experiences and social exchanges may create race, class, and gendered meanings that inform students' social identities and life trajectories relative to peers (Anyon, 1981; Ferguson, 2001). School history, mission, policies, and explicit or tacit values of teachers, parents, and students may shape school climate, culture, and relations that reflect views about youth (Comer, 1995; Jervis, 1996). Shifts in communities' economic or racial makeup, e.g., gentrification, or national restructuring of public education, e.g., privatization and standardization, may influence local school policies and demographics (Hursh & Martina, 2003; Lipman, 2004).

This two-year critical ethnography addressed two focal research questions: (a) How do the relational dynamics of the school's culture frame the present and projected identities of 7th and 8th grade youth in a changing context? (b) How are race and social class being negotiated at Anderson in 2005? Data included critical discourse analyses and thematic triangulation of classroom observation fieldnotes, weekly videotaped student focus groups, audiotaped interviews with students, teachers, parents, and administrators. Seven focus groups, composed of 4–6 self-selected friends, resulted in two groups of Black girls, and one group each of White girls, White boys, Black boys, Boys of Color (Black, Biracial, Latino, Asian), and Girls of Color (Black, Biracial, Latina). Uniquely, this study privileges youth voices, situating their self-constructions within their convergent relationships. It is guided by ecological systems and *critical social constructivist views* (Bronfenbrenner, 1979; Elliott, 2001; Erikson, 1968; Hall, 1997), positing that meanings about the self and identity that are co-constructed within multiply embedded contexts and dynamic relationships. Close, proximal, interpersonal relations (family and peers) *and* distal, structural, societal relations (institutional hierarchies) mutually inform individuals' self-other perceptions, their intersubjectivities and social interactions. Elliott (2001) states, "the self is actively constructed through engagement with other people and the wider world ... social processes are internal to the self ... and the organization of society penetrates to the emotional core of the lives of its members" (p. 48). Holland and Lave (2001) assert, "the energy of enduring struggles" around injustices are "realized in local practice" (p. 13). In this view, relationships, dominant discourses, and racial and class meanings pervade school culture and societal culture, inform policies and practices constituting school life and the ways that youth and adults reciprocally experience and create meanings about themselves and others.

An understanding of Anderson's School culture, the relational dynamics among youth and adults, and societal meanings embedded in social interactions, school policies and practices provides insights into the ways in which race and social class are addressed and inform the social identities of youth. First, I situate Anderson in its historical and social context, as a school committed to diversity and progressive education. Next, through observations and student focus groups, I explore youth identities and social hierarchies created through peer and teacher-student relationships, and related challenges that emerge for youth of color. Third, I examine how race is negotiated, through dominant discourses and forms of social resistance by youth and adults, which shape the cultural landscape and create new possibilities at Anderson.

## ANDERSON HISTORY AND SCHOOL CULTURE

### Situating Anderson School: History and Social Context

Anderson's mission is to "educate students to become creative problem-solvers, confident risk-takers, and independent lifelong learners," with "freedom to interact within a challenging environment . . . [with] knowledgeable teachers to guide them (School Handbook, 2003)." The school's philosophical commitment to progressive education undergirds its commitment to diversity, and is evident as students freely move around combined 5/6th and 7/8th grade, resource-rich, open classrooms, and as teachers promote socially and intellectually animated environs for independent projects, thought-provoking dialogue, inquiry, and synergistic cooperative learning. Anderson is a calm, welcoming place. Its classrooms feel like spaces owned, not merely inhabited by middle school youth and their teachers.

Since its inception, Anderson has been committed to "cultural and economic diversity" and "justice," e.g., by serving poor children from neighboring housing with Head Start funds. Anderson was founded amid the burgeoning civil rights movement and strong economy of the 1960s, when commitment to the social good and uplift of the poor and racially marginalized characterized national sentiment and policy, when affirmative action's race- and gender-conscious measures in education and employment were instituted to redress a history of institutionalized social inequality, when discussions about and struggles against racism, segregation, sexism, and poverty were not only cornerstones of national policy and the democratic ideal, but foundational in the local creation of Anderson School. By 2005, the national climate had changed drastically. It was infused with neoliberal policies that were eroding public education and health care, and federal commitment to the social good was being renounced and supplanted by the corporate privatization of public services, e.g., No Child Left Behind charter schools and managed health care. Democracy as social equality was being redefined as individual choice in the marketplace as individuals and families sought education, medical care, and retirement security in a rapidly changing global economy. The excision of race from the national agenda was central to this process, with anti-affirmative action legislation on the rise and the Racial Privacy Initiative (Proposition 54) proposed to ban institutions from classifying individuals by race. Color-blind ideology and a politics of resentment, were promoted to restore and protect equality for all, while they obscured social inequality, rendered invisible ideological and institutional forms of racism, and silenced opposition to the reality of discrimination (Bonilla-Silva, 2003; McCarthy, 1998). This overhaul of national policy and rollback of social reform created a different context in 2005 than existed in the 1960s when Anderson opened its doors. Pivotal questions emerge: How has Anderson been navigating this new terrain? How are race, social class, and youth identities being negotiated in a changing school context in 2005? What successes, challenges, and possibilities emerged in addressing difference and social equality at Anderson?

### School Culture: Negotiating Diversity

Since the 1980s, Anderson's stable middle- to upper-middle class population shifted from over 60 percent European-American to approximately 65 percent African American, 30 percent European American, 3 percent Latino, and 2 percent Asian and Indian. Worsening conditions in public schools due to the standardization and privatization of public education may account for the increase in African American families seeking private education for their children. In terms of faculty diversity, all of the head middle school teachers were European Americans from working- and middle-class backgrounds, and in the 5th/6th grade classrooms, one assistant teacher was African American and a new assistant teacher was East Indian. Over half of the teachers have been at Anderson for 15 to 30 years. The school administrator's commitment to diversity and progressive ideals articulated in the school mission and policy statements, fostered the search for new faculty of color, the provision of multicultural education, and opposition to high stakes tests.

The *Anderson School Handbook* advocates respect for "difference, multiple viewpoints, cultures, and values," an understanding of history and race, and an anti-bias approach to curricula. This commitment shapes virtually every aspect of school life, including core curricular study of Spanish language, Latino cultures, African American History, partnerships with South African schools, cross-cultural festivals, and student-service initiatives. Curricular efforts are complemented by faculty development initiatives, inservices on race and sexuality, parent-teacher study group responding to a racial epithet, and social justice activities, e.g., immigration march. These and other endeavors are a testament to Anderson's success in implementing broad-based multi-faceted education, sustaining a vibrant, diverse school community, and creating a unique space for youth, families and educators.

Anderson is a microcosm of society, infused with all of the relationships, perspectives, and complex dynamics that contribute to its vibrancy. As one educator astutely stated, "Diversity creates challenges." While teachers and parents are committed to and appreciate Anderson's integrated, progressive nature, the demographic shift to a predominantly African American student body generated concerns about its "limited diversity," the need for Black teachers, and the avowed social class privilege of African American students from middle and upper middle income families. A staff member said: "We can be the best African American school that we can be . . . We need to broaden the diversity of Anderson to include other racial groups. Diversity does not just mean African American." A teacher stated, "They (Blacks) have a monopoly on 'cool.' Our halls are louder than they used to be . . . louder than hallways in other independent schools."

Though diversity is endemic to Anderson, these comments embodied two emergent racial discourses: diversity means more than African American and diversity may be a problem if it is only African American. Implicit concerns of educators and some Black and White parents were "lowered standards," public perceptions of a "Black school," Anderson's economic viability, and social character. On the one hand, the increased enrollment of students of color was fulfilling Anderson's long-standing mission to have a diverse student population. On the other hand, the relative imbalance between majority African American and minority White students may have been perceived as a threat to the preservation and integrity of that long-fought for mission. However, both the administration's concerted recruitment efforts and bourgeoning gentrification that was precipitating demographic changes in surrounding communities, fostered the desired upsurge in White preprimary student enrollment in the fall of 2006, increasing the percentage of White students relative to the percentage of Black students at Anderson.

The challenge of diversity lies in negotiating difference along the lines of race, ethnicity, gender, and sexuality, including explicit and implicit expressions of past and present social inequalities, i.e., "enduring struggles" surfacing on individual, social, and institutional levels. In my early conversations with school personnel, an expression of this challenge surfaced—the problem of social groupings and certain [Black] girls' "social agenda," "popularity," and "sense of privilege." Educators said: "The 'cool kids' are disrespectful and the most popular. Aggressive, powerful kids tease others and outsiders find it hard to defend themselves." "They emphasize dress and focus on . . . cell phones, iPods, computers. They have no time to be quiet in their own heads." "Some students seem to have forgotten that they are privileged and are used to having so much." The adults' race-class coded comments were identity-markers for certain youth and indicators of the challenge of diversity. I heard the educators' frustration and genuine search for answers, but I was cautious of tacit expectations (theirs and mine) that I, as an African American woman, would or should "fix the problem."

Throughout the year, I observed middle school students in eight classrooms with nine teachers and saw their "racial" seating patterns—groups of White and biracial Asian students and groups of African American and biracial Black students, with one White boy and girl in a group with Black students. One morning, I observed what teachers referred to as the girls' "social agenda." Four African American girls, seated in adjacent desks, talked avidly, laughed together, and whisperingly caught the attention of friends nearby, while other students discussed the teacher's guide to their essay revisions. The girls' animated talk and laughter continued until the teacher approached and asked them to quiet down or choose other seats. I thought:

"This is what they mean by 'social agenda.' Why don't they just sit down and do what they're supposed to do?!" I had to process my discomfort in feeling responsible for the girls, for the race, as a Black woman, even though I knew, intellectually, that the burden of "representing the race" or being the "exception" to the essentialized identities of Black stereotypes was a function of racism. It was the flip side of Whites' symbolic privilege, the unfettered ability to "represent themselves neutrally as individuals" sans racial marking (McIntosh, 1970). However, I was perplexed. I thought: "Why is this happening here? These kids know better." As an adult marker of youth identity, the girls' "social agenda" became a thread throughout the ethnography.

## YOUTH IDENTITIES AND RELATIONAL DYNAMICS: SOCIAL HIERARCHIES AND THE RACIAL DIVIDE

The girls' "social agenda" provided a window into the dynamics of race and social class at Anderson, to understand how these middle school youth saw themselves and each other, how they saw and were seen by adults, and what social identities youth were self-authoring or others were ascribing to them in the context of their peer and student-teacher relationships. In this section, I address the first research question presented at the outset of this chapter: How do the relational dynamics of the school's culture frame the present and projected identities of 7th and 8th grade youth in a changing context? In focus group discussions, students identified rather stable peer social groups with names, e.g., Popular Group, Nerds, Smarts, Sports One & Two, and Normals, based on apparent social characteristics, outstanding behaviors, personal qualities, and interests. Their social identities and positions in the social hierarchy were recognized by youth and adults, and informed seating patterns and students' self-selected focus groups. In the first part of this section, I present youth identities and peer relations through three themes that emerged from the focus groups: (a) peer groups and racial-class hierarchies, (b) the racial divide in friendships, and (c) negotiating racial difference. In the second part, I present youth identities and student-teacher relations through two themes: (a) social hierarchies and teachers' differential treatment, and (b) impact of disciplinary bias. In Excerpts #1 and #2, a group of White girls and group of White boys address the racial divide and categorize social groups hierarchically, by race, at Anderson.

### Youth Identities and Peer Relations: Negotiating Social Hierarchies and Difference

#### Excerpt #1: Social Groups and the Racial Divide—White Girls

**Lil:**   The groups are separated by race . . . you'll see it in our classroom, like . . . I don't mean this in any racist way, but all African Americans will sit together and all the White kids will sit together . . . it's almost like there's a divider (Motions a border between two halves).

### Excerpt #2: Hierarchical Social Group and Racial Self-other Identities— White Boys

**Ivan:**     I just split people into two groups . . . um, I have in the top group [Names] . . . kind of the White group. And then we have [Names] . . . kind of the Black group. That's the easiest way to define them.

**Ollie:**     Well, yeah, that yeah, White, yeah we're very segregated.

**Paul:**     Um, OK . . . Ghet-to (laughs) . . . And wait . . . Another thing besides ghetto is people actually try to state that they're poor when they're not . . . they act like they're on welfare or something . . . [Mike] pretends he's poor.

**Ivan:**     He doesn't pretend he's poor. His parents own businesses and he wears clothes that probably cost . . . a hundred dollars.

**Paul:**     OK. OK . . .

**Ollie:**     Let's look at it another way . . . He's talking about, "In the ghet-to, man. I'm rich but I live in the ghetto . . . "
              Yeah, it's sort of prestigious for some reason not to be very wealthy . . .

In Excerpt #1, Lil demonstratively describes the racial divide, with concern that mere talk about race will be taken in a "racist way." In Excerpt #2, as the boys sort the groups, they assign meanings to the self and "the other." Ivan immediately categorizes their social groups hierarchically—the top group is White (self) and implicates the bottom rank of the Black group (the Other). Ollie confirms the social ranking, stating, "we're very segregated," and Paul explicitly identifies the Black group with the pejorative term, "ghet-to." Disparagingly, Paul describes Mike and other African Americans, as students whom he believes feign poverty by their talk and behavior. Opposing this stereotype, Ivan affirms the authenticity of Black students' race-class position. He asserts that Mike does not pretend to be poor, because his parents own businesses and his clothes are expensive. Ollie mocks African American boys' so-called speech and ghetto prestige. The boys construct hierarchical race and social class meanings, e.g., top versus ghetto, and notions of authentic versus inauthentic identities about themselves and "the other." In Excerpt #3, the boys discuss their shifting friendships and sources of the racial divide.

### Excerpt #3: Racial Divisions and Friendships—White Boys

**Ollie:**     Friendships early on are based on parents who are friends, thus, Millie's and Vonceil's parents are friends so . . . they're friends.

**Ivan:**     Uh, I disagree with that . . . my friends when I was little, my parents didn't know their parents . . . In kindergarten my two best friends were both Black . . . and now pretty much all of my friends are White. . . . I think it is kind of a shame . . . being friends with people like Mike . . . broadens my scope.

**Paul:**     Yeah, same with me . . . I was friends with Stanley . . . throughout 1st and 2nd . . . we were pretty good friends back then and then it changed dramatically . . .

**Ivan:**     I . . . assumed that racism . . . happened in school, in my generation . . . I went to a meeting, . . . looked at the parents and . . . they were completely swapped. There was a White table and a Black table . . . I don't really see teachers interacting with each other . . . I . . . only have one [Black teacher] that I have classes with.

In Excerpt #3, the White boys discuss the racial divide among peers and parallel relations among adults. Ivan laments the loss of his early friendship with Mike, a Black boy, and values how their current conversations broaden his scope. Paul notes dramatic changes after second grade. Ollie states that children's friendships are based on their parents' friendships. Ivan observes parents who sit in distinct racial groupings in meetings, teachers who seldom interact across racial lines, and the dearth of Black teachers (Tatum, 1997). The boys drew links between youth and adult relational patterns, while White girls attributed the racial divide and early loss of friends, to somewhat stable personal/familial characteristics, i.e., "personality," "upbringing." Ivan's insight that racism is not confined to youth at school, suggests that racial issues must be addressed by adults across contexts.

In Excerpt #4, African American girls address the challenges of negotiating their self-other identities along race and social class lines, based on how they talk. Their discussion of the meaning and situational appropriateness of speaking "ghetto" extends the White boys' discussion in Excerpt #2, of identities embodied in racialized top/White and bottom/"ghetto" groups. The girls describe the social function of their talk.

### Excerpt #4: Negotiating Difference: Self-other Identities, and Code-switching—Black Girls

**Mina:**   ... I hate when people say to me that I talk proper ... they say that, "well why do you talk like this ... you don't sound, um Black, you sound White" ...

**Amy:**   (Laughs) How do you sound White? I'm still trying to get over that. How do you sound White?

**Sandy:**   You talk proper or you talk ghetto ...

**Amy:**   You can speak ghetto when you're talking to your ... close friends, or, like, your family, you know. You can talk how, like, you want to talk to them, all this slang and stuff. But when you're with people you don't really know, or you're with people you're making a first impression, you don't want to give the people the first impression that you are, like, ignorant Black.

**Kelly:**   I kind of disagree ... you're just gonna speak how it feels most comfortable for you to speak ... like talking ghetto ... [S]ometimes you have to step out of your comfort zone and speak how it is appropriate to speak.

**Mina:**   At that time.

These African American girls discuss using language to negotiate difference, and ways in which others assign meaning to their identities. Mina is offended by others' depictions of her as talking "White," a racial assignation that is not her own. Amy questions what it means to "sound White." Sandy redefines their speech in social class rather than strict racial terms, by making the distinction between "proper" and "ghetto." The girls situate their intentional use of standard and non-standard dialects across varied contexts in their lives. They use "ghetto" speech with family, friends, and people with whom they are comfortable, and "proper" speech to make an impression, e.g., get a job, interact with unfamiliar people. They code-switch to create shared meaning in their talk with others, facilitate relationships across social settings, and mediate social identities ascribed to them by others.

The African American girls embrace and challenge dominant meanings ascribed to them by the White boys' pejorative use of the term "ghetto." The girls denigrate "ghetto" talk as a sign of being "ignorant Black," versus "proper" speech, which affirms the stereotypic social class- and race-based assumption that dialect reflects one's intelligence and cultural value. Conversely, they give new meaning to "ghetto" talk, as a valued "comfort zone" with familiar others and a situation-specific identity-marker. Though all dialects are complex, communicative, and rule-governed, the dominant culture arbitrarily assigns standard and nonstandard dialects, e.g., "proper" and "ghetto," with superior versus inferior value, as inherent class, race, ethnic signifiers of one's position and worth in society (Bakhtin, 1981; Gee, 2005). Though the girls are stigmatized by the inferior status assigned to their dialect, e.g., the White boys' view that African American students pretend to be poor, they define themselves through a sociolinguistic analysis of their own speech patterns. As the girls code-switch from "proper" to "ghetto" talk, they facilitate their sociocultural mobility between dominant and marginalized communities, seek equal access to the opportunity structure, and negotiate their social identities as African Americans across contexts.

The excerpts in this section highlighted peer relations, including students' social groups and hierarchies, racial divisions among them, and shifts in their friendships. They illustrate students ascribing race and class meanings to the self and "the Other," and their efforts to construct new meanings in relation to peers' and adults' views of them. Students forged and contested hierarchical social identities through word usage, e.g., "ghetto," "popular," and "smart," and language-as-social practice, e.g., code-switching and style. They generated explanations for their racialized peer groupings and the racial divide that emerged by 3rd grade, e.g., commonalities, personality, comfortable relationships, upbringing, and adult social patterns. Their efforts to understand the racial phenomena shaping their peer relations, belied nagging, unspoken questions: Why and how did this happen? What impact do these dynamics have on us? How do we deal with this reality at Anderson? They pondered these questions in similar and different ways.

Students addressed the racial divide, either as it emerged in their peer relationships or as they negotiated the ways in which others viewed them. White students discussed changes in their peer relationships, parallels between youth and adult groupings, reactions to shifts in their relative prestige at school, and their views of other youth, along race and class lines. Students of color discussed the consequences of the racial divide for them, dilemmas created by others' views of them, and their efforts to negotiate their relative social position in the school and community. They wrestled with ways to mediate others' negative views of them based on language, while embracing their communicative style and relationships with each other.

These excerpts suggest that diversity at Anderson is not merely a demographic phenomenon, but is a richly textured and fluid relational process, which can enhance the lives of all members of the school community. In schools, as in society-at-large, diversity is complicated by the range of racial perspectives, histories, and dynamics, which permeate students' friendships and interactions, peer and adult social groupings, and students' views of themselves and others. Diversity creates challenges, requiring careful observation and attention to the voices of youth. Their voices provide insights into nuanced interactions and practices that influence the educative relations and experiences of youth across dimensions of human difference. The next section focuses on student-teacher relationships and related challenges that emerged for students of color, which informed students' social identities and negotiations of race and social class at Anderson.

### Youth Identities and Student-Teacher Relations: Negotiating Difference and Social Categories

I pondered whether the "social agenda" noted by educators was "the African American girls' problem," and/or whether there were relational dynamics between these students and their teachers. The striking racial divide described by students suggested that more was going on than meets the eye within this diverse community. In this section, students discussed their differential relationships with teachers based on race, the impact of different treatment, and the implications for youth identities forged in the classroom. The boys of color in Excerpt #5 converse about social groupings and segue into talk about race and teachers' differential treatment.

### Excerpt #5: Social Groupings and Different Relationships with Teachers—Boys of Color

**Alan:** I'm in the Plain Group with like me, Nathan, Ben . . . it's just like plain rather than . . . anything.

**Van:** . . . We're not the Hypocrites . . . the Nerds . . . not the Smarts, definitely . . . I don't think we're that smart.

**All:** (Laugh)

**ME:** What makes a Smart?

**All:** Ideas! They know a lot!

**Ned:** Because they're always raising their hand in class . . . Always making other people feel stupid.

**Alan:** I define them as smart, I think sometimes [teachers do] too, sometimes . . . Like they [teachers] say the world is divided between nerds and stupid people . . .

**Van:** Like just joking . . . But they kind of mean it . . . I think we make each other's identity, like . . . um, like I may dress a certain way and people may not take me as that way and they never will . . .

**Alan:**   You can't change it . . . otherwise everybody'd be like, "Why you be acting that way?"

**Ned:**    It's too late.

**Van:**    [Smarts] . . . uh . . . I don't . . . uh . . . they never get in trouble. [Teachers] just leave them be.

**Alan:**   I think teachers like them. But, I don't think [teachers] like anyone that's quote unquote cool.

**All:**    Yeah.

**Alan:**   [They] just like, people like . . .

**Van:**    Smart, get the work done.

**Ned:**    Yeah.

**Alan:**   [They] don't, [Teachers] don't like you for who you are. [They] like you for like your work.

**Van:**    Yeah.

**Ned:**    And teachers treat them better and talk to them more. They have more conversations with them.

**Alan:**   Like actually have a real conversation with them about school. Like they'll start off the conversation with them a lot, like have a conversation about like school and then end up having a normal conversation.

**ME:**     So what group would you say [teachers] like?

**Van:**    Randy, Darren . . . oh, oh, everyone but . . .

**Ned:**    The White kids.

**All:**    (laughs; shows surprise)

**Van:**    Yeah, yeah, that's kind of right, Oh my God. Yeah, that is kind of true. (all: laugh)

In Excerpt #5, the boys of color identify challenging racial dynamics that affect them at Anderson. They identified racial social groupings and positioned themselves in the social hierarchy as "not Smarts," defined by a teacher as "nerds or stupid people." They discussed how peers see them, and how White teachers' prefer and value those who were White and "smart." They discussed their reactions to these racialized experiences—feeling "stupid" in relation to the "Smarts," who have ideas, and feeling locked into social identities ascribed to them by teachers and others, unable to change how others see them. Van states, "I think we make each others' identity." Alan's statement follows, "You can't change it," and Ned concludes, "It's too late." Their comments reflect their experience that others' views create intractable meanings about the self, which influence how teachers respond to them.

They assert that White students "never get in trouble," and are liked by teachers, while teachers dislike "cool" students, a euphemism for African American students. Most poignant are Alan's statements, "[They] don't like you for who you are. [They] like you for your work." They capture his feeling of being objectified for his work and not being valued for the person he is. His experience of teachers' preferences concur with his self-definition, as "plain . . . rather than anything." Ned astutely observes that teachers treat White students better, "talk to them more," and "have more conversations with them." Alan concurs, noting teachers' willingness to initiate conversations with White students about school, that are "real" and "end up" being "normal." Their experience converged with White boys' descriptions of differential teacher-student relations, based on race and social group. Paul stated: "[You're] normal." Ivan stated: "I'm a nerd! . . . I think teachers like nerds . . . [who] generally like teachers more also. . . . because . . . their intention in school is to grow intellectually." White boys asserted their social identities as "normal," "nerd," an elevated position in the hierarchy, embodying common interests and compatibility with White teachers. Differential relationships and intersubjective experiences between teachers and students instantiated and legitimized the relatively stable racialized student groups and hierarchical social identities of youth in the school.

As the boys of color discussed their relational differences with teachers, revelatory "Aha moments" emerged spontaneously. As Van named the students that teachers liked, Ned noted the racial configuration, "The White kids." Van concurred with surprise, "Oh my God, that's kind of right." Later in the focus group, one student stated "God, it's racist. That was the most amazing thing I've seen at Anderson." Their comments indicated that they were sharpening their reflective lens on their relational experiences, were aware of their socially positioned identities, and recognized that their revelations contradicted their expectations and the dominant discourse on race and diversity at Anderson. I sensed that these boys were as surprised as teachers, administrators, and I were by the subtle racialized incidents that occurred, and by their own incisive insights into dynamics in the classroom that informed their identities.

Students inquired directly about the role of race in teachers' disciplinary decisions or student incidents. During the White boys' conversation, Ivan says that many teachers "will even treat a White student and a Black student differently," and suggests that teachers' views of "the other" determine who is culpable, believable, blameworthy. He states, "[If] . . . a White . . . student did something and a Black student did something, they might be more likely to believe the White student . . . [If] they know that one of them did something they might assume it's the Black student." In vivo, these discriminatory incidents incurred emotions and resistance, as voiced by a group of Black girls in Excerpt #6:

### Excerpt # 6: Impact of Disciplinary Bias—Black Girls

**Mary:** I . . . get . . . annoyed . . . If I get up to go to the bathroom, . . . She acts like I'm going to set a bomb off . . . makes me feel like I want to hurt someone . . . leave . . . I retaliate.

**Ruth:** I get an attitude . . . I'll . . . get on her nerves on purpose . . . It's not . . . fair for some students.

Excerpt #6 reveals "annoyance," sadness, resentment, disconnection, results when teachers unfairly monitor the girls' commonplace requests, e.g., a bathroom visit. Teacher's distrusting and marginalizing her as "Other," incurred Mary's "bomb" analogy, withdrawal, Ruth's attitude, retaliatory desire, and my questions: Was the Black girls' "social agenda" ever retaliation against teacher bias? Were self-authored family-like relations with the girls of color group, (teachers deemed exclusionary an clique), protection amidst stigmatizing experiences?

Sometimes, students were eschewed for "racializing" classroom experiences, i.e., Race is not the issue. In one incident, I observed an African American student ask a White teacher if race had anything to do with her disciplinary decision. In response to his query, the teacher retorted, "It's never about race!" Her definitive statement was a marker, of sorts, of color-blind ideology that seemed to be circulating quietly along side of Anderson's celebratory banner of diversity. Though race was securely placed academically in Anderson's school-wide multicultural curricula, it was not always a discussable topic. The message: Race is not a legitimate topic when issues of discrimination were raised with this White teacher. While both students of color and White students articulated experiences of racial dynamics operating in the classroom, this teacher's statement disputed their experience.

## NEGOTIATING RACE AND SOCIAL CLASS AT ANDERSON

### Dominant Discourses, Social Practices of Resistance, and Identity Renegotiation

As students and educators interactively gave meaning to youth identities, students strove to make sense of their own positionalities and relational dynamics around race and social class. On the one hand, they sought to explain, justify, or resolve manifest race and class differences and inequalities at school. On the other hand, they actively resisted some of the meanings and unequal practices that they were experiencing. This section focuses on the second research question: How are race and social class being negotiated at Anderson in 2005? Focus group discussions and classroom observations revealed ways certain race and class-based identities were supported and contested by students and educators through discourse and social practice. First, I examine the dominant discourses they embraced, to manage race and class dynamics, and shifting social hierarchies and practices. Then, I highlight some thoughtful practices that teachers and students employed to resist inequality, and examine new possibilities that they created to address the complexity of diversity within Anderson School's culture.

### Dominant Discourses

Discourses are ways of representing, valuing, and positioning particular topics, people, institutions, policies. These "clusters of ideas, images, and practices" are symbolic bodies of knowledge, which embody cultural meanings, and determine what sorts of people embody certain characteristics and what related practices are considered contextually appropriate, useful and "true" for the persons, issues, or institutions being referenced (Hall, 1997; Rogers, 2004). Two dominant discourses in society, that emerged after the Civil Rights Movement and resurged with anti-Affirmative Action Movement in the 1990s, also circulated at Anderson. *Color-blind ideology* asserts that race is not relevant in social policy or institutional practices, and that individuals can choose not to see race, and to see only the person. It is reasoned that since race has no biological validity, it has no social validity in structuring societal relations. A *politics of resentment* assumes that an even playing field exists, and asserts that race conscious practices are divisive and unfairly discriminate against Whites. This notion of "reverse racism" equates prejudice, i.e., individual preformed, negative thoughts and feelings about a group, with racism, i.e., the systematic, ideological and institutional subjugation of one group by another. These discourses are productive. Both mask racism, deny social inequality, and protect White privilege and structural inequality (Frankenburg, 1997). Through language and power, they regulate conduct, construct identities, and shape beliefs and social practice.

Discourses surfaced as students discussed their experiences and changing racial dynamics at Anderson. In the White girls' conversation, Millie was unsettled by a shift in the group hierarchies, i.e., the Popular Group was primarily African American. She said: "[T]his isn't meant to be . . . racist . . . but . . . like ninety-nine percent of the people in the quote unquote popular groups are Black women." Disclaiming racism, she implied that it is unfair for Whites to be displaced as the dominant majority, and resented being repositioned from higher to lower status. Her view converges with White teachers' concerns that popular/Black students are "in control," and have a "monopoly on cool," through stylish trendsetting. Excerpts #7 and #8 present other examples of these discourses:

### Excerpt #7: Reverse Racism and Real Racism—White Boys

**Paul:**  This school is I guess pretty racist, you know . . . that is what I think.
**Ivan:**  And you also think it's more racist against White people than Black people?
**Paul:**  In the school . . . Yeah.
**Ollie:**  . . . I feel that I've always taken minority view that White people tend to be the subject of seemingly more racism than Black people attract and this is my view of course, so I'm correct (laughs).
**Ivan:**  . . . It's obvious that not everyone says like "you're Black, you can't be smart," just like no one says, "you're White, you can't be popular" but still these trends keep going . . . I kind of look around more, and I get to see that there is just as much, probably much more actually, real racism against African Americans, uh, that you may not think about it as much. It may seem natural to you, but it is there.
**Ollie:**  I am not alien to racism.

In Excerpt #7, Paul states that the school is "pretty racist." When Ivan asks whether there is more racism against Blacks or Whites at Anderson, the boys'

ensuing conversation embodies their unspoken reference to "reverse racism."
Ollie's self-proclaimed minority position that more racism exists against
Whites, positions them as victims sans privilege. Ivan counters this view, positing that there is more real racism against African Americans. He notes the
subtlety of racism, since no one vocalizes the social identities, "you're Black,
you can't be smart," "you're White, you can't be popular, but the trends continue." Ivan distinguishes between real versus unreal racism or prejudice, and
tells Ollie that real racism against African Americans is there, though he may
not think about it much. These incisive observations and conceptual distinctions indicate his view that racism, like White privilege, gets "naturalized"
and is rendered invisible. Defensively, Ollie says, "I am not alien to racism."
The boys' talk harkens the societal discourse that Whites experience "real
racism" i.e., systemic discrimination, in reverse. "Reverse racism" also
emerged as Black girls' discussed racial injustice, e.g., being followed in stores
as probable stealers. They opposed racism against anyone, agreeing that,
"Everybody has a little racism in them," e.g., Black or White jokes, but distinguished "fully racist" from "not real racism," e.g., segregation versus the
"comfort" of socializing in racial groups. In Excerpt #8, White girls discuss
their feelings about race-conscious events, racism, and homophobia at school:

### *Excerpt #8: Politics of Resentment and Color-blind Ideology—White Girls*

**Millie:** "[W]e celebrate Black History Month, . . . Martin Luther King Day . . . make
a big deal out of it . . . I've always been fine with that . . . but . . . it gets a lot of
dividing because it . . . raises some issues in society today and . . . people tend
to go closer to the things that they are. So . . . looking at . . . the past . . . that's
probably why . . . racist comments . . . will bother them a lot more than someone saying "that's so gay."

**Lil:** " . . . [O]ur teacher said, " . . . I really don't think there should be Black
History Month . . . we're all Americans . . . It doesn't matter anymore." It's an
extremely important part of our history . . . everybody knows it. It's definitely
not as bad as it used to be . . . we're all Americans.

In Excerpt #8, a politics of resentment and color-blind ideology emerge, as
the White girls discuss their concerns about Black holidays. While Millie "has
always been fine" with the celebrations, her disclaimer is that they
foster racial division, raise societal issues, and promote Blacks' greater
opposition to racism than homophobia, e.g., "That's so gay." Her view,
a "politics of resentment" implies that marginalized groups, not racism,
foster "a lot of dividing," and that race-conscious measures, e.g., Black History, are unfair to Whites. Lil embraces her teacher's opposition to Black History Month, under the ideological banner, "We're all Americans," "It doesn't
matter anymore," "It's not as bad as it used to be," alluding to an all-
encompassing national unity that erases difference, denies social inequality,
and embraces colorblindness. The girls seemed uncomfortable when

reminded of the history of privilege and racism made visible during Black History Month and Martin Luther King Day.

Obscuring social inequality, these dominant discourses provided one way to explain, negotiate, or resolve the racial dynamics and tensions experienced. They informed what students considered fair and appropriate school practices, e.g., real vs. "reverse" racism, Black and White jokes, race-conscious holidays, and framed their racialized identities and social hierarchies. While Anderson's school climate provided a context for these dominant discourses to emerge among teachers and students, the school culture also engendered social resistance to discrimination and social inequality. The next section reveals forms of student resistance that challenged these discourses and provided alternative ways to address Anderson's racial dynamics.

### A Culture of Dialogue and Student Resistance: Renegotiating Identities and Social Positions

Students were able to interrogate bias in the classroom and renegotiate social identities, in the culture of dialogue and inquiry promoted by teachers. Though some teachers avoided racial issues, others made pivotal on-the-spot decisions in the classroom, which created a healthy climate for thoughtful inquiry and resistance—for students to address race and class, examine equality in school and society, and explore new meanings about their own and others' identities. In one reading class, students discussed probable rationale for the NBA's proposed dress code, based on a newspaper article, "NBA Makeover." Race became a central issue. Despite the teacher's vocal reservation, "I think this is really provocative. It may not have been the best thing to read," she allowed for an open discussion. She decided to deal with her immediate discomfort, conveying the pedagogical message: In this classroom, the challenging issue of race is a discussable and manageable topic. Students may wrestle with their own and others' viewpoints, within and across racial lines, and can understand themselves and others.

Some students argued that the new dress code implied that, "something is wrong with Black culture . . . it's not civilized" to wear "chains, sunglasses," "do rags," nor "appropriate for kids to see idols dressed this way." They felt that the so-called "professional dress" was designed to "clean up" the League, "so players don't look like they are from the 'hood,'" to provide a "new image for kids" and recruit European players. Students of color and White students deemed the dress code racist: "If they were White, they wouldn't do this." "See how they ban some things and not others . . . how racism is." Students marked and debated racial discrimination embedded in the NBA's targeting particular cultural dress styles. When the teacher ended the discussion, asking, "Would anyone prefer to read?," some students left. Darren, a White student, shifted from the article discussion to their own racial dynamics, asking, "Did anyone notice what just happened?" Ivan, another remaining White student said, "All the White people left." The teacher had created a space for fluid,

honest dialogue about racial assumptions that would go unexamined in a classroom thwarting such discussions. The students' keen observations, willingness
to speak, and rich dialogue occurred in a conducive, teacher-facilitated climate,
engaging inquiry, and attuned pedagogical practice.

In this context, students' resisted current racial practices at Anderson in
direct and subtle ways. They were explicit about race and classroom dynamics, e.g., seating patterns, queried instances that seemed discriminatory, e.g.,
teachers' disciplinary decisions, and challenged discourses that reproduced
inequality at school, e.g., "real racism." Their actions rendered their own
and others' practices visible, discouraged reoccurrences, and defined race as
a discussable topic. Students also employed unique, subtle forms of resistance. They examined their perceptions of teachers' biased behavioral reper-
toires through a student experiment, and renegotiated their social identities
and positions in the school through the exercise of social power.

White and Black 7th/8th grade students conducted an experiment to cor-
roborate their experiences of differential treatment from teachers. A White
and a Black student agreed to leave the room or change seats, to see how
the teacher would respond. If a teacher responded the same to both students,
they concluded that the teacher was fair and did not make decisions based on
race. If a teacher did not respond the same, this confirmed students' hypothesis that a teacher was biased and made decisions based on race. Both African
American and White students observed that teachers responded differently to
the students. White students were not admonished for being out of place;
Black students were stopped and told to return to their seats. Their findings
confirmed their experiences of inequality in the classroom (Excerpts #5 and
#6). Their experiment was an innovative effort to interrogate and oppose bias
and racialized meanings ascribed to their identities.

At Anderson, students used social power to influence others in accessible
arenas, e.g., dress, sports, and popularity, and forge new meanings and positional identities for themselves and others. Black girls described this societal
dynamic while discussing slavery and coping with racism. They recount that
slaves "on the bottom of the food chain," lost "control of [their] identity,"
and assert that African Americans are moving to "the top," emulated by everybody through sports, music, and fashion. The girls suggest that accessing these
social venues complements Black's ongoing efforts to transcend designated
social positions and stereotypic identities. In Excerpt #9, the White boys explicate social power at Anderson.

### *Excerpt #9: Negotiating Relationships and Social Power—White Boys*

**Ivan:**    You don't think that there's any case in which Damen [Black student] would
        have more power?

**Ollie:**    If I were in the same clique as Damen, he might hold power over me … It's
        very easy to identify things within a clique where it's nearly impossible to
        identify one person in one clique is more powerful or less powerful than
        someone in another clique.

**Ivan:**   What if the whole class was . . . locked in a room and you needed to find a way to get out . . . [Y]ou needed to find tools in the classroom. You don't think that Damen would have more . . . ability . . . more power . . . social power to rally the class together and systematically open that door than you?

**Paul:**   Yeah, Damen would . . .

**Ollie:**   Yeah, but that's not social power.

**Ivan:**   Rallying the class together is not social power? . . . What is social power?

**Ollie:**   The capacity to influence other people on a decision within a clique.

**Ivan:**   What about out of a clique, what about the entire classroom? That has nothing to do with social power? . . . it shows that he can control people and people will listen to him . . . it has to do with reputation. I think Damen would have very good luck opening that door compared to Ollie or me . . . or Jody . . . [White students]

In Excerpt #9, the boys conceptualize *social power* as the ability of certain students to influence others. Ivan states that an African American student has greater social power, by his ability to rally the class to open the door, than White students. Ollie resists the idea of being repositioned, by distinguishing between social power inside versus outside of a clique, e.g., students are valued differently across racial groups. Ivan and Paul argue that Damen would have more social power across the entire class. Their explicit reference to Black "social power" and implicit reference to White "intellectual power" hearkens back to their earlier conversations about "popular" and "smart" racialized hierarchical groupings. They explicate the particular form of power or influence, e.g., popularity, which African American students may have in this classroom. As African American girls suggested, "influencing"/social power may embody the struggle for youth to give new meaning to themselves and others, to resist differential treatment, and to reposition themselves in the racial hierarchy. The words of these Black girls and White boys indicate their intersubjective experience of race, identity, and power relations at Anderson.

## CONCLUSION: DIVERSITY AS A DYNAMIC PROCESS OF NEGOTIATION TOWARDS EQUALITY

As of 2005, Anderson School had navigated a 25-year-long history of diversity at the school, documentation of which began in the early 1980s (Slaughter & Johnson, 1988; Slaughter & Schneider, 1986). The studies celebrate the unique history, mission, and structure of an independent school committed to the principles of progressive education and to cultural and economic diversity and "justice." They document some of the determined efforts of teachers, students, and parents to realize these goals in their curricula, school activities, student population, and school culture, amid a changing national climate that was increasingly rolling back social reform for the social good. Through focus groups, observations, and interviews, this chapter addresses the "challenges of diversity," examines the relational dynamics within the school's culture that frame the social identities of middle school youth, and considers ways in which race and social class are negotiated in the twenty-first-century climate.

The words, views, insights, practices, experiences, and social actions of students and educators in this ethnography illustrate that diversity is not just, but more than, a demographic. The attainment of diversity is also a dynamic process of daily interactions and relationships, through which difference and equality are negotiated in school and society. This chapter addresses challenges and triumphs that accompany a committed effort to create a diverse community. These challenges emerged in teachers' concerns about African American "girls' social agenda," in students' experiences and reactions to peer and adult social groups, to hierarchies and racial divide in the school, and in their feelings about racial shifts in their friendships from preschool to middle school. Though intellectually valued by teachers, White students' grappled with their relative social position and power as Anderson became increasingly African American, e.g., "Who experiences more "real" racism?" Negotiating difference, students of color wrestled with reframing their racialized, positional identities, e.g., "How do you sound White?"

This chapter examines youth identities within peer and teacher-student relations, capturing racial, class-based individual and group social identities constructed by students with classmates and adults, e.g., "ghetto," "smart," "top," "bottom," and shared euphemisms used in their discourse, signifying the racial self and other, e.g., "popular," "social agenda," "cool," "nerd," and "normal." Students' revealed discerning experiences of and revelatory reactions to unequal, racialized relationships with teachers, i.e., "[Teachers] treat them [Whites] better." Disproportionate communication and biased disciplinary practices caused youth of color to feel locked into objectified social identities, i.e., "You can't change it," "Teachers like you for your work," and to experience anger, sadness, withdrawal, resentment, i.e., "I retaliate."

Finally, this chapter addresses two dominant societal discourses, color-blindness and politics of resentment, that circulated amidst Anderson's overarching discourse of diversity, and ways that students and educators embraced and resisted. Color-blindness surfaced in a White teacher's response, "It's never about race," a politics of resentment emerged in White students' and teachers' reactions to African American students' "popularity," and White and Black students wrestled with the notion of "reverse racism." As students interactively constructed meanings about themselves and others, and considered the relational dynamics at Anderson, these discursive rationale emerged, obscuring bias and promoting racialized social hierarchies in the school. Simultaneously, students and educators generated interactions, which countered these dominant discourses. Teachers fostered a classroom culture of dialogue and inquiry around race and other social issues, creating a conducive climate for students to pose challenging questions, make astute observations, and explore innovative change strategies. Students interrogated racism and White privilege, negotiated new social identities, and promoted equality at Anderson, through direct queries into bias and debate, classroom experiment, and assertions of social versus intellectual power. Teachers' practices illustrate the enriching role of teacher-student relationships in intellectual and personal development, and the power of fostering students' ability to engage new ideas and ways of being in school and society to address "enduring struggles."

This ethnography indicates that the racial and social class dynamics operating within this independent, diverse, unique school culture, are complex, subtle, and obvious. Anderson's demographic composition and relational culture of diversity created both trials and triumphs. Students and educators negotiated them with committed ethical resolve and ambivalent resistance, persistent inquiry and cursory review, with deep emotion and mild reserve, and animated vocality and still silence, as they navigated the non-linear paths of difference towards equal educational and personal experiences for all youth. The possibilities and challenges that constitute the rich mosaic of life at Anderson in the twenty-first century, not surprisingly, mirror those operating in society at the level of discourse, policy, and social practice.

Through the voices and interactions of students and educators at Anderson, this study illustrates the importance of conversing with youth and addressing issues of difference openly. Invaluable insights into youth experiences, perspectives, and feelings, developed into power dynamics of race and class that inform youth identity construction in schools. Students' voices offer ways to rethink our views of youth, misbehavior, and group dynamics, exemplified by the African American girls and White boys intersubjective experience of "social power." Reexamining the Black girls "social-agenda," initially identified as "a problem," may reveal efforts by students of color to resist inequality, to renegotiate their racialized positional identities, and to be valued for who they are within the school, through social power.

This study champions the foundational springboard that progressive pedagogy and a diverse demographic community can provide for schools: to recognize and engage the challenges of diversity, to reflectively examine underlying assumptions in our pedagogy, disciplinary practices, and ascribed youth identities, and to experience the triumph of resisting inequality and promoting fairness, through thoughtful inquiry and engaging social practice. As students and educators continue to negotiate race and social class at Anderson, they sustain their mission as one of few schools deeply committed to its principles and practice of progressive education and to the vision and reality of economic and cultural diversity.

## NOTE

1. Along with Chapter 2, this chapter contributes to a 25-year view of how race and social class were addressed at Anderson, from 1980 to 2005, by focusing on this issue within the new national climate of the twenty-first century.

## REFERENCES

Anderson School (2003). *The Anderson School Handbook (Available by written request only from E. Brown, c/o D.T. Slaughter-Defoe, 3700 Walnut St., Philadelphia, PA 19104.)*

Anyon, J. (Spring, 1981). Social class and school knowledge, *Curriculum Inquiry*, vol. 11(1), pp. 3–42.

Bakhtin, M. M. (1981) *The dialogic imagination*. Austin: University of Texas Press.

Bonilla-Silva, E. (2003). *Racism without racists: Color-blind racism and the persistence of racial inequality in the U.S.* NY: Rowman & Littlefield Publishers.

Brantlinger, E. (1993). *Politics of social class in secondary schools*. NY: Teachers College Press.

Bronfenbrenner, U. (1981). *Ecology of human development*. Cambridge, MA: Harvard University Press.

Comer, J. (1995). *School power: Implications of an intervention project*. NY: Free Press.

Elliott, A. (2001). *Concepts of the self*. Malden, MA: Polity Press.

Erikson, E. (1968). *Identity: Youth and crisis*. NY: W. W. Norton.

Ferguson, A. (2001). *Bad boys: Public schools in the making of Black masculinity*. Ann Arbor: University of Michigan Press.

Frankenburg, R. (Ed.) (1997). *Displacing Whiteness: Essays in social and cultural criticism*. Durham, NC: Duke University Press.

Gee, J. (2005). *An Introduction to discourse analysis: Theory and method*. NY: Routledge.

Hall, J. (2000). *Canal town youth: Community organization and the development of adolescent identity*. Albany, NY: State University of New York Press.

Hall, S. (ed.) (1997). *Representation: Cultural representations and signifying practices*. Thousand Oaks, CA: Sage Publications.

Holland, D. & Lave, J. (2001). *History in person: Enduring struggles, contentious practice, intimate identities*. Santa Fe, NM: School of American Research Press.

Hursh, D. & Martina, C. (October, 2003). Neoliberalism and schooling in the U.S., *Journal for Critical Policy Studies*, 1(2), http://www.jceps.com

Irvine, J. (1990). *Black students and school failure: Policies, practices, and prescriptions*. NY: Greenwood Press.

Jervis, K. (1996). " 'How come there are no brothers on that list': Hearing the hard questions all children ask." *Harvard Educational Review*, 66(3), 546–576.

Lipman, P. (2004). *High stakes education: Inequality, globalization, and urban school reform*. NY: Falmer Press.

Luttrell, W. (2003). *Pregnant bodies, fertile minds: Gender, race, and the schooling of pregnant teens*. NY: Routledge.

McCarthy, C. (1998). *The uses of culture: Education and the limits of ethnic affiliation*. NY: Routledge.

McIntosh, P. (Winter, 1990). White Privilege: Unpacking the Invisible Knapsack. *Independent School Magazine*.

Rogers, R. (Ed.) (2004). *An introduction to critical discourse analysis in education*. Mahwah, NJ: Lawrence Erlbaum Associates.

Slaughter, D., & Johnson, D. (Eds.) (1988). *Visible Now: Blacks in private schools*. Westport, CT: Greenwood Press.

Slaughter, D., & Schneider, B. (1986, April). *Newcomers: Blacks in Private Schools*. Final report to the National Institute of Education. Volumes 1 & 2. (Contract No. NIE-82—0040). Northwestern University, Evanston, IL. (ERIC Document Reproduction Service Nos. ED 274 768 and ED 274 769).

Tatum, B. (1997). *"Why are all the Black kids sitting together in the cafeteria?": And other conversations about race*. NY: Basic Books.

Valenzuela, A. (1999). *Subtractive education: U.S. Mexican youth and the politics of caring*. Albany, NY: State University of New York Press.

## 3

. . . . . . . . . . . . . . . . . . . . . . . . . . . . . . . . . . . . . . . .

# Whither Go the Status Quo? Independent Education at the Turn of the Twenty-first Century

## Savannah Shange and Diana T. Slaughter-Defoe

### INTRODUCTION

Sometimes educational research has serendipitous origins; it is pursued for no reason other than the researcher's belief that the pursuit is important and will eventually be meaningful. Such is the case here. The second author (Slaughter-Defoe), with the late Dr. Carol Stowe, conducted follow-up interviews with four chief administrators of Chicago-based private schools in the mid-1990s. The intensive original ethnographic study of these four private schools had been conducted 10 years earlier in 1982–83 (Slaughter & Schneider, 1986; Slaughter & Johnson, 1988). In the present chapter, after more than 15 years since the follow-up study, the utility of the original mid-1990s fieldwork is finally realized. Shange and Slaughter-Defoe argue that the values regarding diversity and multiculturalism advanced and articulated in the leadership positions of the two interviewed administrators of independent, private elite schools reflect polarities experienced by directors of independent elite private schools toward the end of the twentieth century.

### THE NATIONAL CLIMATE IN 1990s AMERICAN EDUCATION: THE CULTURE WARS

When Bill Clinton won in an upset presidential election over a Republican incumbent, most education policymakers were still reeling from the damning predictions of *A Nation at Risk* (National Commission on Excellence in Education, 1983). However, Clinton campaigned and won on a "human capital agenda" that placed education at the center of his plan to revitalize America.

The Clinton administration's stance on education made a significant departure from the basic skills thrust that dominated the George Bush Sr. years. The capstone of the "human capital agenda" was Goals 2000, which set benchmarks for states to reach by the turn of the millennium. At the heart of the legislation was equity paired with excellence, reflecting a faith in high expectations and hard work (Smith & Scoll, 1995). While private schools are often sheltered from governmental mandates, Goals 2000 represented a broader vision than traditional national guidelines. This breadth of vision was reflective of the "new federalism" advanced during Clinton's first term in office (Cookson, 1995).

Rather than simply provide an unobtrusive safety net for underserved students through Title I funding, the Clinton administration sought to amplify the federal role in education by guiding policy on a national level. Thus, the paucity of low-income students served by private schools no longer insulated independent institutions from federal education legislation. Indeed, independent schools are implicated in the student achievement benchmark:

> *Every* school in America will ensure that all students learn to use their minds well, so they may be prepared for responsible citizenship, further learning, and productive employment in our Nation's modern economy (H.R. 1804, 1994). [emphasis added]

While the accountability structures developed by steps overwhelmingly focused on publicly administrated schools, it is clear that the independent schools were at least rhetorically included. However, individual school leaders had divergent views on whether and how to integrate the type of reform prescribed.

Therefore, during the last decade of the twentieth century in the United States, the nation was embroiled in a series of battles over controversial litmus-test issues like abortion, gun control, and censorship in which tradition was pitted against progress. Called the "Culture Wars" by James Hunter who defined the antagonists in the battle as "polarizing impulses" (Hunter, 1992, p. 43) of orthodoxy and progressivism in American culture, whereas the former is typified by adherence to "an external, definable, and transcendent authority," which defines "a consistent, unchangeable measure of value, purpose, goodness and identity, both personal and collective . . . It is an authority that is sufficient for all time" (Hunter, p. 44). In contrast, Hunter portrays cultural progressivism as "a spirit of rationalism and subjectivism . . . From their standpoint, truth tends to be viewed as a process, as a reality that is ever unfolding" (Ibid.). Significantly, the Culture Wars were fought far beyond the bounded realm of political wrangling; Hunter's conceptualization of the historical moment emphasizes the moral nature of cultural conflict as it played out in the last quarter of the twentieth century.

The conflict also played out in the discourse of education policy and practice. In this context, we are provided with a glimpse of a dramatically changing American education system. Multiculturalism emerged as a popular, yet contested, curricular strategy with larger implications for administrative practices in and beyond the classroom. Indeed, when addressing the character of the Culture War in higher education, Hunter argues that, "in our own time, the battles in the ivory tower center in many respects on whether to retain an older agreement or to establish a new agreement about what is appropriate for the life of the mind," (Hunter, p. 220) referencing multiculturalism and affirmative action as central conflicts in the academy. Designed as feeder institutions for the nation's top universities, elite private schools provide a new developmental lens to examine the academic battles described by Hunter. With their reputations of excellence and innovation at stake, elite school leaders were thrust into combat over the direction of the field. In mid-1990s interviews with the two independent, private elite school leaders in Chicago, each leader, consciously or unconsciously, chose a side in the battle between tradition and transformation, and thus determined how their academic institutions greeted the twenty-first century.

In addition to legislative history, contemporary academic debates also served to contextualize the choices made by independent school leadership around diversity and race. Education policy served as a venue for the Culture Wars, with the contention focused on curricular content. The Western traditionalists were pitted against multiculturalists; the former stance was essentially conservative in the sense that they wished to continue centralizing the dominance of European civilization, while the latter pushed for the inclusion of global perspectives and critiques offered by scholars of color (Banks, 1993). Trade magazines like *Educational Leadership* sang the praises of multiculturalism (e.g., Adams, Pardo, & Schniedewind, 1991), while Western traditionalists often sparred with proponents of diversity in the popular press (Gates, 1990; Kagan, 1991; MacDonald, 1991). All of these discursive influences converged to form the context for independent school administrative perspectives sampled in 1994.

## METHOD

The questions pursued by the racially mixed interview team in the initial 2-hour interviews conducted in 1982 (Slaughter & Schneider, 1986) addressed: (a) the respondent's educational and occupational background inclusive of future personal educational plans, how the respondent came to be recruited as director or headmaster, and a description of current administrative responsibilities; (b) the respondent's educational goals for teachers and students, including an account of the school's history and traditions; (c) the respondent's perception of how parents, teachers, and students participate and interact in the life of the school, both formally and informally, and with special attention to ethnic and racial minority participation; and finally, (d) the respondent's perceived role in the organization and management of the school, particularly with regard to establishing and implementing school policies.

During the follow-up administrator interviews conducted in fall 1994, section (a) was updated, but only repeated in full at the Roman School where a new chief administrator had been hired. Dr. Slaughter-Defoe participated in all interviews, being accompanied by Dr. Schneider in 1982, and Dr. Stowe in 1994. Although reference was made to information obtained in 1982, in 1994 both existing administrators were encouraged to address the current status of the school, relative to sections (b)–(d). Administrator interviews were taped, transcribed, and reviewed for corrections by Slaughter-Defoe. After the follow-up interviews were transcribed, copies were sent to the respondents in spring 1995 for their records, perusal, and commentary. In addition, Slaughter-Defoe and Stowe discussed the taped interviews; the discussions were taped and also transcribed. These transcriptions, together with copies of the transcribed interviews were available to Shange and Slaughter-Defoe in 2009–10. Obtained follow-up interviews were also analyzed qualitatively in 2009–10.

When Stowe joined Slaughter-Defoe in the follow-up study, Stowe had observed (1993) that educational researchers (e.g., Eisner, 1993) were finally open to permitting the concepts of qualitative research to flourish within the bounds of rigorous empiricism. Consistent with this legacy in qualitative research, the present study used purposive sampling (Maxwell, 2005). We chose to compare and contrast two school sites that were highly representative of private elite education in Chicago during that era: Oak Lawn Academy and Roman School (pseudonyms). From a demographic perspective, the K–8 student enrollment of the two private elite schools had not changed perceptibly in 1994 from the 331 (Oak Lawn) and 564 (Roman) figures in 1981. In the 1981 year, Oak Lawn had 26 teachers, with a 12.7 pupil/teacher ratio; Roman had 44 teachers and a similar pupil/teacher ratio of 12.9. However, 28 percent of Oak Lawn's student enrollment was African American, but Roman's enrollment was considerably lower at 6 percent. From the beginning, Oak Lawn was clearly a desegregated school, and was invited to join the original 1982–84 study; however, Roman's chief administrator, upon learning of the study in 1982, urgently requested participation. This was fortunate as had he not made this request, our chapter would not have been possible because the two other private schools in the study were not independent elite schools.

In the 1994 follow-up interviews, the chief administrators at Oak Lawn and Roman reported no difference in the basic demographics outlined above. In 1994, the new Roman administrator, who had been in his position for about 2.5 years, also reported minimal changes in pupil demographics, but spontaneously offered a remedial strategy, specifically, to first diversify the teaching faculty:

> In the last year we've hired four young African American teachers ... I'm jumping a touch, but we have ... It seemed to me the commitment to diversity here and the growth of the enrollment was—you're kidding yourself unless you have a very strong commitment to a diverse faculty ... a year ago, we had four faculty members of color and I hired eight in a single year.

Despite the initiative, at the time of the 1994 follow-up interview, the school had 12–13 percent ethnic and racial minority children (non-White children), half of whom were African American.

To further explore the evolving diversity practices of independent schools, we engaged the remarkably divergent perspectives of these two Chicago school leaders. Both at the helm of prestigious preparatory schools, these two men articulated not only their administrative practice, but also revealed traces of the ideology inscribed into that practice. Employing the emergent methodology of narrative analysis, we are able to mine the data to provide a "causal link among ideas" (Creswell, 2007, p. 56). Using interview data, we *restory* the ideology and practice of independent school leaders, and situate it in the macro-level national narrative of the Culture Wars. In the restorying process, we seek to examine "the ways in which the stories that rule our lives and our societies are constructed" (Czarniawska, 2004, p. 5). The narratives of school leaders offer a site for the production of cultural discourse, both dominant and dissident. Daiute (2004) argues that all storytelling in a school context is inherently political, and we build on her framework to articulate two opposing typologies of independent school leadership that emerge from a contentious political context.

## FINDINGS

Throughout the data set, two primary themes consistently surfaced: tradition and transformation. While both school sites evince at least cursory elements of both tradition and transformation, there is a large ideological gulf separating their practice. At the height of the Culture Wars in 1994, Oak Lawn Academy's school leadership reflects the traditional goals of the status quo, while Roman School's leadership has embraced the transformational agenda of multiculturalists and progressive educators alike. Through a close reading of longitudinal interview data with school leaders, we seek to map out the discursive and practical moves made by two Chicago-area elite independent schools in response to students and communities of color. As we analyze these conversations, it is important to note the bidirectional nature of organizational leadership; each leader frames the school as he is simultaneously framed by it. Each participant's responses can be viewed as their individual enactment of a role within this specific location (Czarniawska, 2004), and thus, the knowledge they produce is situated and contextual.

## OAK LAWN ACADEMY: A PORTRAIT OF TRADITION

### School Location and History

The educational program of Oak Lawn Academy operated in five buildings located on spacious grounds on Chicago's far South Side. The 20-acre campus includes two athletic fields, and is attractively reminiscent of a small college that is almost cloistered in demeanor. The secluded campus is located in a residential neighborhood, recessed from a busy street; the *Faculty Handbook* described Oak Lawn as a "closed campus" and students were expected to attend lunch in the on-campus dining hall under the supervision of faculty members and student proctors. A fleet of buses was used to transport students who might live as far south as Indiana, and as far north as Waukegan, Illinois. Classrooms comfortably seated no more than 20–25 students, and these rooms, like the administrative offices and hallways, were handsomely paneled in solid wood, conveying a cozy, sedate lived-in atmosphere. In summary, the physical layout of Oak Lawn was proud, commanding, and usually quiet.

Oak Lawn was founded with 10 students in 1873. The growth and development of the school was closely tied to the growth and development of the far South Side of Chicago. A land grant from a development company provided initial support. After a fire in 1874, support came from the developing private university that originally planned to house itself in the area and to attach the school as a preparatory school for the university. Still later, two military colonels with close ties to that same university supported and influenced the school's emergence as a military academy and boarding school; a Charter establishing it as a not-for-profit educational institution was formally granted to the school by the State of Illinois in 1914. The headmaster who was interviewed in 1982 (and again in 1994) observed in 1982 that

> in 1958 at the end of the academic year, 57–58, which was the end of my first year here, the announcement was made that the school would demilitarize...
> We began in the early 60's phasing out the boarding department and by the time I became headmaster in 1966 we had a segment of girls, perhaps 20 or 25% at the most... there was a lot of strong feeling against the move on the part of alumni (who felt) a school that had been extremely rich in tradition lost a lot of tradition at that point... It's been less than 25 years. I think the tradition that has developed since that time is... excellence in education and college admissions. (Slaughter & Schneider, 1986, pp. 241–242)

In this analysis, Oak Lawn represents the prototypical status quo elite school. This school identity is enacted by the school leader's focus on stability, basic skills, and resistance to change. These foci create the infrastructure of an inherently *conservative* educative philosophy, regardless of the demographic make up of the student body. In this sense, "conservative" is employed in its most literal sense—retaining or conserving the existing structure, organization, and management.

### Engaging Students and Families of Color

Both schools in the study cited a marked increase in parental involvement and pressure to hold the school accountable for outcomes. Importantly, in Oak Lawn's case, the headmaster Mr. Edwards (pseudonym) makes it explicit that this is not a result of a change in practice, noting that while, "a higher percentage of parents are more deeply involved in their child's education . . . I don't know that we're reaching out more than we ever did." When contrasted with the research showing that parental involvement is key for the success of Black children, and particularly in view of his open acknowledgement of recent changes in familial life styles, this continuing status quo approach to family engagement may have been a disservice to the school's African American students.

Oak Lawn Academy's hands-off approach is also implicated in the recruitment and retention of students of color. In discussing demographic trends at Oak Lawn, Edwards reports: "Our school is about 25 percent Black. The character of students within those numbers have changed, and we don't do anything to add or detract from them, it's just what happens." Edwards does not boast about the school's student diversity, or even take responsibility for it. Instead, by saying that the presence of children of color is "just what happens," Edwards abnegates institutional responsibility for them, and perhaps by extension, their success.

The theme of laissez-faire diversity extends to Oak Lawn's attention to Black youth's relational needs regarding self-concept development. When asked in 1994 about the racial self-esteem of the school's Black student population, Edwards opines:

> I think the students in our school have their own racial and ethnic identities. [They are] very strong and we don't have to take any special programs for it . . . they're all treated with respect for exactly what they are, so there's never an issue of any need.

His use of the word "special" in regards to culturally sensitive professional development signals that from his perspective, attention to race is something outside the "basic skills" that he has stated as the school's focus. Furthermore, the idea that "respect for what they are" is the litmus test for adequate support overlooks the possible alternative goals of inclusion, accommodation, or transformation. Significantly, Edwards' conception of respect for students of color is limited by his conservatism:

> The funniest thing is to see these Mohammed girls on the basketball court. Their uniform pulled up over their blue jeans and wearing this scarf. To me it's hilarious, hilarious.

In this moment, Edwards is clearly attempting to demonstrate the diversity of the student body, and the equal access to school activities, like physical education, to all students. However, his description of Muslim children as "funny" and "hilarious," when added to his lack of familiarity with the proper terminology for a major religion puts Edwards at odds with the trend toward multiculturalism in the mid-1990s.

### Teacher Development and Classroom Practice

In consideration of the role of faculty in the educative process, Oak Lawn puts a premium on formal qualifications in the hiring process, and teacher autonomy in the classroom. Teachers are expected to have superb instructional competence: "We expect them to do what they are supposed to do, teach the basic skills, and then beyond that the methodology and all the rest is really up to them." Thus, even within the conservative thrust of Oak Lawn's leadership, there would ostensibly be space for individual teachers to take up a more transformative approach to teaching the "basic skills."

As a nod to the contemporary trend toward cultural inclusion, Edwards indicates the influence of diversity on his direction of classroom practice:

> What roles do the Blacks and Orientals and so forth play in history? What contributions do they make to the arts, how have they been involved in the sciences? How does it affect their lives? And we insist that the curriculum is multicultural so that you don't have to rely on a course that might attract 3% of your student body.

Certainly, Edwards is asserting an integrative approach to multicultural education. However, he is also dismissing the power of courses focused on communities of color to "attract" a large number of students, which is presupposed as a requisite for a successful course. Further, language like "contributions" and "roles played" connotes that Edwards' conception of "multicultural" is along the lines of a Heroes and Holidays approach (Lee et al., 1998), rather than a substantive revision of canonical knowledge.

### Leadership Style and School Identity

Perhaps, the arena in which Oak Lawn's traditional approach seems most salient is the school's organizational identity, attended by the leadership style of Mr. Edwards. When speaking of his relationship to other Oak Lawn staff, Edwards states that, "I'm viewed here by the faculty as extremely conservative." Significantly, Edwards does not reference any attempts to come to a middle ground with teachers, or to modify his approach to reflect the perspectives of the staff at large. Quite the contrary, he paints a portrait of the school as an unchanging, and perhaps even unchangeable entity:

> We're here. The church has changed, the public schools changed, the neighborhood changed and all these other things. Oak Lawn Academy is Oak Lawn Academy.

In an oblique reference to the major demographic shifts brought to Chicago by "White flight" and urban underdevelopment, Edwards identifies his institution as a proud anachronism anchored to a time gone by. When placed in

Hunter's taxonomy of the Culture Wars, Edwards' declaration evidences cultural orthodoxy and its commitment to an "unchangeable measure of value, purpose, goodness and identity."

Further, as Edwards himself is a White Anglo-Saxon male, he is representative of historically dominant power structures in Chicago, as well as the nation more broadly. While it may seem that his interests are at odds with those of Black and other communities of color, his conservative approach may also serve the needs of particular families of color. Through his demographic and positional power, Edwards can socialize young people into the norms of U.S. power which may be exactly what African American parents seek in sending their children to Oak Lawn Academy.

Located less than twenty miles north of Oak Lawn Academy, the Roman School represented a remarkably different response to the Culture Wars, economic restructuring, and demographic shifts in Chicago in the last third of the twentieth century. Rather than embracing tradition and a conservative educational approach, our analysis finds that the Roman School administrator represented a progressive challenge to the status quo. The transformational approach of this institution is anticipated by the school leader's marked commitment to change the school environment, and even leverage the resources of the school, in order to create more equitable outcomes for students of color.

## ROMAN SCHOOL: A PORTRAIT OF TRANSFORMATION

### School Location and History

Founded shortly after 1882, the Roman School in 1982 was an optional educational institution for the children of families living in the most prestigious downtown Chicago neighborhoods. It enrolled over 900 children in grades pre-K–12. The campus was comprised of two principal buildings, the first housing children in grades pre-K through 5, the second housing children in grades six through 12. The colorful elementary school building, acquired in 1926, also housed administrative offices, a faculty work room, an art studio, a library, gymnasium, and dining facilities. An annex acquired by the school in 1969 supported conference and reception facilities, offices for the parents' organization and for the business manager and staff. Because there was no playground, neither of the principal school buildings evoked images of a "school building." Students used the city nearby park and grounds for their recreational activities. In the high rise, the small classrooms were fully carpeted, equipped with wide windows. The "school" appeared to have "the same design quality of an urban multi-dwelling home rather than a traditional school building" (Slaughter & Schneider, 1986, p. 270).

The Roman School was founded

> in a living room located in Chicago's most exclusive neighborhood area (by) a
> group of parents who wanted a good education for their boys ... A woman,

brought in from the East, in 1888 was the first headmaster. Her task was to educate a handful of young boys so that they might go to the most fashionable college preparatory schools of the time, e.g., Choate, St. Paul, Andover, and Exeter . . . a separate school was also established (later) for girls. These two separate schools existed for over 50 years. There was no corporate nor curriculum connection between the two schools until 1952, when they merged for educational and economic reasons. (Ibid., pp. 270–271)

Both the headmaster and teachers reported in 1982–83 that throughout its history, the tradition at Roman had been upon "classical education," "college preparatory," and "high academic standards" (Ibid., pp. 272–273). In addition, in 1953, a Parents' Council was founded, with the purpose being to "promote mutual understanding and cooperation by offering the opportunity for parents, faculty, students, administrators and trustees to exchange ideas and to work together to serve the best interests of the school" (Ibid., p. 276).

### Engaging Students and Families of Color

In 1994, the Roman School had a student body that was 17 percent of color, roughly half of whom were African American. Jacobs observed: "Well, across the board, throughout the school, I think it's about seventeen of [*sic*] percent." While the proportion of Black students was lower at Roman than at Oak Lawn, the former institution's approach to educating students of color was very different and the socioeconomic status of families served was far more diverse than that of Oak Lawn.

At Oak Lawn, Mr. Edwards seemed to take a kind of laissez-faire approach when he insisted that his school was not increasing outreach to families of color, but rather noting that "we don't do anything to add or detract from [African American students], it's just what happens." Mr. Jacobs references a similar tradition at Roman, lamenting that in terms of student recruitment, "We for a long time just took orders. We sat in our neighborhood and people came and signed up their kids." Critiquing this kind of laissez-faire approach to student diversity that many administrators seemed to take, Jacobs sought to change this practice at Roman, shifting to recruiting at upwards of 60 feeder schools, and mentioning that "we're recruiting in Hyde Park for the first time."

Hyde Park is a well-established multiracial neighborhood that includes middle to upper-middle income Black families on the South Side of Chicago. It is on the opposite side of town from Roman in terms of both geography and social status. The median income in Hyde Park was $31,571 compared to $51,274 in the North Side neighborhood where Roman is located (U.S. Census Bureau, 2000). Jacobs' choice to not only reach out to African American communities, but to centralize this strategy as part of his narrative of leadership signals, for us, the transformational nature of his approach to the educational leadership of his school.

Jacobs views Roman in partnership with, and even in service to, the Chicago Public Schools. As part of a diversification strategy, Jacobs started a High Jump feeder program, modeled after Prep for Prep, a New York City program that coaches high-achieving, low-income public school students for entrance into the city's most elite independent schools. Jacobs described High Jump as "a community outreach program" serving "all kids of color from the community," and he even contemplated starting Roman satellite campuses around the city.

Certainly, Jacobs did not undertake or even conceive of these large-scale projects alone; he cites his experience at the National Association of Independent Schools' national institute for faculty and students of color, "We took ten people . . . When we came back I formed an advisory committee of parents and alumni of color to address broad issues." Through this kind of meaningful engagement and participation of families of color, Jacobs is creating the kind of school environment truly conducive to parental involvement in schools, and presumably, to the optimal development and learning of their African American children.

### Teacher Development and Classroom Practice

Central to Jacobs' approach to staff development was shifting the demographic composition of the faculty. Taking an even more aggressive tack than he did with student recruitment, Jacobs secured a special budgetary flexibility from the Board to hire teachers of color, even if the school was fully staffed. His perspective was that even if a school is invested in a more racially diverse student body,

> You're kidding yourself unless you have a very strong commitment to a diverse faculty. A year ago we had four faculty members of color and I hired eight in a single year.

By any measure, a twofold increase in staff of color is more than progress; it is a sea change. Significantly, these waves of change do not stop with changing the color of the people in the classroom, but actually bringing a broader range of hues to the curriculum itself, with Jacobs arguing that Roman needs to teach "a more inclusive view of the world." In keeping with that vision, Jacobs helped to shift the required coursework so that

> In history there are core requirements on Western, non-Western, and American . . . there's an option to take two non-Western.

Here we see a fundamental distinction between Roman and Oak Lawn in terms of curricular response to the rising tide of multiculturalism. While Edwards at Oak Lawn Academy dismissed the idea of separate courses focusing on people of color because they would not be well attended, Jacobs has been at the helm of an institution that not only requires in-depth study of histories beyond Europe, but actually creates a pathway for students to complete requirements *outside* of the canon of Western civilization.

### Leadership Style and School Identity

Possibly, this cleavage between the two headmasters' leadership styles is rooted in their social location and relationship to power. As a White man excluded from the "old boy's network" because of his Catholic faith, Irish heritage, and urban upbringing, Jacobs quite possibly viewed his own rise to power as a shift from elitist tradition. This shift was extended into the school structure by aggressively hiring faculty of color and creating pipelines for students of color. Strikingly, Jacobs does not see himself as being "charitable" or giving to those who are "less fortunate" with these programmatic initiatives. Rather, he describes himself acting in solidarity with communities of color, recounting these thoughts about a Black Roman student's chances for success:

> There is an Irish Catholic from Rogers Park heading the Roman School. That's one generation... It is just as likely that you, as a young, African American man, one generation from now could be heading the Roman School.

Of course, there are significant differences between the social trajectories of Irish and Black communities in Chicago that should not be minimized, but even in this romantic light, Jacobs is still doing important ideological work. When compared to Edwards' declaration that "Oak Lawn Academy is Oak Lawn Academy," it is clear that the primacy Jacobs places on transformation, even at the risk of ceding his own hard-won leadership position, puts Roman on an alternate trajectory to their fellow independent school, Oak Lawn.

Jacobs puts it very plainly, stating that "this is a racist society" in which "the power group doesn't easily give up its power." In the context of independent schools a quarter century ago, Jacobs evidences a relatively radical perspective that may be rooted in his own life experience, or in his inclination toward scholarly inquiry. Still contemplating pursuing a doctorate later in life, Jacobs asked a rhetorical question that seems to be the impetus for so much of his work, "It's this whole process, I mean, what is excellence?" In seeking the answer, Jacobs also created a dynamic, progressive environment committed to extending the promise of an elite education to African American children even beyond the cloistered ranks of the bourgeoisie.

## EPILOGUE[1]

Over fifteen years after these conversations took place, both the Roman School and Oak Lawn Academy mark racial diversity as an element of their school identity, but in remarkably different ways. When we examine the contemporary public persona of each school, as communicated through the respective institutional websites, the presence of students of color is unmistakable; on both websites, visitors are greeted with a slideshow of idyllic campus scenes, studious poses, and triumphant athletic performances, with students of color prominently featured in four of ten images for the Roman School, and three of seven for Oak Lawn Academy. Indeed, the Oak Lawn site includes this in a pastiche of quotes from community members:

> Friends brought us to the academy. What we found there were impressive students who were Black, White, Hispanic and Asian; affluent and not-so-affluent. With this diversity on top of the strong academics we were sold.
> —N.S., parent

By reproducing the phrase "we were sold," the Oak Lawn staff explicitly connects the presence of students of color with the economic investment families make when they choose an independent school. However, while racial diversity is touted as a marketable quality of the school, it is only mildly referenced in the core documents of the school. There is no demographic information about the student body available online, nor is there any mention of race in terms of faculty recruitment or retention. While Oak Lawn has recently named a Director of Diversity, it seems that the role is only one of many other "hats," including teaching at least three classes each semester. These elements combine to form a portrait of Oak Lawn that is only a slight departure from the conservative institution led by Edwards at the turn of the last century, with diversity seen as an unintentional added bonus, rather than a programmatic necessity.

Conversely, the Roman School foregrounds racial diversity not only as a selling point, but as central to its mission. There is a clearly visible page of the website entitled "Diversity at Roman," where we learn that not only has the school recently created a position for Dean of Multicultural Affairs, but that Roman "intentionally seeks to admit students and families of various identities and backgrounds." That intention seems to have borne fruit:

> [Roman] also is dedicated to increasing diversity in all aspects of school life. Currently, across all three divisions, 26 percent of [Roman] employees and 27 percent of students self-identify as being people of color.

Compared to the demographics in 1994, there has been a 50 percent increase in students of color across the school, and the percentage of staff of color has more than doubled. Key here is the rhetorical pairing of student diversity with faculty diversity, a clear connection to the transformative approach to hiring that Jacobs brought as a school leader. Further, these numbers are not comprised of only entry-level staff positions; the current Director of Admissions and Financial Aid at the Roman School is a Black woman. Sixteen years ago, Jacobs mused that a "young, African American man, one generation from now could be heading the Roman School." Given the progress the school has made toward his vision, that day may come soon.

## NOTE

1. The 2010 website pages for both Chicago-based schools were examined for purposes of this section of our chapter. However, to preserve confidentiality, these websites were not included in the references.

## REFERENCES

Adams, B.S., Pardo, W.E., & Schniedewind, N. (1991). Changing "The Way Things Are Done Around Here." *Educational Leadership, 49*(4), 37–42.

Banks, J.A. (1993). The Canon Debate, Knowledge Construction, and Multicultural Education. *Educational Researcher, 22*(5), 4–14.

Cookson, P.W. (1995). Goals 2000: Framework for the new educational federalism. *Teachers College Record, 96*(3), 405–417.

Creswell, J.W. (2007). *Qualitative inquiry and research design.* Thousand Oaks: Sage Publications.

Czarniawska, B. (2004). *Narrating the organization: Dramas of institutional identity.* Chicago: University of Chicago Press.

Daiute, C. (2006). Stories of conflict and development in US public schools. In C. Dauite, Z. Beykont, C. Higson-Smith, & L. Nucci (Eds.), *International perspectives on youth conflict and development.* (pp. 207–224). New York: Oxford University Press.

Eisner, E. (1993). Forms of understanding and the future of educational research. *Educational Researcher, 22*(7), 5–11.

Gates, H.L. (1990, December 9). A campus forum on multiculturalism: Opening academia without closing it down. *The New York Times,* p. 45.

Glaser, B., & Strauss, A. (1967). *The discovery of grounded theory: Strategies for qualitative research.* New York: Aldine.

Goals 2000: Educate America Act of 1994, H.R. 1804, 104 U.S.C. §3 (1994).

Hunter, J.D. (1992). *Culture Wars: the struggle to define America.* New York: Basic Books.

Kagan, D. (1991, May 4). Western values are central. *The New York Times,* p. A30.

Lee, E., Menkart, D., & Okazawa-Rey, M. (Eds.). (1998). *Beyond Heroes and Holidays: A Practical Guide to K–12 Anti-Racist, Multicultural Education and Staff Development.* Washington, D.C.: Teaching for Change.

MacDonald, H. (1991, October 6). Multiculturalism divides more than it unites. *The New York Times,* p. 16.

Maxwell, J.A. (2005). *Qualitative research design: An interactive approach.* (2nd ed.). Thousand Oaks: Sage Publications.

National Commission on Excellence in Education. (1983). A nation at risk: The imperative for educational reform. *Chronicle of Higher Education, 26,* 11–16.

Slaughter, D., & Johnson, D. (Eds.). (1988). *Visible Now: Blacks in private schools.* Westport, CT: Greenwood Press.

Slaughter, D., & Schneider, B. (1986). *Newcomers: Blacks in Private Schools.* U. S. Office of Education (formerly National Institute of Education), Office for Educational Research and Improvement. Vols. I (13 chapters) and II (appendices). (ED 274 768, ED 274 769).

Smith, M.S, & Scoll, B.W. (1995). The Clinton human capital agenda. *Teachers College Record, 96*(3), 389–404.

Stowe, C. (1993). *Qualitative research*. Unpublished paper. Available from: D.T. Slaughter-Defoe, 3700 Walnut St., Philadelphia, PA 19104.

Stowe, C. (1994). *Stories of community*. Unpublished doctoral dissertation, Northwestern University, School of Education and Social Policy, Evanston, Il.

U.S. Census Bureau, Census 2000, Summary File 1 (SF 1) and Summary File 3 (SF 3).

# 4

. . . . . . . . . . . . . . . . . . . . . . . . . . . . . . . . . . . . . . . . . . . . . . .

# "There Is a Subliminal Attitude": African American Parental Perspectives on Independent Schooling

*Howard C. Stevenson and Edith G. Arrington*

## INTRODUCTION

In predominantly White school settings, where African Americans are distinctly in the minority in the student (and faculty) population, African American students need a buffer from racial politics. Research has found that while the best learning varies in many public and private schools, racial stress remains problematic for Black students from preschool to college education settings (Advancement Project, 2005; Arrington, Hall, & Stevenson, 2003; Cole & Arriola, 2007; Gilliam, 2005; Rosenbloom & Way, 2004). The burden of shouldering this perceived and actual hostility is not solely confronted by youth as many African American parents also worry about the emotional costs their children may pay as they develop intellectually, socially, and emotionally within predominantly White elite school settings. Many African American parents struggle with the decision of how to select the best learning environment for their children in terms of (resources, etc.) that is as congruent with their family's cultural background as is possible.

This chapter will review the perspectives of parents concerned with the school experiences of African American students in predominantly White, independent elite schools (PWIS). Their stories were examined through the Success of African American Students (SAAS) study—a longitudinal, mixed-method, collaborative research project between a university research team and several independent elite schools in the Northeast. Data from focus groups, surveys, and individual interviews with parents, teachers, and school administrators will illuminate: (1) parental beliefs on the benefits and challenges of an independent school education; (2) the processes by which parents perceive, acknowledge and engage with the tension that can arise from dynamics pertaining to race, racism, culture, and ethnicity in their child's schooling; and (3) how parental racial/ethnic identity and racism is related to their socialization practices.

### Independent Schools as Contexts of Black Parental Choice and Racial/Ethnic Socialization

Predominantly White educational contexts may be appropriately framed as racially dissonant contexts for Black students in that the racial composition ratios remain one-sided throughout their schooling experience with regard to student-peer and student-teacher relationships. The best schools in U.S. society are defined by economic resources, small student-teacher ratios, newer books, latest technology, and modern facilities. African American parents who enroll their children in the "best schools" want what all parents want for their children—an educational advantage that leads to access to the best institutions of higher learning (Gray-Little & Carels, 1997). Access to top colleges and universities in the United States is a key step toward future social and economic mobility. Many of the graduates of predominantly White, independent elite schools (PWIS) do continue their education at those institutions of higher education deemed most prestigious in U.S. society. Despite the educational advantages that exist in these settings, PWIS are similar to all school contexts in that they do not escape the trappings of institutional racism, the denial that accompanies it, and the interpersonal interactions that can thwart the psychological well-being of young African American students (Arrington, Hall, & Stevenson, 2003; Arrington & Stevenson, 2006; Hall & Stevenson, 2007; Stevenson & Arrington, 2009).

For decades, the socialization or cultural transmission of values has been a factor in understanding how African American families function differently than other families in U.S. society with respect to schooling (Bowman & Howard, 1985; Hughes et al., 2006; Johnson, 1988; McAdoo, 2002; McKay, Atkins, Hawkins, Brown, & Lynn, 2003; Neblett, Philip, Cogburn & Sellers, 2006; Spencer, 1983, 1984; 1990). Racial/Ethnic socialization (R/ES) research developed in the 1990s and extended the racial awareness work of the doll studies of Clark and Clark and the Black racial identity work of the 1970s and 1980s (Bentley, Adams, & Stevenson; Stevenson, 2011). Recent agendas have illuminated the challenges and benefits of explicit Racial/Ethnic socialization (R/ES) as an invaluable mediator of developmental and child psychosocial competence (Neblett et al., 2008; Spencer, 1983; 2002; Stevenson & Arrington, 2009). Parental R/ES is believed to hold protective buffering and reframing benefits for Black people, and particularly Black youth, for managing societal antagonism and racism, influencing racial identity and self-esteem (Johnson, Spicer, & Hughes, 2009; Neblett, Smalls, Ford, Nguyen, & Sellers, 2009) and enhancing racial coping and agency (Stevenson, 2003). It is likely that future research will identify peers, authority figures, and youth, not simply parents, as powerful and reciprocal agents of racial socialization, Furthermore, schools are no less powerful a stage for these communications and interactions to take place than youths' homes or neighborhoods.

Parenting Black youth becomes even more complex when the larger societal context of race-based inequities is unconsciously perpetrated by well-intentioned authority figures such as teachers, and other school administrative staff. While these inequities are not consciously identified by children, they are most certainly impacted by them (American Psychological Association, 2008; DHHS, 2001). Perceived and actual racism experiences contribute to the justification of R/ES in the minds of many African American parents who wish to protect their children and themselves from negative physical and emotional health consequences (Stevenson & Davis, 2003; Williams & Williams-Morris, 2000).

Brown and Greenwood (2010) report that while increases in students (from 19% to 21.9%) and faculty of color (from 9.6% to 12.1%) has increased in National Association of Independent Schools (NAIS) from 2001–2002 to 2007–2008, there are regional and type of school (boarding versus day types) that reveal a more telling picture. In fact, the greatest growth in student and faculty of color appears to be in the West, not in the Northeast. As in all schools, PWIS are racially socializing environments in dire need of illumination on "race matters" that differentially impact the functioning of African American students or other students of color as compared to their White peers (Arrington et al., 2003; Gray-Little & Carels, 1997).

We studied the relationships of parental racial identity and racism experiences to parental R/ES and emotional functioning. The major hypothesis here is that the more parents experience racism and are more racially conscious, the more they are likely to socialize their children around race. Another expectation from our work is that there would be variability among Black parents regarding their identification of racial politics as a problem within their child's school.

## METHOD

### Participants

As a part of the Success of African American Students in Independent Schools study (SAAS; Arrington & Stevenson, 2006), both qualitative and quantitative data were collected over several years of exploring African American student social and emotional adjustment. Two waves of parents were administered surveys at least 12 months apart in psychosocial adjustment, perceptions of child school experiences, and personal experiences with racism and racial socialization. The first cohort of 69 parents completed the surveys at Time 1 (T1). The average age of the T1 participants was 45 years old. Most of the participants were female (79.5%) and African American (90%), with a minority of White parents (8.2%). Slightly more than half of the sample was married (57.7%) followed by single/never married (20.5%), divorced (13.7%), widowed (4.1%), and separated (2.7%).

About half of the sample had at least one other family member who attended an independent school. Only 12 percent of the mothers in the T1 sample attended an independent school while 15 percent of the fathers had done so. A sizable portion of the T1 sample reported over $105,000 in total family household income (41%). With regard to family composition, half of the sample was single-child households, while 33 percent had two children, and 17 percent had three or more.

A total of 59 Time 2 (T2) participants completed the surveys with 39 of those parents having also completed surveys at T1. Of these participants, 86 percent received at least a college diploma (with 35% completing a master's degree and 12% a doctoral degree). As compared to the T1 cohort, 50 percent of the parents reported an income level above $100,000. Over 75 percent of the T2 parents were married, 13 percent never married or single, and 12 percent were divorced. Only 16 percent of the mothers in the T2 sample attended an independent school while 19 percent of the fathers had done so. With respect to family composition, 44 percent of the T2 sample was single-child households, 37 percent of the families had two children, and 19 percent had three children or more. Parents were compensated $20 for filling out each packet of measures with questions about their personal and family racial identity, coping, and socialization experiences, which were administered once in T1 and once in T2.

### Measures

#### Parent Experience of Racial Socialization (PERS, 2002)

The PERS (follows the teenage version identified by Stevenson, Cameron, Herrero-Taylor & Davis, (2002) which asks youth how often they have heard their family tell them how to handle racial issues.) The difference is that parents are the target about how much they deliver these messages to their children. The parents can answer "Never," "A Few Times," or "Lots of Times" to 40 statements on racial messages. The Overall Parent Racial Socialization Experience score was utilized in this study (Cronbach's $\alpha = .91$ at T1 and .80 at T2).

#### Perceived Racism Scale (PRS)

The PRS is a 52-item, multidimensional measure of perceived racism for parents (PRS) and youth (PRS-A) (McNeilly, Anderson, Armstead, Clark, Corbett, Robinson, Pieper, & Lepisto, 1996). The PRS-A assesses work, academic, public and racist statements experiences including: frequency of exposure to types of racist incidents, affective responses to racism, and behavioral coping responses. The frequency items used a 6-point Likert scale ranging from "Not applicable" to "Several times a day" ($\alpha = .94$ for both last year and lifetime subscales). The emotional response to racism items used a 5-item Likert scale ranging from "Not at all" to "Extremely" ($\alpha = .83$ for school and public, $\alpha = .96$ for work, and $\alpha = .80$ for the racist statements domains). All parent racism variables including frequency of exposure to types of racist incidents, affective responses to racism, and behavioral coping responses were reliably assessed with $\alpha$ coefficients ranging from .67 to .96 for Time 1 and Time 2 variables.

### *Multidimensional Inventory of Black Identity-Adult versions (MIBI) (Ham & Sellers, 1999)*

The MIBI is a reliable and valid measure of the Multidimensional Model of Racial Identity (Sellers, Smith, Shelton, Rowley, & Chavous, 1998) and covers three aspects of racial identity: how a person defines themselves in terms of race (centrality), how a person evaluates their racial group (public and private regard), and how they think members of the racial group should act (ideology). Only the centrality and regard scales were used in this study. Participants use a 5-point Likert scale to respond to items. The Parent version of the MIBI yielded reliability coefficients of .82 for centrality, .78 for public regard, and .70 for private regard at both Time 1 and Time 2, respectively.

### *Qualitative Content Analysis*

To understand the parental perspectives of R/ES, the SAAS research team conducted five focus groups of parents of Black (including biracial) children and adolescents attending independent schools. These focus groups were conducted with parents of students from two participating SAAS schools. Most parents were Black though each focus group had at least one White parent. At both schools, Black faculty and/or administrators participated in the focus groups because their children attended the schools. Focus groups lasted approximately 90–120 minutes and were audiotaped and videotaped. The protocol for the focus groups consisted of questions that covered varied topics. Through analysis of the videotapes and resulting transcriptions, themes were identified.

## RESULTS

### Qualitative Analyses of Parent Focus Groups

Analysis of the parent focus groups confirmed the importance of the content of R/ES and the racial challenges within the school context. Parents discussed the tension between taking advantage of the educational opportunities independent schools provide and the concern they have about how attending these PWIS impacts: (1) the way their children view themselves, and are viewed, as members of the Black community and (2) their social and academic success as students in independent schools. Whenever a few parents disclosed their concerns, the more the disclosures triggered repressed memories of discrimination for other parents. This recalling of repressed racial discrimination was identified with Black mothers socializing their preschoolers about racial awareness and coping (Stevenson & Abdul-Kabir, 1996). Participants slowly remembered experiences as they felt safe within the immediate interviewing context, perhaps because socially, we are less prepared to openly discuss racial hostility. In our review of the focus group transcripts, three R/ES and communication themes stood out: (1) buffering racial/ethnic identity through protection and affirmation; (2) reappraising racial/ethnic politics by teaching racial coping and agency strategies; and (3) awareness of independent schools as racially socializing environments.

The first theme identified as buffering racial/ethnic identity through protection and affirmation, reflected parental desires to socialize their children by adding what schools often leave out of their educational agenda, namely racial/ethnic pride and legacy teaching. The experience of discrimination politics was not just a phenomenon of early and late adolescent youth. Sometimes, seemingly "minor" discriminatory events stay with children and their parents for a long time. One parent remarks about needing to protect her child from a teacher's insulting comment as they were rehearsing for an elementary school play.

> Yeah, I had to have a real serious talk with my daughter. She had an incident with racism with one teacher, something about her skin color—there was a play about bears or something, she wanted to be a polar bear and [the teacher] said, well, you can't be a polar bear because of the color of your skin. And it was a lot of other little things that were tied in with that incident.

One parent remarked "We need to provide the racial correctives at home." Parents were aware of cultural discontinuities in the school and home environments and were not shy in discussing these mismatches of ways of being and knowing. One example of a protection/affirmation comes from a parent who wanted her child to internalize her African and African American heritage in order to promote her self-empowerment and self-appreciation.

> And maybe it's because I'm one of those people, but I had to start from the jump arming her with the fact that she was going to be a queen, a king, you know, if she wanted to be. I mean the fact that she didn't necessarily ever have to view herself as subservient, you know what I mean. And there are certain times, she's come to me when she's let me know that I may be a bit on the militant, you know. [laughter] ... and so we've been educating each other ... and I mean this child's been going to Africa since she's been three years old and hasn't gotten there yet ... But I also try to show where people in our family, on their own scale—and she just has this mission as far as I'm concerned, I hope

she really internalizes it, that her mission is to do what they were always told, that each generation has to widen the path for the one that's coming behind . . . you know, she's just got to be positive and you know the color of her skin, you know, may be an impediment to some, but it's definitely not for her . . . We've got to empower them because . . . It's even one of those situations so far when she needs running to people who are not of color, not totally understanding things.

There are past, present, and future worries embedded in this parent's rationale for R/ES that cover a spectrum of experiences from social rejection to self-actualization across within- and cross-race/ethnicity dimensions. Moreover, the definition of self is an "extended self," one in which the daughter is representative of family and culture and in many ways both parent and daughter are being socialized by this communication process. In "both-and" fashion, protection and affirmation socialization are competing tensions as parents attempt to buffer the tragedy of inevitable societal discrimination while touting the brilliance of their children's talent.

A second R/ES theme identified includes communications regarding reappraising racial/ethnic politics by teaching racial coping and agency strategies. This theme promoted the experiences of parents having to help youth see or resituate discrimination within school and neighborhood settings as the problem of the oppressor, not the oppressed. This reappraisal process helps parents to reframe the discrimination moment as an event to be managed, conquered, and transcended rather than one to be internalized. One parent remarked that a direct discrimination experience is the best way for youth to comprehend racism when she states, "I don't think they have the same sensitivities until they get smacked in the face." Still, as these moments are painful for youth and parent alike, they reflect a unique form of social rejection (Macdonald & Leary, 2005). Not only are parents led to protect and affirm youth, they are led to teach them how to survive and thrive amidst the dynamics of racism.

> When we were looking for our first home . . . and having . . . a Caucasian person walking up the street with their animal and the kids going near it, having this person walk away and go the other way. And having a lot of other little incidents . . . and having our oldest son say, "are we going to get this house" and have us say, "no," and explain to him that it wasn't an issue of money or other factors, it was an issue of not being welcomed in this neighborhood, and why. And that was a serious conversation we had. And he cried.

Another parent remarked at how she and her husband used R/ES to protect the psyche of their child, but also to teach their son strategies of coping while reappraising the racial insult.

> It's pretty much around protecting his feelings. And sometimes he notices, well, this kid is able to do this and I'm not—little subtle things like that. So we pretty

much talk to him about how to protect his own feelings, how to handle dialogue, not to be personally afraid of the consequence, that his parents will always back him, you know, 100 percent, as long as he's doing the right thing. Yeah, just he comes home a lot of times and his feelings are hurt and we pretty, not much clean up the mess, so to speak, but we try to avow him and try to build him up so he feels strong . . . We try to teach him how to go back and just tough it out and work on techniques and you know, pick up skills to combat scenarios and situations.

Other parents had concerns about stereotypes as demonstrations of the presence of racial hegemony and engaged in communication focused on alertness to discrimination and coping with antagonism. One parent convinced her son to keep achieving by stating, "You will make the status quo happy, if you are an academic failure, on drugs, in jail, or dead."

Finally, there are often racial socialization comments about how to reappraise and cope with the ignorance of others about the differences in Black self-care and grooming. Two parents discussed how being on the swim team can be a socio-political experience for Black girls. One parent stated:

In lower school, she had an interesting experience where she was with some of her White girlfriends . . . but they were talking about pouring water on their hair and they were trying to encourage my daughter to do it. And she came to us and said . . . what took place and she's always felt it was important to keep her hair together and straight, together and looking right. And I said, if you do that, it will frizz up. Your hair is not like theirs. . . . I said if you do that, you will have mom working on that hair for a long time, it won't look the way it looks now, it's just not the same as if you wet your hair the way they wet theirs.

The third racial socialization theme among the focus groups was that of understanding how PWIS are racially socializing environments. Parents are aware of how schools can project a fair and neutral stance on racial issues, but in reality are sending messages that they do not want to address those issues, what Arrington & Stevenson (2006) identify as the "niceness isn't always kindness" motif. One parent described that process as "controlled diversity." Another parent who was not one to racially socialize her lower school child began to wonder if it made sense as other parents were talking about its importance. It triggered a reflection of her childhood independent school experience which seemed to bring back memories of subtle racial intolerance—repressed, denied, or forgotten.

We came to school armed with what we needed to be there and to be able to survive there and succeed there . . . and I was going to private school during that time when I got everything I needed to know about being Black at home. And I didn't need to go to school to learn any more about being Black. And, in fact, went to school because that was a refuge where I didn't really have to be Black, I could just be there and forget about race, forget about color. And it was that, oh, we don't see color here, type of thing . . . the private school was that refuge and you didn't go there to be Black . . . But then there were issues that came up. And it was an unreal world because that world that we were living in while we were there from 9 to 3 was not the real world at all.

Perhaps, the most salient R/ES influence of the schooling experience was the lack of African American presence. Arrington & Stevenson (2006) discuss the unique challenges of how density of African American students within independent school schools shape the learning and emotional safety climate within classrooms. These tensions influence their parents as well.

> It breaks my heart that my daughter has been the only African American girl in her class since kindergarten and this goes to identity; even when there is a nurturing environment, there can still be a dominant pull . . . Until we have a critical mass, we will have a different dynamic; it affects not only my daughter but me also; there is a *subliminal attitude postulating failure instead of success*.

Other parents are clear that density determines if they expect to remain in the school environment and battle the racial politics or leave.

> And I've been very up front and vocal about that, that we're making a decision about whether to stay . . . He's very happy, but I'm concerned about this loss in diversity as you go up [the grades]. And that would be a major reason why he wouldn't stay.

Another parent chimes in, that

> we keep losing these children. I just think that it speaks volumes of the kids when they come to this school and all the Black males they see are cleaning and they've got maybe two teachers, but the rest of them are cleaning. That sends a message not only to your Black male child but also to the White children.

Overall, the focus groups illuminated the depth of the importance of a variety of R/ES practices toward the successful coping of African American students in independent schools.

### The Relationship of Parental Psychosocial Factors to Parental Racial Socialization

#### *Racial Identity and R/ES*

Parental racial identity factors at Time 1 were significantly related to R/ES. Parents who believed that the public held a negative view of African Americans as a racial group more frequently discussed discrimination alertness to their children ($r = -.24$, $p < .05$). As expected, parents who felt positively about being a member of the African American racial group, more frequently racially socialized. High private regard parents reported greater coping with antagonism ($r = .34$, $p < .01$), cultural pride ($r = .39$, $p < .01$), and cultural legacy ($r = .44$, $p < .0001$) socialization. Similar patterns were found for parents with high levels of racial centrality. That is, parents with high racial centrality reported higher scores in coping with antagonism ($r = .26$, $p < .05$), cultural pride ($r = .30$, $p < .05$), and cultural legacy ($r = .38$, $p < .003$) socialization. Conversely, at Time 2, race centrality was inversely related to mainstream socialization ($r = -.30$, $p < .003$). Parents who were more race-centric would less frequently socialize their children about the importance of racism discussions, cultural legacy, or education at PWIS.

### Emotional Responses to Racism and Racism Experience

Overall, emotional responses to racism were influential in the higher reporting of parental racial socialization. Time 1 Parents who reported high scores on measures of feeling sad ($r = .32$, $p < .05$) and ashamed ($r = .28$, $p < .05$) in experiencing racism also scored higher in coping with antagonism socialization. Time 1 Parents who reported feeling hurt ($r = .27$, $p < .05$) and strengthened ($r = .42$, $p < .001$) when experiencing racism scored high in cultural pride socialization. Parents who reported feeling hurt ($r = .29$, $p < .05$), powerless ($r = .26$, $p < .05$) and hopeless ($r = .28$, $p < .05$) when experiencing racism provided frequent mainstream fit socialization. Parents who reported feeling ashamed when experiencing racism provided frequent cultural legacy socialization ($r = .26$, $p < .05$). Parents who reported feeling angry ($r = .29$, $p < .05$) and ashamed ($r = .25$, $p < .05$) when experiencing racism reported frequent alertness to discrimination socialization to their children when experiencing racism. Unexpectedly, racism within the last year or lifetime was unrelated to the racial socialization of parents, except for one finding. Time 1 Parents who reported more experience with racism within the last year scored lower in frequency of coping with antagonism socialization ($r = -.27$, $p < .05$).

With respect to Time 2 analyses, parents who reported feeling sad ($r = .44$, $p < .004$; $r = .35$, $p < .003$) and ashamed ($r = .43$, $p < .005$; $r = .37$, $p < .05$,) when experiencing racism scored higher on frequency of parental alertness to discrimination and cultural pride socialization. Parents reporting higher scores in feeling strengthened when they experienced racism also reported frequent cultural pride ($r = .34$, $p < .05$) and mainstream ($r = .41$, $p < .01$) socialization. Only parental alertness to discrimination was found to be positively related to frequency of racism experience within the last year.

The consistent finding across the T1 and T2 groups included the relationship between parents feeling strengthened when experiencing racism and frequent CPR socialization and parents feeling ashamed when experiencing racism and frequent alertness to discrimination socialization.

## DISCUSSION

In this chapter, we identified the relationship of parental R/ES practices and several key psychosocial parental factors including experiences with and emotional responses to racism, and parental endorsement of Black racial identity. Our goal has been to identify parental concerns about enrolling their children in predominantly White independent schools and how they cope with it. This study contributes to the R/ES literature by illuminating multiple avenues for future research in racially dissonant educational contexts.

The qualitative investigation of parental concerns about their children's independent schooling reveals that their communications to youth have protective, affirmative, and reappraisal characteristics to ensure that their children's emotional well-being is secured. Parents' comments revealed that many maintain a keen eye on the school as an agent of R/ES, albeit a positive and/or negative one. These findings support assumptions of earlier research by Arrington, Hall, & Stevenson, (2003) on African American students in independent schools suggesting that schools are racially socializing contexts and when these dynamics are ignored, schools are unprepared for understanding the academic striving of Black students.

The density or presence of students of color within a particular school context can determine how comfortable they feel to achieve and succeed (Gray-Little & Carels, 1997). Ironically, Gray-Little and Carels' notion of dissonance also referred to how social contexts vary with regard to other contextual factors that influence school achievement and self-esteem of Black and White students including "level of social support, the opportunities for friendship, and the number of people with a shared value system (p. 109)." Research on how parents feel about this dissonance is lacking.

Parental racial identity and its multiple facets continue to mediate the stressful experiences that parents and societal institutions raise for youth (Sellers et al, 1998). Newer research is isolating how various facets of public regard, private regard, and centrality are differentially influenced by R/ES processes (Rodriguez, Umana-Taylor, Smith, & Johnson, 2009; Stevenson & Arrington, 2009). Profile analysis strategies may be helpful to understand how parents and students use a combination of racial/ethnic stereotyping, protective, affirmative, reappraisal, and competence teachings to manage the complexity and tension of diversity conflicts within PWIS educational and social settings. Not all of these settings are ignorant of racial/ethnic politics or unprepared for the need for support. Where parents are on the racial identity continuum appears to influence how frequently they find it necessary to engage in racial socialization. Race-centric parents may feel that they have to provide more racial coping strategies along with their children's educational experiences, no matter how elite those experiences and opportunities.

The quantitative analysis demonstrated that the trauma of confronting racism as a Black person and talking about racial matters with one's children appears to affect the emotions of Black parents. The more parents reported feeling ashamed, helpless, sad, hurt, and hopeless when faced with racism, the more they reported delivering all of the racial socialization types at both Times 1 and 2. The one discrepancy was for parents who felt strengthened when experiencing racism; they tended to report greater cultural pride socialization at Times 1 and 2. In general, racial socialization is stressful for parents and this area of study demands much more exploration in future R/ES research (Stevenson, 2011). Future research might consider how parents who experience the practice of R/ES as stressful can receive support for such practices. Moreover, explaining to parents the potential emotional consequences of R/ES, practicing how to accomplish these communications with therapeutic support until parents feel competent, and therapeutic emotional processing of the multiple trauma concerns for their children can be very useful strategies to minimize the stress of R/ES.

Parents are not static participants in the R/ES process as they watch their children undergo tragic and painful discriminatory experiences (Coard & Sellers, 2005). It appears parental experiences with racial discrimination over time promote greater communication regarding racial exclusion and bias. Hughes and Chen (1997) found similar results when parental experiences of racial bias in the workplace promoted more racial communications to their children. Parents who do not personally encounter racial discrimination may take an "if it ain't broke, don't fix it" approach to the R/ES process. The challenges to this approach may be not protecting or preparing youth to deflect indirect and subtle communications of Black inferiority.

Tracking parental racial socialization across time seems to yield stable results that demonstrate how these practices continue to be influenced by parental racism experiences and racial identity (Hughes & Chen, 1997).

The limitations of this research include the small sample size of parent and children pairs, the potential variability in mission and philosophy of the selective sample of independent schools, and the lack of long-term qualitative interviewing or ethnographic observation of parent and youth experiences with racial/ethnic challenges and triumphs in raising a child of color within a PWIS. Despite these limitations, this research represents an initial step into the world of Black student emotional and interpersonal adjustment in PWIS settings.

This study investigated how African American parents responded when their children experienced racial challenges in independent schools. Under stress, parents teach youth to expect, seek out, and attach to their own sources of racial pride and support. The analysis of parental R/ES processes supports theoretical models that unite identity to context and parental teaching to child racial/ethnic emotional and coping outcomes. We believe that tacit racial socialization processes occur all the time, but that explicit processes are necessary to balance out negative stereotypical views of Blackness. Ultimately, a model that appreciates the stress appraisal, self-efficacy, and racial negotiation competence of parents and youth can close the gap of ignorance and ambivalence when racially tense conflicts occur within the school context (Stevenson, 2011). If parental R/ES practices are influential in how children make meaning of racial tensions and uplifts, then it is possible that their own personal life triumphs with racial stress play a major role. Future work should explore how these parental coping strategies may contribute to the academic adjustment of Black youth.

It is strongly encouraged from the summary of research that the emotional development of African American youth is enhanced when they are taught how stigmatization processes undermine their emotional well-being. While there has been critique of bringing stereotype dynamics to the awareness of individuals because of its potential to increase the belief in stereotypical myths (Pinel, 1999), we believe that research has understudied the role of racial/socialization as a buffer of protection and affirmation of racial identity or as a mediator of reappraisal and competence in racial/ethnic negotiation (Stevenson, 2011). The implications for intervention development that integrates parental racial/ethnic socialization to counter stereotypes implicit within schooling politics and build racial negotiation social skills are promising.

## REFERENCES

Arrington, E.G., Hall, D.M., & Stevenson, H.C. (Summer, 2003). The success of African-American students in independent schools. *Independent School Magazine, 62*, 10–21.

Arrington, E.G., & Stevenson, H.C. (2006). *Success of African American Students in Independent Schools: Final Report.* Technical Report No. OO1. SAAS Project, University of Pennsylvania, Graduate School of Education, Philadelphia, PA, http://repository.upenn.edu/gse_pubs/23

Brown, A.C., & Greenwood, J.J. (Winter, 2010). Changing the face of the academy: Innovative approaches to faculty recruitment. *Independent School Magazine.*

Coard, S.I., & Sellers, R.M. (2005). African American families as a context for racial socialization. In V. McLoyd, K. Dodge, & N. Hill (Eds.), *Emerging issues in African-American family life: Context, adaptation, and policy* (pp. 264–284), *Duke Series in Child Development and Public Policy,* (K.A. Dodge & M. Putallaz, Series Editors). New York, NY: Guilford Press.

Cole, E.R., & Arriola, K.R.J. (2007). Black students on White campuses: Toward a Two-Dimensional model of Black Acculturation. *Journal of Black Psychology, 33, 4,* 379–403.

Gray-Little, B., & Carels, R.A. (1997). The effects of racial dissonance on academic self-esteem and achievement in elementary, junior high, and high school students, *Journal of Research on Adolescence, 7*(2), 109–132.

Hall, D.M, Cassidy, E., & Stevenson, H.C. (2008). Acting "tough" in a "tough" world: The validation of a fear of calamity measure among urban African American adolescents. *Journal of Black Psychology, 34*(3), 381–398.

Hughes, D. (2003). Correlates of African American and Latino parents' messages to children about ethnicity and race: A comparative study of racial socialization. *American Journal of Community Psychology, 31,* 15–33.

Hughes, D., & Chen, L. (1997). When and what parents tell children about race: An examination of race-related socialization among African American families. *Applied Developmental Science, 1,* 200–214.

Hughes, D., Rodriguez, J., Smith, E.P., Johnson, D.J., Stevenson, H.C., & Spicer, P. (2006). Parents' ethnic-racial socialization practices: A review of research and directions for future study. *Developmental Psychology, 42*, 747–770.

Macdonald G. and Leary, M.R. (2005). Why does social exclusion hurt? The relationship between social and physical pain. *Psychology Bulletin, 131*, 202–23.

McAdoo, H. (2002). Village talks: Racial socialization of our children. In H. McAdoo (Ed.) *Black children: Social, educational, and parental environments* (2nd ed.) (pp. 73–96); Thousand Oaks, CA: Sage Publications.

McKay, M.M., Atkins, M.S., Hawkins, T., Brown, C., and Lynn, C.L. (2003). Inner-city African American parent involvement in children's schooling: Racial socialization and social support from the parent community. *American Journal of Community Psychology, 32*(1/2), 107–114.

National Association of Independent Schools (2008) NAIS Member Schools Facts at a Glance www.nais.org/resources/statistical.cfm?ItemNumber=146713.

Neblett, E.W., Phillip, C.L., Cogburn, C.D., & Sellers, R.M. (2006). African American adolescents' discrimination experiences and academic achievement: Racial socialization as a cultural compensatory and protective factor. *Journal of Black Psychology, 32*, 199–218.

Pinel, E. (1999). Stigma consciousness: The psychological legacy of social stereotypes. *Journal of Personality and Social Psychology, 76* (1), 114–128.

Rodriguez, J., Umaña-Taylor, A., Smith, E.P., & Johnson, D.J. (2009). Cultural processes in parenting and youth outcomes: Examining a model of racial-ethnic socialization and identity in diverse populations. *Cultural Diversity and Ethnic Minority Psychology, 15*(2), 106–111.

Rosenbloom, S.R., & Way, N. (2004). Experiences of discrimination among African American, Asian American, and Latino adolescents in an urban high school. *Youth & Society, 35*(4), 420–451.

Sellers, R.M., Smith, M., Shelton, J.N., Rowley, S.J., & Chavous, T.M. (1998). Multidimensional model of racial identity. A reconceptualization of African American racial identity. *Personality and Social Psychology Review, 2*, 18–39.

Stevenson, H.C. (2011). *Recasting racially stressful encounters: Theorizing the conflict reappraisal role of racial/ethnic socialization.* Manuscript plan submitted for publication accepted and manuscript in preparation.

Stevenson, H.C., & Abdul-Kabir, S. (1996). *Reflections of hope from the "Bottom": Cultural strengths and coping of low-income African American mothers.* Proceedings of the Roundtable on Cross-Cultural Psychotherapy, Teachers College, Columbia University, New York, 61–69.

Stevenson, H.C., & Arrington, E.G. (2009). Racial-ethnic socialization mediates perceived racism and the racial identity of African American adolescents. *Cultural Diversity and Ethnic Minority Psychology, 15*(2), 125–136.

Stevenson, H.C., Cameron, R., Herrero-Taylor, T., & Davis, G.Y. (2002). Development of the teenage experience of racial socialization scale: Correlates of race-related socialization from the perspective of Black Youth. *Journal of Black Psychology, 28*, 84–106.

Stevenson, H.C. and Davis, G.Y. (2003). Racial socialization. In R. Jones (Ed.), *Black Psychology*, (4th ed.) Cobb & Henry: Hampton, VA.

Stevenson, H.C., McNeil, J.D., Herrero-Taylor, T., & Davis, G.Y. (2005). Influence of neighborhood cultural diversity on the racial socialization experiences of Black youth. *Journal of Black Psychology, 31*(3), 273–290.

# 5

· · · · · · · · · · · · · · · · · · · · · · · · · · · · · · · · · · · · · · ·

# "More Than What We Read in Books": Black Student Perspectives on Independent Schools

*Edith G. Arrington and Howard C. Stevenson*

## INTRODUCTION

Research into the social context of schools highlights how economic resources, neighborhood environment, and demographics influence students' engagement in their school settings. The racial composition of the student body is also an integral aspect of the social context of schools (Carter, 2010; Stearns, 2010). Schools where a student's racial group comprises less than 20 percent of the student population have been described as "racially dissonant" (Gray-Little & Carels, 1997). For Black students, schools in suburban areas as well as private and independent elite schools, are more likely to be racially dissonant given contemporary patterns of residential segregation and socioeconomic realities (Orfield & Lee, 2006).

The number of Black parents who have taken advantage of the educational resources that exist in private (such as parochial) and independent elite schools has gradually increased over time resulting in the higher visibility of Black students in these schools (Slaughter & Johnson, 1988). Despite the increasing visibility of Black students in private and independent elite schools, these institutions have traditionally been, and continue to be, predominantly White. Black students average approximately six percent of the student body at independent schools with the total population of student color standing at approximately 25 percent (National Association of Independent Schools, 2009).

In order to better understand the multiple factors thought to impact how Black students navigate the independent school environment, the Success of African American Students (SAAS) in independent schools project was initiated. SAAS was a longitudinal, mixed-method, collaborative research project between a university research team and several independent elite schools in the mid-Atlantic region. Student, parent, faculty and staff, and alumni perspectives were obtained using qualitative and quantitative research methods over the course of approximately five years. Students were interviewed individually and also completed survey questionnaires that assessed variables including: students' sense of self, connection to the school community, racial identity, encounters with racism, and experience of distress and anger. The SAAS research team defined success as a positive sense of self by students across social contexts, a strong sense of community and membership in school, and a racial identity that could be used as a resource particularly when confronting racism and race-related stereotypes. Our research was guided by the idea that the socialization that takes place within the school is important to the school success of all students, but is of particular interest to students from racial and ethnic minority groups.

By socialization, we are referring to "the acquisition and reproduction of ways of being in the world" (Pelissier, 1991, p. 81). Slaughter-Defoe (1995) described the places where lessons are learned about how to "be" as a person "contexts of socialization." Alongside the home and neighborhood, the school setting is arguably one of the most important contexts of socialization in which youth develop. In the home and at school, youth are learning how to be as a person who is a member of a specific family and a unique individual with certain attributes. They are also learning how to be as a person who belongs to one or more racial communities. This latter form of socialization, that is, racial socialization, takes place in school as well as the home. In previous work, we assert that schools not only socialize children and youth academically, but racially as well (Arrington, Hall, & Stevenson, 2003).

Racial socialization is just one of several processes in play as parents of Black students make decisions about selecting a school for their children. We argue that the process by which parents make choices related to their child's education is influenced by where parents are situated within the broader social context in which factors such as race and socioeconomic status matter. We believe that parental beliefs about race and socioeconomic status shape how they negotiate various social contexts—including their children's educational settings. We expanded on the above assertion in our other work on the factors related to Black parents' decision to enroll their children in predominantly White, elite independent schools and their perspectives on the independent school context while their children were students (Stevenson & Arrington, 2011). In the current chapter, we turn our attention to the perspective of Black students attending predominantly White independent schools.

A Black male high school student testifies to the unique and different experience of being an African American student in predominantly White schools:

> It's just . . . an interesting, like different experience and very few people have this experience, you know . . . [To] be an African American in a predominantly White school. It's just a unique experience. It's hard to explain. So, it's different.

This experience is one that is compelling yet often untold. Part of what makes this story so compelling is how race and diversity are constructed in the independent school setting as well as how Black students negotiate race and racism in schools (Arrington, 2005). Race certainly matters in American society and as such, racism continues to impact the development of all individuals—particularly, youth of color. For instance, in a study of 810 Black families, Simons, Murry, McLoyd, Lin, Cutrona, and Conger (2002) reported that many of the children encountered various aspects of racial discrimination ranging from being physically assaulted (18%) to being called an insulting name (67%).

This chapter presents some of the findings from the SAAS project from the student perspective. It is believed that this data will inform the discussion of independent schools as options for educating Black youth. The chapter aims to provide insight into students' beliefs on why and how they, and their parents, made the decision to attend an independent school and their viewpoints on what it is like to be a Black student at an independent school.

### Participants

#### Qualitative

Individual interviews with 54 Black students[1] in grades six to twelve were conducted over a two-year period. Forty-eight students were male and six were female.[2] Each interview took place at students' schools and lasted on average approximately one hour (range: 40 minutes to two and one-half hours).

#### Quantitative

Survey questionnaires were collected from students over multiple years in four schools. The first year of quantitative data collection across multiple schools will be reported here. At Time 1, 108 students completed surveys; 49 of the students were male and 59 were female. All students were in grades five through twelve at the time they completed the surveys. The mean age for the Time 1 cohort was 14.8 years.

#### Procedure

Student, parent, faculty and staff, and alumni perspectives were obtained during the SAAS project through a variety of qualitative and quantitative research methods over the course of approximately five years; two waves of quantitative data collection had the most substantial yield for both students and parents. Students were interviewed individually and also completed survey questionnaires that assessed many variables including: students' self-esteem, psychological sense of school membership, racial identity, encounters with racism, and experience of distress and anger. Student interviews were audiotaped and transcribed. After the interviews were transcribed, data was analyzed using thematic analysis as described by Boyatzis (1998). For the interview data presented in this chapter, themes were derived from the SAAS team's research efforts within independent schools. Themes reflected the unique context of independent schools and the realities regarding race that existed for the Black students in their school communities.

A cover letter explaining the Success of African American Students (SAAS) project and a consent form were sent to families from four independent elite schools in the Northeast. Consent was obtained when parents and students signed and returned consent forms to the SAAS research office. Students were administered the survey in paper-and-pencil format either individually or in a small group. A member of the SAAS research team was present during the administration in order to answer any questions and to review the survey once the student was finished to check for skipped items or any other inconsistencies. Students were paid $10 for participating in the study.

### Measures

**Demographic Questionnaire.**   A questionnaire that gathered racial/ethnic background, socioeconomic, school, neighborhood, and friendship information was administered to students.

**Hare General and Area-Specific Self-Esteem (HARE) Scale (Hare, 1996).**   The HARE is a 30-item scale that uses a 4-point Likert scale to assess students' levels of self-esteem in general, as well as in specific areas (with peers, at school, at home). Examples of items include "I am an important person in my classes" (school esteem) and "I am an important person to my family (home esteem)." With a Cronbach's alpha of .88, the overall HARE was found to be a valid and reliable measure for students participating in the SAAS project.

**Perceived Racism Scale—Adolescent Version (PRS-A) (McNeilly, Anderson, Armstead, Clark, Corbett, Robinson, Pieper, & Lepisto, 1996).**   The PRS-A is a 52-item, multidimensional measure of perceived racism for adolescents. It is a modified version of the Perceived Racism Scale that is used with adult populations. The dimensions of the PRS-A are: frequency of exposure to types of racist incidents, emotional responses to racism, and behavioral coping responses. Each dimension is assessed over the past year and over the individual's lifetime in the following domains: employment, academic, public, and exposure to racist statements. The academic domain of the PRS-A, which is comprised of 17 items, was the only domain used in this study. Adolescents responded to each item using a 6-point Likert scale ranging from "Not applicable" to "Several times a day." Items in the academic domain of the PRS-A include "My academic success has suffered because of my race" and "People think that I will act out their stereotypes of how they think a

Black person is supposed to act (school sports, style of dress, speech, etc.)."
With a Cronbach's alpha of .90, the academic domain of the PRS-A was valid
and reliable for study participants.

***Psychological Sense of School Membership (PSSM) Scale (Goodenow,
1993).***     The PSSM is an 18-item measure of school belongingness for adolescents. Adolescents respond to items such as, "I feel very different from
most other students here" and "People here notice when I'm good at something" using a 5-point Likert scale. With a Cronbach's alpha of .91, it was
found to be a valid and reliable measure.

### Results

#### *Qualitative*

Using interviews, focus groups and surveys the SAAS team was able to hear
the voices of Black students in independent schools over the course of several
years. Students shared their insight into how they came to attend an independent school and what their experience in the schools was like as a young Black
person.

> I've learned a lot more than just, I guess what we read in the books. What we
> learn in the books. Just in general about interacting with different races and not
> having as many people of the same race to identify with but still having to do
> well and be successful. It taught me a lot.

The quote above is from a Black male in his senior year at an independent school
participating in the SAAS study. It illustrates one of the tenets that the SAAS
research team posited in their prior work; that is, that schools socialize students
racially as well as academically. In the case of independent schools, the academic
socialization provided to students is grounded in the wealth of economic resources that students can take advantage of during their school tenure. The tuition paid by families and the schools' endowments facilitate the resource-rich
academic environments in which independent school students find themselves
developing. Characteristics of this type of resource-rich environment include,
but are not limited to, small teacher-student ratios, expansive campus settings
that are clean and safe, the latest technology and textbooks, a wide array of athletic and extracurricular offerings, and dining options where healthy and diverse
food options abound.

Access to resource-rich school environments was one of the major themes
that arose in the parent component of the SAAS study (cf., Stevenson &
Arrington, 2011). The students participating in the SAAS study also spoke
about the advantages of attending resource-advantaged schools. For instance,
a Black male high school student said:

> I think it's been a good experience because, I mean, I know I have to work with
> lots of people, different people every day. I mean, the education's great, the

facilities are nice, and you can do, I mean there's so many, so many options to increase your learning, like so options at your disposal. Like computers, and books, great teachers and kids are pretty nice too.

Often when talking about the reasons that they attended independent schools, the students participating in the SAAS study made comparisons to what type of education they believed they would have received in a public school. For instance, one male high school student commented, "Academically I feel that I've been enriched [here] and gone beyond what I believe they do in public school." Another male high school student said, "Once I got here, pretty much everything changed. I mean, the academics were much harder." A middle school student also compared his middle school experience in independent schools to a public school context:

> Like at public school you would get 2 or 3 pieces of homework a week, but here you get books that you carry back and forth, you have to read books, but the other thing I like was that it seems I learn more things faster. But they said about here what you learn for 4th grade at public school you learn in 2nd grade here, cause they teach you more stuff faster.

The "they" referred to by the student could be a parent, a teacher, or peer at the school. What is significant about this quote is the construction of the independent school educational context as better than the public school environment—in this case, the idea that in independent schools, students are challenged academically in ways that their same-grade peers in public school are not is what has been conveyed via the socialization that takes place in school and larger society.

Another male high school student reported a conversation he had with his mother about the lack of other Black students in his school. He said his mother replied, " 'I understand that,' but she was like, 'But you know this would be a great opportunity.' " That the mother of this student emphasizes the opportunity that exists in the independent school environment is not surprising given the historical relevance of education in the Black community. Educational opportunity has been a consistent theme in African Americans' pursuit of equality in the United States that dates back to their experience of chattel slavery through segregation and the subsequent Civil Rights Movement and into the modern era. Some variation of "obtain the best education possible" has been repeated in countless Black homes as a way to pursue upward mobility. Arguably, it is a component of the racial socialization messages that Black parents transmit to their children. Through our interviews and focus groups with Black students in independent schools, we saw that many students did receive the message from their parents that obtaining the "best" education was a strategy for them to be successful in life. One male high school student said:

> Education here is excellent. I mean, you can't really find many schools much better than this one in this area, and a lot of students here take advantage of that, but [I've]

been taught to take it, you know, to use my education here to further me in life. Not just, "Okay, I'm here, you know, so what, just go along with it." I'm gonna to try to get as much out of it as I can.

How is the "best" education defined? One of the first responses many students gave to the question about the positive aspects of attending an independent school was a variation of "the education" or "you get a good education." A few students followed their brief assertion by elaborating on attributes of the school setting that characterized "good education." One student said, "It's a small school so you can get like individual attention from the teachers and it's very easy to and they pretty much look out for you." Another stated, "The academics are probably the best, cause the things that 'm doing here, people keep on telling me, they haven't done these things 'til they were in college or later than that." The physical environment of the school was an additional aspect of independent schools that students spoke of in relation to getting a good education. For example, a male student spoke about the safety of the school campus, "Just like from, from like the city. I can come here and you know not feel worried about something happening me to after school or something like that."

Independent schools seem to be viewed by the Black students attending them as academically rigorous places, particularly as compared to other school settings they may have attended. For example, a male high school student said:

> Because being in this school, it threw me for a loop, because I'm not... I wasn't always used to studying or working cause when I went to public school, Catholic school, it was so easy and I got into this school and thing... I mean, for the first couple of years, things were fine. And then when I hit 9th grade, it kinda threw a little twirl at me. And so I decided this year I try to make an effort to improve upon myself.

Part of the reason that Black students and their families choose to attend independent schools then is to take advantage of an academic environment that is perceived to challenge students in terms of how and what they learn more so than a public or Catholic school setting.

Many students described the opportunities they believed existed within the independent school context as part of a "good education" as well. The following quote from a male high school student illustrates this point:

> Great education, get a great education, lots of opportunities. Opportunities I wouldn't have gotten anywhere else. Like I take Spanish and last year I went on a Mexican Exchange Program. I went to Mexico for a whole entire month... And just these type different things, I wouldn't be able to do if I had still been in a Catholic... a Catholic high school or public high school.

Aside from the actual process of academic socialization, students discussed the benefits they believed attending independent school would have on their educational journey after high school. One male high school student said, "Well, pretty much, you're able to go to any college as long as you work hard. You just have to keep up your grades and (inaudible), I guess you can say. So you have the ability to get in several colleges, good colleges." The idea that independent schools are effective training grounds for college admissions was reflected in the comments of other students as well. The following quote from a male high school student is an example:

> Like this is such a great steppingstone for college. And students come back and they talk to us and they say, you know, with a lot of public schools, in order to get in, they have to be in like the top like 5% of their class. And then you have [students] from like prep schools and . . . you get like ten kids [from the same prep school in the college class] . . . They're not top of their class, but like they're just well-prepared.

Beyond college preparation, students spoke about the other benefits of attending independent schools—such as the diversity of the student body as well as the social connections that can arise while attending these schools. In terms of diversity, one Black male high school student said, "[This school] opens up your eyes to all different types of cultures and religions and races and things like that. And the school just prepares you well for college and just for the real world in general." Another student, a Black male in high school, spoke more at length about the benefits of a relatively diverse student body:

> Well yeah, you make a lot of friends, that's a good thing, and your friends just aren't like a certain type of people. Like if I thought I went to like a public school, I'd probably hang out with mostly Black kids, but since I go here, I just don't have Black friends, I have White friends, Asian friends, Indian friends, Jewish friends, so I mean I think that's a total positive. And it shows you how to interact with people in the working world too.

Along with the diversity being an asset of independent schools, students spoke to the existence of social connections that might prove beneficial to them in the future. A Black male high school student offered the following perspective:

> The connections that are formed here. Cause I mean, there's . . . alumni [of this school] everywhere. If you go anywhere and just say I go to [this school], you're guaranteed a lot more things if some kid says I go to [the neighborhood public school]. So this school may like close doors for you as far as being diverse and being yourself, but it opens so many other different things like the business world and stuff.

The latter part of the quote above is a succinct description of the trade-off described by some Black students in regard to their experience in the independent school setting. In our interviews, students spoke compellingly to the ways in which their schools can be challenging places to negotiate as Black people even while they are able to take advantage of the academic and social benefits to attending independent schools. While one female high school student sums up the benefits of attending an independent school when she says: "I really like it. There is so much [this school has] to offer"; another female student in her senior year commented:

> Well, I think for some kids here, some of your average students here, it's not too hard to find someone that's exactly like they are. If they want to find someone that's exactly like they are, it wouldn't be too hard. But I think that's impossible for me, at this school. And that's something that I've had to deal with.

This "both–and" dynamic—the existence of race-related stressors that may close doors for students alongside academic and social opportunity that should open doors for students—must be acknowledged in order to obtain an accurate representation of Black students' lived experiences in their schools.

The findings from the quantitative surveys administered to the students participating in the SAAS project illustrate the "both–and" experience of Black students in independent schools. We will now take a closer look at some of the race-related stressors that Black students report encountering in independent schools, as well as their perceptions of themselves and their school community.

### *Quantitative*

In terms of perceived racism in the school setting, participants reported encountering an average of ten events (out of the 17 possible situations) over the lifetime. With respect to the frequency with which students report experiencing racism in the school, the range and standard deviation of the responses suggests that there was a wide array of experience with racism among the participants. It is of note that only seven students (out of 108 or 6% of the sample) reported experiencing no racism in school over their lifetime.

The event encountered by the largest percentage of students over the past year and their lifetime was "People think I will act out stereotypes of how Blacks act." Nearly half had experienced this over their lifetime. The event encountered by the smallest percentage of students over the lifetime was "When I go to see a guidance counselor at school, he/she tells me to get technical training instead of go to college." None of the students reported encountering this several times a year or more over their lifetime. What is interesting about students' reports of perceived racism is that the encounters are not overt or crude expressions of racism. Students in the SAAS study reported experiences that pertained to social constructions of race and the often limiting and stereotypical way in which being Black is viewed by others. The stress of identifying how race matters in a situation and making meaning of what it means to confront racial stereotypes is a part of the racial stress engagement process that we believe is particularly salient to Black youth in racially dissonant contexts such as independent elite schools.

The SAAS team wanted to explore how being a Black student in racially dissonant schools might relate to students' sense of self. We examined the level of students' self-esteem across academic, peer, and home contexts. The students in the SAAS project reported moderately high levels of self-esteem across school, peer, and home contexts. Student report of self-esteem across peer, home, and school contexts was high ranging from a relative low of 3.11 (on a 4-point scale) for school esteem to a high of 3.52 for home esteem. A multiple analysis of variance (MANOVA) was conducted to ascertain if there were differences on peer, home, or school esteem by gender, by being biracial, or by neighborhood racial composition. No significant differences were found. We then explored the relationship between students' experiences with racism and their sense of school membership. Bivariate correlations indicate that there was a strong, negative relationship between the experience of school racism and PSSM ($r = -.50, p < .0001$).

## DISCUSSION

To echo one of the students cited earlier in the chapter, Black students in independent schools, as is the case with students across all types of school settings, learn more in their school environment than what they read in books. As critical contexts of socialization, schools are sites where young people learn how "to be" as members of a community and society-at-large. For Black students attending predominantly White, independent elite schools the learning process is a multifaceted one.

The students we spoke to as part of the Success of African American Students (SAAS) in independent schools project discussed an array of topics as reasons for attending independent schools. These topics included access to resources, educational opportunity as a mechanism for social mobility in the form of college preparation and social connections, perceptions of a more academically challenging environment, and exposure to diverse peers.

Alongside their reports of advantages to attending an independent school, the Black students participating in the SAAS study also described some challenges related to attending their schools. The most pertinent challenge included encounters with race-related stressors made particularly salient by their racial minority status within their school settings. An examination of students' reports of perceived racism in their schools indicates that many students highlighted others' beliefs that they will act out stereotypes related to

Blacks as the stressor they confront most often. Additionally, reports of racism increased from one school year to the next for students.

Despite encounters with race-related stress, Black students in the SAAS project still reported relatively high levels of self-esteem at school as well as at home and with peers. As with all students, Black students possess various levels of personal characteristics—such as self-esteem across important contexts and achievement motivation—that likely buffer them from the effect of different stressors. How students understand themselves as an individual member of a racial group, in other words, their racial identity, is just one personal characteristic that might serve as a protective function when encountering stress (including race-related stressors). Alongside students' personal characteristics, we believe that the socialization students receive from their families about being Black helps counteract the adverse consequences that may arise during the racial stress engagement process (Stevenson & Arrington, 2009).

The adults that students interact with in their school settings also play a role in socialization processes—including racial socialization—that influence students' experiences in their schools. In order to promote successful schooling for Black students, educators and parents need to be aware of the aspects of the social context that shape how students experience their schools. This is important whether students attend predominantly White, independent schools or a neighborhood public school where youth of color are the majority of the student body.

The racial composition of the student body (as well as the faculty) or the prevailing socioeconomic status of the school setting influences youth and the socialization they encounter in pursuit of a "good education." The students participating in the SAAS project spoke eloquently to us about their school experiences. The information we gathered from our interviews with students and the surveys they completed confirmed our belief that when parents make choices about where their children will attend school, it is important to recognize and acknowledge the many ways in which race matters to students in their schools and society-at-large.

## ACKNOWLEDGMENTS

This research was supported by grant PO1 #MH-57136 from the National Institute on Mental Health, Howard Stevenson and Margaret Beale Spencer, Principal Investigators. We would be remiss if we did not thank our colleagues who made SAAS a truly collaborative effort. Without support and insight from Sherry Coleman, Jacquelyn Hamilton, Rita Goldman, John Dover, and Diana Bonner, as well as many others over the course of the years, we could not have done this work.

## NOTES

1. Participating students identified as Black or biracial (that is, having one Black parent); participating students will be referred to as Black throughout the chapter.

2. The majority of students interviewed were male due to the original project's focus on understanding why Black male students were leaving independent schools at a seemingly disproportionate rate. As more funding for the study was obtained, the research team was able to include female students in the work.

## REFERENCES

Arrington, E.G. (2005, August). Race and racism in the lives of Black students in predominantly White schools. In H.C. Stevenson (Chair), *Adolescents Making Meaning: Issues of Race, Gender, and Identity*. Symposium conducted at the 113th Annual Convention of the American Psychological Association: Washington, DC.

Arrington, E.G., Hall, D.M., & Stevenson, H.C. (2003). The success of African American students in the Independent-Schools Project. *Independent School Magazine, 62*(4), 11–21.

Boyatzis, R.E. (1998). *Transforming qualitative information: Thematic analysis and code development*. Thousand Oaks, CA: Sage.

Carter, P. (2010). Race and cultural flexibility among students in different multiracial schools. *Teachers College Record, 112*(6), 1529–1574.

Cunningham, M., Hurley, M., Foney, D., & Hayes, D. (2002). Influence of perceived contextual stress on self-esteem and academic outcomes in African American adolescents. *Journal of Black Psychology, 28*(3), 215–233.

Goodenow, C. (1993). The psychological sense of school membership among adolescents: Scale development and educational correlates, *Psychology in the schools, 30*, 79–90.

Gray-Little, B., & Carels, R.A. (1997). The effects of racial dissonance on academic self-esteem and achievement in elementary, junior high, and high school students, *Journal of Research on Adolescence, 7*(2), 109–132.

Hare, B.R. (1996). Hare general and area-specific self-esteem scale, In R.L. Jones (Ed.), *Handbook of tests and measurements for Black populations*: Vol. 1 (pp. 204–206). Hampton, VA: Cobb & Henry Publishers.

McNeilly M.D., Anderson, N.B., Armstead, C.A., Clark, R., Corbett, M., Robinson, E.L., Pieper, C.F., & Lepisto, E.M. (1996). The perceived racism scale: A multidimensional assessment of the experience of White racism among African Americans, *Ethnicity & Disease, 6*, 154–166.

National Association of Independent Schools (2009). NAIS FACTS AT A GLANCE. Retrieved from http://www.nais.org/files/PDFs/NAISMemFacts_Salaries _200910.pdf

Orfield, G., & Lee, C. (2006). *Racial transformation and the changing nature of segregation*. Cambridge, MA: The Civil Rights Project at Harvard University. Retrieved from http://www.nais.org/files/PDFs/NAISMemFacts_Salaries _200910.pdf

Pelissier, C. (1991). The anthropology of teaching and learning. *Annual Review of Anthropology, 20*, 75–95.

Simons, R.L., Murry, V., McLoyd, V., Lin, K., Cutrona, C., & Conger, R.D. (2002). Discrimination, crime, ethnic identity, and parenting as correlates of depressive symptoms among African American children: A multilevel analysis. *Development and Psychopathology, 14*, 371–393.

Slaughter, D., & Johnson, D. (Eds.). (1988). *Visible Now: Blacks in private schools.* Westport, CT: Greenwood Press.

Slaughter-Defoe, D. (1995). Revisiting the concept of socialization: Caregiving and teaching in the 90s—A personal perspective. *American Psychologist, 50*(4), 276–286.

Stearns, E. (2010). Long-term Correlates of High School Racial Composition: Perpetuation Theory Reexamined. *Teachers College Record, 112*(6), 1654–1678.

Stevenson, H.C., & Arrington, E.G. (2011). "There is a subliminal attitude:" African American Parental Perspectives on Independent Schooling, In D. Slaughter-Defoe, H.C. Stevenson, E.G. Arrington, & D. J. Johnson (Eds.). *Black educational choice in a climate of school reform: Assessing the private and public alternatives to traditional k-12 public schools.* Santa Barbara, CA: ABC-CLIO Praeger Press.

Stevenson, H.C., & Arrington, E.G. (2009). Racial/ethnic socialization mediates perceived racism and identity experiences of African American students. *Cultural Diversity and Ethnic Mental Health, 15*(2), 125-136.

Watts-Jones, D. (2002). Healing internalized racism. The role of a within-group sanctuary among people of African descent. *Family Process, 41*, 591–601.

**6**

. . . . . . . . . . . . . . . . . . . . . . . . . . . . . . . .

# The Black-White Achievement Gap in Highly Selective Independent High Schools: Towards a Model Explaining Emergent Racial Differences

*Peter Kuriloff, Amanda C. Soto, and Rachel Garver*

## INTRODUCTION

Disparities in academic performance between Black and White students have typically been referred to as the achievement gap. Explanations offered for the gap include differences between White students' and Black students' social and cultural capital (Coleman, 1988; Stanton-Salazar, 1997), fears of "acting White" (Fordham & Ogbu, 1986), avoidance of academic endeavors for fear of suffering the shame of academic failure (Ferguson, 2007), adherence to cultural forms of survival that de-prioritize academic success and require students to "code-switch" in school (Anderson, 1999; Reichert, Stoudt, & Kuriloff, 2006), culturally insensitive pedagogy and instruction (Ladson-Billings, 1995), and stereotype threat leading to increased anxiety and a perceived inability to succeed in school (Ferguson, 2003; Steele & Aronson, 1995). Despite the various explanations for the phenomenon, dramatically disparate expenditures between school districts with predominantly White student bodies and those with predominantly Black student bodies suggest the phenomenon also might be attributed to a resource gap (Anyon, 1997; Kozol, 1991).

However, highly resourced elite environments pose a challenge to some of these explanations. Some common explanations for the achievement gap, such as negative dispositions toward academic success (Fordham & Ogbu, 1986) or poor preparation are not relevant, while others, such as disparities in social capital (Coleman, 1988; Stanton-Salazar, 1997), may be salient. Most notably, material and human resources are no longer of concern at elite independent schools. The schools' enormous resources (e.g., class sizes of 10 to 18, a large majority of the teachers with advanced degrees, extensive libraries; science, arts and sports facilities) that would be the envy of many small colleges and their students' deep academic commitment, high performance and strong test scores (Cookson & Persell, 1991), suggest that whatever is going on, at least in part, is being constructed within the school settings.

Most achievement gap research has explored racial differences in public school settings, typically focusing on the low academic performance of students of color in urban, low-income environments where schools are under-resourced. Very little research has looked at the achievement gap in independent schools. What happens in such elite schools where highly selective admissions processes create diverse[1] student bodies with relatively similar incoming GPAs and scores on the Secondary School Admissions Test (SSAT) and the Preliminary Scholastic Aptitude Test (PSAT)? Through the use of mixed-methods, we explore the following questions: How does the achievement gap manifest in highly selective populations? To what extent do the most common explanations offered for the gap hold in these settings? Can a better understanding of the achievement gap in elite independent schools inform our understanding of the same phenomenon in public schools?

In this chapter, we describe how we noticed an achievement gap in several independent schools that we have observed and were told about by knowledgeable informants.[2] These schools annually select fewer than 25 percent of their applicants to student bodies between 400 and 1000. By analyzing over a decade of student achievement patterns drawn from one published research project (De Jarnett, 2006), we confirmed the existence of a gap we had observed anecdotally in other schools. We then set out to develop a model designed to explain it based on an intensive review of relevant literature. Where possible, we supported claims with quotes, interviews, and focus groups reported in the few qualitative studies that have been done with elite independent school students (De Jarnett, 2006; Gaztambide-Fernandez 2009; Maloberti, 2010; Ottley, 2005; Richmond, 2011).

We propose a model that identifies factors potentially contributing to the achievement gap both at the student and school levels. At the school level, certain variables are institutionalized (e.g., grading systems, the minority status of Black students), while others are interpersonal and suggest greater individual agency (e.g., teacher feedback). In this sense, the school context is not a static structure, but rather a product of the interaction and accumulation of individual actions and institutional decisions and traditions, giving promise to the potential for school level reform. At the student level, many of the variables involve having not (yet) acquired elements of an upper-class habitus (Bourdieu, 1984; Kuriloff & Reichert, 2003) or what we have come to call "knowing how to do prep-school"—habits of mind and heart that these schools require for success.

### Establishing the Existence of a Gap

In order to determine whether or not an achievement gap existed, we examined 13 years of archival data at "The School," drawing on the research of De Jarnett (2006).[3] We then tested to see if Black and White students, who entered The School (as De Jarnett calls it) with roughly comparable entrance exams and grades, earned equivalent grade point averages (GPAs) when holding their scholastic aptitude scores constant. If their scores were made statistically equivalent, a difference in their grades at The School would indicate an achievement gap, while proportional representation among both low and high achieving students would indicate that the students' grades follow similar patterns regardless of their race.

The student sample consisted of 91 Black students and 1439 White students from the classes of 1990 to 2003. Our data include student grades (cumulative GPA and course GPA), PSAT scores (administered in the 10th and 11th grades), and demographic information. We used these data systematically to test our anecdotal observations and the information provided to us by school heads about the existence of a race-based achievement gap. Table 6.1 presents differences in GPA by Race across Subjects.

In our sample of 1520 students, the average of Black students' cumulative GPAs was lower than their White peers' by approximately 0.30; this difference is both statistically significant ($p < 0.01$) and meaningful. Earning an additional three-tenths of a point (on a 4.0 point scale) can have important implications for a student's academic future, impacting his or her college choices and competitiveness for scholarships. For individual courses, White students earned 0.3–0.5 higher GPAs than Black students in math, science, and English courses.

**Table 6.1**
**Differences in GPA by Race across Subjects**

|          | N    | Mean | SD    |
|----------|------|------|-------|
| **Math**     |      |      |       |
| Black    | 91   | 2.51 | 0.755 |
| White    | 1439 | 2.87 | 0.656 |
| **Science**  |      |      |       |
| Black    | 91   | 2.38 | 0.647 |
| White    | 1437 | 2.89 | 0.648 |
| **English**  |      |      |       |
| Black    | 91   | 2.74 | 0.502 |
| White    | 1439 | 3.12 | 0.490 |

Grade Point Average differed across groups ($p < 0.01$) in each course.

This difference in GPA between groups could reflect a natural variation in the student body or may be evidence of a systematic difference between Black and White students' performances in class. To determine whether or not the difference in grades operated independently of student's "aptitude" (as measured by the PSAT), we used analysis of covariance (ANCOVA). We conducted a one-way, between-groups ANCOVA to compare the grades of Black and White students incorporating PSAT score as a covariate. Table 6.2 shows there was a significant race effect on GPA after controlling for the effect of PSAT score, $F (2,1585) = 199.513$, $p < 0.01$.

**Table 6.2**
**Differences in GPA Holding PSATs Constant**

| | Analysis of Covariance Summary | | | | |
|---|---|---|---|---|---|
| Source | Sum of Squares | df | Mean Square | F | Eta Squared |
| Ethnicity | 3.535 | 2 | 1.767 | 11.660** | .011 |
| PSAT | 76.800 | 1 | 76.800 | 506.641** | |
| Error | 240.266 | 1585 | 0.152 | | |

$**p < 0.01$

The accumulated quantitative data indicate that students entered The School with roughly comparable abilities. Black students were among the very highest achievers in their feeder schools. They did not enter with fear of failure (Ferguson, 2007). They also were motivated to compete and succeed academically. The School and other elite independent schools of the same caliber are certainly not under-resourced (Anyon, 1997; Cookson & Persell, 1985; Kozol, 1991). Clearly, the achievement gap develops in the schools. To build an explanatory model of this phenomenon, we carefully reviewed the literature and supplemented it with interviews and focus group data drawn from several published qualitative studies.

### Developing an Explanatory Model

Our inquiries yielded two major variable categories: one pertaining to the youths' experiences as they become students at elite independent schools, the other pertaining to the schools as they address (and failed to address) the process of becoming an independent school ("prep") student. The literature and the qualitative data we uncovered suggest some Black students begin school feeling intensely that they are academically behind their peers and that they suffer shame and guilt when they fail to "measure up." In addition, some Black students come to see they lack key skills involved in "doing prep school"— skills which include help-seeking, acquiring study skills, connecting to teachers, self-advocacy and feeling entitled to challenge teachers. The second major category, concerning the school, suggests that some teachers fail to fully appreciate Black students' experiences, which include understanding the differential impact of feedback on Black versus White students, the power of the teacher's role and the importance of avoiding stereotyping. The school category also includes the importance of fostering connections by opening space for discussions in the classroom—sometimes by strategically interrupting the dominant class culture—and the imperative of explicitly helping Black students learn to do prep school.

### Student Variables

#### Behind from the Start. Students' Academic Expectations Are High[4]

One White male student defined failing as getting a C, while another expressed shock at receiving a C+. He, along with two other White students, described an important part of the transition to their school as gradually becoming more comfortable with failure and not performing at the top of the class. Maloberti's (2010) interviews suggested that some Black students felt behind from the start, felt stressed by that and never got used to getting lower grades. This qualitative evidence is supported in the research of Ronald Ferguson (2007), who found that many Black students believe they are less academically successful than their White classmates, which may negatively affect their academic performance.

Students Maloberti (2010) interviewed expressed the belief that classmates who came from elite, demanding middle schools were used to the level of work and already acculturated to their new environment. Gaztambide-Fernández (2009) suggests Black students, especially the majority entering elite prep schools from public schools who are accustomed to being at the top of their class and completing academic work with ease, can be in for a shock. Zweigenhaft and Domhoff (1991, 2003) found that Black students quickly experienced academic angst and a sense of failure when they received lower grades in a more academically rigorous environment. Not understanding that an important dimension of doing elite school is learning to be comfortable not being at the top, those students who were not able to reach out for help or otherwise find support rapidly felt (perhaps realistically) they were underprepared and (unrealistically) less capable than their White classmates.

If these observations have merit, the common explanatory discourse for the achievement gap that claims minority students lack the skills and knowledge to "do school" may not be completely accurate. The Black students at elite independent schools have been adept at doing public school. Doing school in an elite environment requires learning an upper-class habitus—habits of mind and heart that align with the demands of an upper class education (Kuriloff & Reichert, 2003). The elite habitus predominant at these schools is not only exclusive in its relationship to wealth, but also to race; race and class being inextricably linked in the elite status of these settings, which historically have been places created and populated by the White upper class (Gaztambide-Fernández, 2009; Kuriloff & Reichert, 2003). Symbolic reminders of the marriage of wealth and Whiteness in such spaces are not only seen in enrollment statistics, but also seen in the pictures of old White men adorning their hallways (Horvat & Antonio, 1999).

### *Personal and Family-based Feelings of Guilt and Shame*

Students are likely to feel shame about their lower academic performance if they are used to performing well at their prior schools (Zweigenhaft and Domhoff, 1991, 2003). Two Black female students in Maloberti's (2010*) study described how the adjustment to receiving lower grades was not only hard on themselves, but also on their parents. These students had to deal with the parental disappointment in addition to their personal shame in receiving lower grades. In turn, pressure from home may have contributed to feelings of guilt and shame.

Black students in independent schools often carry the burden of opportunity for their family and community (Herr, 1999). Herr also found that students can understand their difficulties around managing academically and psychologically disparate school and home cultures as an inherent weakness within themselves. This may evoke stereotype threat as they may feel shame if they believe they are fulfilling negative stereotypes (Steele & Aronson, 1995). Both this burden of opportunity and the internalization of the struggle to manage the home-school conflict may contribute to feelings of shame for poor academic performance at school. In turn, some Black students may avoid seeking help as it can draw attention to their academic trouble.

### *Help-Seeking Shame*

The shame associated with asking for help, along with a lack of knowledge about how to benefit from support structures, may contribute to some Black students' tendency to avoid the support available at elite prep schools and, in turn, weaken their academic performance. Students who attended less demanding middle schools and achieved all A's may be unfamiliar with the need to seek extra support and have to learn to seek it. One Black female in Maloberti's (2010*) study reported that in her middle school, students who talked to teachers after class were seen as brown-nosing. In contrast, students who came from independent feeder schools were well aware of the importance of building relationships with teachers and seeking help from them outside of class (Maloberti, 2010). Furthermore, some Black students who come to elite schools may not have had academic support structures available at their previous public schools (Zweigenhaft & Domhoff, 1991, 2003).

### Study Skills Challenges

De Jarnett (2006) proposed that students in the lowest quartile at the independent school he studied arrived lacking the necessary study skills to succeed, and explicitly teaching such skills was largely overlooked in the curriculum. As a result, low-performing students were left feeling that their lack of skills betrayed a personal failure and that developing them was a personal responsibility.

### Reading Teachers, Building Connections

Several studies that involved interviewing Black prep-school students (De Jarnett, 2006; Maloberti, 2010; Ottley, 2005; Richmond, 2011; Schoeffel, van Steenwyk, Kuriloff, 2011; Richmond, 2011) described understanding the teacher's expectations as a key to academic success. However, it is clear that knowing what a teacher expects is a central challenge for students. Honing in on a teacher's preferences and style is especially challenging in schools where it is common to change teachers every term. While several of the students interviewed by Maloberti (2010) and Richmond (2011) believed that teachers look favorably upon those who attend teacher conferences because it shows effort and care, proactively building relationships with teachers can be time consuming. This may prove especially difficult for Black students who may not access academic support resources at prep-schools because they do not feel they have the extra time to do so (Ferguson, 2007). The difficulties for some Black students go beyond time. As one young Black woman told Maloberti (2010*), she tended to build stronger relationships with adults at her school who were not in the classroom, such as admissions staff. One serious obstacle to building relationships with teachers, she explained, is the frequency with which teachers change. Moreover, this student came from a middle school in which it was not typical, expected, nor particularly encouraged for teachers and students to build personal relationships. She realized that those students who are closer to the teachers feel more comfortable speaking up in class, which might partly explain why she tends to be quieter.

Many studies have found that a student's sense of connectedness to school *and* to home will influence their academic performance (Akos & Galassi, 2004; Libbey, 2004; Schneider & Shouse, 1992; Stanton-Salazar, 1997; Valenzuela, 2005). Often coming from a home culture and economic class distinct from the majority of their classmates, Black students can feel isolated at school, and, at the same time, from their families and community members who may perceive them as transformed by their new school experience (Anson, 1987; Cookson & Persell, 1991; Gaztambide-Fernández, 2009). Although Black students may feel comfortable committing themselves to academics at school, this commitment can often create distance between them and their family and community members. Andre Robert Lee captured this feeling of estrangement from his family in his film *The Prep School Negro* (Lee, 2009), which depicts his experience as a Black scholarship student at an elite independent school.

Such tensions often create a situation where Black students can be doubly marginalized both in school and in their home community. Gaztambide-Fernández (2009) found that at one elite institution notions of intelligence were intertwined with class status in that lower-income and minority students were often perceived as being condescending when they returned home: "Ambivalence about being 'smart' is bound up with anxiety about upward mobility and a reluctance to be seen as a wealthy person" (p. 73). Accordingly, teachers and administrators may not notice the economic and psychological impact of expecting students to buy expensive attire for school events or adorning school walls with pictures of elderly white figures (Horvat & Antonio, 1999). As Gaztambide-Fernández (2009) explains, connectedness was a zero-sum game; becoming more connected to school meant losing part of oneself. In order to assume the privileges that came with attending a highly selective school, students had to align themselves with an environment where excellence, or "distinction," was created and perpetuated by a system of exclusion based on race, class, and gender (Gaztambide-Fernández, 2009).

Kuriloff & Reichert (2003) quote Black students making the same claim at a different elite school. Walton and Cohen (2007) demonstrate that when students feel that they have few relationships in their lives, they may experience "belonging uncertainty" which negatively affects their motivation and persistence. This general sense of disconnectedness—from school and home—therefore may help explain the achievement gap at these elite prep schools.

### Self-advocacy and Feeling Entitled to Challenge the Teacher

Building connections can shade off into self-advocacy, something some Black students shied away from. One Black female student explained that students are most likely to attend student-teacher conferences when urged by their teacher, especially when they are invited through written feedback. Moreover, she believed that the students most likely to be found at conferences are the higher performing ones. She noted that students who go to conferences to lobby for their grades understand the personal advantage of knowing the teacher well. More broadly, this student complained that the benefits of conferences had not been made explicit by the school, and as a result, they may be intimidating or seem irrelevant to students (Maloberti, 2010).

The Black female student who described students lobbying for grades mirrored what other students (both White and Black) reported: that a group of economically privileged White students were the ones most likely to dominate class discussions, talk back to teachers, and protest their grades, and that this entitlement influences the voices of Black students. Blacks and other minorities can feel constricted in the classroom and in confronting teachers. One Black student commented that she usually accepts the grades she receives, as opposed to questioning them like some of her classmates (Maloberti, 2010*). Of course, such feelings on the part of students do not exist in a vacuum; they reflect some of what the students experience within the context of elite schools.

### School Variables

#### *Misunderstanding the Meaning of Feedback*

Black students at elite schools may be more sensitive to the expectations and feedback of teachers than many of their White peers (Ferguson, 2007). Richmond (2011) found Black students were more invested in the opinion of their teachers—whether negative or positive—than White students. More than the White peers, the Black students reported trying to please their teachers and felt ashamed upon receiving negative feedback in an update report. Further, Black students who received negative update reports often expressed the belief that they deserved them. White students tended to downplay the importance of the teacher's feedback and felt more comfortable blaming the teacher for poor academic performance rather than internalizing the responsibility. This differential attitude toward teacher feedback seems to be exacerbated by the fact that Black students received fewer teacher update reports than White students and those that they did receive were overwhelmingly negative in contrast to those received by White students. Not realizing that his experience was typical of other Black students in the school, one Black male student reflected on the use of the update reports: "I think some teachers just use it to highlight the bad parts of people and not the good parts" (Richmond, 2011, p. 137). These results must be read cautiously, however, as Harber (2010) found that a "positive feedback bias" may exist when White teachers give more positive feedback to Black students than to White students in order to look egalitarian and avoid the appearance of being racist. It seems reasonable to assume both kinds of teacher behavior exist and each in its own way is problematic as it fails to provide unclouded feedback to Black students.

Casteel (2000) found that Black students focus on pleasing their teachers in their work to a much greater extent than White students. Jussim, Eccles, & Maddon (1996) found that "the estimated impact of teacher perceptions is almost three times as great for Black students as for whites" (as quoted in Ferguson, 2007, p. 126) indicating that, perhaps, differences in cultural values between home and school "immunize" some students from teacher views and increase sensitivity to teacher feedback for others (Weinstein, 1985, p. 344). Negative teacher feedback may be doubly hurtful when Black students also encounter teachers' negative stereotypes.

#### *Teacher Stereotypes*

In several independent schools, our interviews found that most students and teachers claimed that grading is fair and unbiased.[5] Yet, we have noted racial differences in how feedback is delivered and received that suggest some teachers experience a disparity between their belief in the potential of Black students and their experience of student classroom performance. For example, one teacher Maloberti (2010) interviewed lauded the in-class insights of his Black male students, but lamented that such ideas were rarely well-communicated or presented through writing:

> What I am conscious of with a lot of these guys [Black males] is the disparity between their insight in class and what they can get down on paper. And, some of them come around, but some of them, there is always a gap between what their test performance indicates and what I see is their capacity for managing information and making interesting connections. (p. 114)

Such statements suggest that some teachers perceive the achievement gap directly and may then over generalize. Here, professional development may be needed to help them nuance their understandings of the performance of individual Black students. Yet, even when Black students' efforts are rewarded by high grades, their performance often has to be outstanding to appear average to the teacher (Datnow & Cooper, 1997).

Some teachers' generalizations may contribute to constructing a "bias in a teacher's expectation of a student's performance that affects that performance" (Ferguson, 2008, p. 124). Teachers' perceptions of student performance may also influence students' feelings of guilt and shame. Zweigenhaft and Domhoff (1991, 2003) found that teachers at elite independent schools expressed a sense of inevitability when the Black students struggled academically. Such processes may be particularly influential given the weight Black students give to teachers' opinions (Casteel, 2000; Jussin, Eccles & Madden, 1996).

### School Culture as Stereotype Threat

Steele and Aronson's (1995) notion of stereotype threat, the stress accompanying the fear one's performance will reinforce negative stereotypes about one's racial group (or any identity category), may point to factors in school environments that can contribute to the achievement gap.

Simply occupying a minority status can trigger stereotype threat. Steele explained that a population of students is often susceptible to stereotype threat if it falls below a critical mass; a number that varies depending on the environment. Notably, Black students comprise a small minority (6% to 10%) at these schools. In addition to minority status stigma, Gaztambide-Fernández (2009) found that Black students were often constrained to the stereotype of Blacks as anti-intellectual. He described a discourse at an elite school that positioned "diversity" and "intelligence" as antithetical, suggesting that White students and faculty generally perceived students of color as intellectually unworthy. Students of color also believed they were largely admitted to the prep school "in order to create diversity and, thereby 'enrich' the curriculum" (p. 165), thus, creating (and selling) the best environment or experience possible for majority students rather than for reasons of equity and social justice (p. 166).

### The Power of the Teacher's Role

Black students who have negative interactions with teachers may feel a sense of futility in their academic work (Beady & Beady, 1993), if the interactions are not countered by positive encouragement. Indeed, for most of the students Richmond (2011) interviewed, grades and update reports were highly important and affected the students' dispositions towards the school and their teachers. She found that students interpreted teacher feedback as indicative of their relationship with the teacher, while teachers viewed the feedback as instrumental for communicating with students. This disconnect around the relational weight of teacher feedback suggest that some teachers may be unaware of the emotional power of their feedback.

### Setting High Standards

Of course, the power students give teachers can work to their advantage as well. One Black male student Maloberti (2010*) interviewed recounted that the time he had a Black teacher, and was pushed harder and held to a higher standard, was a fulfilling experience for him. Of course, White teachers can hold such standards and help students meet them as well, but this comment does underline the importance of doing it and suggests that having a more diverse faculty could help counter some of the cultural misunderstandings we have outlined.

### Lack of Listening and Caring

Schneider and Shouse (1992) found that students' experiences of support can be colored by race. Through the use of the National Educational Longitudinal Study Data (NELS, 1988) and ethnographic methods, Schneider and Shouse (1992) studied independent school students who generally had a positive perception of their school and shared in school spirit. Despite the sense that their teachers were fair and praised them, over twenty percent of the Black students felt that their teachers were not genuinely interested in their well-being. Black students were more likely than the White, Hispanic, or Asian students to report that their teachers did not listen to them. Other studies (Valenzuela, 2005; Marseille, 2009) have shown that minority students often feel their teachers care about their academic performance, but not their well-being as people. Taken together, these findings suggest that dimensions of connection have a cultural quality that may require differential attention if teachers hope to have all youth experience them as caring. The major area in which this may be accomplished is the classroom where some students feel neither listened to nor appreciated.

### Creating Safe Classroom Spaces

Finally, our research suggests teachers may need to take a more active role in creating safe spaces within classroom discourse for Black students (Kuriloff & Reichert, 2003). Given their minority status, Black students are not likely to be the most verbal members of classrooms in elite schools. This can be compounded when teachers fail to interrupt dominant White (often male) student voices that uncritically presume the world is as they see it and sometimes express painful stereotypes. Horvat & Antonio (1999) found that the dominant culture at school was not only established by teacher comments and actions, but also reinforced when teachers left White students' hurtful comments towards Black students unaddressed; Gaztambide-Fernández (2009) found the same phenomena at Weston. Correcting this will mean opening up discussions to other students' views; it will mean making room within the classroom to discuss race. One male student who identified as "mixed Cherokee, Black, and White," applauded his school for making one's race irrelevant. However, he also explained that he could not find a receptive audience or the opportunity to talk about the kind of racial discrimination he had experienced at his previous school (Maloberti, 2010*).

## USES OF THE MODEL: DISCUSSION AND CONCLUSIONS

Our discovery of an achievement gap at elite prep schools shows that some of the dominant discourses concerning the gap in public schools are inadequate to explain it in elite schools. There is no resource gap. Black students are academically competitive with the White students from the start. They know how to do (public) school. They do not subscribe to the code of the street and therefore do not need to be hyper-alert, and they are not resisting "acting White." Instead, we found Black students who needed to learn upper-class habits of mind and heart that enable them to do prep school, as well as schools that need to help their teachers become more culturally knowledgeable and more adept at interrupting the dominant culture which entitles certain students within their classrooms. More broadly, we found that schools could help Black students do much better by teaching explicitly the *doing* of elite school. Despite the marginalization and stress for Black students that can come with adopting an elite habitus, the advantages that come with acquiring it through attending such elite schools often explicitly motivate the choice to attend by Black parents and students alike (Kuriloff & Reichert, 2003; Ottley, 2005).

Our model needs testing in a more systematic fashion and we plan to do that going forward. Assuming we confirm what we have argued here, it will have direct implications for intervention. The model suggests that teaching and learning are transactional; that both teachers and students must be part of the remedy. All students, and certainly those who are not from privileged backgrounds, need to be taught the process of becoming an elite student—that many people start out feeling behind and that there is nothing to be ashamed of as one develops mastery of a new and challenging environment. Students need to learn—and be taught—study skills and how to advocate for themselves. Schools need to reflect on how their actions or inactions affect Black students and be willing to make the changes Black students' presence may inspire—to make themselves more welcoming and effective places for all students. Teachers and students need to learn how to foster connections and how to appropriately challenge teachers' authority and students' silence. Most important, schools need to understand that helping students to develop an explicit meta-understanding of doing elite school is the bedrock of acquiring an upper-class habitus—the habits of mind and heart that are the very essence of preparing them to succeed in high school, college, and career. Working together to uncover this central aspect of a school's "hidden curriculum" may be as important as learning the academic subjects which constitute a school's open curriculum. Indeed, while all the discourses seeking to explain the achievement gap in public schools may be necessary for understanding it, they may not be sufficient without considering the necessity of helping students develop a meta-understanding of doing school.

## NOTES

1. As early as the late 1970s Doyle (1981) showed that independent schools had better racial and ethnic diversity than many White, suburban public schools. This discrepancy has only grown over the years since that period.

2. These include heads of schools who have enrolled in the University of Pennsylvania's Graduate School of Education's Mid-Career Doctoral Program, as well many heads with whom the senior author is author is friends.

3. De Jarnett conducted his study at an elite prep school, which for purposes of anonymity, he called "The School." He was also very careful to eliminate any ways to trace back data to individuals. Thus, the data he provided us were thoroughly "sanitized." Further, all the other studies we draw on for case material were equally careful to protect the names of their research sites (schools) and the identities of their informants.

4. Maloberti graciously provided us access to his raw interview data. When we discuss interviews drawn from them, we indicate it with an * in the citation. They are accessible to other scholars (with appropriate precautions to preserve their anonymity) on request. Other cites to the author are drawn directly from his dissertation.

5. We have conducted such interviews at five different elite schools.

## REFERENCES

Anderson, E. (1999). *Code of the street: Decency, violence, and the moral life of the inner city*. New York: W.W. Norton & Company.

Anson, R.S. (1987). *Best intentions: The education and killing of Edmund Perry*. New York: Vintage.

Anyon, J. (1997). *Ghetto schooling: A political economy of urban education reform.* New York: Teachers College.

Beady, C.H., & Beady, M.O. (1993). *A systemic approach for creating an effective environment for African American students: Lessons from a private school.* Cleveland, OH: Cleveland State University, Urban Child Research Center.

Bourdieu, P. (1984). *Distinction: A social class critique of the judgment of taste.* London: Routledge and Kegan Paul.

Casteel, C.A. (2000). African American students' perceptions of their treatment by Caucasian teachers. *Journal of Instructional Psychology, 27,* 143–148.

Coleman, J.S. (1988). Social capital in the creation of human capital. *American Journal of Sociology, 94,* S95–S120.

Cooksen, P.W. & Persell, H.P. (1991). Race and class in America's elite preparatory boarding schools: African Americans as the "outsiders within." *The Journal of Negro Education, 60*(2), 219–228.

Datnow, A. & Cooper, R. (1997). Peer networks of African American students in independent schools: Affirming academic success and racial identity. *The Journal of Negro Education, 66*(1), 56–72.

De Jarnett, R. (2006). *A comprehensive thirty-four year longitudinal study of the academic progress and academic school experiences of boys in a highly selective secondary school population.* Unpublished doctoral dissertation, University of Pennsylvania, Philadelphia, PA.

Doyle, D.P. (1981). A Din of inequity: Private schools reconsidered. *Teachers College Record, 82*(4), 661–673.

Ferguson, R. (2003). Teachers' perceptions and expectations and the Black-White test-score gap. *Urban Education, 38*(4), 460–507.

Ferguson, R. (2007). *Toward excellence with equity.* Cambridge, Massachusetts: Harvard Education Press.

Fordham, S., & Ogbu, J. (1986). Black students' school success: Coping with the burden of "acting white." *Urban Review, 18*(3), 176–203.

Gaztambide-Fernández, R.A. (2009). *The best of the best: Becoming elite at an American boarding school.* Cambridge: Harvard University Press.

Harber, K.D. (2010). *The positive feedback bias.* Unpublished paper at Rutgers University.

Herr, K. (1999). Private power and privileged education: De/constructing institutionalized racism. *International Journal of Inclusive Education, 3*(2), 111–129.

Herrnstein, R.J., & Murray, C. (1994). *The bell curve.* New York: The Free Press.

Horvat, E.M., & Antonio, A.L. (1999). "Hey, those shoes are out of uniform": African American girls in an elite high school and the importance of habitus. *Anthropology and Education Quarterly, 30*(3), 317–342.

Jowett, S., & Cockerill, I. M. (2003). Olympic medalist's perspective of the athlete-coach relationship. *Psychology of Sports and Science, 4,* 313–331.

Jussim, L., Eccles, J., & Madon, S. (1996). Social perception, social stereotypes, and teacher expectations: Accuracy and the quest for the powerful self-fulfilling prophesy. In M.P. Zanna (Ed.), *Advances in experimental social psychology* (pp. 281–388). San Diego, CA: Academic.

Kozol, J. (1991). *Savage inequalities: Children in America's schools.* New York: Crown.

Kuriloff, P., Reichert, M.C., Stoudt, B., & Ravitch, S. (2009). Building research collaboratives among schools and universities: Lessons from the field. *Mind, Brain and Education, 3*(1), 34–44.

Kuriloff, P. & Reichert, M.C. (2003). Boys of class, boys of color: Negotiating the academic and social geography of an elite independent school. *Journal of Social Issues, 59*(4), 751–769.

Ladson-Billings, G. (1995). Toward a theory of culturally relevant pedagogy. *American Educational Research Journal, 32*(3), 465–491.

Lee, A.R., Lee, B., Ewing, H., Grady, R., & Lynch, S. (Producers), & Lee, A.R. (Director). (2009). *The prep school Negro* [Motion Picture]. United States: (Available from Andre Robert Lee).

Libbey, H.P. (2004). Measuring student relationships to school: Attachment, bonding, connectedness, and engagement. *Journal of School Health, 74*(7), 274–283.

Maloberti, G.W.M. (2010). *Making the grade in a competitive boarding school: Exploring practice and perception.* Unpublished doctoral dissertation, University of Pennsylvania, Philadelphia, PA.

Marseille, W. (2009). *Coming in first, finishing last: African-American male perceptions of relationships with coaches and teachers and the impact on academic and athletic performance.* Unpublished doctoral dissertation, University of Pennsylvania, Philadelphia, PA.

Ottley, L.A. (2005). *Outsiders within: The lived experience of African American students at the Shipley School.* Unpublished doctoral dissertation, University of Pennsylvania, Philadelphia, PA.

Reichert, M.C., Stoudt, B., & Kuriloff, P. (2006). Don't love no fight: Healing and identity among urban youth. *The Urban Review, 38*(3), 187–209.

Richmond, M. (2011). *Feeding back: Looking at an independent school feedback system through a relational lens.* Unpublished doctoral dissertation, University of Pennsylvania, Philadelphia.

Schneider, B., & Shouse, R. (1992). Children of color in independent schools: An analysis of the eighth grade cohort from the national education longitudinal study of 1988. *The Journal of Negro Education, 61*(2), 223–234.

Schoeffel, M., van Steenwyk, M., & Kuriloff, P. (in press). Students share their beliefs about success through participatory action research at The Shipley School. *Independent School Magazine.*

Stanton-Salazar, R.D. (1997). A social capital framework for understanding the socialization of racial minority children and youth. *Harvard Educational Review, 67*(1), 1–40.

Steele, C. M., & Aronson, J. (1995). Stereotype threat and the intellectual test performance of African Americans. *Journal of Personality and Social Psychology, 69,* 797–811.

Tatum, B.D. (2003). *"Why are all the black kids sitting together in the cafeteria?" A psychologist explains the development of racial identity.* New York: Basic Books. (Originally published 1996.)

Valenzuela, A. (2005). Subtractive schooling, caring relations, and social capital in the schooling of US-Mexican youth. In L. Weiss & M. Fine (Eds.), *Beyond silenced voices: Class, race, and gender in United States schools* (Rev. ed.) (pp. 83–94). Albany: SUNY Press.

Walton, G.M., & Cohen, G.L. (2007). A question of belonging: Race, social fit, and achievement. *Journal of Personality and Social Psychology, 92*(1), 82–96.

Zweigenhaft, R.L., & Domhoff, G.W. (1991). *Blacks in the white establishment? A study of race and class in America.* New Haven: Yale University Press.

Zweigenhaft, R.L., & Domhoff, G.W. (2003). *Blacks in the white elite: Will the progress continue?* Maryland: Rowman & Littlefield.

# 7

# The Influence of Private and Public School Contexts on the Development of Children's Racial Coping

*Deborah J. Johnson, Diana T. Slaughter-Defoe, and Meeta Banerjee*

## INTRODUCTION

Families and schools are linked by their interdependent roles in the socialization and preparation of children. As primary socializers of their children, African American parents know that their success is partially dependent upon preparing them to face the exigencies of discrimination. School is a partner in this process that either furthers the goals of parents or undermines those goals. Schools are secondary socialization contexts where racial/ethnic socialization messages are either intentionally or unintentionally communicated as well. Selecting nonpublic schools presumably allows parents to choose environments, where at the minimum, their parenting goals will not be undermined and in some cases, will be promoted. The Comer School Development Program (SDP) intervention provides an enhanced environment to public school children and their families where the transformed and adjusted school climate should impact the positive and proactive development of racial coping skills, as well as facilitate the more rapid acquisition of these skills. Parental and school racial socialization messages are interpreted and translated by children into strategies for negotiating their status and racialized experiences in the world. Necessarily, the racial coping strategies that children develop are influenced by the character and culture of the schools they attend. No work has been conducted that compare the acquisition or articulated use of racial coping skills among public schools, inclusive of Comer school settings, and private school children in homogeneous

African American settings. This chapter represents an initial exploration as we report on and compare the articulation or use of racial coping strategies (RCSs) among public and private elementary school children.

### Racial Coping as Social Problem Solving

Children's racial coping is the product of parental socialization processes, particularly in early development. Racial/ethnic socialization has been defined and operationalized in a number of ways (Hughes, Rodriguez, Smith, Johnson, Stevenson & Spicer, 2006), including the shaping of children's positive racial/ethnic identity, the forging of strong linkages to own group or the development of their cultural authenticity. The concept of racial socialization (as defined by preparation for bias and cultural development strategies) is reflected in the intentional and unintentional messages, child rearing behaviors, and other parent-child interactions that communicate about how the child should perceive, process, and respond to discrimination, prejudice, and other barriers based upon race. While the home is a mainstay context of these processes, the school context is the next major environment where race-related socialization of children occurs (Johnson, 1988b, 2005). We are proposing that racial coping skills among children are the expected outcomes of these home/school experiences and processes. As children mature, increasingly these skills are linked to peer and community transactions, as well as to their interpretive lenses (Hughes et al., 2006; Johnson, 2005).

Going to school in the primary grades is a gradual process of transition in which children, with support from parents and teachers, learn adult-like strategies for managing and resolving social problems presented in school communities (e.g., Comer, 1980). Most social problem solving and prosocial activities involve settling arguments over rules in play, determining fairness, likability, support, and morality among playmates and classmates. For African American children, racial stimuli may have salience for characterizing how children/youth approach social and prosocial problem solving with peers. Racial coping is an understudied category of social problem solving skills where some of the solutions have prosocial qualities. Individual race-related coping strategies (RCS) incorporate aspects of cooperation, conflict resolution, and moral reasoning in response to situations cued or perceived as race-based. These elements are inherent in social and prosocial skill development among children (Eisenberg & Fabes, 1998). Moreover, we anticipate that the development of racial coping skills are aided by underlying developmental processes that parents recognize and adjust their messages to accommodate (Hughes & Chen, 1997) and have been shown to vary by age among children (Johnson, 2005). This chapter presents data on public and private school children's perceptions of how fictive children like themselves should cope with social dilemmas.

Culture influences prosocial skill development (Aviezer, Van Ijzendoorn, Sagi, & Schuengel, 1994; Knight & Kagan, 1977) and this is no less true for racial coping strategies (Johnson, 2005; Johnson & Spicer, 2009). Kim (1999) found that preferred strategies of diverse groups of 3rd grade children differed and were associated with cultural socialization and experiences with prejudice. That African American families use cultural approaches to instill race-related coping skills in their children has been documented in several studies (e.g., Hughes et al., 2006).

School peers are influential in this development as is the relationship between children and teachers. Peers reinforce moral behavior and help with problem solving (Furman & Masters, 1980; Tesson, Lewko, & Bigelow, 1987). Positive, supportive relationships between teachers and children increase prosocial skills among preschoolers and elementary grade children (Howes, Matheson, & Hamilton, 1994; Solomon, Watson, DeLucchi, Schaps, & Solomon, 1988). School programs directed towards children's positive conflict resolution find that, at least for a time, these programs are more powerful than other influences or developmental trajectories that ultimately increase children's prosocial orientation (Solomon et al., 1988; Solomon, Watson, Battistich, Schaps, & Delucci, 1996). In schools where there is a positive climate (extending to a positive racial climate) (Slaughter & Carlson, 1997), or contexts where discrimination/exclusion experiences are reduced or buffered, we expect the increased usage of racial coping strategies (RCSs) as associated with prosocial skill elements (i.e., RCSs: engage, moral reasoning both racial and nonracial, explore the problem, and persistence). In other words, more proactive strategies will likely evolve in these more positive environments. The basis for these expectations is located in the conceptual and theoretical foundation of the work.


### Theoretical Model

Developmental research involving children has become decidedly ecological over the last 40 years and in the last 15–20 years more contextual, even though culture or social stratification factors remain somewhat elusive. Garcia Coll, Crnic, Lamberty, Wasik, Kenkins, Garcia & McAdoo (1996) proposed a model where social stratification factors (i.e., social position, racism, segregation, etc.) were more central, and were essential as distal influences on the experiences and development of competences of children of color. In the model, at least three ideas are central to the work being presented here, (1) that among African American children, racial coping skills are critical competencies to develop irrespective of social-economic family background; (2) that the promoting or inhibiting influences of contexts of schools and communities are multiplicative on the development of children's competencies; and (3) that distal social stratification factors have influence regardless of the racially or economic homogenous or heterogeneous school and community contexts of daily experience. This last point suggests that majority experiences, real or anticipated, are historically meaningful to those influential adults across the child's environments, if not to the child.

## Racial Stress and Coping: Triangulation on the Child

Parents attempt to prepare children for the experiences of devalued status in the society while balancing and protecting the child's sense of self. They anticipate the events of discrimination and develop childrearing strategies, messages, and goals to help their children combat them. In a promoting school setting, these strategies and goals of parents have continuity because they are supported in the school. In inhibiting school settings, these goals and cultural experiences are discontinuous, undermining the development of proactive RCSs (Stevenson & Arrington, 2009). This relationship between family and school triangulates on the child and also represents the bidirectional natures of these influences (Johnson, 2005; Johnson et al., 2003). Moreover, this set of dynamic relationships exists in an ecology of "racial stress" (Peters & Massey; 1983; McAdoo, 1983). This ecology of racial stress is constantly impinging on these relations. Children's race-related coping skills emerge from this reality. African American private schools may more often represent these continuous promoting environments.

## School and Racial Coping

As the Garcia Coll et al. (1996) model indicates, school is an important socialization context. Empirical linkages have been made between the schooling environment and elementary children's racial coping orientations (Johnson, 1994; Marshall, 1995). For instance, Johnson (1994) found that among African American children who were in three types of private school settings (private elite, parochial, and Pan African), preferred strategies varied by school. Adolescents in racially heterogeneous independent schools were affected by racism experiences (Arrington & Stevenson, 2006). Studies of college students and adolescents have suggested linkages between the development of racial coping skills, personality characteristics, and success in school (Pollard 1989; Bowman & Howard, 1985; Gurin & Epps; 1975). Pollard's (1989) study of urban high school students directly linked individual and family strengths, as well as coping strategies with achievement. Bowman & Howard (1985) found that racial barrier awareness was associated with higher school grades. They concluded that the coping orientation transmitted by Black parents to their children was an important component of their motivation, achievement, and career aspirations. Many of these studies highlighted the relationship between racial socialization and achievement in more typically lower-income public school contexts and have often excluded middle-income families and children. Racial coping strategies are shaped by the stressors and supports present and working in the school context (e.g., Stevenson & Arrington, 2009).

## Comer's School-based Intervention Model

As a model of transformation, the Comer's school-based intervention model emphasizes positive, collaborative partnerships among teachers, administrators, families, and students (Comer, 1980). Improved relations between school personnel and families or other community constituencies fuel trust among families, children, and schools. Positive attributes of the school climate are increased and ultimately the learning environment as well as learning for children. Of critical importance here is the emphasis on parental empowerment among public school parents which may enhance the connection between the private schools studied and the intervention schools. Also, more trust among adults increases trust in children and this likely reduces peer tension and conflicts. Along with these changes in school climate, accompanying changes in children's racial coping strategy maturation and the school's support and monitoring of coping strategies would likely influence RCS development. A basic tenet of Comer's philosophy is that schools have failed in the past because of social, moral, and psychological considerations. Given immersion in a well-implemented program, children's ability to cope with race should also be affected by this model as a set of skills that fuse social, moral, emotional/psychological, and cultural factors, beliefs, and behaviors into the strategies utilized. Although the Comer intervention strategy does not explicitly focus on race, the normative developmental structures that underlie a child's ability to cope effectively with race are targets of the intervention. Since the intervention was intended to have an impact on overarching social and prosocial competencies in the course of normal development, racial coping skills would also be affected.

What do we expect from our private school contexts? Private or independent schools can be challenging and threatening environments to children's sense of self (Arrington & Stevenson, 2006; Slaughter, 1991; Slaughter & Carlson, 1997). Our anticipation is that this threat is offset by the homogeneous racial if not the cultural context of all-Black schools. The challenges here may emit from peer demands for cultural authenticity in some form (Fordham & Ogbu, 1986) and the issue of continuity/discontinuity with the home/family (Johnson et al., 2003). We expect the Comer environment to better support the development of proactive RCSs by comparison to the nonintervention schools. The Comer model should transform public school environments in ways that are comparable to independent schools or some intermediary form of independent schools with respect to RCSs and prosocial skill development, but how big is the gap between these public and private spaces even under the best of circumstances?

## METHOD

To emphasize the influence of school type and contexts on racial coping, we have conducted a largely descriptive analysis that focuses on two factors: school type and children's racial coping strategies.

### Data and Description of School Contexts

African American children's racial coping strategies were assessed in separate studies conducted in Chicago at two different points in time (1986–87 and

1992–1996). One study was conducted in private schools during the late 1980s and the second study was conducted in a group of public schools nearly five years later in the early 1990s.

### Private School Study Description (Johnson, 1988b, 1994)[1]

In this school setting, the racial coping strategies of 41 African American children between 5–14 years old (median age 9–10 years) attending three types of all-Black private schools (cultural immersion/Pan African, private elite, and parochial) were assessed. Families in the study were economically diverse, 80 percent of families were above median income in two of the schools and in the parochial school, a mission school, and about 70 percent of families were below the median.

### Public School Study Description (Slaugher-Defoe & Carlson, 1997)[2]

In the second study, 19 public schools participated in a four-year evaluation study of Chicago-based Comer model and matched comparison schools beginning in 1991–2 and including nearly 3,468 assessments of individual children in grades 1 and 3 from 1992 through 1996–7. Many of these schools were predominantly African American but in some schools, the distribution of ethnic groups was more diversified with significant numbers of Latino and Euro American students. The study was designed to compare the potential success of the Comer School Development Program (SDP) intervention with matched schools with no Comer intervention. In this chapter, we share information on only Comer "Model Implemented Successfully" schools (n = 6)[3] and Comparison schools (n = 9). Taken together, the present sample includes 1,239 grade 3 children. Importantly, the Comer model emphasizes school-level changes in school climate, inclusive of greater participation in educational decision-making and structural and social changes that are comparable to those aspects of some democratically-run private schools (Slaughter and Johnson, 1988).

### The Racial Stories Task (RST)

Children were administered the Racial Stories Task (RST & RST II), a series of race-related social situations and asked to resolve the problem presented in four types of scenarios (Johnson, 1988a; 1994; Johnson, D. J., Slaughter-Defoe, D., Pallock, L., and Kim, E. [2001, April]). Each of the vignettes depicts an overt racial conflict involving another child. The stories are of two types: between-group conflict characterizes four of six vignettes and the remaining two vignettes are within-group conflict. Each story requires the child to make decisions about what the character in the story should do and provide that response. The coping domains were developed and reliability conducted in previous work in the private school's study (Johnson, 1988a, 1994, 1996, 2005) and became the standard upon which reliability of the RST and coping domains were established in the public school Comer Intervention study. Though domains have been established reliably elsewhere, the individual strategies will be presented here. The stories reflect the experiences and themes of cultural authenticity, racialized verbal assaults and name calling, stereotypes and counter-stereotypes, and race pride. These strategies are detailed in a chapter in *Visible Now: Blacks in private schools* (Johnson, 1988b) and elsewhere.

### Approach

Though public and private school types vary within each grouping, only the averaged information for all private schools is provided. Comer poorly-implemented schools were eliminated from the findings presented as well-implemented Comer schools were thought to be more meaningful to the analysis. Importantly, it was clear early on that strategy generation by children could vary widely across settings with uneven "Ns". As such, understanding proportions of use would be more valuable than strict presentation of frequencies and these are used in Table 7.1. The numbers represented in Table 7.1 reflect this "usage" proportion that is comparable within strategy providing descriptive information about the strategy's relative importance across all these school types and is much less tied to numbers of participants. In addition, rankings based upon frequencies will be presented as well to demonstrate significance in variation of individual RCSs by school type, the analytical strategy is described in the next section.

### Public and Private School Comparisons: Rankings

Comparing observed and expected rankings among the three types of schools will provide some guide as to the relative usage factor for each strategy across schools types. Table 7.1 indicates that the averaged-frequencies or proportions of articulated RCSs were examined for the three school types: Private, Public—Comer Implemented Successfully, Public—Matched Comparison No Comer Implementation. To compare rankings, first, each RCS average will be ranked 1, 2, or 3, according to which of the three groups had the highest, next highest, and lowest average. Second, the highest (1) or lowest (3) ranks were inspected to determine which RCSs had a school group that was 10 or more percentage points higher or lower than the other two school groups.

## SUMMARY OF FINDINGS

In this section, we provide a brief summary of the variations within school types first in private and then in public schools (see Table 7.1). In an initial analysis (Johnson, Slaughter, Pallock, & Kim, 2001), poorly-implemented

Table 7.1
Distribution of Children's Racial Coping Strategies by School Type

| Coping Strategies | PRIVATE (n = 41) | PUBLIC Comer Implemented (n = 567) | PUBLIC Comparison (n = 672) |
|---|---|---|---|
| Assert Selfhood | 43.9%* | 29.1% | 34.5% |
| Avoid Conflict | 9.8% | 33.7% | 41.5% |
| Conform | 22.0% | 14.3% | 12.4% |
| Defer to Authority | 58.5% | 55.0% | 49.6% |
| Authoritative Directive | 7.3% | 4.6% | 2.8% |
| Engage Authority | 34.1%* | 10.8% | 9.5% |
| Change Environment | 14.6% | 22.2% | 25.6% |
| Explore | 12.2% | 8.5% | 6.1% |
| Ignore | 43.9%* | 33.7% | 32.6% |
| Project Inferiority | 4.9% | 6.0% | 5.2% |
| Legal Reasoning | 2.4% | .2% | .1% |
| Moral Reasoning (Non-racial) | 19.5% | 33.2% | 25.6% |
| Moral Reasoning (Race-related) | 17.1% | 12.7% | 10.9% |
| Negate Racial Group | 2.4% | 1.1% | 1.6% |
| Persist | 9.8% | 28.0% | 29.9% |
| Physical Confrontation | 19.5%* | 3.9% | 4.3% |
| Strategic Planning | 34.1%* | 17.3% | 17.6% |
| Racial Pride | 12.2%* | 3.7% | 4.0% |
| Subvert | Not Coded | .5% | 1.5% |
| Project Superiority | 14.6%* | 3.2% | 2.7% |
| Develop Support Systems | 12.2% | 15.7% | 22.9% |
| Verbal Confrontation | 14.6% | 12.0% | 15.3% |
| No Racial Coping Strategies | 19.7% | 10.4% | 19.8% |
| Total # of Schools | 3 | 6 | 9 |

*RCSs in which Private school students led the Public school students by 10 or more percentage points.

Comer schools were included as a third category. This information is not presented here to better underscore the public school experience, and any parallels between the private and public school experience that might exist due to the Comer SDP intervention. Next, we highlight some key points of variations in distribution of children's racial coping strategies in these two public school contexts and information about analyses in which developmental differences were assessed. Finally, we compare and contrast the incidence of racial coping strategies between the three school types: (1) Private, (2) Public—Comer Intervention, and (3) Public—Matched Comparison, non-Intervention. We will address specifically what public and private school settings appear to be offering or perhaps, diminishing in the coping skills development of African American elementary school children.

### Private Schools

#### *School Type*

The responses of private school students revealed a broad spectrum of strategies where proactive strategies incorporating use of authorities, multilayered planning, self-assertion, and bring others together were frequently employed (Defer to Authority, Assert Personal Selfhood, Engage Authority, Strategic Planning). There was also the extensive use of Physical Confrontation, a strategy that involves endorsing hitting other children as the appropriate response. Racial coping strategies that required metacognitive perspective taking were also utilized more regularly including Ignoring (a problem) and Conforming (to particular expectations).

School types were distinctive among the private schools, but only insofar as particular RCSs might distinguish them and fit with the character/philosophy of the school. So for instance, children in the Catholic school were highest in their thinking about the "right thing to do when others are involved" (Moral Reasoning–Non-racial). Children in the Pan African school had the most truncated use of all strategies and emphasized Racial Pride themes more than other schools in their coping. In the Private Elite school, children by their strategy, think of themselves as doing as well as or better than other racial groups (Project Superiority), particularly Euro Americans, for example.

Among the youngest group of children, their strategies were tied to their limited experience and to the protective coping of their parents, so a frequent strategy involved a lot of deferring to "Mom" for help (Defer to Authority). Among the middle childhood group (9 and 10 year olds), the emergence of autonomy and the beginnings of peer influence was observed in the distribution patterns of the strategies. In the oldest early adolescent group, parents' influences were still prominent in the coping patterns, but emerged as more diffuse or indirect in their coping. The children's own assertive strategies and strategies demonstrating their self-assuredness were indicated by increased used of the RCSs; Assert Selfhood and Engage Authority, for example, became prominent at this age.

### Public Schools

*School Type*

In the analysis of RCSs by school type (groups defined as Comer implemented, and comparison schools), main effects demonstrated clearly and statistically that RCSs differed by school types. Post hoc comparisons revealed that children in Comer implemented schools reported higher incidence of Moral Reasoning (racial and non-racial) and lower conflict avoidance (Avoidance) than both the non-implemented and comparison schools. Children in the Comer implemented schools used Physical Confrontation at levels that were low, but indistinguishable from the comparison group. Comer school children had a better repertoire of racial coping strategies and need for additional peer supports (Develop Support Systems) in relation to comparison schools. Use of Persistence was significantly higher in the Comer non-implemented schools than in the Comer implemented schools. On the whole, children in the Comer implemented schools used more proactive strategies and this effect was intensified as the intervention progressed.

*Developmental*

Following a subset of children from grade 1 to grade 3, it was possible to assess how strategies changed over a period of time. Here, we will summarize the findings from analyses conducted with MANOVA on Comer and comparison schools. Comer children were more challenging to adults and grew in their inquiries over time such that they were more likely to use the RCS, Engage Authority, in which they might question adults, such as teachers, when faced with an unfair situation. Children in the comparison school showed no instances of the use of the Engage Authority. Over time, Comer school children stopped using the Negate Racial Group Membership coping strategy; this strategy indicated the denial of group membership. By the time the children completed grade 3, there was minimal use of the strategy among comparison group children. Moral Reasoning, both racial (explicitly applied to race) and nonracial (emphasizing fairness or "being right") were two RCSs incorporated into one domain or category. Children in Comer schools used the Moral Reasoning strategies at higher rates in year 1 and lower rates in year 3. The interaction effect on the Moral Reasoning category stems from the change in comparison schools that were low in year 3, but again match the Comer implemented schools in year 3.

The children's use of strategies across the three schools were most distinguished by four strategies that best distinguished schools regarding development (Defer to Authority, Physical Confrontation, Change or Choice of Environments, and Negate Racial Group Membership coping strategies) as indicated by a three-way interaction effect. Defer to Authority is a strategy that younger children employ a great deal and it is expected that their deference to adults would lessen as their peer relations and self-confidence become stronger. As the Comer intervention proceeded, use of this strategy was increased among grade 3 children. Among comparison school children, there was no change in usage over time. As mentioned above, Physical Confrontation is a rarely used strategy in the public school context, but is more prominent in comparison schools. Change of Environment is a strategy that seeks to escape conflict by bettering perceived supports. Here, comparison schools begin much higher and in two years, their use of this strategy is significantly reduced. Comer school children were infrequent users in wave 1 and their reduction in usage is not as dramatic in year 3.

### Private and Public Comparisons: Rankings

The distribution of ranks between Private versus Public schools (referring to Table 7.1) was significant beyond chance: $X^2 = 38.786$, 2 d.f., $p < .001$. The Chi-square analysis suggested rejection of the hypothesis of essentially no difference in the distribution of RCS rankings between the two separated groups, notably, private versus public schools. The Private school group led the three groups 14 times (i.e., with 14 different RCSs), and 7 of these 14 RCSs bested both Public school groups by 10 or more percentage points. These 7 RCS are starred (*) in Table 7.1. In addition, the Private school group had a lower average by 10 or more percentage points in comparison to both Public school groups for two RCSs. The RCSs were Avoid Conflict, Change Environment, and Persist.

In contrast, the Public school group–Comer Implemented took second position behind the Private school group 14 times. This school group took first position only twice, with the following RCSs: Project Inferiority, and Moral Reasoning (Non-racial). The second and third groups for both of these RCSs were, respectively, Public–Matched Comparison, and Private. Importantly, however, fewer average numbers of youth in this Public school group reported having "No Racial Coping Strategies"—averaging 10.4 percent in comparison to 19.8 percent and 19.7 percent respectively for the Public–Matched Comparison, and Private groups.

Finally, the Public–Matched Comparison group led the other two school group types only seven times, reaching the 10 percent cutoff twice. This group was highest on the use of the Develop Support Systems, and lowest in the use of Defer to Authority.

In sum, either the private school setting or a school-based intervention that focuses on enhancement of school climate in a direction comparable to that experienced in high quality private schools (e.g., Comer Model), support the effective emergence and development of prosocial coping strategies among African American elementary school children. A key finding for public schools is that Comer intervention schools showed patterns indicating more maturity and growth and an edge on competencies being fostered in those enhanced climates. When compared to the patterns of the private school children, there appears to be a chasm of difference between these two types of experiences. Distinctive patterns among the private school children depart greatly from children in the two public school contexts on proactive strategies. Of note, private school children were much higher on being able to engage adults (Engage Authority) for what the child needs (Assert Selfhood, and the complex pattern of multistep plans (Strategic Planning) to achieve an outcome. Two other racial coping strategies were in much higher proportions among private school children, although of general low usage across all other school types. These included Racial Pride and similarly, Project Superiority with an RCS signifying a sense of "as good as or better."

Unanticipated differences in the patterns among the two school types was the much higher proportion use of Physical Confrontation at 19.5 percent among the private school children and less than 5 percent among the public school children. Private school children again seemed to demonstrate higher levels of efficacy, competence, and sense of control by comparison with public school youth, such that proportions of Avoidance of Conflict, Conform, and any sense of inferiority regarding racial group membership (Project Inferiority or Negate Racial Group) was very low among them.

## DISCUSSION AND CONCLUSIONS

Although descriptive and exploratory in nature, the research reported here demonstrated that public and predominantly African American private schools are likely to be vastly different contexts in which the development of children's racial coping skills evolve. Private school contexts can certainly be inhibiting school environments especially when children are lodged in more predominantly Euro American schools where more incidents of racism may occur (Arrington & Stevenson, 2006). Private school students in this study were in all African American institutions and with the exception of their confrontational strategies, proactive strategies among these youth were highly developed. These contexts may be the most continuous environments for African American youth with respect to parental goals and values for children and the least racially volatile with respect to experiences of racism allowing proactive strategies to flourish. Alternatively, these more privileged youth may arrive at school with more self-confidence and general coping resources; the disentanglement of these factors is ripe for future study. When this continuity does not exist between families and schools, then African American families with resources must work harder to both buffer their children's experiences and to achieve these problem solving pinnacles among their children (Stevenson, & Arrington, 2009).

The higher rate of the RCS, Conform among private school children was unexpected. Studies of class alone would indicate that lower SES families are more likely to value conformity (Luster, Rhoades, & Haas, 1989;

Hoff-Ginsberg & Tardiff, 1995). A subset of those children were in a parochial school and were of lower income which might explain why Conform was elevated in the private school group. Also, the dynamics of conformity in the success of middle class children should be further investigated among African American and more diverse groups of peers. We also found that the rates of conformity for the Comer children were slightly elevated as well, but not nearly as much as among the private school children.

Comer school children appear to have surpassed comparison school children in their use of a couple of key proactive strategies and the reduction of other more nonproductive and short-term success strategies. Pallock & Johnson (1998) have shown that as African American children grow older, their feelings of trust diminish, especially for adults at school. This deterioration in trust among children in middle childhood typically corresponds to a decline in their use of racial coping strategies that call upon adult authority (parents and teachers) to intervene on their behalf. Among Comer school children, there was an increase in the use of the Defer to Authority or adult authority racial coping strategy. Possibly, students in Comer schools maintain a healthy trust of adults and have internalized a belief that their intervention will be effective. Of course, children did not rely on adult authority exclusively in solving problems as there were simultaneous increases in usage in other proactive strategies overall.

Comer intervention schools indicated more inconsistent findings with respect to children's racial coping, but generally demonstrated that the development of social skills is at an elevated level for children on some strategies. There were a number of strategies that revealed trends in the direction of positive Comer effects, but with no directional test here for significant differences, these trends could not be verified. Still, the proportions indicate typical patterns for the development of social and prosocial skills.

With respect to racial socialization, has the choice of an African American school setting been in any way an advantage to Black families? Our work here indicates, in the most rudimentary way, that it very well may be the advantage that some families were seeking. This study requires systematic follow-up to address design flaws like uneven sample sizes between school types, age group differences in the private versus public school youth, or some lack equivalence in historical cohorts that might account for more advanced usage of racial coping strategies. Still, there is evidence worthy of future investigation.

Here, in the context of the late 1980s and early 1990s we tentatively suggest that African American families choosing all or predominantly Black non-public school settings as educational environments for their children may have done well. The enhanced continuity between home and school goals for their children likely accelerates children's coping skills for negotiating racialized environments and experiences. Importantly, this is not an argument for racial resegregation of elementary schools. Rather, it is an argument suggesting we should expect more of schools that educate African American children than an exclusive focus on academic achievement. Notably, these findings suggest that the schools may be advancing a climate that supports the development of these youths' prosocial and racial coping skills, especially given the larger societal contexts in which the children are expected to mature and ultimately, lead competent adult lives.

## NOTES

1. Dr. Johnson's data on private schools were obtained from her study conducted at Northwestern University in 1988, and entitled *Identity development and racial coping strategies of Black parents and their children: A stress and coping paradigm.* Contact Dr. Johnson, chapter author, for an expanded synopsis of this study. Data collected in the original private schools study (Johnson, 1988a), yielded 22 strategies. In the Comer study (Johnson et al, 2001; Slaughter-Defoe & Carlson, 1997), a new strategy emerged "Subvert" or "Subversive" increasing the strategy codes/definitions to 23. While a distinct code, it was a very rarely coded strategy and did not emerge in Milwaukee public school study, a large urban public school system. For these reasons, codes for this strategy only appear within the Comer study.

2. As co-principal investigator of the Chicago Comer School Development Research Evaluation Project funded by the MacArthur Foundation (Drs. Thomas Cook and Charles Payne were colleagues and co-investigators), Dr. Slaughter-Defoe became the organizer and convener of three poster symposia focused on "Examining the outcomes of the Chicago Comer School Development Program." Two symposia were international, and based, respectively, in Brisbane, Australia (June 10–14, 2002, Third International Conference on Child and Adolescent Mental Health), and Amsterdam (June 18–22, 2002, International Society for Cultural Research and Activity Theory (ISCRAT), Fifth Congress). Both Drs. Johnson and Slaughter-Defoe presented papers in each of these symposia, as the Racial Stories Task (RST) was administered to all available first and third graders in the participating schools. The third symposium, upon which an earlier version of this paper was presented, was national (April, 2001, Society for Research in Child Development, Minneapolis, MN). This paper, authored by Johnson, Slaughter-Defoe, Pallock, and Kim was entitled: *Longitudinal analysis of the Comer intervention on children's race-related social and prosocial problem solving.*

3. Dr. Thomas Cook developed a 10-item measure, administered annually to school staff, to assess the effectiveness of school administrative and management groups in the school, indicators of effective communication and school community, of cultural and racial inclusion, and of the use of child development knowledge by school staff. Each school had a designated slope (repeated measures general linear model with the measure as the within-subject factor and SDP status as a between subject factor) based upon four years' worth of assessments). Results obtained from this measure developed by Cook were supported by the qualitative ethnographic study of the degree of Comer intervention implementation of the nine participating Comer schools that was conducted by Dr. Charles Payne. These findings were used to classify Comer schools as more or less successfully implemented. In addition, in her specific focus on primary grade children in the overall context of this evaluation research, Dr. Slaughter-Defoe studied primary grade children's perception of school climate (Slaughter-Defoe & Carlson, 1997). Obtained data supported children's perceptions

of more favorable school climate in schools designated by Cook and Payne as "Comer Model Successfully Implemented" schools.

## REFERENCES

Arrington, E.G., & Stevenson, H.C. (2006). *Success of African American students in independent schools: Final report* (Tech. Rep. No. 001). Philadelphia. University of Pennsylvania. Graduate School of Education. SAAS Project, http://respository.upenn.edu/gse_pubs/23

Aviezer, O., Van Ijzendoorn, M.H., Sagi, A. & Schuengel, C. (1994). "Children of the dream" revisited: 70 years of collective early child care in Israel Kibbutizim. *Psychological Bulletin, 116*, 99–116.

Bowman, P.J., & Howard, C. (1985). Race-related socialization, motivation, and academic achievement: A study of black youths in three generation families. *Journal of the American Academy of Child Psychiatry*, 24, 131–141.

Comer, J.P. (1980). *School power: Implications of an intervention project.* New York, NY: Free Press.

Eisenberg, N., & Fabes, R. A. (1998). Prosocial development. In W.A. Damon, (Editor-in-Chief), N. Eisenberg (Volume Ed.), *Handbook in Child Psychology: Social, Emotional, and Personality Development*, (5th ed, vol. 3, pp. 701–778). New York, NY: John Wiley & Sons.

Fordham, S., & Ogbu, J. (1986). Black students' school success: Coping with the "burden of 'acting white.' " *Urban Review*, 18(3), 176–206.

Furman, W., & Masters, J. C. (1980). Peer interaction, sociometric status, and resistance to deviation in young children. *Developmental Psychology, 30*, 905–911.

Garcia Coll, C., Crnic, K., Lamberty, G., Wasik, B.H., Jenkins, R., Garcia, H.V., & McAdoo, H.P. (1996). An integrative model for the study of developmental competencies in minority children. *Child Development, 67*, 1891–1914.

Gurin, P., & Epps, E. (1975). *Black consciousness, identity and achievement.* New York, NY: John Wiley and Sons.

Hoff-Ginsberg E., & Tardif, T. (1995). Socioeconomic status and parenting. In M.H. Bornstein (Ed.), *Handbook of Parenting*, (Vol. 2, pp. 161–188). Mahwah, NJ: Erlbaum.

Howes, C., Matheson, C.C., Hamiliton, C. (1994). Maternal, teacher, and child care history correlated of children's relationships with peers. *Child Development, 64*, 264–273.

Hughes, D., Rodriguez, J., Smith, E.P., Johnson, D., & Stevenson, H. (2006). Parents' ethnic/racial socialization practices: A review of research and directions for future study. *Developmental Psychology, 42*(5), 747–770.

Hughes, D., & Chen, L. (1997). When and what parents tell children about race: An examination of race related socialization among African American families. *Applied Developmental Science*, 1, 200–214.

Johnson, D. J. (1988a). *Identity formation and racial coping strategies of Black children and their parents: A stress and coping paradigm.* (Doctoral Dissertation, Northwestern University, 1987), *Dissertation Abstracts International, 48*, 2581A.

Johnson, D.J. (1988b). Parental racial socialization strategies of Black parents in three private schools. In D.T. Slaughter & D. J. Johnson (Eds.), *Visible Now: Blacks in Private Schools* (pp. 251–267). Westport, CT: Greenwood Press.

Johnson, D.J. (1994). Parental racial socialization and racial coping among middle class Black children. In J. McAdoo (Ed.), *XIII Empirical Conference in Black Psychology* (pp. 17–38). East Lansing, Michigan: Michigan State University.

Johnson, D.J. (1996). *The Racial Stories Task: Situational racial coping of Black children.* Paper presented at the meeting of the International Society for the Study of Behavioral Development, Quebec City, Quebec, Canada.

Johnson, D.J. (2001). Parental characteristics, racial stress, and racial socialization processes as predictors of racial coping in middle childhood. In A. Neal-Barnett, J.M. Contreras, & K. A. Kerns (Eds.), *Forging links: African American children clinical developmental perspectives* (pp. 57–74). Westport, CT: Greenwood Press.

Johnson, D.J. (2005). The ecology of children's racial coping: Family, school and community influences. In T. Weisner (Ed.), *Discovering successful pathways through middle childhood: Mixed methods* (pp. 87–110). Chicago, IL: University of Chicago Press.

Johnson, D.J., Jaeger, E., Randolph, S.M., Cauce, A.S., Ward, J., & The NICHD Early Child Care Research Network (2003). Studying the effects of early child-care experiences on the development of children of color in the US: Towards a more inclusive agenda. *Child Development, 74*(5), 1558–1576.

Johnson, D.J., Slaughter-Defoe, D., Pallock, L., and Kim, E. (2001, April). Longitudinal analysis of the Comer intervention on children's race-related social and pro-social problem solving. Unpublished paper presented at the biennial meeting of the Society for Research in Child Development, Minneapolis, MN.

Johnson, D.J., & Spicer, P. (Eds.). (Special Section, 2009). Racial/Ethnic socialization, identity, and youth outcomes: Excavating culture. *Cultural Diversity and Ethnic Minority Psychology, 15*(1); 1–10; 27–50; *15*(2) 106–157.

Kim, E. (1999). *Ethnic minority children's racial coping: Cultural context, school context, and developmental processes.* Unpublished master's thesis, University of Wisconsin-Madison, Madison, Wisconsin.

Knight, G.P., & Kagan, S. (1977). Development of prosocial and competitive behaviors in Anglo-American and Mexican-American children. *Child Development, 48*, 1385–1394.

Luster, T., Rhoades, K., & Haas, B. (1989). The relation between parental values and parenting behavior: A test of the Kohn hypothesis. *Journal of Marriage and the Family, 51*, 139–147.

Marshall, S. (1995). Ethnic socialization of African American children: Implications for parenting, identity development, and academic achievement. *Journal of Youth and Adolescence, 24*, 377–396.

McAdoo, H.P. (1983). Societal stress: The Black family. In H. I. McCubbin & C.R. Figley (Eds.), *Stress and the family, Vol. 1: Coping with normative transitions.* New York: NY: Brunner/Mazel.

Pallock, L., & Johnson, D.J. (Feb, 1998). *Racial Socialization Newsletter.* Vol. 1, No. 1. Principal Investigator, Deborah J. Johnson.

Peters, M.F., & Massey, G.C. (1983). Mundane extreme environmental stress in the family: The case of the Black family in White America. In H. McCubbin, M. Sussman, & J. Patterson (Eds.), *Stress and the family: Advances and developments in family stress theory and research* (pp. 199–218). New York, NY: Hayworth.

Pierce, C. (1975). The mundane extreme environment and its effect on learning. In S. G. Brainard (Ed.), *Learning disabilities: Issues and recommendations for research* (pp. 1–23). Washington, D.C.: National Institute of Education.

Pollard, D.S. (1982). *Perspective of Black parents regarding the socialization of their children.* Unpublished manuscript, University of Wisconsin–Milwaukee, Milwaukee, WI.

Slaughter-Defoe, D.T. (1991). Parental education choice: Some African American dilemmas. *Journal of Negro Education, 60*(3), 354–360.

Slaughter-Defoe, D., & Carlson, K.G. (1997). Young African American and Latino children in high-poverty urban schools: How they perceive school climate. *Journal of Negro Education, 65*(10), 60–70.

Slaughter, D., & Johnson, D. (Eds.). (1988). *Visible now: Blacks in private schools.* Westport, CT: Greenwood Press.

Solomon, D., Watson, M.S., Delucchi, K.L., Schaps, E., & Battistich, V. (1988). Enhancing children's prosocial behavior in the classroom. *American Educational Research Journal, 25*, 527–554. doi: 10.3102/00028312025004527

Solomon, D., Watson, M.S., Battistich, V., Schaps, E., & Delucchi, K.L. (1996). Creating classrooms that children experience as communities. *American Journal of Community Psychology, 24*, 719–748.

Stevenson, H. C. & Arrington, E.G. (2009). Racial/ethnic mediates perceived racism and the racial identity of African American adolescents. In D.J. Johnson, and P. Spicer, (Eds.). (Special Section). Racial/Ethnic socialization, identity, and youth outcomes: Excavating culture. *Cultural Diversity and Ethnic Minority Psychology, 15*(2), 125–136.

Tesson, G., Lewko, J.H., & Bigelow, B.J. (1987). The social rules that children use in their interpersonal relations. *Contributions of Human Development, 18*, 36–57.

# PART II

. . . . . . . . . . . . . . . . . . . . . . . . . . . . . . . . . . . . . .

# Understanding Parental Educational Choices for African American Children

Education, for African American families, has historically represented the great divide between access to the middle and upper echelons of U.S. society or relegation to places of little or no choice. And "choice," as it applies to education, has traversed decades of hardship, exclusion, and school failure to ultimately offer a narrow passageway through which families might push their African American children onward to better lives with more options for success.

The chapters in Part II emphasize school choice as process, as decision making, as advocacy, as motivation, and as movement toward achieving success. As parents make educational choices within and outside of public school systems, the chapters in Part II emphasize some of the experiences of children and families in independent, charter, and public schools. In the commentary, we learn that African American families continue to have an intense urgency regarding the education of their children. Throughout the chapters, African American parents of Black children whether economically marginal or middle class, biological or White foster parents of youth often considered "Black," all have the same sense of urgency about their children's futures—they cannot await change or risk the mediocrity of poor quality schooling experiences. As such, the chapters collectively depict the processes and reasons for families becoming public school leavers, public school advocates, or maintaining the legacy of Black families in non-public schools.

· · · · · · · · · · · · · · · · · · · · · · · · · · · · · · · · · · · · ·

# 8

# Commentary: We Can't Wait for "Superman": The Importance of Parental Involvement in Schools

## Karen G. Carlson

As a former urban school administrator (principal, associate superintendent, and superintendent), I believe children are our most valuable resource. In my experience, suburban and urban parents will do whatever they possibly can to ensure the best for their children.[1] As noted earlier, parents with means, such as African American parents who can enable their children to attend private, selective enrollment public magnet, or charter schools do not gamble on their child's education. Even in such settings, however, parents and families frequently do not have all the information needed on how race and inequality can affect their children's experiences in those schools.

Several documentaries, for example, have been released recently that allude to the need for superhuman qualities to reform our public schools. In *Waiting for Superman*, we follow five families in their desperate quest to get a coveted seat for their child in excellent public charter schools. Winning a seat in one of these "great" schools is like winning the lottery. Few people win. The documentary, *Waiting for Superman*, highlights the anguish of parents and children trying to escape the public schools for what are perceived to be better charter schools. All too quietly, the movie states that only one in five charters get "amazing" results; this data is obscured in the film. Researchers at Stanford University's Center for Research on Educational Outcomes (2009) found that only 17 percent of the nation's charter schools outperform their public school counterpart; many others may actually do worse. Parents who have choices do not have time to wait for a school to get good enough for their children.

Since the release of *A Nation at Risk* (1983), parents who were able, found a number of alternatives for their children's education. Many middle-class parents of all races left urban centers and resettled in the suburbs where schools were safer and had proven track records preparing children for higher education. Those who could not leave or who chose to remain in the city, sought alternatives to their neighborhood school, choosing private elite schools, parochial schools, magnet and selective enrollment schools, and when that did not work, some decided to pursue home schooling. In Chicago, even public school teachers chose to send their own children to private, parochial, and magnet schools at a rate much higher than the general public, 38.7 percent compared to 22.6 percent (Doyle, D. P., Diepold, B., & DeSchryver, D. A., 2004).

In Chicago, the late 1980s were a time of great upheaval for the public schools. After a very long teacher strike and a visit by then-Secretary of Education William Bennett claiming Chicago's schools were the "worst in the nation," parents, community members, the business community, and teachers joined forces legislatively to topple the public school bureaucracy to create democratically run schools led by local parent-dominated boards called local school councils. Many of these schools, particularly at the elementary level, began to improve. A new brand of principal leadership emerged which was more customer-driven; concomitantly, parents became more involved in their children's schools. But while some schools improved dramatically and others improved only somewhat, not enough schools were "good enough" for all children, especially at the high school level, where parochial, private, and selective enrollment magnet schools had better outcomes, especially for children of color. In 1995, additional legislation gave control of the Chicago public schools to the mayor. Influenced by the business community, accountability strategies were employed and a serious push began to bring the middle class back to the public schools.

Market-driven strategies of competition and accountability were developed to attract families back to the public schools; these led to a number of reforms and new school models including magnet clusters within neighborhood schools, charter schools, contract schools, and performance management models. Additionally, in other urban areas, vouchers were pushed. Policy leaders and school reformers recognized that our democracy could not thrive unless every school was good enough for every child. With the passage of the 2001 legislation of No Child Left Behind (NCLB), serious achievement gaps between subgroups (race, poverty, gender, disabilities, etc.) were identified. A number of promising research-based strategies have been identified that public schools have employed over the last two decades to attempt to close the achievement gap and ensure that every school educates every child to high standards.

The Consortium on Chicago School Research (2006) found 100 Chicago schools[2] in advantaged and disadvantaged neighborhoods showed improvement when at least three of five essential supports are present: leadership, instruction, professional capacity, parent involvement, and school climate. Carlson, Shah, and Ramirez (1999) identified 13 leadership strategies that successful Chicago public school principals employed that led to far better results, including the essential supports cited above. Unfortunately, school change is messy, complex, and slow. Added to that dilemma, seats in coveted magnet and selective enrollment public schools are in short supply. Several authors in this volume point to the complexities linked to parent choice and involvement along dimensions of race and inequality within public and non-public schools.

For these reasons, until we get it right in public schools, I think middle-class parents and upwardly mobile parents of all races will "vote with their feet" whenever necessary or possible, and will continue to choose the best option possible for their precious children. Regrettably, those motivated, involved families and their children are exactly what the public schools really need to become successful and improve student outcomes. Epstein and Sheldon (2006) would argue I believe, that such families are essential to the newer emphasis on school, family, and community partnerships that is severely needed for children's successful academic experiences in non-public and public schools.

## NOTES

1. Inquiries about this chapter should be directed to Dr. Karen G. Carlson, Dominican University in River Forest, IL.
2. There are 675 schools in the Chicago Public School District.

## REFERENCES

Carlson, K.G., Shah, S., & Ramirez, M. (1999). *Leave no child behind: A Baker's Dozen Strategies to Increase Academic Achievement–An examination of Chicago's most improved schools and the leadership strategies behind them*. Chicago: Chicago Academic Accountability Council. (ERIC Document Reproduction Service No. ED436615).

Center for Research on Educational Outcomes (2009). *Multiple choice: Charter school performance in 16 states*. Stanford: CREDO. http://credo.stanford.edu/reports/MULTIPLE_CHOICE_CREDO.pdf

Chilcott, L. (Producer), & Guggenheim, D. (Director). (2010). *Waiting for Superman* (Documentary). United States: Paramount Vantage and Participant Media.

Doyle, D.P., Diepold, B., & DeSchryver, D.A. (2004). Where do public school teachers send their kids to school? *Arresting Insights in Education 1* (1). Washington, D.C.: Thomas B. Fordham Foundation and Institute. (ERIC Document Reproduction Service No. ED485524).

Epstein, J.L., & Sheldon, S.B. (2006). Moving forward: Ideas for school, family, and community partnerships. In C. F. Conrad & R. Serlin (Eds.), *SAGE Handbook for research in education: Engaging ideas and enriching inquiry* (pp. 117–138). Thousand Oaks, CA: Sage Publications.

National Commission on Excellence in Education. (1983). *A nation at risk: The imperative for educational reform*. Washington, DC: Government Printing Office.

Sebring, P., Allensworth, E., Bryk, A., Easton, J., Luppescu, S. (2006). *The essential supports fort school improvement*. Chicago: Consortium on Chicago School Research. *http://ccsr.uchicago.edu/content/page.php?cat=3&content_id=46*

# 9

. . . . . . . . . . . . . . . . . . . . . . . . . . . . . . . . . .

# The Power of Positionality in the Educational Marketplace: Lessons from the School Choices of African American Mothers

*Camille M. Wilson*

## INTRODUCTION

> I would never send my kids to a regular public school. I don't care what area it's in, whether it's way out far with all the White kids, or whatever, I wouldn't. If it's a magnet school I would. I like some of the magnet schools—they're good—but not a regular public school, no way!
>
> —an *African American Catholic school mother*

For over twenty years school reformers, scholars, and policymakers have engaged in a contentious debate over market-based school reforms, such as school vouchers and charter schools—reforms that proponents stress will benefit African American families and others who have long been denied educational liberties. The voices and perspectives of African American parents, however, have been nearly absent from the debate. In this chapter, I reflect on data from my 2000 study of the school choices of low-income and working-class African American mothers to describe how they navigated an inequitable educational marketplace and constructed their school choices. The mothers include 14 women who chose among traditional public, magnet, charter, and private schools in the Los Angeles Unified School District. In light of changes and consistencies in the school choice arena since 2000, I explain how the mothers' data shed light on the potential of charter schools and school vouchers to offer equal educational opportunity then and now. Most importantly, I emphasize how their stories illustrate how their positionality as raced, classed, and gendered choicemakers powerfully influenced their educational decision making and their school choice experiences. Hence, I build upon the data and Black feminist theories to propose that African

American mothers make *positioned* school choices and further suggest that school choicemaking often represents educational motherwork, a strategy of political resistance that entails fighting for the power to secure educational opportunities that will allow children to flourish both in schools and in society-at-large. School choicemaking for these mothers reflects the education for liberation tradition that has long influenced African American parents (Cooper, 2005, 2007, 2009; Stulberg, 2008). It also represents an important form of advocacy that educators and policymakers often negate that must inform school choice research and policies in order to fully provide African American families adequate educational options.

## THE PROMISE OF SCHOOL CHOICE REFORM

By 2000, both charter and voucher reforms were popular and controversial school choice measures that, to differing extents, relied on rules of supply and demand and constructed parents and students as education consumers. Advocates for these policies, many of whom were conservatives, claimed that the autonomous and competitive nature of market-based school choice reforms would make choice schools more accountable to the public, thereby providing a higher quality and more equitable option for all (Manno et al., 1998; Peterson, 1999). Critics suspected that underprivileged parents were destined to face defeat in a competitive educational marketplace given their limited socioeconomic resources (Henig, 1994, Wells et al., 1999). Some further suggested that parents of color were pawns in the political games of free-market proponents. They contended that market-oriented school choice reforms were inequitable and exploited parents of color by capitalizing on their hopes and desperation for better schooling, while advancing conservative political agendas that would fail to serve the parents' interests (Apple, 2001; Carl, 1994, 1996; Henig, 1996). Low-income and working-class African American families, who were the subject of many of the school choice policy debates, demonstrated interest in choice reforms—as evident by their enrollment in charter schools and participation in both publicly and privately funded voucher programs. Yet, their perspectives rarely informed either popular, academic, or policymaking debates. Consequently, I conducted in-depth qualitative study of African American mothers' school choices, experiences, and views in an effort to step back from the contentious rhetoric that both school choice proponents and critics fueled to better understand parents' standpoint. I wanted to offer the very parents that choice proponents promised to help—and critics believed would be hurt—the opportunity to define their own educational goals, needs, resources, strategies, experiences, and opinions. I hoped that such a study could offer a small, but powerful snapshot of how school choice options actually affect African American families' lives and compel educators, researchers, and school choosers to consider the school choice debate in more contextualized and careful ways.

Now that we are well in to the new millennium, debates regarding the merits of school choice reforms continue. School choice options have grown

(Wells, 2009); academic data regarding the achievement outcomes of choice schools has been collected (see Ballou, 2009; Figlio, 2009; Wells, 2009); an recent U.S. Supreme Court rulings have further deregulated the educational marketplace (see *Zellman v. Simmons-Harris*, 2002; *Parents v. Seattle*, 2007). Still, educational inequity persists, along with achievement gaps that reveal that too many African American children are struggling to academically succeed. In addition, an overwhelming amount of school choice research remains devoid of data from African American parents.

## MARKETS, EQUITY, AND AFRICAN AMERICAN PARENTS

According to a market-based paradigm—a paradigm greatly informed by rational choice theory—parents enter the educational marketplace as education consumers to shop for schools (Neiman & Stambough, 1998; Schneider, Teske, & Marschall, 2000; Vergari, 2007). Parents, consequently, set goals, seek information, evaluate prospective schools, and select their preferred school. Parents also enter the marketplace with differing values, beliefs, information, and resources (Schneider, Teske, & Marschall, 2000; Vergari, 2007).

My research on African American mothers' educational views, experiences, and choices show that race, class, and gender factors are critical to their school choicemaking and educational experiences. They also contribute to the mothers perceiving traditional public schools as sites of sociopolitical and cultural resistance. This all points to the salience of mothers' positionality and their tendency to make *positioned* school choices, rather than choices that are merely rational.

*Positionality*, a term that comes from feminist scholarship, refers to how one is socially located (or positioned) in relation to others given background factors such as race, class, and gender (Maher & Tetreault, 1993; Martin & VanGunten, 2002). A person's positionality relates to the extent to which they are privileged, resourceful, powerful, and thus able to navigate and succeed within the dominant social structure.

My notion of positioned school choice, which is also influenced by Black feminist thought (Collins, 1994, 1998, 2000), conceptualizes a highly subjective parental school choice process that is inextricably linked to choicemakers' positionality. Positioned school choices are emotional, value-laden, and culturally relevant. They are informed by how parents are politically situated within greater society and the educational structure. Furthermore, when mothers make positioned school choices to combat inequity and advocate for the safety, opportunity, and/or wellbeing of their children, those choices constitute "motherwork" (Cooper, 2007).[1] Motherwork encompasses the strivings of mothers, particularly mothers of color, to challenge inequities by enacting agency and protecting and uplifting their children (Collins, 1998).

# MOTHERS' STANDPOINT AND CHOICEMAKING CONTEXTS

To capture the school choice perspectives of African American mothers, I designed a qualitative study that incorporated feminist methodological principles. I sought to identify the shared perspective—or *standpoint*—of 14 low-income and working-class African American mothers (see Harding, 1991; Smith, 1987). This group included grandmothers who were legal guardians of their grandchildren. All of the mothers had children who previously attended traditional, elementary public schools, but were enrolled in different types of middle schools at the time of the study. I interviewed everyone twice for an average two hours each interview, gathering nearly 60 hours of data.

The Los Angeles Unified School District (LAUSD) provided the educational marketplace in which the mothers in this study functioned. At the time I conducted this study, LAUSD served 720,000 students making it the second largest school district in the nation.

LAUSD operated under a state open enrollment policy, adopted in the early 1990s, that allowed students to attend any California public school as long their families provided transportation and there was available space. In addition, LAUSD offered its own school choice options to parents as a result of its court-ordered desegregation plan, including 150 magnet programs that admitted 20 percent of applicants. Nearly 60 charters schools also functioned in the district though most of them were located outside of inner city areas; and, while the State of California has never funded school vouchers, a company operated a private voucher program in the Los Angeles area during the time of the study. So, ostensibly, LAUSD offered public school parents a range of school options, yet it proved to be a very challenging educational marketplace to navigate, and was criticized for being low-performing, inefficient, bureaucratic, and unresponsive to diverse students' needs (Birdsall, 1999).

The mothers in this study chose distinct schools given their diverse life circumstances and understanding of their options. The first set of mothers chose Walker Middle School, a traditional public school. In 2000, Walker Middle School had one of the lowest rates of student performance and parent involvement in Los Angeles and a high rate of teacher turnover. Most of its nearly 2000 students came from low-income families, and almost half of its student population was African American. The second set of mothers sent their children to Hillsdale Charter School, a racially mixed school known for its academic excellence situated in an affluent, predominantly White residential community. Hillsdale first operated as a public magnet school and then converted to a charter school in the early 1990s. Third, were the mothers who chose Imani Academy, an Afrocentric private school located just five minutes away from Walker Middle School. Almost 100 percent of Imani's 300 students were Black. Imani also enjoyed a reputation for academic excellence and offered small class sizes. Imani's annual tuition was $5,000, which mothers stressed they struggled to pay. Last, were the mothers who chose Trinity Catholic School, located in the same South Central Los Angeles region as the Imani and Walker schools. Like the academy, Trinity had approximately 300 Black students and a student's enrollment was contingent upon their parents volunteering 40 service hours a year. All three mothers paid Trinity's $200 monthly tuition, using funds from their income, child support, and/or extended family assistance; only one of the mothers said she was attracted to the school because of its religious focus.

## THE VALUE OF EDUCATION AND POSITIONED SCHOOL CHOICES

All of the mothers stressed the value of education and linked educational attainment to their children's chances of socioeconomic advancement and life success; thus, the prospect of their children attaining a quality education carried high stakes. One mother asserted that with an education, society's powerholders "can't deny you from nothing." Most of the mothers, in fact, explained that they were motivated to choose good schools for their children because doing so would enable their children to become independent; compete against more affluent peers; protect and defend themselves in a racist society; and have more prosperous life options than they themselves had (Cooper, 2005). The mothers' motivations and goals directly reflected their positionality, particularly the hardships they faced that they attributed to race, class, and gender factors. For instance, Ms. Carter, one of the mothers who placed her child at the Afrocentric academy, reflected on her reasons for withdrawing her son from a public school.[2] She asserted:

> It was like being a Black boy was something that was not good, and you have to feel good within yourself to succeed . . . And you'd be surprised how you trust your kid with a teacher, and the teacher's with him more than you are. They're with him the majority of the day and for someone to just really lower your child's self-esteem was horrible.

The mothers also emphasized what they perceived to be the inadequacy of urban, traditional public schools. They recounted numerous negative encounters they and their children had within such schools, particularly those involving teachers they characterized as unqualified, uncommitted, uncaring, and/or biased towards their children (Cooper, 2003). Most mothers associated educators' biases with the negative opinions they held about their children's racial background, disability, and/or single parent households.

In total, the mothers shared an adamant belief that their positionality, and that of their children, disadvantaged them in schools and within the educational marketplace. The mothers' positionality colored the lens through which they saw and interacted with the world. Their choices were constructed based on culturally relevant factors and their concern for their children's emotional wellbeing and academic needs; hence, they made positioned school choices.

Data from the mothers further show that their positionalities were connected to their emotional and financial hardships. The 12 single mothers in the study stressed the numerous sacrifices they made to financially provide for their families, such as working overtime each week, working two jobs, or taking public transit rather than buying a car. Furthermore, the grandmothers spoke of accepting that part of their life was on hold in order to raise their grandkids. Most of the mothers agreed with one's statement that child rearing and school choicemaking duties fall "all on me." Still, they emphasized their resolve to make the sacrifices necessary to secure the best education possible for their children.

## MOTHERS' CHOICEMAKING PROCESS

Facing the prospect of choosing a middle school inspired many of the mothers to heavily contemplate the feasibility and advantages of placing their children in a public or private school. The mothers took the initiative to investigate and evaluate their children's educational options before selecting a school. This involved calling schools and district offices and visiting prospective schools to tour the facilities or observe classrooms. A few of the private school mothers explained that they selected their child's middle school based on the referrals of others.

Data from the four grandmothers at Walker Middle School and the mothers at Hillsdale Charter School showed that these women had been active school choicemakers though they functioned within the public system. The grandmothers initially enrolled their grandchildren in Walker Middle School because it was the site closest to their residence, yet each Walker grandmother soon became disappointed with the traditional middle school. Wynda Johnson remarked:

> As far as public schools [go], I believe that a child can make it in public schools, I just don't believe that the majority will.... I mean, I see it every day. I just knew I wanted him [her grandson] to get out of this school. He never has homework. He never has books. All of this money that LAUSD has, the kids don't have books. I don't understand that. And I just don't see that the teachers and parents work together.

The other grandmothers concurred with Johnson's remarks and further noted Walker Middle School's overcrowded conditions and high teacher turnover rates. While at Walker, the grandmothers learned more about LAUSD's open enrollment policies and then pursued alternative, public school options. When I interviewed the grandmothers for the second time during the same school year, all but one had decided to transfer their grandchildren to other public middle schools.

Contrary to the Walker Middle School grandmothers, the Hillsdale Charter School mothers said their children's neighborhood public schools turned them off from the very start. The mothers perceived the schools as unsafe and having poor academics and/or inappropriate special education programs for their children. The three mothers who had children with special needs explained that they were aware of open enrollment policies and their right to select a school that could accommodate their children. These mothers agreed that obtaining information about their school choice options via word-of-mouth was often easier than getting it from district officials. Jenay Adams, whose son had autism, asserted:

> No one wants to tell you anything. It's like if we [the school district] tell you that this is available you might ask for it and it'll cost money, so we're not going to tell you.... No, no, no, they don't tell you anything! I learned about everything from other parents, but a lot of times that happens too late.

The other charter school mothers agreed that the choice process could be "discouraging." The six private school mothers had limited experience choosing among Los Angeles's public schools. In fact, all but one sent their children to only one public school before transferring them to Imani Afrocentric Academy or Trinity Catholic School. Consequently, the most significant school choice the private school mothers made was choosing to exit the public school system because, as they insisted, their children were not being "challenged." Ms. Mathis, a Catholic school mother, explained that she preferred private schools because they are "smaller, it's more of a unity, it's more organized, and people are more involved because public schools act like they don't care if they want parents." Whereas the three Imani Academy mothers contended that, unlike in public schools, Imani's administrators and teachers maintained very high expectations of Black students and expressed sincere interest in their academic performance and personal well-being.

A school's racial composition also proved to be important to several mothers. Mothers from each of the four schools stressed the value of their children gaining cultural "exposure" and "getting along" with other racial/ethnic groups so they could excel in a diverse society. The Imani and Trinity mothers further noted their children had access to Black teachers and "role models," thereby helping them to flourish in a culturally affirming environment. Finally, just a few mothers said high test scores or percentile rankings were a significant choice criterion.

The concept of positioned school choice accounts for the fact that the mothers in this study maintained a holistic view of quality schooling, which previous school choice literature rarely acknowledges or validates (Doyle & Feldman, 2006; Garcia, 2008; Smrekar, 2009). The fact that some mothers had to make school choices that involved protecting their children's physical and emotional welfare before worrying about test scores and academic rankings does not mean they were unwise choicemakers. Instead, it reflects the social and political realities of their environment, their lives, and the status of urban, public schools.

## MOTHERS' VIEWS OF CHARTERS SCHOOLS AND SCHOOL VOUCHERS

While market advocates contend that charter schools and public school vouchers can help level the playing field for parents like the mothers in this study (Van Heemst, 2004; Vitteritti, 1999), the mothers' views and experiences cast doubt over such assertions. In 2000, charter schools were a relatively new school option; still, it was surprising that most of the mothers (aside from those at Hillsdale) had never heard of them. Hence, I overviewed the charter school idea for them and noted the advantages and disadvantages that proponents and opponents claim. The charter school idea impressed almost all of the mothers since, at the time of the study, the schools were autonomous, known to be more responsive to parents, and had small student populations (Nathan, 1996; Vitteritti, 1999). Mothers from all four schools perceived charter schools as offering benefits to individual students and families, but said they were not convinced that charters could spark competition among public schools and lead to significant reform overall. Interestingly, Ms. Rogers, a mother at Hillsdale Charter School, commented that LAUSD sends a "confusing" pamphlet to district parents each year that describes various school choice options and reform policies. She asserted that the information is "Greek" to most Black parents who "just don't know."

The mothers were much more aware of the school voucher concept and the heated debate surrounding it. With some reservations, a few mothers explained that they favored the adoption of publicly funded school vouchers. Ms. Chiles, an Afrocentric Academy mother, asserted that vouchers would give working-class parents like herself the financial boost they need to afford private school tuition. Yet, she stated that a voucher "may help you get a shorter line, but it's not going to be your ticket to get in." She added that many Black families would still be "left out of the loop," but indicated that it is better to adopt a school choice policy that benefits some African American families rather than help none. Similarly, another mother from Imani asserted:

> Vouchers would really help supplement [my efforts to pay tuition], whereas putting her in a public school that's not up to par—to me—I'm doing my child a disservice . . . It's almost like every man for himself really. . . . I do feel bad about that, but I can't hold my child back because of that.

The majority of mothers expressed their disapproval of public school vouchers and doubted that many parents could afford to pay the rest of the tuition since they themselves would be unable to do so. Indeed, five mothers were particularly familiar with the voucher concept given that they explored private voucher options through a private voucher association. Four of these mothers, however, lacked the funds and access to transportation to make the private voucher worthwhile.

Ms. Rogers, from Hillsdale Charter School, explained that "the scholarship was something like $1,500 each, which on a tuition of $8,000 for the year, wasn't a drop in the bucket." Ms. Barrett, a Catholic school mother, who applied for a private voucher and was denied, insisted:

> They need to take that money and improve the public school system, and then we can take our kids out of these private schools, honestly. If they could put the money into the schools around here, and have them where they're safe, and have them where the classrooms are small, and they have teachers there that can control their classrooms, then [my daughter] would be getting dropped off every morning at a public school and picked up from a public school.

Like Barrett, most of the mothers who provided anti-voucher remarks pointed to ways that policymakers should reform urban public school systems rather than "abandon" them.

## LESSONS LEARNED

The data from the mothers in this study indicate the diversity of views African American parents have about the merit of market-based, school choice reforms. At the same time, the mothers offered an important shared standpoint from which researchers and policymakers can learn. The mothers pinpointed the key limitation of school choice initiatives—their capacity to assist only a small segment of the African American working-class or low-income population. Parents are clearly not advantaged by reform initiatives they distrust or know little about. Nevertheless, the mothers in this study held out tremendous hope that educational attainment would improve their children's lives, and they made significant sacrifices to pursue alternatives to traditional public schools. The mothers also stressed the importance of improving traditional, urban public schools and emphasized the need for educators to serve all African American children well. Still, they said that they cannot rely on education powerholders to serve their interests; consequently, the mothers served as school choice-makers and active advocates for their children in various school settings.

All but three of the 14 mothers chose to withdraw their children from the traditional public school system by the end of this study. Their choice to exit the public school system reflected their frustration and unwillingness to have their children miss out on educational opportunities while reformers and policymakers debated about how to improve the traditional system. Indeed, the educational market's competitive forces did not drive the educational decision making of the mothers in this study, nor did the rhetoric of school choice proponents and critics. Mothers were driven instead by a quest for equal educational opportunity and school choice initiatives offered the mothers hope. The mothers' hope of gaining the power, resources, and opportunities their children need to advance in an unequal society motivated them to make positioned school choices. Their choicemaking efforts further constituted "motherwork"—an important form of political and cultural resistance (Cooper, 2009).

While the findings from this study cannot be generalized to all African American mothers, even a decade after the study, the data offers valuable insight and important theoretical implications regarding school choice. Data show that the school choice standpoint of the mothers is inextricably linked to the meaning they made from their racial, class, and gender identities and life contexts. The fact that their positionality deeply impacted their standpoint and school choicemaking accords with the idea that race, class, and gender are interlocking features of Black women's identities and epistemology for which the notion of *positioned choice* accounts (Cooper, 2005, 2007).

The positioned choice concept helps one contextualize the mothers' decision making. It does not negate African American mothers' rationality or logic; rather, it helps analysts understand that the mothers (and others like them) are very rational, but in more complex and sophisticated ways than many educators, scholars, or policymakers typically identify.

## IMPLICATIONS FOR TODAY'S SCHOOL CHOICE ARENA

Since I completed my study of African American mothers' school choicemaking in 2000, public school choice options have increased for parents, including the establishment of more charters schools throughout the nation, the endorsement of charters schools in No Child Left Behind legislation, and the backing of charter schools by both Republican and Democratic leaders (Goldring, 2009; Wells, 2009). On the other hand, the U.S. economic recession has constrained the resources of millions of families since 2007, decreasing their ability to afford private school (Kuznia, 2011), and school vouchers options are few. Publicly funded voucher programs only exist in Florida, Milwaukee, and Cleveland while some small-scale, privately funded voucher programs operate throughout the country (Figlio, 2009). In all, public magnet school programs remain the most popular school choice option in the United States (Goldring, 2009); but, as I note below, various options have not necessarily decreased the inequities of the educational marketplace.

### Inconclusive Academic Outcomes

The satisfaction rates of parents whose children attend choice schools are higher than those who attend traditional public schools (Goldring, 2009; Figlio, 2009), yet the academic achievement rates for choice school students are not generally higher. With regard to the academic outcomes of charter school students, Wells (2009) stresses that "the preponderance of evidence is that student achievement is highly uneven in charter schools and generally not significantly higher than that of similar students in regular public schools" (p. 156). Likewise, the academic data regarding magnets are largely inconclusive but, like charter schools, they do reap some positive effects depending on curriculum, structure, and grade levels (Ballou, 2009). Nevertheless, as the data from the mothers in my study supports, standardized academic data is not all that matters to African American parents. Non-academic issues, such as diversity, the moral and/or religious values of educators, curricular preferences, and social fit matter as well (Cooper, 2009; Figlio, 2009; Pedroni, 2005). These issues, while not measured by tests, influence the overall schooling experience of students and shape how parents assess school quality.

### Absence of Parental Voice in Research and Policy

School choice reform undoubtedly remains a crucial aspect of education policy and is a hot topic among education researchers. The few researchers who have studied African American school choicemaking and/or African American choice schools since 2000 have found that African American parents' desire for school choice has not wavered. Many African American families are still willing to struggle and sacrifice to flee low-performing schools, secure educational opportunities for their children, and enact agency by taking advantage of school choice options (Pedroni, 2005; Stulberg, 2008).

Pedroni's (2005) research is one of the only other studies that explicitly examines the school choices of Black women. He specifically investigates Black women advocates of Milwaukee's school voucher program and affirms the significant educational influence that Black mothers have had. He further explains that their agency, along with their raced, classed, and gendered identities, have not been adequately captured by either conservatives or liberals, nor by choice proponents or opponents. Pedroni calls upon critical educators to "envision strategies for rearticulating marginalized families' educational concerns to ultimately [spark] more effective, meaningful, and democratic educational reform" (p. 104). I support much of his analysis, yet further suggest that the "rearticulation" of African American families' perspective is not needed as much as the deeper examination and *reinterpretation* of their standpoint.

Educators, scholars, and policymakers must give Black families more credit for their wisdom, intelligence, strategies, and risk taking and thus, provide parents greater opportunities to articulate their own views. Only through better understanding how parents construct and exercise school choices can equitable, high-quality school choice options be devised and more fairly implemented.

## ACKNOWLEDGMENT

An earlier version of this chapter appeared as Cooper, C.W. (2005). School choice and the standpoint of African American mothers: Considering the Power of Positionality. *The Journal of Negro Education, 74,* 174–189. Excerpts reprinted with permission from *The Journal of Negro Education,* © 2005 Howard University. Website: www.journalnegroed.org.

## NOTES

1. For an extensive discussion of the historical contexts related to school choice and African American parents, see Cooper 2005, 2007, 2009. The Cooper 2007 and 2009 articles also respectively emphasize how African American mothers' choicemaking can help educators reconceptualize notions of advocacy, parent involvement, and care.
2. Pseudonyms are used for all mothers and schools.

## REFERENCES

Apple, M.W. (2001). *Educating the "right" way: Markets, standards, god, and inequality.* New York: RoutledgeFalmer.

Ballou, D. (2009). Magnet school outcomes. In M. Berends, M.G. Springer, D. Ballou, & H.J. Walberg (Eds.), *Handbook of research on school choice* (pp. 155–178). New York: Routledge.

Carl, J. (1994). Parental choice as national policy in England and the United States. *Comparative Education Review, 38*(3), 294–322.

Carl, J. (1996). Unusual allies: Elite and grass-roots origins of parental choice in Milwaukee. *Teachers College Record, 98*(2), 266–285.

Chubb, J.E., & Moe, T.M. (1990). *Politics, markets, and America's* schools. Washington, D.C.: The Brookings Institute.

Cobb, C.D., & Glass, G.V. (1999). Ethnic segregation in Arizona charter schools. *Education Policy Analysis Archives, 7*(1). Retrieved October, 2000 from http://www.olam.ed. asu.edu/eppa

Collins, P.H. (1994). Shifting the center: Race, class, and feminist theorizing about motherhood. In E.N. Glenn, G. Chang, & L.R. Forcey (Eds.) *Mothering: Ideology, experience, and agency.* New York: Routledge.

Collins, P.H. (1998). *Fighting words: Black women and the search for justice.* Minneapolis: University of Minnesota Press.

Collins, P.H. (2000). *Black feminist thought: Knowledge, consciousness, and the politics of empowerment.* (2nd ed.). New York: Routledge.

Cooper, C.W. (2003). The detrimental impact of teacher bias: Lessons learned from African American mothers. *Teacher Education Quarterly, 30*(2), 101–116.

Cooper, C.W. (2005). School choice and the standpoint of African American mothers: Considering the power of positionality. *Journal of Negro Education, 74*(2), 174–189.

Cooper, C.W. (2007). School choice as "motherwork": Valuing African-American women's educational advocacy and resistance. *International Journal of Qualitative Studies in Education, 20,* 491–512.

Cooper, C.W. (2009). Parent involvement, African American mothers, and the politics of educational care. *Equity and Excellence in Education, 42*(4), 379–394.

Diamond, J.B. & Gomez, K. (2004). African American parents' educational orientations: The importance of social class and parents' perceptions of schools. *Education and Urban Society, 36*(4), 383–427.

Figlio, D. (2009). Voucher outcomes. In M. Berends, M.G. Springer, D. Ballou, & H.J. Walberg, (Eds.) *Handbook of research on school choice* (pp. 321–337). New York and London: Routledge.

Garcia, D.R. (2008). Academic and racial segregation in charter schools: Do parents sort students into specialized charter schools?*Education and Urban Society 40*(5), 590–612.

Gewirtz, S., Ball, S.J, & Bowe, R. (1995). *Markets, choice, and equity in education.* Buckingham, UK: Open University Press.

Goldring, E.B. (2009). Perspectives on Magnet schools. In M. Berends, M.G. Springer, D. Ballou, & H. J. Walberg (Eds.), *Handbook of research on school choice* (pp. 361–378). New York and London: Routledge.

Harding, S. (1991). *Whose science? Whose knowledge? Thinking from women's lives.* Ithaca, NY: Cornell University Press.

Henig, J. (1994). *Rethinking school choice: Limits of the market metaphor in education.* Princeton, NJ: Princeton University Press.

Henig, J. (1996). The local dynamics of choice: Ethnic preferences and institutional responses. In B. Fuller, R. Elmore, & G. Orfield (Eds.), *Who chooses, who loses? Culture, institutions, and the unequal effects of school choice.* New York: Teachers College Press.

Kuznia, R. (2011, Jan 10). Recession tied to private school declines. *Daily Breeze.* Retrieved online from http://www.dailybreeze.com/news/ci_17043255

Levin, H.M. (1991). The economics of educational choice. *Economics of Education Review, 10*(2), 137–158.

Lewis, D., & Nakagawa, K. (1994). *Race and educational reform in the American metropolis: A study of school decentralization.* Albany: State University of New York Press.

Maher, F.A., & Tetreault, M.K. (1993, July). Frames of positionality: Constructing meaningful dialogues about gender and race. *Anthropological Quarterly, 66*(3), 118–126.

Manno, B.V., Finn, C.E., Jr., Bierlein, L.A., & Vanourek, G. (1998). Charter schools: Accomplishments and dilemmas. *Teachers College Press, 99*(3), 537–558.

Martin, R.J., & VanGunten, D.M. (Jan–Feb, 2002). Reflected identities: Applying positionality and multicultural social reconstruction in teacher education. *Journal of Teacher Education, 53*(1), 44–54.

Miller, J.J. (1992). Whose choice? School choice has its natural opponents. Hint: they're not black parents. *National Review, 44*(24), p. 44 (2 pps.).

Moe, T.M. (Ed.) (1995). *Private Vouchers.* Palo Alto, CA: Hoover Institute Press.

Nathan, J. (1996). *Charter schools: Creating hope and opportunity for American education.* San Francisco: Jossey-Bass.

Neiman, M., & Stambough, S.J. (1998). Rational choice theory and the evaluation of public policy. *Policy Studies Journal, 26*(3), 449–465.

Parents Involved in Community Schools v. Seattle School District No. 1, 551 U.S. 701 (2007).

Parker, L., & Margonis, F. (1996). School choice in the US urban context: Racism and policies of containment. *Journal of Education Policy, 11* (6), 717–728.

Pedroni, T.C. (2005). Market movements and the dispossessed: Race, identity, and subaltern agency among Black women voucher advocates. *Urban Review 37*(2), 83–106.

Peterson, P. (1999, Oct 4). A liberal case for vouchers. *New Republic*, p. 29.

Schneider, M., Teske, P., and Marschall, M. (2000). *Choosing schools: Consumer choice and the quality of American schools*. Princeton and Oxford: Princeton University Press.

Smith, D. (1987). *The everyday world as problematic: A feminist sociology*. Boston: Northeastern University Press.

Smrekar, C. (2009). The social context of magnet schools. In M. Berends, M. G. Springer, D. Ballou, & H. J. Walberg (Eds.), *Handbook of research on school choice* (pp. 393–408). New York: Routledge.

Stulberg, L.M. (2008). *Race, schools & hope: African Americans and school choice after Brown*. New York: Teachers College Press.

Trent, S.C. (1992, Oct). School choice for African-American children who live in poverty: A commitment to equity or more of the same? *Urban education, 27*(3), 291–307.

Van Heemst, D.B. (2004). *Empowering the poor: Why justice requires school choice*. Oxford: Scarecrow Education.

Vergari, S. (2007). The politics of charter schools. *Educational Policy, 21*(1), 15–39.

Vitteritti, J.P. (1999). *Choosing equality: School choice, the constitution, and civil society*. Washington, D.C.: Brookings Institute Press.

Wells, A.S. (1993). The sociology of school choice: Why some win and others lose in the educational marketplace. In E. Rassell & R. Rothstein (Eds), *School choice: Examining the evidence*. Washington, D.C.: Economic Policy Institute.

Wells, A.S. (2009). The social context of charter schools. In M. Berends, M. G. Springer, D. Ballou, & H. J. Walberg (Eds.), *Handbook of research on school choice* (pp. 155–178). New York: Routledge.

Wells, A.S., Lopez, A., Scott, J., & Holme, J.J. (1999). Charter schools as postmodern paradox: Rethinking social stratification in an age of deregulated school choice. *Harvard Educational Review, 69*(2), 172–204.

Wells, A.S., Holme, J.J., Lopez, A., & Cooper, C.W. (2000). Charter schools and racial and social class segregation: Yet another sorting machine? In R. Kahlenberg (Ed.), *A notion at risk: Preserving public education as an engine for social mobility*. New York: The Century Foundation.

# 10

## Parental Choice and Involvement in the Education of Sudanese Unaccompanied Minors

*Meenal Rana, Deborah J. Johnson, Laura V. Bates, Desiree B. Qin, and Andrew Saltarelli*

### INTRODUCTION

The connection between school and home is a key factor in school success in Western countries (Epstein, 1987). Parent involvement in school is often related to the social class of the parents (Lareau, 2000). Parents who are well-educated and have financial means are not only more involved in their children's school, but also have the power to choose school environments and make educational choices not open to less affluent parents (Kleitz, Weiher, Tedin, & Matland, 2000; Lareau, 2000). They can choose leading schools by moving into better school districts, by paying for private schooling, by using resources to enable attendance in charter schools, or by initiating school transfers. In addition to selecting good quality schools for their children, parents can be involved in schools and the educational process in many ways (Bronfenbrenner, 1979). This includes advocating for their children, meeting with teachers, helping children make class choices, and serving as board members (Epstein, 1987). There may be different levels of parent involvement in school (Lareau, 2000).

The Sudanese refugee youth, often referred to as the "Lost Boys of Sudan," came to the United States in 2000–2001 unaccompanied by their biological families and were placed with U.S. foster parents who were primarily White and middle class. Their adjustment to the American context included swift introductions to a number of status phenomena, including both class and race. The process of "becoming American" for these youth included the experience of assigned status that interlaced their refugee/ambiguous orphan statuses with intermittently prescribed status as African American. Sometimes, they are "just Black" imbued with the meaning of marginalized status but more generically and historically than for native African Americans. Therefore, the role of foster parents intersects with class, race, and the immigrant experience. Given the role of parents in children's education, how do children succeed academically when parents are absent during their initial school years? What happens to their schooling when they migrate to a different country without their biological and cultural parents? The present study explores educational choices and involvement of foster parents in the schooling of their Sudanese foster youth in the United States. In this inquiry, we particularly note where the intersections described earlier arise for the foster parents.

## BACKGROUND

The civil war in Sudan separated the Sudanese youth from their parents and in 2000–01, their resettlement with U.S. foster families began. During the war, the youth witnessed and experienced deprivation and extraordinary displacement (Bixler, 2005). Children separated from parents endured trauma and adversity during a 1,500-mile trek made on foot through three African countries (i.e., Sudan, Ethiopia, and Kenya). The children were eventually placed in refugee camps where they lived for many years without much adult support (Luster, Johnson, & Bates, 2008). In the Kakuma refugee camp (Kenya), children were able to attend schools opened by the United Nations (UN) on a more frequent basis. However, these UN schools lacked resources and were often disrupted by war (Luster et al., 2008). At best, adults in the refugee camps sometimes provided informal counseling to the children. Children who attended the school in Kakuma were either self-motivated or prodded by their peers and camp counselors. The Sudanese youth not only had very limited educational experience in Africa (Luster et al., 2008), but also encountered numerous challenges when they began to attend in schools in the United States. These difficulties included limited English skills, academic challenges related to inadequate educational preparation, an unfamiliar school system, financial constraints, mental health issues, and adjustment with peers in schools (Rana, Qin, Bates, Luster, & Saltarelli, 2011).

Given their inadequate educational experiences in the past and new challenges in the United States, it is critical to explore how U.S. foster parents of Sudanese youth—the majority of whom were White and middle class, helped them make school choices and complete their education. The context of the study is unique in that even though the foster parents were empowered by their race, education, and social class to make educational choices for these youth and be involved in their education—race, immigration status, and language could easily put the Sudanese youth at risk for interpersonal and institutionalized racism and school failure. Another unique aspect of the study is that although these youth migrated without their parents and were therefore at risk, they were also somewhat advantaged over other immigrant children by having American foster parents who were familiar with the education system in the United States. Residing with immigrant parents would have meant learning to navigate the system along with them (Sluzki, 1979).

We used Hirschman's framework (1970) to understand the educational choices of foster parents caring for Sudanese refugee youth. This framework emphasizes a consumer model of educational choice where the relationship between customer satisfaction and the quality of any service organization are critically linked to the reactions of customers. In this study, we consider parents as customers and schools as service organizations. According to Hirschman, when customers are powerful and can afford to make different choices if dissatisfied, they can respond in two different ways to low quality services at schools: They could "exit" from that school and look for a better quality of services in other public or private systems, or they could demand improvement in the quality of services by advocating for changes to improve academic standards and address individual needs.

According to the 2000 U.S. Census, about 10 percent of all children enrolled in middle and high school in the United States attend non-public schools; 11 percent of Asian and European Americans, 6 percent of African Americans and Latino children are enrolled in private schools (U.S. Census, 2000). Research on the educational choices of African American parents indicates that those who select private over public schools for their children are concerned about low quality of education and lack of resources in public schools (Ascher, 1986). The factors that attract these parents toward private schooling are: (a) higher academic or disciplinary standards; (b) better academic preparation for good jobs; (c) networks and social skills, and (d) environment to strengthen racial identity (Ascher, 1986; Carter, Jones-Wilson, & Arnez, 1989; Lee, Chow-Hoy, Burkam, Geverdt, & Smerdon, 1998). Parents also make choices to be involved in their children's education.

This study is an extension of Epstein's (1987) model of parent involvement—the uniqueness lies in how White parents became involved for the first time in their Sudanese foster children's education when the youth were adolescents. Many parents in this study were, like the youth they fostered, confronting marginalization based upon race or skin color for the first time. This nebulous "blackness" ascribed and given meaning by the communities and school institutions around them would be new experiences for these parents. As parents negotiate school choice and involvement, would their class and race capital be challenged or would they wield these resources despite the new circumstances? Importantly, would they respond to the schooling experiences of their Black foster children in ways similar to those of U.S. African American parents?

## METHOD

This study is part of a larger research project on Sudanese *Lost Boys* initiated in 2001, focusing on their risk, resilience, and adaptation to a new culture. Data for this paper are drawn from in-depth interviews with U.S. foster parents seven years after resettlement of the Sudanese youth.

## Participants and Setting

With the assistance of the resettlement agency, 19 Sudanese refugees, and 20 parents from 15 foster families in the United States were recruited and participated in our interviews. Altogether we interviewed five couples, three married mothers where fathers were not present at the time of interviews, two single fathers, and five single mothers. Most of the foster parents were European Americans (75%); 10 percent of the parents were African American, and 15 percent identified as being from other ethnic groups (second generation Mexican, Asian, and Middle Eastern; first generation African). In data analyses, we emphasized only the perspectives of White foster parents. However, we do present data from two African American parents and one African immigrant parent anecdotally in our discussion to suggest comparisons with the majority White parents.[1]

## Interviews

The 2.5-hour semi-structured parent interview focused on their experiences as foster parents and the help they provided to the youth. At the time of resettlement, the mean age of the youth was 15 years (SD = 2.34), and the youngest child was 11 years[2] old. Data for this chapter were drawn from responses to questions on the ways foster parents were involved in youth's education and made choices to enhance their school experiences and how their foster parents' educational choices affected their school experiences. All interviews were taped with their consent and later transcribed. Original interviewers examined the transcripts for accuracy before they were coded.

## Data Analysis

Two members of the research team conducted thematic analysis of the transcribed interviews. A three-step coding procedure was used: open, axial, and selective coding (Strauss & Corbin, 1990). The context and processes were also carefully examined while coding the data. The individual coders achieved consensus on the key stories told by the participants.

# RESULTS

The results are presented in three parts: We first describe the parents who made educational choices for their foster children; then, we discuss the types of educational choices that these parents made; and last, we share how the foster parents were involved with their youth's education.

**Description of Parents Who Made Educational Choices**

In our study, five youths went to private schools, one attended a school of choice, and 13 attended public schools in seven different districts. Besides references to youth who participated in our study, foster parents also talked about the schooling of the other Sudanese refugee youth who had lived with them. At least four of the 15 foster families in the study chose private schools for youth living with them. Irrespective of the type of school youth attended, most parents encouraged the youth to finish their schooling by communicating that in the United States, the pathway to upward mobility and a better life is through education.

Parents who chose to send their foster children to private schools worked hard to make it happen. All the parents reported using their savings and loans to send these youth to private schools. In the words of one of the parents, "We took our foster care money and paid for a private school for them and then just used our own money and loans from family." One of the parents, a single father, chose five different schools for each of his five foster youth in various parts of the city. When we asked him about how he managed to do that, he shared with us:

> I would drive them all to school each morning, and it took me an hour and a half, and then I would drive to work. I think by doing this [making choices of school] I helped my kids. I didn't just say, well we live in this neighborhood so you're gonna go to that school. I understand the importance of school and I will drive my kids across town to get them to the best school.

One parent wanted to put all his foster children into a Christian school, but financial limitations caused him to send only the youngest of his three Sudanese foster children to the school. He reasoned that this child would have to spend many years in school—thus, he would need a positive environment for a longer duration. Parents who sent foster youth to various public schools reported different experiences of working with the school system depending on the youth's abilities and the neighborhoods where they lived.

**Types of School Choices**

Parents in our study made two different types of school choices, either they selected private schools for the youth residing with them or they chose a public school district that catered to the unique needs of youth in their care. These types of choices seemed linked to the immigrant/refugee nature of their experiences and the need for more attentive and individualized environments. Some parents were satisfied with the public schools that their foster children were attending; others were less satisfied, and thus, they were highly involved in the school community through their service on school boards or through their advocacy efforts for additional support for the Sudanese youth.

The foster parents made educational choices based on various factors. These factors can be categorized into two main groups: (a) positive experiences and perceptions of private schools, and (b) negative experiences and perceptions of public school environment and educational quality.

### Experiences/Perceptions of Private Schools

Some parents opted for private schools because of their positive perceptions of their educational and/or social climate or because they believed these schools had better educational support.

### *High Academic Standards*

Private schools provided rigorous academic standards, according to the parents who decided to send their foster children to these schools. They were viewed as having better preparation for college and better supports for English language learners. One of the parents viewed private schools as having the potential to better serve the individual needs of the youth because their high academic standards were a better match for the youth's talents and intellectual abilities. In his words:

> [Name of the youth] was an incredibly bright kid and I didn't want to put him in [Name of the district] public school, so I paid to put him in Catholic school—just because I could see that this is a bright kid, and I want him to get the best education.

### *Nurturing Environment*

Besides higher academic standards, foster parents perceived that youth would be better socialized with other highly motivated children attending the private schools. These parents also perceived that past trauma of the youth due to war and violence in Africa and limited education in camps would require a more supportive environment to fill the gap in their education. One of the parents provided the following insights:

> I mean a lot of these kids walk out, because they've got all the things that should push them in the wrong direction are already there. Nonexistent parents cause they are always working, mental health issues, behavioral issues, they've seen war, violence, etc. it's all present, but if they can get into a nurturing environment, a lot of those things turn into benefits and turn into tools that they could use.

### *Good Resources and Staff*

The foster parents perceived private schools to have more resources to support youth's academic pursuits. They also indicated that staff seemed dedicated to spending extra time helping the youth to "catch up" academically.

In reflecting, one parent said, "I know they [the school staff] made exceptions for the boys, they definitely gave them a whole lot attention—they really really embraced them."

### Experiences/Perceptions of Public Schools

Some parents made educational choices based on negative perceptions of, or experiences with, public schools. In the public school context, they frequently chose to "voice" their concerns within their school districts.

#### *Lack of Resources/Ill-prepared Schools*

Some parents found that the school districts were not ready for the Sudanese immigrant youth—the budgeting process for the school year had already been completed prior to the arrival of the youth, and thus, no allocation had been made to support the additional needs of the youth, such as ESL assistance. Due to lack of ESL services in many school districts, some of the youth were required to join special education classrooms. Some of these public schools also lacked proper reading and writing materials. One of the parents expressed her frustration:

> They [school] would send him [the youth] home with these math worksheets that I couldn't read because the print was so fine and then the copy was so poor, it was like, I can't read it—10th generation photocopy, you know.

Another parent shared, "They [school staff] weren't prepared, children of that age, teenagers, who couldn't read, maybe more than a second, third, fourth grade level. So this was a real undertaking on their part, not financially having the money."

#### *Low Expectations of Teachers*

The parents whose youth went to public school perceived that some of the teachers in their school districts had very low expectations for them. A parent whose child did not finish his homework talked with his ESL teacher about it. According to this parent, the ESL teacher conveyed her lower expectation for the youth as such, "Oh, he [the youth] turned in [his homework]. I told him he did a great job. You know in the spring he could barely write sentences, at least now he's punctuating and capitalizing." Another parent shared how one of the teachers did not have high expectations and made her child sit in the back of the classroom. Parents mentioned that some teachers indicated that they [the teachers] did not have enough time to pay individual attention to the youth.

#### *Less Motivated Peers*

Parents were challenged by the intersection of ascribed race and class distinctions of the youth in the form of external expectations for them. Some of the parents feared that their youth would end up in the company of unmotivated peers. One of the foster parents reported, "[Youth's name] was even threatened because he was making good grades in school and other kids didn't appreciate it." Some parents' own stereotyped lenses created fears about the educational climate in public schools. These parents had negative perceptions of public schools in low income and minority communities. They feared that the youth would adopt poor behavior and learning practices learned from their school peers: "The kids [Sudanese] come buttoned up, very polite and then walk out of [name of a school district] as gang members." These perceptions may have been related to the youths' adoption of practices associated with "youth culture" as it exists currently in U.S. schools.

Many youth who went to public schools reported incidences of racism in school. Their parents also talked about the racism that youth had to face due to lack of diversity in some of the public school districts. One of the parents shared her apprehensions by saying, "How would they [youth] adapt to going to the school where the only other minority students are, if somebody else has a foster kid, cuz those are the only Blacks in this school are foster children."

### Public School Quality Choices

Some parents in our study selected school districts with higher academics than those of schools that were located in their neighborhood school district. A parent whose foster son spoke a different language than English put him into a city school where the youth's home language was taught. This parent did not compromise on the quality of public school for his foster youth. In his words:

> I hate the public school in my neighborhood. It has got a bad reputation. I met with the principal when I got my first domestic kid [foster child] and I was not impressed. And I vowed to myself that I would never send any of my kids here, and I never have.

Some parents, who were either teachers or were on the school board, shared how different school districts had different levels of academic standards, resources, and support to help refugee and immigrant populations. This awareness aided them in making school choices and in determining the level of school involvement required on their part. Having compared many school districts before selecting a good school for one of his foster children, one parent shared with us:

> I was just checking the MEAP scores for all the high schools in [name of the city]. Two thirds of the kids in that school do not speak English as their primary language. They're the fourth highest MEAP score out of all the high schools in [name of the city]. The principal and the teachers are the best.

## Public School—No Choice

There were a few parents who were satisfied with the academic standards and support of their school districts. They were appreciative of staff and administrators of the schools—who worked with the youth to meet their academic and ESL needs. The appreciation of one such parent was clear:

> The teachers in the school were so excited that some of the Lost Boys were going to be coming, and they just went out of their way to help with the boys. One of the teachers would give [name of youth] oral exams because he had trouble with reading and writing and doing everything in the time limit, so she went out of her way to give him special tests, most of the teachers were really great.

There were also some parents who were not satisfied with the public schools that their children were attending, but did not, or could not, make a different choice. Based on the experience with their school district, these parents were involved at different levels to support academic pursuits of the youth. Next, we discuss how the foster parents in our study were involved in their foster children's education. Generally, positive experiences in school required less involvement in school. Level of involvement also depended on the personal characteristics of the youth.

## Parent Involvement

### Home Involvement

Foster parents played a large role in acclimating youth to various cultural norms and to the day-to-day routines of U.S. life. Foster parents helped youth in variety of ways after they had arrived in the United States (e.g., enrolling the youth in school, opening an account, and filling out financial aid forms, etc.). Parents also provided structure in the youth's lives, helping them develop a daily routine, and encouraging them to avoid unnecessary distractions.

Many of these parents, regardless of where their youth went to school, were involved with schoolwork. The youth needed a lot of help in writing and grammar outside of school. The parents helped them with homework—in particular with the unfamiliar subjects taken in the U.S. context (i.e., U.S. history and government). Also, parents drove them to various appointments and to different sports camps.

### School Involvement

Most foster parents were involved in the education of these youth beyond just attending the parent teacher conferences. One parent noted, "I believe that you've gotta really advocate for your kid because they [Sudanese youth] don't speak English as their primary talking, and so I always made it a point to be at all [parent teacher conferences]". Another parent said that she wanted to make her youth as comfortable as possible by being involved in the school:

> Part of it was school, helping her feel comfortable because she was an outsider coming in, number one she was Black, number two she was a foreigner, and number three she spoke a different language and was learning English. So I think there were challenges there. I worked with the superintendent.

Additionally, effective and appropriate levels of involvement required that parents understand how their foster youth were being perceived. Here, the parent melds the issues of racial status and immigrant status and with other categories of difference. In this example, these experiences are additive, that is, deficits aggregating the perceptions of others—"Black" is added to "foreign" is added to "language barriers." Some parents were teachers in the same school districts, whereas others served on school boards. Given the limited previous educational experience of many of these youth, their parents advocated for their English learning, classes selection, and accommodations for English as second language test takers. One of the parents said: "We got together and went to the school board, and shortly after that they pulled one of the English teachers and she agreed to teach ESL." Some parents also created awareness about the background of the youth that were coming to them. For example, a parent said:

> I was on the school board, so I sat down one time with the superintendent and some of her administration, and some of the teachers regarding the adjustment problems that these kids were having in school. I shared some of the stories that I had heard from these youth what they had gone through when they were young. I was trying to put a different perspective, helping them understand where these kids were coming from.

Many parents were able to find someone among school staff to work with their children closely by being constant advocates for them. One parent stated:

> The counselor was pulling out resources that are on the books for those kids who really really struggle . . . those things really worked for us . . . I think if schools were to examine that, rather than I think a number of schools didn't even try to do that. And we were just blessed because this man was willing to put that time in.

### Community Involvement

Most of the parents in our study were White, middle class Americans who were able to use their social capital for their foster youth. Some of the extended family members also supported the youth living with these families in a number of ways including providing some extra money to youth, sharing their skill sets with them, or connecting them further with peers and important contacts. Many parents involved their youth in various sports (e.g., soccer) through personal connections with coaches, teachers, and parents of other American youth.

## DISCUSSION

We found that parents in our study took several different approaches to educational choices for their foster youth. Some parents chose to put their children into private schools because of perceived deficiencies in the public schools and beliefs that private school was a more supportive learning environment. Some parents made different choices for different children based on their abilities and needs. Some placed their children in the local public schools, but acted as advocates to obtain the supports and services needed to improve educational outcomes of the youth if the public schools were thought to be lacking. Parents perceived several problems with public schools, including low academic expectations, poor school climate, lack of accommodation to children's learning needs, and negative peer influences. Parents' choices and their reasons for choosing private school or community involvement were consistent with Hirschman's (1970) theoretical perspective of consumer behaviors in response to quality of educational contexts.

Parents' educational choices and school involvement patterns were at many junctures intermixed with issues of class and race. Most often these perceptions and challenges emitted from external sources, such as schools and communities. Occasionally, the parents' own stereotypes influenced their assessments of school quality. For the most part, parents seem to understand the exigencies of race and its implications for their wards in the school setting. Despite the new experiences linked to the lowered racial statuses of their Sudanese youth, parents seemed able to maintain their social capital in promoting at least minimal success for the youth in their care. These successes, though sometimes stunted by further discrimination in the society (e.g., part-time work, jobs), largely helped to promote school completion and not infrequently, higher education.

In our sample, there were three parents with immigrant backgrounds and two African American parents. We thought it might be important to anecdotally address how cultural, racial and immigrant experiences affected educational choice and involvement for immigrant and African American parents, but because there were so few parents, results should be interpreted with caution.

Our interviews with the first- and second-generation immigrant families suggest that they placed a strong emphasis on the value of education for the purposes of social mobility. Numerous examples of these "teachings" and the corresponding instrumental aid to the youth were evident in the interviews. For example, one of the parents was particularly angry with the school for having low expectations for her foster sons. Our findings confirm other research indicating immigrant parents move to the United States to find educational opportunity and a better future, thus making a major investment in their children's education (Sy et al., 2007).

The African American families provided instrumental help to the youth who lived with them; and they also emphasized the value of education. However, the instrumental help was offered in the context of an emphasis on independence and self-sufficiency. Specifically, the perception of the youth's pre-existing self-sufficiency (i.e., as related to communal peer care-taking in the camps) was appreciated. An emphasis on race made a brief appearance in one African American parent's interview regarding the potential of racism to affect these youth by virtue of the stereotypes built around their immigrant and African origins, and as intertwined with skin color. One parent said, "... low expectations might be a form of racism." In contrast, White parents observed the phenomenon of "low expectations," but did not label it as a form of racism. One African American parent articulates the struggle "... trying to tell them about the need to talk about race, and I chose not to ..." such that her decision to refrain is based in the complex of racialized experience, but also "elevated" status associated with immigrant social positioning and the possibility of "finding a different kind of America" as a new kind of Black/Brown American. The social capital afforded to White American parents and viewed as big "leg-up" to educational success, was expressed by one African American parent, "if they had been in a White family their view of the world may have been you know, 'I could do anything.'" The African American parents *did* see their educational choices and strategies as reflective of the realities of race and class stratification.

That some African American parents viewed the youth as more self-sufficient compared to U.S. youth their age may explain a less "hands-on" approach consistent with cultural views of balancing independence and collective values believed necessary competence for success in U.S. society among middle-income African Americans (Arnett, 2003; Taylor, Hinton, & Wilson, 1995). This is different from the attachment emphasis of the White American families interviewed. Further, Ascher's work (1986) indicated that African American parents might choose private school as a consequence of pushing against more negative features of public schools, but in our anecdotal interviews we had no African American parents who chose private schools— they also did not problematize the public school setting in any major way.

More research is required to determine how consistent this approach might be across a larger sample of middle-class African Americans fostering immigrant adolescent youth. Our findings suggest that intensity of views or values and differences in experiences might influence the messages African American parents give to Sudanese refugee youth about how to be successful in schools. The views could also drive the school choices of racially different foster parents of Black youth.

School choice as associated with the fostering of this unique group of Sudanese children appeared to interface between the general experiences of middle-class parents and those of immigrant parents. Their values regarding education and ensuring positive outcomes were handled much the same way as adoptive and biological U.S. families with a range of special concerns—language, social perceptions, cultural and racial stereotyping. As such, these "special concerns" do influence the challenges associated with preparing the youth to succeed academically. The choices made by all foster parents in this study were economically and socially contextualized with the common objective of helping their foster children achieve academic excellence (Kleitz et al., 2000).

## ACKNOWLEDGMENT

We want to take this opportunity to acknowledge and remember our dear mentor, colleague, and friend, Dr. Tom Luster, who passed away in March 2009. We gratefully acknowledge his leadership in this research.

## NOTES

1. It is important to understand the uniqueness of youth-parent dyads, with an assumption that these middle-class foster parents might have been privileged in making choices for their foster children, who had a different race, culture, and those who came from a different part of world. Parents' educational practices/choices that might be cultural or associated with their minority experience are addressed anecdotally in the discussion, as there were so few parents with these backgrounds.

2. For youth who did not know their exact age, we used the age estimated by the UN based on their level of physical maturity when examined in the refugee camp. Academically, these 19 youth had been successful. At the time of the interviews, 12 youth were enrolled in college, 2 had graduated from four-year institutions, 1 had obtained a training certificate from a community college, and 4 were not currently enrolled but planned to return to school. Four of the youth were parents themselves, including both females.

## REFERENCES

Arnett, J. (2003). Conceptions of the transition to adulthood among emerging adults in American ethnic groups. In J. Arnett & N. Galambos (Eds.), *Social issue: Exploring cultural conceptions of the to adulthood: New directions for child and adolescent development* (pp. 63–76). San Francisco, CA: Jossey-Bass Publishers.

Ascher, C. (1986). Black students and private schooling. *Urban Education Research Information, 18*(2), 137–145.

Bixler, M. (2005). *The lost boys of Sudan.* Athens: The University of Georgia Press.

Bronfenbrenner, U. (1979). *The ecology of human development.* Cambridge, MA: Harvard University Press.

Carter, R.T., Jones-Wilson, F.C., & Arnez, N.L. (1989). Demographic characteristics of Greater Washington, D.C. area Black parents who chose nonpublic schooling for their young. *Journal of Negro Education, 58*(1), 39–49.

Epstein, J.L. (1987). Toward a theory of family school connections: Teacher practices and parent involvement. In K. Hurrelmann, F. Kaufmann, & F. Losel (Eds.). *Social invention: Potential and constraints* (pp.121–136). New York: deGruyter.

Hirschman, A.O. (1970). *Exit, voice, and loyalty: Responses to decline in firms, organizations, and states.* Cambridge, MA: Harvard University Press.

Kleitz, B., Weiher, G., Tedin, K., & Matland, R.E. (2000). Choice, charter schools, and household preferences. *Social Science Quarterly, 81*(3), 846–854.

Lareau, A. (2000). *Home advantage: Social class and parental intervention in elementary education* (2nd ed.). New York: Rowman & Littlefield Publishers.

Lee, V.E., Chow-Hoy, T.K., Burkam, D.T., Geverdt, D., & Smerdon, B.A. (1998). Sector differences in high school course taking: A private school or Catholic school effect? *Sociology of Education, 71,* 314–335.

Luster, T., Johnson, D. J., & Bates, L. (2008). Lost boys finding their way: Challenges, changes, and small victories of young Sudanese refugees in the United States. In R. L. Dalla, J. De-Frain, J. Johnson, & D.A. Abbott (Eds.), *Strengths and challenges of new immigrant families* (pp. 265–286). Lanham, MD: Lexington Books.

Rana, M., Qin, D.B., Bates, L., Luster, T., & Saltarelli, A. (2011). Factors related to educational resilience among Sudanese unaccompanied minors. *Teachers College Record, 113*(9).

Sluzki, C. (1979). Migration and family conflict. *Family Process, 18*(4), 379–390.

Strauss, A.C., & Corbin, J. (1990). *Basics of qualitative research: Grounded theory procedures and techniques.* London: Sage Publications.

Sy, S.R., Rowley, S.J., & Schulenberg, J.E. (2007). Predictors of parent involvement across contexts in Asian American and European American families. *Journal of Comparative Family Studies, 38*(1), 1–29.

Taylor, L., Hinton, I., & Wilson, M. (1995). Parental influences on academic performance in African American students. *Journal of Child and Family Studies, 4*(3), 293–302.

U.S. Census Bureau (2000). SF4 Data Files. Washington, DC: Author.

# PART III

. . . . . . . . . . . . . . . . . . . . . . . . . . . . . . . . . . . . . . . . . . .

# The Consequences of Choice: Educational Benefits to Children—To Communities? Special Focus on Charter Schools

Between 1950 and 1976 emphasis was on the 1954 *Brown v. Board of Education of Topeka, Kansas* decision that declared segregation in public schools unconstitutional. Concerns have been expressed that rather than encouraging desegregation, the decision had exactly the opposite effect, beginning with the White private academies created in Southern communities. However, magnet schools were created in response to prevailing notions that high standards and school desegregation could not coincide.

By the 1980s, public experimentation with choices and the increased cultural and social diversity of all schools emerged as national trends. Both trends challenged the deleterious effects of particular neighborhood schools. First, advantaged by the presence of magnet schools, and later, charter schools, African American families could join with likeminded families independent of particular neighborhoods. Second, the increments in educational options theoretically permitted more attention to the needs and talents of individual Black children. Presently, these trends are accompanied by a shift in focus from debate surrounding desegregation, to debates about the relationship between educational standards, identification and measurement of these standards, and the proper education of African Americans. Today, the largest percentage of African American students who do not attend neighborhood public schools, attend public, decentralized, charter schools. Chapters in Part III focus on preliminary analyses of the consequences of the choice of education in charter schools, assessed through quantitative researches, several qualitative studies focusing on school organization, inclusive of support for parental empowerment, and the cultural and racial contexts in which attempts are made to sustain these schools.

# Do Charter Schools Work for African American Children? Separating the Wheat from the Chaff

*Valerie C. Lundy-Wagner and Herbert M. Turner III*

## INTRODUCTION

Charter schools afford disenfranchised communities relegated to poor per-forming traditional public schools with an opportunity to attend other public schools that are more autonomous and accountable in terms of teaching and learning, as well as with reference to state and local regulation. For African Americans in particular, charter schools have been an important alternative to traditional public schools (Hoxby & Murarka, 2009; Gleason, Clark, Tuttle, & Dwoyer, 2010). In fact, according to the National Center for Edu-cation Statistics (NCES) (Aud et al., 2010), during the 2007–8 academic year, approximately 26 percent of charter schools had student populations that were more than 50 percent Black, whereas the proportion of Black students in all public schools was only 17 percent. Furthermore, 55 percent of charter schools were located in cities during the 2007–8 academic year (Aud et al., 2010), locations, where according to The Great City Schools (a coalition of the 66 of the largest urban public schools), African Americans represent nearly 35 percent of students (Uzzell, 2010). Given those data, charter schools clearly offer African American families and students an alternative to traditional public schooling, both engendering hope and giving promise to improve Black students' academic achievement, decrease high school dropout rates, and increase postsecondary education and training.

Whether charter schools are delivering the hoped-for changes and improve-ments in African American student learning and achievement has largely been considered "premature" (Hill, Angel, & Christensen, 2006, p. 139). For exam-ple, in a review of research on charter schools and achievement between 2000 and 2006, none presented data on longer-term outcomes, like persistence, high school graduation rates, or postsecondary matriculation (Hill et al., 2006). In addition, while most research on charter schools rarely focuses on African American student achievement explicitly, in some cases, the sample population under review is almost exclusively comprised of this racial group. In those cases, the research presents an opportunity to characterize African American student performance in charter and other public schools.

Critics of educational research generally, and charter school research specifically, often cite the lack of rigorous research designs (i.e., randomized controlled trials [RCTs], quasi-experimental designs [QEDs] or longitudinal analyses). In addition, the variability of each charter school (i.e., institutional goal and mission, pedagogical approaches, curricular foci, hiring policies, political climates, geographic location, and student populations) highlights the myriad student- and institution-level characteristics that affect achievement. Since each of these elements has the potential to impact students' educational opportunities, the inability to disentangle their individual and combined contribution to student learning and achievement is problematic. As such, making strong statements about the aggregate worth of charter schools on student achievement is unreliable. Further, when charter school effectiveness findings are identified, differences are often mixed and/or statistically insignificant (Hill et al., 2006, p. 140)—especially when considered in the aggregate (i.e., charter schools in one state).

The variability in charter school composition and structure contributes to one notable limitation of charter school research: the lack of attention to a scientifically based protocol. Specifically, the notion of causal inference fails to permeate the body of research on charter schools, especially via the federally suggested design of RCTs (Petrosino, Boruch, Soydan, Duggan, & Sanchez-Meca, 2001). That is, as of 2010, relative to the body of research on charter schools, relatively few could definitively attribute variation in student achievement to charter school attendance. Also complicating this research is authors' failure to explicitly disclose any vested interests in charter school research outcomes.

Given the storied history of African American education in the United States, and the African American presence in many charter schools, a systematic examination of charter school research is warranted. Furthermore, since Black students comprise nearly 35 percent of students in the largest urban school districts (Uzzell, 2010), and many of the worst performing public schools are in urban districts, where the proliferation of charter schools is often significant, researchers must devote some acute attention to African American students and charter schools. Thus, the primary goal for this chapter is to clearly illustrate the use of scientific research to separate the evidentiary "wheat from the chaff" when interpreting research on charter schools and their impact on Black students. After providing some additional background on the history of Black education and the charter school movement, we present a comparative evaluation of selected charter school research. The secondary goal is to use this analysis to make recommendations for future research and inform the policy debate on whether charter schools cause higher Black student academic achievement relative to comparable students attending traditional public schools.

## BACKGROUND

### African American K–12 Education and School Choice

Prior to the Civil War, African Americans were largely forbidden to engage in formal educational activities. The notion of school choice was essentially nonexistent for the Black community and virtually all other Americans as well. However, as emancipation loomed, African Americans began to formally educate themselves in the mid-1860s, establishing institutions known more contemporarily as historically Black colleges and universities (HBCUs) (Gasman, Lundy-Wagner, Ransom & Bowman, 2010). Affiliated with both White and Black leadership and religious organizations (e.g., Presbyterians, Methodists, and Episcopalians), these institutions afforded African Americans of means (and primarily those residing in the South), with a legal option of schooling (Gasman et al., 2010). HBCUs and some other institutions helped establish an initial conception of African American school choice—primarily that if African Americans wanted to obtain a U.S. education, they would have to receive it within their own community.

Approximately 100 years later, the notion of African American school choice evolved from existing solely within the Black community onto the national scene with implications for all American families. The landmark 1954 *Brown v. Board of Education* desegregation ruling afforded African American's access—albeit limited—to schools outside their community. In response to the mandated desegregation of White public schools, White reactions ranged from individual acts of violence to systematic sabotage at the elementary, secondary, and postsecondary levels. The 1954 ruling dismissed the "separate but equal" status quo of the mid-twentieth century, where African American students were relegated to public schools that by and large had fewer resources, less funding, and fewer certified teachers than their White peer schools. Local governments were forced to allocate money and other resources to Black public education, sums considered paltry in comparison to the appropriations for Whites. Nonetheless, by the late 1960's, "school choice" meant that African American students were legally permitted to enroll in public schools besides those that had been all-Black, and specifically schools that were better resourced and had previously been for Whites-only under Jim Crow.

Despite the *Brown* ruling and subsequent Civil Rights and Elementary and Secondary Acts of 1965, by the 1990s, Black children remained highly segregated in American public schools. Among other things, White flight and residential segregation contributed to racial isolation in American public schools. The result was similar to that of the pre-1964 African American educational opportunity: on average, Black students were in schools that had lower academic achievement, more destitute facilities, fewer White and more economically disadvantaged students, fewer appropriately credentialed teachers, and significantly less funding. Although the notion of choice existed for African Americans legally, the social status quo in many ways reintroduced Black educational segregation. With the myriad reform issues (i.e., pedagogy, teacher quality, decentralization, community control, curriculum, and whole school reform) of the mid-twentieth century, critics of the K–12 education system felt underserved communities deserved alternatives to traditional public schools. Rhetoric surrounding the persistent Black–White achievement gap also fueled demands for alternative schooling options with the implication that nontraditional methods and approaches would result in more achievement (as measured primarily by standardized test scores).

### Emergence of Charter Schools

The 1983 publication of "A Nation at Risk" presented a scathing critique of U.S. education, energizing and emboldening alternative schooling advocates. Between then and the 1990s, various school reform measures (e.g., magnet schools, gifted and talented schools, community decentralization, community-parent empowerment, parent-school partnerships, and privatization) were considered to improve educational environments, all with the hopes of increasing student achievement. Despite the numerous strategies available for improving public K–12 education, charter schools became popular. As defined by the U.S. Department of Education (2010):

> A charter school is a publicly funded school that is typically governed by a group or organization under a legislative contract or charter with the state; the charter exempts the school from selected state or local rules and regulations. In return for funding and autonomy, the charter school must meet the accountability standards articulated in its charter.

The first charter school was established in Minnesota in 1991 to enhance previous notions of school choice and provide students, especially those in low-performing schools with alternatives. Despite the geographical limitations of school choice, proponents perceived choice as especially beneficial for African American students who were and often continue to be over-represented in low-performing schools. Though the composition of critics and proponents has varied over time (Lubiencki & Weitzel, 2010), opponents often consider charter schools as a mechanism for circumventing deeper educational issues related to improving government bureaucracy and positively influencing teaching and learning in the classroom, and not about choice. Furthermore, the resultant notion of school choice was bolstered with the passage of the 2001 No Child Left Behind (NCLB) Act, which legally grants students in failing schools admission to higher performing schools in their district (McDonald et al., 2007).

Often considered a monolithic group, charter schools vary considerably in terms of their origination and can be characterized as startups or conversions. Conversions are essentially traditional public schools that have a modified relationship with the district. In this case, the school *can* retain teaching staff, serve the same students, and in some cases operate on the same site, and enjoy freedom in terms of curriculum, staffing, budgeting, and other operating policies. Alternatively, startup charter schools are new—that is, the administration recruits students, teachers, and staff from the larger population. Unlike conversions, startups are generally unaffiliated with districts and their facilities. This issue of charter school origination may be critical for many reasons, but primarily when considering the highly debated relationship between teacher quality and achievement (Baker & Dickerson, 2006). Besides charter origination, critics suggest that a multitude of factors influence student success in charter schools.

Despite the criticisms of charter schools, they are undoubtedly a small, but fast-growing part of the U.S. school system. In fact, since the early 1990s, charter schools have proliferated in 40 states and the District of Columbia, educating upward of 1.5 million students, approximately 3 percent of all public school children. During the 2009–10 academic year, 39 states opened 419 new charter schools (CER, 2010), indicating that charter schools are an important element of publicly funded K–12 education. Although the average charter school student may not be African American, in urban school districts where African Americans are overrepresented, Black students often constitute a majority of charter school applicants and enrollees (Uzzell et al., 2010).

Besides an option for school choice, some suggest that charter schools in the context of NCLB instigate a market where schools compete for students. That is, charter and traditional public schools compete for parents' favor and student enrollment by advertising approaches to teaching and learning expected to cause higher student achievement. Implicit within this competition is the assumption that schools will expend energy improving teacher quality, pedagogy, the curriculum, or engaging parents, for example, to facilitate higher academic achievement. Although evidence of this competition is undocumented, it does not detract from the notion of school choice.

In addition to those important aspects of charter schools, attention to charter school admissions is also warranted. Take for example, the background characteristics of students attending KIPP (Knowledge Is Power Program) schools. According to some, many teachers reported nominating their highest achieving students to KIPP and similarly high-profile charter schools. This suggests that some academic achievement gains by charters over other publically-funded schools (charter and not) may be masked by "cherry picking" during recruitment and admissions (Metzger, 2002). For example, the low representation of English language learners and special education students in charter schools may also contribute to some of their purported successes. This, and related issues of charter school student composition highlight the need for high quality research that differentiates between startups and conversions, accounts for prior student achievement, and considers admissions and enrollment criteria.

### Scientific Evidentiary Standards and Education Research

In the 1970s, U.S. education stakeholders sought evidence of program effects to justify use of expenditures on federally funded initiatives (e.g., Head Start), which instigated criticism of educational research. Critics were disappointed with the lack of emphasis on elements of research design, including causal relationships, randomization, replication, and measurement (Delandshare, 2009). In effect, failure to incorporate these elements of the scientific standard permitted the proliferation of educational research that could not answer the most relevant counterfactual: Will students who have not received the intervention have made different gains (compared to those who did receive the intervention)?

Although the critique of educational research has been ongoing since the 1970s, NCLB (2001) established a federal standard on scientific research in education as "the use of randomized controlled trials to provide solid evidence of what works in education to policy makers, teachers, parents, researchers, and other consumers of research" (Delandshare, 2009, p. 35). In addition, the Institute for Education Sciences (IES), the research arm of the Department of Education, was established in 2002 under the Education Sciences Reform Act to improve the quality of educational research and evaluation. Other entities like the Campbell Collaboration (Petrosino et al., 2001) and What Works Clearinghouse (Boruch & Herman, 2006) further support the use of these federal standards in the production of scientifically based education research.

In the context of charter school research and academic achievement, incorporation of causality would provide three key standards. First, it would find that any statistically significant changes in academic achievement are due to attending the charter school. Second, that attending the charter school is the only possible explanation for significant changes in academic achievement. And third, that variation in the attendance patterns (i.e., attending or not attending charter schools) is related to the variation in the effect (i.e., changes in achievement).

## PRIOR EVALUATIONS OF CHARTER SCHOOL ACHIEVEMENT RESEARCH

Whether charter schools are effective for African American children in grades K–12 is an important, but premature question for one important reason—the time horizon. Although charter schools grew exponentially after 1991, a critical mass of students was necessary to identify and monitor samples at the national, state, regional and district levels to implement an appropriate research design. This has undoubtedly, although not exclusively, contributed to the lack of scientifically based rigor in charter school research. Carnoy and colleagues (2006) provide an excellent critique of National Assessment of Educational Progress (NAEP) data presented by the American Federation of Teachers (AFT), highlighting some of the methodological barriers and limitations to charter school research: overuse of elementary compared to middle or high school data, unmatched students, and the omission of admissions criteria and school origination (e.g., whether the charter is a conversion or startup and how long since it opened), school context (e.g., funding/resources, mission, management system, pedagogical focus, or curriculum), and data (e.g., achievement scores for fewer than two years). The authors also point out that despite these limitations, the research findings are mixed and often not significant, though they do mirror state-level research (Carnoy et al., 2006).

State-level research can be useful considering charter schools' local context. Hill and colleagues (2006) conducted a review of 40 publications related to charter schools and test scores between 2000 and 2006. They found that only 13 of the 40 states and jurisdictions that have charter schools were examined. Besides that, the conclusion of most state-level studies is that there is no definitive achievement advantage for students attending charter schools (Carnoy et al., 2006).

By law, charter schools are required to meet the same achievement standards as the traditional public schools. This mandate coincides with a primary but implicit assumption about the charter school movement and research, namely, that these schools *can* cause higher student achievement. Given the effort required to circumscribe the existing public school system (e.g., pass state charter law), some suggest that the effects of charter schools on student performance should be greater than, and not just equal to the effect of attending a traditional public school. To better contextualize the body of charter school research in relation to African American student achievement, we review a subset of the extant literature, focusing on causal relationships, where applicable.

## PURPOSE AND SEARCH METHODOLOGY

Considering the history of African American education, the importance of charter schools for Black students, and the lack of causal research, we present a qualitative evidentiary review guided by the following question: Given the existing evidence on charter schools, what can we conclude about their effectiveness for African American children in grades K–12 in the United States? To answer the research question, we conducted a systematic literature review on charter school effectiveness for African American students (Wade, Turner, Rothstein, & Lavenberg, 2006). The literature search was limited to quantitative studies, and specifically sought studies that acknowledge African Americans and incorporate RCTs (randomized control trials), QEDs (quasi-experimental designs), or longitudinal studies. This resulted in a three-phase review process detailed below.

First, we identified ten repositories that would include publications related to the research question. Specifically, we relied on EconLit and Psychinfo, which include scholarship from ten outlets, including the Education Resources Information Center (ERIC), the Social Science Research Network (SSRN), the National Bureau of Economic Research (NBER), the National Center for School Choice (NCSC), and the National Charter School Research Project (NCSRP).

Second, we identified a set of search terms that would sufficiently capture keywords related to the research question, including: "charter school," "school choice," and "school voucher." Besides using those primary search terms, we combined those phrases with secondary terms anticipated to identify quantitative research: "achieve*," "effect," "eval*," and "impact*." This resulted in a number of articles, reports, working papers, dissertations, etc.

Third, we applied screening criteria to the list of documents on charter schools published after 1990, identifying the research design, opting to keep scholarship that employed an experimental design. Since this identified only a few documents and the noted databases largely focus on peer-reviewed research articles, we included other unpublished and informally published documents regardless of research design to represent the diversity of charter schools research. Taken together, the five documents selected represent notable differences in the design, methodology, and analysis of charter school research.[1] Table 11.1 presents a summary of the five articles included in this qualitative synthesis.

Given the variability in publication status, the number of schools included, outcome measures, student samples, and percent of Black students included in each piece (see Table 11.1), this chapter should not be considered an exhaustive review of research on charter schools and African American students, but rather a narrative on a subset of the extant literature as of September 2010. This qualitative synthesis of student outcomes research provides an opportunity to shed light on the state of and challenges to charter school research. A summary and critique of the five studies is presented in the following section.

## RECENT RCTS, QEDS, AND LONGITUDINAL STUDIES

Some of the limitations with charter school maturity and the challenges of selection bias have been addressed through recent research (Albert-Green, 2005; Gleason et al., 2010; Hoxby et al., 2009; Tang, 2007, and McDonald et al., 2007), although, the findings, conclusions, and policy implications of this research is varied.

The work by McDonald and colleagues (2007) yielded positive effects of charter school attendance on student achievement, as well as other outcomes (e.g., climate, pedagogy) at the end of two years in one new elementary, middle, and high school (in one state). In their study, McDonald and colleagues (2007) use a matched-case research design and an ANOVA framework on a sample of

**Table 11.1**
**Summary of Selected Documents on Charter Schools**

| Author Name(s) | Year of publication | Approximate student sample size[1] | % Black students | Grade span(s) | No. of schools | Primary outcome variable(s) | Publication status |
|---|---|---|---|---|---|---|---|
| Albert-Green | 2005 | 24 | — | 6–8th | 2 | Perceptions of effectiveness | Unpublished dissertation |
| Tang | 2007 | 7,000 | 15% | 211th | 185 | State achievement tests | Unpublished dissertation |
| McDonald, Ross, Bol, & McSparrin-Gallagher | 2007 | 500 | 94% | K–3rd, 6–7th, 7–8th | 3 | State achievement tests | Peer-reviewed article |
| Hoxby & Murarka | 2009 | 33,000 | 63% | 3–8th | 42 | State achievement tests | Informally published agency report |
| Gleason, Clark, Tuttle, Dwoyer, & Silverberg | 2010 | 2,300 | 16% | 6–8th | 36 | State achievement tests | Informally published agency report |

[1]Student sample size includes the total number of students in each document; however, in each document different analyses may have only included a subset of the sample.

approximately 500 students. Children at charter schools were matched with similar students in the nearby traditional public schools on key characteristics, including prior school attendance, grade level, race, gender, free or reduced lunch eligibility, and prior achievement where possible. Among the 18 comparisons, 12 were statistically significant. There were positive results for students in first grade, new sixth and seventh graders, and in both subjects (reading/language arts and math). There were also significant and positive results for second-year seventh graders in reading/language arts, but not math. Among the high school students starting the school in eighth grade, charter school students had significantly higher achievement scores in both math and reading/language arts.

Students included in this urban district and study were overwhelmingly African American (approximately 80% and 90%, respectively), indicating that the charter schools in this area may indeed have a positive impact on African American achievement (McDonald et al., 2007). While pretest achievement scores were statistically insignificant for middle and high school students, effect sizes for each grade level were relatively large, and sample sizes were small (e.g., high school sample $n = 134$), leading the authors to suggest two things. First, while the findings are promising and positive, additional research is needed to *properly* judge educational outcomes over time beyond each school's developmental stage. Second, research focusing on the mechanisms of success, not just documentation of it, is necessary in order to fully capture success for replication.

In a much larger study, Hoxby and Murarka (2009) conducted an extensive review of charter and public school students in New York City using administrative data from the State Department of Education. The sample included student data both prior to and after applying for admission to 42 of the 47 city charter schools between the 2000–01 and 2005–06 academic years. This study is especially informative given the size of the sample population and with respect to African American students, as the percentage of Black students who apply to New York City charter schools is approximately 64 percent even though they only comprise 32 percent of public school students (Hoxby & Murarka, 2009). In this study, researchers attempted to estimate the causal effect of charter schools on state test scores, focusing on the effect of time enrolled in the charter school. Results indicate that students attending New York City charter schools between third and eighth grade experience significant improvements in mathematics and reading scores, after considering expected gains had they attended traditional public schools (Hoxby & Murarka, 2009). Careful not to extrapolate the findings to students outside of the study period and New York City context, the results revealed consistency of the positive effect across race and gender groups (Hoxby & Murarka, 2009). Despite these positive aggregate results, the authors also highlight the large variance in school-specific effect estimates for math and reading scores (Hoxby & Murarka, 2009).

In another study, Tang (2007) investigated the effect of charter schools on student achievement (measured by standardized test scores) in San

Diego, California. Overall, the results suggest that charter schools in San Diego perform as well as traditional public schools with some variation based on grade level, type of charter school, and years since charter school opened (Tang, 2007). The largest positive gains by grade level are in high school reading, and the largest losses are in middle school reading. The data also suggest that the largest achievement losses are made during the first three years of charter school attendance, regardless of startup or conversion status (Tang, 2007). In terms of demography, the results indicate that African American, Latina/o, and White middle school students perform worse in reading at conversion schools, and have higher gains in startups. Tang (2007) also noted that gains were relatively consistent after charters had been in operation for four or more years. In sum, the positive effect of startups and the negative effect of conversions on student achievement when combined suggest that attendance in charter and traditional public schools results in similar achievement. Assuming the non-significant aggregate effect of charter schools found in this study is confirmed with other work, Tang (2007) advocates for cost effectiveness analysis for the two publically funded approaches, implying that the least effective among charter and traditional public schools be modified or even eliminated.

Albert-Green (2005) presents yet another study that attempts to address limitations of past research on charter schools by focusing on *perceptions* of exemplary open-enrollment charter schools in Texas. An effective or exemplary open-enrollment charter school is defined as having at least 90 percent of the students passing (including all minority groups) and a dropout rate of less than 1 percent. In this study, 11 previously established characteristics of school effectiveness are examined from the perspective of students, parents, and teachers at two exemplary open-enrollment charter schools. Survey responses indicated that students agreed with 6, teachers agreed with 8, and parents agreed with 9 of the 11 characteristics of effective charter schools.

All three groups agreed that the exemplary charter schools provided a safe and orderly environment, benefited from a positive environment, exhibited high expectations, and maintained an emphasis on basic skills (Albert-Green, 2005). Due to the role of parent/student selection into charter schools via open enrollment and the random selection of study participants, the use of open-enrollment exemplary status omitted the need for proof of effectiveness on academic achievement.

The findings indicate that although a charter school may satisfy the criteria for being effective, perceptions of these characteristics vary slightly among stakeholders. As such, the author recommends including more research using data triangulation to identify perceptions of effectiveness at exemplary charter and effective traditional public schools among students, parents, and teachers.

A recent study by Mathematics and IES found somewhat less flattering results (Gleason et al., 2010). Using data from 36 charter middle schools that had been in operation for at least two years in 15 states, Gleason and colleagues (2010) compared achievement outcomes of lottery winners and losers at each school site. Using a rather simple analytical approach, standardized achievement effects at each school were compared for analysis; in addition, these data were combined to construct an aggregate charter achievement impact values. The results revealed no significant differences in average student achievement, behavior, and progress among charter school lottery winners and losers (Gleason et al., 2010). Somewhat explaining this was the significant variability in student achievement across schools (Gleason et al., 2010). Furthermore, the authors found an important inverse relationship between family income and academic achievement. Specifically, there was a positive and significant effect on lower-income students' second year math scores, and a negative and significant effect on test scores in math and reading for students who did not qualify for free or reduced lunches (or higher-income students). With regard to demography, there were no significant differences in achievement gains (or losses) based on race or gender.

Despite the various sample sizes and contexts, these five studies highlight the varied approaches to charter school and academic achievement research. Given the recent calls for use of rigor in educational research and the results of these studies, arguments could be made both for and against charter schools. In the remainder of this chapter, we provide an in-depth comparison of the studies presented above, focusing specifically on the methodological approaches and research designs to highlight reasons for the differences in outcomes.

## COMPARATIVE ANALYSIS OF FIVE STUDIES

Education evaluation work is fundamentally shaped by the research design. Issues like data collection and analysis are just as critical to the results as the methodological approach. In the following sections, we consider potential sources of influence on findings in the five studies of charter school effectiveness on academic achievement.

### Methodological Comparisons among the Studies

The characteristics of the charter and traditional public schools, students, teachers, and parents in the five studies are summarized in Table 11.1. Potential variations in charter school benefits with regard to race and ethnicity should be considered cautiously. In addition, unlike the extant research on charter schools that typically focuses on students in elementary grades, the samples in these highlighted studies included youth spanning elementary, middle, and high schools.

Besides demography, features of the study designs and measures for these studies are summarized below. To help account for self-selection, matched-samples were used to compare students in multiple cases (McDonald et al., 2007; Tang, 2007). In other studies, when data were more exhaustive and available on lottery winners and losers, achievement scores were examined based on charter school application status (Hoxby & Murarka, 2009; Gleason et al., 2010). Another strategy by Albert-Green (2005) included random selection of student, teacher, and parent samples in successful open-enrollment schools. The Albert-Green (2005) strategy of random selection of study participants is used to remove any bias related to responses on the perceptions of exemplary charter schools. Both the McDonald-led (2007) and Tang (2007) research also incorporated some indicator of student switching into and out of charter and public schools to avoid misrepresenting the role of self-selection into and out of charter schools. If analyses in the matched sample studies (e.g., Tang, 2007) had focused only on charter school students, results could have been misleading because students who attend charter schools must have motives for attending charter schools that to some degree were related to anticipation of improved academic achievement.

Although academic achievement was not the only outcome measured in these studies, it was assessed similarly (Hoxby & Murarka, 2009; Gleason et al., 2010; McDonald et al., 2007; Tang, 2007). In the latter two studies, academic achievement was measured using standardized test scores for reading and mathematics. In Albert-Green's (2005) work, the outcome measure related to perceptions of effectiveness, with charter school effectiveness having been defined upfront by state terminology. Furthermore, each source of data surrounding the notion of academic achievement has strengths and weaknesses. Namely, the capacity of standardized measures of academic achievement to reliably and accurately capture the impact of teaching and learning in the classroom was neither examined, nor has been proven in the context of longer-term outcomes.

The five studies also used different methods and criteria to evaluate the statistical significance of school effects on outcome measures. In the Albert-Green (2005) study, only descriptive (and not inferential) statistics were used to summarize the perceptions of charter school effectiveness. In the Hoxby and Murarka (2009) study, authors used lottery fixed effects in all regressions to account for the inherent random assignment of a lottery, and the non-random participation in a charter school lottery. Also, test score comparisons were conducted using the Hotelling's $T^2$ test (set at the 95% level). McDonald and colleagues (2006) work compared achievement scores for students in charter and public schools using either ANOVA or MANCOVA. The significance of the findings were evaluated using effect sizes, which were calculated for both adjusted and unadjusted mean differences for each subject area and each grade level using Cohen's $d$.

The criteria employed in the Tang (2007) study reflect a more traditional approach to tolerating the probability of a Type I error (attributing an effect of charter schools that does not exist, and is instead due to change). Minimizing risk for Type I error would be useful for decision-makers in determining charter school effectiveness. However, minimizing Type 1 error increases the chance of making Type II error, or failing to attribute an effect (e.g., improved achievement) to an intervention (e.g., attending a charter school) that it does achieve. The Tang (2007) study used a more stringent level of Type 1 probability for identifying effects as statistically significant (*p*-value less than .05 or .01). Also, in this fixed-effects model, Tang (2007) cautiously includes a lagged dependent variable (i.e., test scores), which resulted in use of the Anderson and Hsiao (1982) estimation model to reduce bias and inconsistency.

In the Gleason-led research (2010), an ordinary least squares (OLS) strategy was employed on district-wide data using a relatively large sample and controlling for observed demographic data. The second part of this study included a matched comparison group approach that included a propensity score estimation procedure that excluded many cases and thus, led to less statistical power than the OLS (Gleason et al., 2010). Based on the different research questions and designs represented in these five studies, we cannot examine how the findings compare when uniformly applying the criterion for statistical significance that was used in any one study. In effect, there is greater consistency in charter school effectiveness within individual studies, rather than across them.

Three of the five studies also tested for differences in charter school effectiveness for subgroups. In Tang's (2007) work there were some variations by ethnicity/race; Black middle school students, like their White and Latina/o peers, performed worse in reading at conversion charter schools, and had higher reading gains in startup charter schools. Albert-Green (2005) found small differences in perceptions of two exemplary open enrollment charter schools among students, parents, and teachers. In the Gleason-led (2010) and Hoxby and Murarka (2009) studies, there were no observed significant difference between African American and Latina/o, or male and female students achievement. However, since McDonald and colleagues' (2006) work used matched pairs a priori (e.g., ethnicity/race, gender, free and reduced lunch status), there were no tests for differences in subgroups.

## Making Sense of the Findings

Overall, the data presented here neither strongly champion nor harshly criticize the work of charter schools as a viable alternative to traditional public schools, for all students or African American students specifically. In conclusion, there are two reasons why research on charter school effectiveness should be considered with caution. First, there remains relatively little data on students in charter and traditional public schools that can be incorporated into a scientifically based experimental research design, although this body of work is growing. The data are often limited in terms of time horizon, grade span, agency type, and locality, thereby preventing evaluation of both short- and long-term outcomes. Second, while some research shows charter schools do provide students with an educational environment that has a positive effect on achievement, these results vary based on the type of charter school (i.e., startup or conversion), student grade level, subject area, and students' background demographic and achievement characteristics. Clearly, more work should be done to characterize and understand the role of charter schools on student achievement. We believe the earlier work led by Anthony Bryk (Bryk, Lee, & Holland, 1993) comparing public and parochial schools is an excellent example of a research methodology and design that could inform the charter school debate. In addition, replication efforts may also provide an opportunity to showcase relevant and appropriate information on the potential benefits or drawbacks of charter schools. Furthermore, areas affected by Hurricane Katrina currently offer educational researchers an opportunity for extensive consideration of charter schools and their role in Black academic achievement.

## RECOMMENDATIONS

Families, teachers, and policymakers require high quality evidence as they consider resource allocations of school-based interventions, like charter schools. Despite the lack of consensus on whether charter schools positively affect African American achievement, this analysis highlights key areas that warrant careful consideration in the decision-making process. Parents should be cognizant of their students' academic needs in the context of school resources (e.g., funding, structure, and teacher quality), at charter and non-charter schools. Administrators, researchers, and policymakers must focus on developing a body of research that includes: a standard nomenclature for achievement research and evaluation; data collection that will allow for disaggregation; longitudinal studies incorporating lottery-based assignment; differentiation between predictors and mechanisms of success; and the cost-benefit analysis of charter versus traditional public schools.

## CONCLUSION

While education has been an important source of pride and upward mobility for African Americans since the nineteenth century, the role that charter schools will play during the twenty-first century has yet to be determined. Besides indeterminate evidence and less than ideal data, the variability of each charter school context in terms of mission, origination, management, funding, student population, hiring, admissions, curriculum, and pedagogical focus makes identification of the positive (or negative) effects difficult to decipher and highlight. Furthermore, few have acknowledged the implicit assumptions about charter schools. That is, if charter schools do not raise student achievement (especially that of disadvantaged and African American students in particular), then is state or district bureaucracy really implicated in the problems we have with lower school achievement among racially and socially marginalized youth? Regardless, whether or not Black students attending charter schools will make gains beyond those they would have made in traditional public schools has yet to be resolved. Despite the challenges exemplified in this review of research, charter schools do offer African American children and families with a choice of publically funded educational options and hope for greater achievement.

## NOTE

1. The systematic review of citations and abstracts focused primarily on two databases, EconLit and PsychInfo, and a three-phase screening process. In Phase 1, citations and abstracts were screened for keywords which elicited approximately 1,100 documents from the two databases (e.g., "charter*achieve" = 366, "school choice*achieve" = 579, and "school voucher*achieve" = 116). Of those documents, citations and abstracts considered irrelevant (i.e., those not about charter schools, not quantitative studies, and published prior to 1990) were excluded, resulting in 108 documents.

During Phase 2 and 3, citations and abstracts were screened to identify only those documents employing an experimental design. This resulted in five documents, of which two appeared to be RCTs based on the citation and/or abstract, and three could not be excluded. After a review of these documents in their entirety, it was determined that none employed a RCT research design, and two were reviews of research. As such, two well-known recently published quantitative works were included in this chapter (e.g., Gleason, P., Clark, M., Tuttle, C.C., Dwoyer, E., Silverberg, M., 2010; Hoxby & Murarka, 2009), of which the former is an RCT. This resulted in five diverse quantitative studies about charter schools and student achievement.

## REFERENCES

Albert-Green, D. (2005). Teachers', parents', and students' perceptions of effective school characteristics of two Texas urban exemplary open-enrollment charter schools. Unpublished dissertation. Texas A&M University. UMI #: 3189555.

Anderson, T.W., & Hsiao, C. (1982). Formulation and estimation of dynamic models using panel data. *Journal of Econometrics, 18*(1), 47–82. doi: 10.1016/0304-4076 (82)90095-1

Baker, B.D., & Dickerson, J.L. (2006). Charter schools, teacher labor market deregulation, and teacher quality: Evidence from the schools and staffing survey. *Educational Policy, 20*(5), 752–778. doi: 10.1177/0895904805284118

Boruch, R. & Herman, R. (2006). The Institute for Education Sciences' What Works Clearinghouse. In R.F. Subtonik, & H.J. Walberg, *The scientific basis of educational productivity* (pp. 269–282). Greenwich, CT: Information Age Publishing.

Boruch, R., May, H., Turner, H.M., Lavenberg, J.G., de Moya, D., Grimshaw, J., & Foley, E. (2004). Estimating the effects of interventions deployed in many places. *American Behavioral Scientist, 47*(5), 608–625. doi: 10.1177/0002764203259291

Bryk, A.S., Lee, V.E., & Holland, P.B. (1993). *Catholic schools and the common good.* Cambridge, MA: Harvard University Press.

Carnoy, M., Jacobson, R., Mishel, L., & Rothstein, R. (2006). Worth the Price? Weighing the evidence on charter school achievement. *Education Finance & Policy, 1*(1), 151–161. doi: 10.1162/edfp.2006.1.1.151

Delandshere, G. (2009) Making sense of the call for scientifically based research in education. In R. Winkle-Wagner, C.A. Hunter, & D.H. Ortloff (Eds.), *Bridging the gap between theory and practice in educational research: Methods at the margins* (pp. 35–46). New York: Palgrave.

Gasman, M., Lundy-Wagner, V., Ransom, T., & Bowman, N. (2010). *Unearthing promise and potential: Our nation's historically Black colleges and universities*. ASHE Higher Education Report, *35*(5). San Francisco: Jossey-Bass.

Gleason, P., Clark, M., Tuttle, C.C., & Dwoyer, E. (2010). *The evaluation of charter school impacts: Final report* (NCEE 2010–4029). Washington, D.C.: National Center for Education Evaluation and Regional Assistance, Institute of Education Sciences, U.S. Department of Education.

Hill, P.T., Angel, L., & Christensen, J. (2006). Charter school achievement studies. *Education Finance & Policy, 1*(1), 139–150. doi: 10.1162/edfp.2006.1.1.139

Hoxby, C.M., & Murarka, S. (2009). *Charter schools in New York City: Who enrolls and how they affect their students' achievement*. National Bureau of Economic Research Working Paper 14852. Cambridge, MA.

Lubienski, C.A., & Weitzel, P.C. (2010). *The charter school experiment: Expectations, evidence, and implications*. Cambridge, MA: Harvard Education Press.

McDonald, A.J., Ross, S.M., Bol, L., & McSparrin-Gallagher, B. (2007). Charter schools as a vehicle for education reform: Implementation outcomes at three inner-city sites. *Journal of Education for Students Placed at Risk, 12*(3), 271–300. doi: 10.1080/10824660701601282

Metzger, M.R. (2002). School accountability or school choice: A bad cocktail? *Oklahoma Policy Studies Review, 3*(1), 20–25.

Petrosino, A., Boruch, R.F., Soydan, H., Duggan, L., & Sanchez-Meca, J. (2001). Meeting the challenges of evidence-based policy: The Campbell Collaboration. *Annals of the American Academy of Political and Social Science, 578*, 14–34. doi: 10.1177/000271620157800102

Tang, Y.E. (2007). *Essays in empirical microeconomics*. Unpublished dissertation. University of California, San Diego. UMI #: 3284312.

U.S. Department of Education, National Center for Education Statistics, Common Core of Data (CCD), *State Nonfiscal Survey of Public Elementary/Secondary Education, 1996–97 and 2006–07*. (This table was prepared October 2008.)

U.S. Department of Education, National Center for Education Statistics. (2010). *The Condition of Education 2010* (NCES 2010–028), Indicator 32.

U.S. Department of Commerce, Census Bureau, Current Population Survey (CPS), October Supplement, 2008. http://factfinder.census.gov/servlet/ADPTable?_bm=y&-geo_id=04000US48&-qr_name=ACS_2008_3YR_G00_DP3YR5&-ds_name=ACS_2008_3YR_G00_&-_lang=en&-_sse=on

Uzzell, R., Simon, C., Horowitz, A., Hyslop, A., Lewis, S., & Casserly, M. (2010). *Beating the odds: Analysis of student performance on state assessments and NAEP*. Washington, D.C.: Council of the Great City Schools.

Wade, A.C., Turner, H.M., Rothstein, H.R., & Lavenberg, J.G. (2006). Information retrieval and the role of the information specialist in producing high-quality systematic reviews in the social, behavioural and education sciences. *Evidence and Policy: A Journal of Research, Debate and Practice, 2*(1), 89–108. doi: 10.1332/174426406775249705

. . . . . . . . . . . . . . . . . . . . . . . . . . . . . . . . . . . . . . . . . . .

# 12

# Charter Schools in New York's Black Communities: Managing Resources in Local Organizational Fields

*Luis A. Huerta, Bruce Fuller, Lynette Parker, and Chad d'Entremont*

## INTRODUCTION

Early advocates for charter schools, going back two decades, promised that liberation from bureaucratic rules and union contracts would spark the creation of inventive schools and offer parents direct accountability (Nathan, 1996; Kolderie, 1992). Yet, contemporary enthusiasts increasingly argue for stiffer quality controls, whether regulated by government or charter management organizations (CMOs; Fuller, 2010; Huerta & Zuckerman, 2009). Nationwide, urban school districts now press rules and forms of accountability, while earmarking greater support for charters within this widening mixed-market of schools.

The growing worry over quality is especially acute among charter schools that serve predominately African American communities. Our earlier research, drawing on a national sample of charter schools, found that those serving Black children often faced problems in acquiring sufficient resources and building institutional credibility within their neighborhoods (Bodine et al., 2008). We found that teachers working in charters serving Black students were less likely to be fully credentialed, and the ratio of students per teacher was thinner, compared with charters mainly serving White students. Still, the principals of Black charters reported longer school years and more after-school programs than charter peers serving Whites.

Black charter schools increasingly face a tough organizational dilemma. On one hand, they define their mission and grassroots legitimacy, in part, by building from the heritage and child-rearing practices of Black

communities. These charters were created by conscientious parents or educators who sought more effective teachers, safer and more human-scale schools,
and a culturally rich curriculum built on the African American historical
experience and values rooted in their communities (e.g., Yancey, 2000). However, charters cannot live on cultural assets and neighborhood legitimacy
alone. They need money.[1] So, charter principals must connect with local
school district and state officials, and they must approach foundations and
families to obtain necessary material resources.

The rub comes when financial sponsors push Black charter schools in ways
that may alienate these schools from their local roots. This chapter describes
the case of New York, where an activist mayor and school chiefs, backed by
major foundations, continue to push charters to rationalize their management, routinize curricula, lift test scores, and work with a "reform partner"
or charter management organization. But the elite reformers that press these
contingencies for funding typically hold little appreciation for the symbolic
resources and rooted nature of charters that serve Black communities (Scott
& DiMartino, 2010).

We focus on three New York charters that bring this organizational
dilemma to life. Each school operates in a local organizational field (Scott &
Meyer, 1994) in which accountability pressures are growing more intense.
To frame these stories of charter development, we use neo-institutional
theory, stemming from the work of sociologists and political scientists (Scott,
2002; Rowan, 2006). This framework helps to illuminate (a) the ways in
which charter principals define symbolic and material resources, (b) how the
local field of charter funders and regulators defines the behavior required of
charter leaders, and (c) the dilemma now experienced by Black charter principals who seek to maximize material resources which are controlled by city
officials and funders, while not pulling-up stakes or alienating their own
Black constituents.[2]

We begin with the conceptual tools that help frame the story of resource
acquisition among charter schools. We then focus on the struggles of three
New York schools to acquire symbolic legitimacy and hard resources in their
local organizational field, without divorcing their mission from the commitments that originally motivated their work inside Black neighborhoods.
Finally, we discuss implications for how reform elites go about lifting and
rationalizing charter schools, shifting a movement that once sprouted from
the grass roots.

## CONCEPTUAL FRAME: CHARTER SCHOOLS
## NEGOTIATE LOCAL ORGANIZATIONAL FIELDS

All organizations must acquire and deploy resources in ways that advance
their legitimacy or benefit their clients or customers. Organizational theorists, working in schools since the 1970s, once argued that school "systems"
are loosely coupled, that principals or district officials can sustain legitimacy

in the eyes of taxpayers and political leaders without necessarily being effective or technically efficient (e.g., Meyer & Rowan, 1977; Meyer, Scott & Deal, 1983). Yet, the push for accountability, first by state leaders and then under the No Child Left Behind legislation, has bolstered technical-efficiency pressures that emanate from this macro-organizational field. That is, government officials and private funders expect charter schools to produce specific outcomes and lift test scores (Fuller, 2009; Rowan, 2006). This pressure on charter advocates grows more intense as three national studies now show no advantage for students attending charter schools, on average, relative to peers in regular schools (Miron, 2010).[3]

Yet, neo-institutional theorists remind us that firms must conform to the demands set by resource providers if they are to maximize resource flows (Powell & DiMaggio, 1991; Scott, 2002). If city leaders or state charter officials push local principals to focus on "core" curricular topics or regularize accounting procedures, then legitimacy suffers when charter leaders fail to conform. Courting a CMO or attending the right conferences might advance visibility in the local field. However, these actions respond to the institutional or symbolic demands of the field; they do not necessarily boost the technical efficiency of the charter organization. Still, successfully playing the game with donors and government officials does not necessarily advance a school's legitimacy or reputation with local parents (Huerta & Zuckerman, 2009).

By the late 1990s, big-city mayors and district school boards began to view charters as one element of their reform agenda—"greased" by foundation funding and lent political punch by CMOs. This shift created a more complex local organizational field, dominated by financiers, regulators, and local politicians. These players may grant dollars, while others define the terms of organizational practices that charter principals must follow to look legitimate.

Charter educators still operate within the wider organizational field of public education, seeking resources and visibility with state and federal governments. Large CMOs, like Knowledge Is Power (KIPP) or Green Dot charters also work closely with national foundations. State rules governing charters continue to spread, including uniform finance formulae, rules for admitting students, standardized testing, allocation of public facilities, and regulation of Web-based "virtual charters" (Huerta & d'Entremont, 2010). The Obama administration has required that state legislatures remove caps on the number of authorized charters in order to compete for (unrelated) federal dollars. Local governments, like New York over the past decade, are playing a more intense role, approving public funding, allocating facilities, requiring management "partners," and generally defining what a legitimate charter school must look like and how it must organize its work (Wohlstetter & Smith, 2010).

We must recognize that the local field's demands on charter schools are socially constructed and do not necessarily advance a school's technical efficiency. In New York City, for example, when charters are urged to select teachers from Teach for America or other alternative-pathway programs, it is not based on evidence of stronger effectiveness. Yet, conforming to this push from downtown reformers does signal legitimacy—that one leads a charter school that is in the game. When charters are required to "partner" with a reform organization, no clear evidence shows that this boosts test scores. However, cooperating with this requirement lends credibility in the eyes of local reformers who distribute dollars.

This leads to the core questions of our study: How do charter school principals define useful resources, and how do they go about acquiring them? This search for resources—dollars or labor (material) and organizational practices that yield legitimacy (symbolic)—occurs largely within the local organizational field (DiMaggio, 1988; Burch, 2007; Schneiberg & Clemens, 2006). At the same time, charter principals in all communities—of color or White—attempt to scaffold up from the local preferences of parents and neighborhood activists when it comes to hiring teachers, deciding the language(s) of instruction, the architecture of curricula, and expectations pressed on students.

## RESEARCH METHOD: EXAMINING HOW BLACK CHARTER SCHOOLS DEFINE AND ACQUIRE RESOURCES

Our research design—allowing us to delve into how charter schools in Black communities seek material and symbolic resources—builds from how state or local governing authorities construct differing forms of charter schools. We purposively sampled nine charter schools in two states (New York and California), drawing from three types of charters: (1) regular public schools that convert to charter status (conversion schools); (2) charters that belong to a for-profit network (market schools); and (3) non-profit charters that are unattached to a CMO (mission-driven schools). Interviews were conducted over a period of 18 months, at least four days in each school, including in-depth conversations with the principal, at least two teachers, a board member, and parents. All interviews were recorded and transcribed, and then codes were attached pertaining to conceptions of material, social, and symbolic resources and the processes by which these resources were acquired.

Our earlier work details how conversion charters, often closely aligned with the practices of regular public schools, while still linked to their district office, enjoy greater access to public funding (Bodine et al., 2008). These schools, on average, provide higher mean salaries for teachers and employ larger shares of teachers who are fully credentialed and more experienced. Conversions draw down larger shares of categorical aid than market or mission-driven schools (Krop & Zimmer, 2005). But the latter two kinds of charters tend to be adept at acquiring resources from foundations and rely on CMOs for support and legitimacy in local organizational fields (e.g., KIPP, Aspire, or Green Dot; see Bulkley, 2004; Wohlstetter et al., 2005).

This chapter focuses only on the three New York schools which originally served proportionally large numbers of Black students. The conversion school is a former public school in one of New York City's outer-boroughs where parents, educators, and local community members worked together to achieve charter status. The mission school is a start-up charter located in Manhattan with an active board, established political connections, and relationships with a number of successful non-profit organizations. The market school is a for-profit charter which has partnered with a nationally recognized CMO, located about 80 miles from New York City.

## PURSUING RESOURCES IN NEW YORK'S BLACK COMMUNITIES

### Shifting Charter Policies and New York's Evolving Organizational Field

New York offers a useful setting for tracking the pursuit of charter school resources, inside and outside Black communities.[4] First, similar to most states, New York charters receive less public funding than traditional public schools. Charters were entitled to 100 percent of local operational expenditures when we conducted our field work, but they were prohibited from receiving categorical aid. Charters also receive less funding than school districts for full-time special education services (Jacobowitz & Gyurko, 2004).

Second, state law encourages resolution of budget shortfalls through private fundraising and entrepreneurial activities.[5] New York City has expanded access to public and private resources, municipally funded charter school networks, facilitating public-private partnerships, and granting unprecedented access to public facilities.[6]

Third, the city encourages charters to engage in formal partnerships with intermediary organizations, in some cases requiring partnerships as a condition of re-chartering (Huerta & d'Entremont, 2010). Given this endorsement of intermediaries in helping to manage charter schools and the new requirement for all traditional schools to partner with support organizations, it is reasonable to predict that agencies granting charters will give preference to new charter schools that have joined with an intermediary.

Overall, these policies—pressed in the organizational field in which Black charter leaders must operate—hold direct implications for how these schools must conform to routinizing the curriculum, linking pedagogy to standardized tests, and managerial practices. This isomorphism with the local field is required to obtain material resources and official legitimacy, whether it advances a school's credibility with parents or neighborhood leaders, or not.

Next, we outline each school in three stages of their evolution. First, we describe the local organizational field and how each school's mission is supported by symbolic and material resources in their local context. Second, we outline the active decisions made by school administrators in seeking alternative resources and how the acquisition and use of new resources may challenge a school's mission. Lastly, we describe how securing additional resources may force schools to conform to symbolic institutional demands (linked to technical efficiency) at the expense of their ties to the community (socially constructed legitimacy).

### The Conversion School: A "Mom and Pop" Charter Risks Institutional Legitimacy

The first case—what we call Conversion School—was previously a regular public school located in an outer borough of New York City. The school served 524 students when we conducted our interviews: 22 percent African American; 41 percent Latino; 17 percent Asian; and 19 percent White. The school has a history of innovative practice and its leaders strongly believe that learning is a collaborative process based on the common experiences of community members. The school converted to charter school status to provide parents and teachers with an increased role in shaping educational outcomes. The decision was widely supported and, consistent with state law, voted on by the larger school community. Parents favored conversion by a margin of 320 to 6. The school's new charter introduced a flattened administrative hierarchy with a principal and four co-principals. With the autonomy offered by conversion to a charter school, its leaders sought to exploit their new freedoms to engage with their most valuable resource: the local community. A co-principal of the Conversion School explains what autonomy meant to the school:

> Freedom to do anything—freedom from the restraints of a district office. Freedom to spend the money the way we wanted to spend the money. Freedom to work with parents the way in which we wanted to work with parents. . . . the school is parents.

Parents and teachers gained an increased role in school decision making, including reserved seats on the school's board of trustees. In addition, parents were recognized as a resource that could transmit the culture and values advanced by the school. A co-principal explains:

> On the one hand, the parents become the talent pool to a large extent of what's happening. On the other hand, by being inside and being in the armpit of the school and seeing it from the inside view, in many ways, many of them silently transmit the values of the school to other parents who therefore open up passive back and forth communication.

As the school evolved, its strong community ties became more then simply a vision of the school, but also a necessity in order to leverage resources for some of its most basic offerings. Conversion to charter school status also reduced access to state and local funds. While the school continued to draw on some in-kind resources, such as food service, transportation, and testing, and retained the use of its facility for a nominal fee, a number of important programs and services became unavailable. For example, the school lost state funding for English language learners, and it was no longer covered by the district's insurance policies. Increasingly, the school was forced to rely on informal community relationships to supplement its budget and cover expenses outside its core curriculum. A number of local arts organizations provided money and materials for the school's art classes. A prominent New York City foundation offered an architectural consultant. And, the school reached an agreement with a nearby college to provide leadership training in exchange for students working as unpaid staff. These new in-kind resources were essential if the school was to provide the same educational experiences as a fully funded district school. Beyond material resources, the school benefited from the connections to social capital in the community that also yielded material resources. These social ties were reflected in the school's board membership. As one of the school's co-principals explains:

> The board members, one's a dean of a college, one's the head of a local library, one's deeply attached to a community-based organizations. So we don't have so much formal relationships with those organizations, but yet, the perspective of the organizations is deeply resonated in the character and the viewpoint of the board members.

Despite an admitted need for additional resources, school leaders remained reluctant to solicit large donations, apply for private grants, or establish formal partnerships. In part, their decision to go it alone was based on the school's belief that such activities demanded an intensive time commitment from staff, but rarely bore fruit. The school had been fairly active in pursuing smaller grants for the arts and was clearly frustrated with the realization that a full-time employee was likely needed to secure awards as small as $2,000. More importantly, the school feared that relying on external partnerships would threaten its autonomy and mission. As one co-principal explains, "the minute you bring somebody else in, well, they may have deep pockets, they may be able to write you a big check, but they're also going to control you, too, and that's the tradeoff."

Thus, the school draws a clear distinction between informal relationships with local community organizations and partnerships with larger private businesses and foundations. The former are perceived as a natural outgrowth of the school's reliance on parents as a resource and their important link to the wider community. Even prior to the school's conversion, a significant number of parents volunteered their time and expertise and were hired on as staff when positions became available. The latter operate outside the larger school community and are therefore viewed with skepticism.

The school is well aware of the consequences of its self-imposed limitations. Refusing revenues reduces flexibility—91 percent of the school's budget is spent on personnel—and may place unfair demands on staff. In addition, by resisting the dominant funding strategies of some of the most well-known charter schools in New York City who partner with management organizations, foundations and other intermediaries, the school opened itself up to questions about its direction, stability, and legitimacy as a learning institution. As one co-principal comments:

> A number of charter schools have a management company and their management company has a big structure and they support the charter school. We're really interested in staying the way we are so that we have the autonomy . . . That makes us wonderful in one sense and poor in the other sense.

During the reauthorization of the school's charter, conflicts emerged when the chancellor's office tried to impose a number of new regulations on the school including district approval of future board members and expenditures over $25,000, and a strong urging to partner with an intermediary organization. The authorizer also wanted another $25,000 to be put in an escrow account in case the school was dissolved, even though at no time during the reauthorization process was the school found to be in financial trouble.

The school emerged from the reauthorization process battle weary. The principal noted that the school enrolls a significant number of middle class students with above average test scores, and he questioned whether charter schools with different student populations would be able to follow the school's example. The school's co-principals spoke of the necessity of building charter school networks to support similar "Mom and Pop" operations that were not interested in joining more formal charter management organizations (CMOs). Possibly, the Conversion School will never vigorously pursue private resources, regardless of the sacrifice, because it considers corporate partnerships to be fundamentally incompatible to the school's mission.

Conversion School was conscious of the changing policy context in New York City where the chancellor's endorsement of CMO-partnered charters was fueling an expansion of intermediaries that threatened self-described "Mom and Pop" charters. Yet, the school was willing to resist the coercive pressures to uphold newly emerging definitions of effective schooling (in this case, newly emerging institutionalized definitions of effective resource partnerships), potentially jeopardized their long term sustainability (Powell & DiMaggio 1991; Meyer & Rowan 1977). Conversion School did succeed in building a strong community network of socially constructed resources from diverse sources within their local organizational field (arts organizations, museums, and local universities) that support and defend the goals and practices of the school.

### The Mission School: Material Resources Flow as Community Ties Loosen

Mission School is a start-up, elementary charter school that originally hoped to locate in a large Dominican community in Manhattan. The school partnered with a local Latino community organization and adopted a dual language curriculum to provide students with fluency in both English and Spanish. School leaders perceived their charter as an investment in their community and culture. Unfortunately, finding an appropriate facility proved difficult and the school was moved a few miles south to a largely African American community. Presently, the school serves 360 students, 65 percent who are African American and 33 percent who are Latino. Requests to hold separate lotteries for English and Spanish speakers were denied, forcing administrators to immediately change the school's educational program. As the principal of the charter school board explains:

> To have a dual language school, you need bilingual students. We started in [a neighborhood] with an English monolingual student population that made the dual language program an educational impossibility, and right now … the overwhelming majority of our kids continue to come from [the neighborhood] and continue to be monolingual English kids.

Moving to a neighborhood with student demographics that were unaligned with the original mission of the school proved challenging, not only in delivering a dual language curriculum to mostly monolingual students, but also in recruiting and relying on community resources that could support the school's mission. For example, the school principal explained the difficulty in engaging parents in basic school activities:

> In terms of parents, they try. They really try. So sure, they'll volunteer, if they have time. We've had our PA [Parent Association] and we have representatives on the board of trustees … and we're supposed to have a school planning council. So it's very sporadic. It isn't anything consistent.

The disconnect and inability to draw resources from their local community, coupled with insufficient public resources, forced the school to seek additional support from non-traditional venues. A school co-principal explains, "we don't get enough money from the state to cover our costs here, are you kidding? We would be out on the street, if we were not going out and actually pursuing other grant money.

Few relationships emerged with the local community. Instead, school leaders relied on associations with more distant Latino community organizations including their co-founding partner. At first, familiarity bred trust and flexibility, but over time informal interactions became more complicated. School personnel found themselves exhausting personal favors in other areas where they were deeply invested. Thus, as a result of distance and necessity, the school's relationships with outside organizations evolved into formal public/private partnerships where specific resources were clearly identified and provided. A prominent immigrant community organization helped support an after school program and extracurricular activities. The National Council of La Raza offered a consultant to administer professional development to teachers. Opportunities to secure small private grants emerged. The school principal estimated that the school had secured roughly $30,000 from a federation of various Latino organizations. These relationships produced vital social resources, but the modest yield of revenues demanded the school become more entrepreneurial in seeking additional resources.

As the school matured, school leaders recognized the need to tap into revenue sources outside the Latino community. Again, the school's approach was to build external partnerships and pursue increasingly larger private grants. External partnerships provided both indirect and direct benefits. For example, the Center for Charter School Excellence helped the school locate and hire its current principal, an individual with significant experience in private fundraising. External partnerships also made the school more attractive to private foundations reluctant to fund schools directly, alleviating some risk. Of course, it remained entirely possible for the school to devote considerable time and energy to a grant application and receive no pay out. But even as the school was being recognized as adopting funding practices endorsed by the district, it was still challenged in securing legitimacy and funds from larger donors.

Still, when the school's grant seeking efforts were successful, they greatly improved educational services. The State University of New York's Charter Schools Institute (CSI) reported that from 2000 to 2004 the school received $940,775 in private grants and donations, not including funds for capital expenses. At the time of our interviews, the school had recently secured a commitment in excess of $4 million from the New York City Council to help purchase a second school building and potentially open a middle school. While these funds would be publicly provided, the deal was premised on the school's ability to raise an additional $9 million. School leaders commented that their success in building new relationships and raising private revenues was essential to gaining the City Council's support.

The school's shift in focus toward private grants and donations did not preclude acquiring additional public resources. Yet, public grants remained less attractive, because they are generally viewed as more time consuming, less sustainable, and less suitable to external partnerships. A number of administrators commented that financial and academic success can eliminate important public funding streams. In contrast, private resources, which may also be temporary, are more flexible and easier to incorporate into long-term strategies to build brand recognition, develop lasting partnerships and most importantly, legitimacy in the local organizational field. School leaders looked around the city and noted that the more successful a charter school becomes, both in terms of academic performance and financial viability, the easier it becomes to perpetuate continued success and earn legitimacy. The school principal explains:

> There's the KIPP Academy. There' the Harlem Children's Zone. They're two
> of the more highly-recognized and I believe more successful charter schools in

the city.... So, if you have that kind of caché, and you have the kind of people who are involved in those programs, then, it's my impression—I could be totally wrong—but things come to them.

The school's interest in private fundraising has provided substantial financial security, but has also transformed the school's original mission. In the last few years, the school has removed all vestiges of its original dual language curriculum, adopted New York City learning standards, and begun annual testing, which it initially eschewed. In part, these changes helped satisfy the school's authorizer and facilitate reauthorization, while also addressing the legitimate needs of the school's students. The principal explains how these decisions were direct responses to centralized demands:

> So in order to get re-chartered ... we had to adopt an assessment system that they had to okay.... So we have invested considerable resources in test prep for our kids that happens on Saturdays, training for teachers, and test preparation.

These changes have also led to teaching and learning methodologies that are more closely aligned with some of the City's most well known charter schools, including KIPP Academy. In addition, the school has nurtured a high-profile student performance group reminiscent of extracurricular activities at the Harlem Children's Zone.

As a result, the school has redefined its mission to principally focus on the students it enrolls (primarily African American students). When discussing their students, administrators and staff frequently evoke references to family and community. However, this passion is no longer easily extended to the larger community beyond the school's doors. When the principal of the school's board of trustees was asked to reflect on whether the school had changed, he commented:

> Oh, my gosh! We stopped being a dual-language school and became a foreign language school. We abandoned the co-principal structure to a head-of-school structure. We totally standardized our curriculum throughout the school, to meet New York State Regent standards. We redid the school.

These changes reflect the tradeoffs that most charter schools confront. On the one hand, Mission School was successful in exploiting its new legitimacy as a viable investment in the eyes of funders so that it could attract private resources. On the other hand, accepting grants from organizations that were disconnected with the community transformed the school. The school consciously abandoned its original mission and conformed to a standardized curriculum aligned with definitions of effective schooling shared by its intermediary foundation partners and the mayor's office. What resulted is a school that was successful in maximizing material resources available in an evolving local organizational field filled with a diversity of funders and intermediaries. However, acquiring new resources and institutional legitimacy was at the expense of not connecting with the symbolic and cultural roots in its local African American community. While the social assets of the community could have proven to be vital in building a school that might nourish and sustain the cultural identity of the African American community, the material resources from private foundations and the accompanying institutional legitimacy proved more valuable in immediately sustaining the school.

### The Market School: A For-profit Firm Manages Resource Flows

Market School was founded in partnership with a national for-profit CMO (the school serves 250 students, 48 percent are African American, 38 percent are Latino, and 17 percent are White). This relationship has greatly influenced the school's pursuit and use of educational resources, as well as the teaching and learning methodologies it employs. The CMO partnership also buffers the school against competition from surrounding local districts. Unlike the Conversion and Mission Schools described above, Market School is located outside of New York City, where support for charter school reform is tentative. At times, disputes over educational resources with local districts have become contentious. For example, state law requires that all school districts within a 15-mile radius of a charter school must provide public transportation to charter students. However, this does not prevent districts from setting up transportation schedules that inconvenience charter students. Market School's principal explains how in "most districts we've been able to resolve some of the problems of arrival and departure of our students. But there are still one or two districts who I'll say are playing games with the transportation."

Given such conflicts, the process of building community relationships is limited. Instead, the CMO partnership provides access to material resources and a wider network of CMO-partnered schools without working through local districts, thus drawing resources from a local organizational field that is made up of other networked schools.

The disconnect between schools networked with for-profit management organizations and traditional schools is driven by both the shared culture advanced by networked schools, and by what Market School's principal describes as formal practices and polices that limit charters from drawing public resources. For example, Market School was prohibited from joining a publically funded regional education service provider. The principal explains that:

> we wanted to become a member of the region's Boards of Cooperative Educational Services [BOCES], and then subsequently the state association, and that's what we asked for. What we were told was that we could attend the Boards of Cooperative Educational Services programs, but we have to pay at the non-member rate.

The exclusion from this important public association precludes charters from networking and joining relevant conversations about education with all public schools. The school's non-member status sends a message that charters exist on the periphery. The principal feels that their marginalized status is further exacerbated by state-level policies that offer charters limited support and push charters further from collaborating or networking with traditional public schools. He explains:

> Look at the charter school legislation to determine whether or not the policies and procedures are supportive of or detrimental to the existence of charter schools ... charter schools, as far as New York State is concerned, are pariahs of schools in the state of New York.

Thus, a paradox exists within Market School. The school is noticeably isolated from the larger public education system in the community where it operates. In fact, the school attracts low-income and minority parents who feel their children were neglected by their assigned public school and were placed in low-academic tracks and remedial programs. The school takes great pride in providing an alternative to unsatisfied families. Conversely, the school does not see itself as providing an educational program that is any different from a traditional public school. The school utilizes the same basic funding, applies a curriculum aligned with state standards, and relies upon a CMO, much like a school district, to perform administrative duties. The principal comments:

> I've said to my board and I've said to my staff, "what makes us any different than any other elementary school?" And while they were trying to answer I said, "save your energy: Nothing! ... Reading, math, science, social studies, physical education, et cetera, just like the other elementary school."

Remarkably, the school that takes fullest advantage of private partnerships provides the most traditional educational program and devotes little time and energy to locating new funding sources or engaging in the promotion of innovations in its teaching and learning methodologies.

Specifically, the school relies almost entirely on revenues generated through student enrollments to cover operational costs. While the school is committed to providing high quality education, its leaders view students as important revenue sources and acknowledge the necessity of adopting cost-efficient programs. The school's principal explains his understanding of charter school funding:

> Again, remembering that the way that charter schools are funded is through tuition. ... so if you have 500 kids here, you get $5 million. If you've got 200 kids here, you get $2 million, the more kids you have, then it generates more funds. For example, if three kids give us $30,000, a program for it could cost us $10,000, so you're $20,000 ahead of the game. But if you only had one kid and a program cost $10,000, then you would absorb everything by that one youngster.

The principal's comments reveal that educational programs and practices are unaltered by student enrollment characteristics, helping the school to stay in good standing with its CMO and take full advantage of its partnership, while also legitimizing its practices within the network schools.

The CMO provides the school with three main resources. The first is a standardized curriculum aligned to state standards and testing requirements, as well as lesson plans, textbooks and worksheets, and a host of other class-room materials. Second, the CMO administers and interprets a monthly assessment program that tracks student progress. Tests are given and inter-pretations are immediate, allowing staff to better assist struggling students. Third, the CMO provides professional development for teachers including on-site training, on-line training, and national and regional conferences. Programs are offered for both administrators and teachers and cover topics ranging from guided discovery learning to classroom management and disci-pline to building an inspiring learning environment. The resources provided by the CMO are not additions to the school's budget as the school pays for these services. However, staff administrators express confidence that this partnership lowers costs, assures quality, and establishes a level of stability that is generally unavailable to a small independent school.

Market School's dependency on its CMO for additional resources and serv-ices is clear. The principal explains how readily the CMO will assist them:

> The daily and the routine needs are taken care of through the establishment of the budget, but those unexpected things that might occur, we don't have the resources to handle that. So we'll go back to our CMO and say, we need some funds . . . tack it onto the bills that you have to pay down the road. But they have the ready cash to do so.

In exchange, Market School pays a high price, essentially trading their autonomy for resources. This compromise stems from limited access to pub-lic sector resources that are prescribed by regional and state policy restric-tions, but is also linked to the school's active pursuit of legitimacy within the immediate local organizational field of CMO-networked schools.

Market School exemplifies how increased autonomy, coupled with ani-mosity linked to competition for scarce public resources, may work to isolate charter schools and further reduce access to public funding. Market School's contentious relationship with neighboring public schools limited its ability to tap in to economies of scale for special services within their local district, as well as draw resources from the regional service provider (BOCES).

Instead, Market School relied on the centralized supports of the CMO, which promoted both a governance structure similar to that of a traditional district office, and a standardized curriculum and professional development system well aligned to institutional definitions of effectiveness. These prac-tices would yield institutional legitimacy for Market School within its local organizational field and allow the CMO to expand operations to additional charter schools in the region. However, the school further distanced itself from drawing community resources or forging local relationships that could work to address some of the wider cultural tensions that initially drew students to Market School.

## IMPLICATIONS FOR CHARTER SCHOOLS, BLACK COMMUNITIES, AND ELITE BENEFACTORS

These cases illustrate how conditions of scare resources, coupled with the autonomy that charters are bestowed, encourages charter leaders to be entrepreneurial in seeking alternative resources and building relationships with players in their local organizational field. These relationships reflect the norms, behaviors, and practices advanced by charter leaders in Black and other communities, along with the sources of legitimacy pressed by partner organizations and funders (major actors in the field). For charters serving predominantly Black populations, navigating this contemporary marketplace of resources and symbolic currency can prove especially challenging. The charters are forced to reconcile the need to retain the values and commitments of their host communities, while engaging in the pragmatic search for material resources which risks alienating them from their local roots.

We have detailed how dispersed accountability, coupled with conditions of scarce resources under the decentralized charter model, have led to the creation of local organizational fields where charters not only seek dollars but also legitimacy from non-official sources, including parents, community and business groups, CMOs, and foundations. Some of these resources are socially constructed or symbolic and include moral, cultural, and community-based resources tied to a school's mission and neighborhood credibility. These resources may prove vital for principals and other school leaders as they try to shape a locally rooted educational program—one promise of early charter school advocates. Yet, other resources may flow from partnerships in the marketplace of funders and intermediaries, including CMOs and foundations. These resource providers must adhere to the priorities and social forms pressed by official agencies that seek legitimacy for their reform efforts, stressing the importance of a regularized curriculum, standardized tests, and rationalized forms of management. Lastly, by focusing on the actions of school-level leaders, we have illuminated how the process of institutionalization (the pressure to conform) is mediated by actors in the local field.

Charter leaders in Black communities will continue to face challenges in obtaining material resources that can sustain their school organization and retain human-scale ties to their community. School leaders must also navigate the evolving local policy context that favors specific types of partnerships that yield institutional legitimacy, while at the same time draw from social and cultural resources rooted in their community.

Finally, the elite benefactors of charter schools—under rising pressure to show that charter schools can deliver on their promises of organizational innovation and stronger student performance—will continue to press certain organizational forms. This includes, as our study shows, an emphasis on a more standard curriculum and set of pedagogical practices, reliance on standardized tests, and more rationalized management structures. This may indeed help lift test scores. Whether these intensifying pressures with the local organizational field advance or reinforce a charter school's engagement with its own parents and neighborhood commitments, remains an open question.

## ACKNOWLEDGMENTS

Data collection in California and New York was financed by the Hewlett Foundation's support of Policy Analysis for California Education (PACE) and by Teachers College, Columbia University. Professor Fuller's time is aided by the Institute of Human Development at the University of California, Berkeley.

Appreciation is expressed to those who helped in conducting school visits and interviews, then transcribing many pages of the voices captured in this chapter. In addition, we acknowledge those whose important conceptual contributions and research assistance were part of our earlier research efforts on this topic. Collectively, this includes Edward Bodine, Maria Fernanda Gonzalez, Megan Silander, Sandra Park, Sandra Noughton, and Laik Woon Teh.

Corresponding authors: Luis Huerta, lah2013@columbia.edu, and Bruce Fuller. b_fuller@berkeley.edu.

## NOTES

1. For a complete discussion on funding distribution and inequities in charter schools, see Huerta & d'Entremont, (2010).

2. Profs. Scott and Meyer have used the phrase "institutional field" to describe the population of organizations that affect sources of material resources and social legitimacy that dominate (or participate in contestation) within a field. We prefer the phrase "organizational field," since both technical-efficiency and institutional-legitimacy pressures are typically operating in fields.

3. Charter schools facing stronger parental demand, or those situated in cities that provide sustained organizational supports as in New York City, have shown encouraging results for students, both in higher test scores and graduation rates among charter high schools, compared with students attending regular public schools (Hoxby, Muraka, & Kang, 2009). But these findings cannot be generalized to the average charter school nationwide.

4. The New York Charter Schools Act of 1998 set an initial cap of 100 schools. Yet growth was rapid; the state hit this cap in January 2006. The state legislature increased this cap to 200 charter schools in April 2007.

5. The Charter Schools Act of 1998, Article 56 states, "The board of trustees of a charter school is authorized to accept gifts, donations or grants of any kind made to the

charter school … private persons and organizations are encouraged to provide funding and other assistance to the establishment or operation of charter schools."

6. Entrepreneurial activity has lead to funding disparities among charter schools. For example, the Thomas B. Fordham Foundation (2005) reported that in 2002–03 the average New York charter school spent $10,881 per student, whereas the three most well-funded charter schools in the analysis—the Child Development Center, the Harlem Day Charter, and the KIPP Academy Charter—spent between $17,985 and $22,686 per student.

## REFERENCES

Bodine, E., Fuller, B., González, M.F., Huerta, L.A., Naughton, S., Park, S., & Teh, L.W. (2008). Disparities in charter school resources: The influence of state policy and community conditions. *Journal of Education Policy, 23*(1), 1–33.

Bulkley, K. (2004). Balancing act: Education management organizations and charter school autonomy. In K. E. Bulkley & P. Wohlstetter. (Eds.), *Taking account of charter schools: What's happened and what's next* (pp. 121–141). New York, NY: Teachers College Press.

Burch, P. (2007). Educational policy and practice from the perspective of institutional theory: Crafting a wider lens. *Educational Researcher, 36*(2), 84–95.

DiMaggio, P.J. (1988). Interest and agency in institutional theory. In L.G. Zucker (Ed.), *Institutional patterns and organizations* (pp. 3–21). Cambridge, MA: Ballinger.

Fordham Foundation & Institute (2005). *Charter school funding: Inequity's next frontier.* Washington DC: Thomas B. Fordham Foundation & Institute.

Fuller, B. (2009). Policy and place: Learning from decentralized education reforms. In B. Schneider, G. Sykes & D. Plank, (Eds.), *Handbook of education policy research.* New York: Routledge.

Fuller, B. (2010). Palace revolt in Los Angeles? Charter and Latino leaders push unions to innovate. *Education Next, 10.* Retrieved from http://educationnext .org/palace-revolt-in-los-angeles/

Hoxby, C.M., Murarka, S. & Kang, J. (2009). How New York city's charter schools affect achievement, August 2009 Report. (Second report in series.) Cambridge, MA: New York City Charter Schools Evaluation Project.

Huerta, L.A., Gonzalez, M. F., & d'Entremont, C. (2006). Cyber and home school charter schools: Adopting policies to new forms of public schooling. *Peabody Journal of Education, 81*(1), 103–139.

Huerta, L.A., & Zuckerman, A. (2009). An institutional theory analysis of charter schools: Addressing challenges to scale. *Peabody Journal of Education, 84*(3), 414–431.

Huerta, L.A., & d'Entremont, C. (2010). Charter school finance: Seeking institutional legitimacy in a marketplace of resources. In C. Lubienski & P. Weitzel (Eds.), *The charter school experiment: Expectations, evidence, and implications* (pp.121– 146). Cambridge, MA: Harvard Education Press.

Jacobowitz, R., & Gyurko, J.S. (2004). Charter School Funding in New York: Perspectives of Parity with Traditional Public Schools. The New York University Institute for Education and Social Policy: http://steinhardt.nyu.edu/iesp/ publications/pubs/charter/ CharterFinance.pdf (accessed February 19, 2007).

Kolderie, T. (1992). Chartering diversity. *Equity and Choice. 9*(1), 28–31.

Krop, C., & Zimmer, R. (2005). Charter school type matters when examining funding and facilities: Evidence from California. *Education Policy Analysis Archives, 13*(50).

Meyer, J.W., & Rowan, B. (1977). Institutionalized organizations: Formal structure as myth and ceremony. *American Journal of Sociology, 83*( 2), 340–363.

Meyer, J.W., Scott, W.R., & Deal, T.E. (1983). Institutional and technical sources of organizational structure: Explaining the structure of educational organizations. In J.W. Meyer & W.R. Scott (Eds.), *Organizational environments: Ritual and rationality* (pp. 45–67). Beverly Hills, CA: Sage.

Miron, G. (2010). Performance of charter schools and implications for policy makers. In C. Lubienski & P. Weitzel (Eds.), *The charter school experiment: Expectations, evidence, and implications* (pp. 73–92). Cambridge, MA: Harvard Education Press.

Nathan, J. (1996). *Charter schools: Creating hope and opportunity for American education.* San Francisco, CA: Jossey-Bass Publishers.

Powell, W.J., & DiMaggio, P.J. (1991). The iron cage revisited: Institutional isomorphism and collective rationality in organizational fields. In W.J. Powell, & P.J. DiMaggio (Eds.), *The new institutionalism in organizational analysis* (pp. 63–82). Chicago, IL: University of Chicago Press.

Rowan, B. (2006). The new institutionalism and the study of educational organizations: Changing ideas for changing times. In H.D. Meyer & B. Rowan (Eds.) *The new institutionalism in education* (pp. 15–32). Albany, NY: State University of New York Press.

Schneiberg, M., & Clemens, E.S. (2006). The typical tools for the job: Research strategies in institutional analysis. *Sociological Theory, 24*(3), 195–227.

Scott, J.T., & DiMartino, C.C. (2010). Hybridized, franchised, duplicated, and replicated: Charter schools and management organizations. In C. Lubienski & P. Weitzel (Eds.), *The Charter school experiment: Expectations, evidence, and implications* (pp. 171–196). Cambridge, MA: Harvard Education Press.

Scott, W.R. (2003). *Organizations: Rational, natural, and open systems (5th ed.).* Upper Saddle River, NJ: Prentice Hall.

Scott, W. R., & Meyer, J. W. (Eds.) (1994). *Institutional environments and organizations.* Thousand Oaks, CA: Sage.

Wohlstetter, P., Smith,, J. Malloy, C., & Hentschke, G.C., (Eds). (2005). *Charter school partnerships: Eight key lessons for success.* Los Angeles, CA: Center on Educational Governance.

Wohlstetter, P., & Smith, J. (2010). Uncommon players, common goals: Partnerships in charter schools. In C. Lubienski & P. Weitzel (Eds.), *The charter school experiment: Expectations, evidence, and implications* (pp. 147–170). Cambridge, MA: Harvard Education Press.

Yancy, P. (2000). *Parents founding charters schools: Dilemmas of empowerment and decentralization.* New York, NY: Peter Lang Publishing.

# 13

. . . . . . . . . . . . . . . . . . . . . . . . . . . . . . . . . . . . . . . . . . .

# When Community Control Meets Privatization: The Search for Empowerment in African American Charter Schools

*Janelle T. Scott*

## INTRODUCTION

The charter school experiment is two decades old, and there are currently over 4,000 charter schools operating in 40 states, the Washington, D.C., and Puerto Rico. Under the Obama administration's *Race to the Top* program, which incentivized states to increase their charter school numbers along with other reforms, and with significant philanthropic support, the urban charter school reform movement stands to grow rapidly in the coming years. A particular and somewhat controversial growth area is that of charter schools managed by for-profit or non-profit educational or charter management organizations (MOs).[1]

From its inception, charter school reform enjoyed support from advocates who held differing ideological stances (Wells, Grutzik, Carnochan, Slayton, & Vasudeva, 1999). Some advocates favored allowing teachers, parents, and community members to shape schooling according to their sense of the needs of their children, while others argued public school systems were inherently wasteful and bloated and would be more creative and innovative with fewer resources if freed from districts and given to the private sector.

As the charter school movement has expanded and matured over the last two decades, teachers' union leader Albert Shanker's original vision of a teacher-led model (Shanker, 1988), has given way to a more privatized model, with significant tensions over control ensuing (Ascher et al., 2001; Bulkley, 2005). Community based charter school advocates often wish to offer a more culturally representative and responsive pedagogy than offered in traditional public schools. In comparison, MOs have specific school designs, governance structure, and curricula that they seek to bring to scale across schooling franchises, sometimes in multiple states. These schooling models might not map onto or include space for community, teacher, or parental preferences. As such, the proliferation of MOs in urban school districts warrants much closer scrutiny in terms of its effects on community engagement and empowerment in the resulting charter schools (Scott & DiMartino, 2010). These privatization efforts have been popular with parents and communities of color, but also have been contested by the same populations.

Much of the research on charter schools operated by MOs has focused on the achievement outcomes (Garcia, Barber, & Molnar, 2009; Gill, Zimmer, Christman, & Blanc, 2007). While this research is important for determining school effectiveness in terms of test score data, it often gets mired in methodological debates. In addition, achievement studies cannot engage the political tensions that have often accompanied attempts to privatize schools serving communities of color (Scott & Fruchter, 2009), nor can they consider the multiple purposes of public education beyond test scores (Engel, 2000).

As yet the research literature has not adequately explored the issues of empowerment between predominantly African American communities and the MOs that operate their schools. We know far too little about what voice or influence parents, teachers, and community members have once they become involved in a privately managed charter school.[2] This chapter considers such issues in two predominantly African American charter schools. The case studies reveal that market advocates' claims that choice results in parental and community empowerment are challenged by the lived experiences of these school communities, who struggled for control. First, I discuss the chapter's conceptual framework, which considers empowerment from the perspective of teachers and communities. Next, I examine professional and community empowerment in two charter schools. The chapter ends with a discussion of the policy implications raised by the two cases.

## CHARTERS, MOS, AND EMPOWERMENT

Empowerment has been a prominent theme in educational reforms, and particularly important in African American struggles over schooling. At various points in the history of education policy, school reformers, policy makers, teachers' unions, grassroots organizations, and market advocates have supported reforms that shifted power from centralized state and school district bureaucracies to local school communities (Tyack & Cuban, 1995). African American teachers, parents and principals have often been central in those struggles (Murtadha & Watts, 2005; Walker, 1996). In contemporary debates about school choice, however, the voices of African American educators and community members are often muted.

Two central arguments undergird school choice. First, theorists posit that when parents are allowed to choose schools for their children that best cohere to their values and desire for quality, schools will be forced to compete for their patronage or risk closure. Another assumption is that providing parents with choice in their children's schooling—usually limited to district boundaries—is tantamount to fulfilling the promise of the Civil Rights Movement (Arons, 1989; Blackwell, 2007; Bolick, 1998).

The market-based empowerment arguments invoke normative ideals: democracy, choice, and equality. Yet, some advocates of choice and privatization embrace the language of the Civil Rights Movement without holding any explicit commitment to making schools more participatory. While they favor parental *choice* of schools, they do not necessarily advocate for parental or teacher *voice* in school-level decision-making, governance, curriculum, personnel, or discipline policy. In fact, in 1990, Chubb and Moe famously argued that the central problem facing public education was that it was too democratic; allowing different stakeholders to fight over their visions for schooling was detrimental to school quality. More recently, former New York City Schools Chancellor Joel Klein echoed this argument, asserting it was not desirable to run schools by "plebiscite" (Chubb & Moe, 1990; Cramer & Green, 2010).

Some progressives argue that the modern school choice movement taps into the long history of African Americans seeking to realize alternative educational institutions (Forman, 2005). Indeed, many African Americans have been active in charter school reform, such as the Black Alliance for Educational Options (BAEO). Increasingly, Democratic African American policy makers have also supported the expansion of school choice—a sea change in what has traditionally been seen as a largely white and Republican policy issue. And the relatively recently formed advocacy group, Democrats for Educational Reform, which was started by wealthy donors, has promised to only support candidates who endorse charter schools and other related reforms. Progressive charter school advocates have supported more voice and control for local communities, but they are less interested in completely dismantling public education systems, and instead want to reinvigorate them. The risk is that operating a charter school under the auspices of a private provider could result in re-regulation under new management (Handler, 1996).

This school choice support might be understood as a need for the "strategic engagement" of African American parents and communities who might not fully align with the conservative policy agendas, yet choose to engage in school choice order to secure the best options for their children in a context where quality educational options are few (Pedroni, 2007). Some African American choice advocates argue that traditional civil rights' leadership is out of sync with the desperation of poor parents who are people of color (Holt 2000). These grassroots communities and activists of color see school choice and privatization as a means to greater power and voice (Sullivan, 2000).

Traditional civil rights groups have typically been tepid supporters and detractors of school choice. The National Association for the Advancement of Colored People (NAACP) has opposed vouchers for over thirty years, and in 2010, joined with a coalition of civil rights groups to oppose many of the Obama administration's educational reforms. These allies caution against the use of charter schools as a systemic educational reform because of the mixed achievement data, and the underrepresentation of special education students and English language learners in charter schools (Lawyers Committee for Civil Rights under Law et al., 2010).

## DESCRIPTION OF THE STUDY

This qualitative case study had four points of inquiry in order to engage the empowerment claims offered in support of charter schools: (1) to understand the motivations from charter school communities for entering into partnerships with MOs; (2) to explore the goals of the MOs and the school communities in terms of their agendas for the schools and for public education; (3) to learn how the MO and school community negotiated governance; and (4) to explore the educational environments of the schools in the context of their cities and districts. The study was conducted in two Californian urban school districts where the percentage of African American students was in decline. This context proved to be important as the school founders formed the charter schools to serve African American students who they felt were getting lost in the districts. In addition, because California's charter school law did not guarantee founders access to start-up funds, the impetus to go it alone was balanced by the need to secure a stable management partner and/or donor (Scott & Holme, 2002). The schools shared an MO, The Better Tomorrows Education Fund (BTEF).[3]

### The Management Organization: The Better Tomorrows Education Fund (BTEF)

The Better Tomorrows Education Fund was a non-profit organization founded in 1994. A multi-millionaire donor who favored school choice funded the MO. The BTEF began targeting charter schools in primarily religious, urban communities of color, promising management and technical support, seemingly on a philanthropic basis. At the time of the study, there were 15 charter schools around the country that were partnered with the BTEF. Foundations Elementary Charter School and the Southside Learning Center were two of them.

### Foundations Elementary Charter School

Foundations Elementary Charter School was located in the Mission Unified School District (MUSD). The school was located in a predominantly African American, working-class community where many of the district's charter schools were located, prompting an African American MUSD board member to wonder if charter school reform was merely yet another means of "experimenting" on "black and brown children." The charter school was housed at the Vista Christian Church. The K–7 school served 700 students who were almost exclusively African American. The students' families were predominantly church members. Some teachers favored the racial and religious homogeneity of the school, while others wanted more diversity. All the parents I spoke with, however, explained that the racial make-up of the school was one of the main factors they used to choose the school for their children.

### The Southside Learning Center

The Southside Learning Center (SLC) was a part of the Larga Unified School District (LUSD). The school served 120 K–2 grade students; nearly all were African American. The teaching staff was all African American men and women. The BTEF had contacted one of the community leaders, asking her to form a focus group to discuss the educational needs of African Americans in LUSD. From these conversations, the BTEF and the SLC agreed to partner. The school's board, all African Americans, had connections to school district leadership, community organizations, and the private sector. The CEO of the BTEF also served on the board. The charter showed that the school's board of directors would "establish the school's objectives," while delegating the responsibility for meeting those objectives to the teachers and school-site management.

### Findings: Community and Professional Empowerment

The data revealed that stakeholders vied for at least two forms of empowerment: community and professional. Yet, the empowerment rhetoric surrounding charter school reform did not neatly align with community or professional control in the two schools. Political and social contexts shaped power distributions. For example, at SLC, where the district played a strong regulatory role, and where the governing board had powerful social capital, professional, and community empowerment were more evident. At Foundations, where the district played a less regulatory role, and the governing board was inactive, community empowerment was slightly more evident, with the MO and church leadership team assuming most of the decision-making over the wants of teachers, and some community members.

### Professional Empowerment

With multiple layers of regulation, from the district and MO, teachers felt their work was constrained. Teachers reported feeling most professionally empowered at the SLC after it terminated its relationship with the BTEF. The charter school professionals balanced their control with MO officials, school district officials, and parents in the school. Moreover, the expertise the BTEF purported to bring to local schools was often found lacking by the teachers themselves, and BTEF officials were not guaranteed to be any more responsive than school district officials.

Teachers at both schools were likely to be new to the profession, uncertified, and earned less than neighboring public school teachers. Teachers reported that the BTEF failed to provide them with professional development or classroom resources. At Foundations, the teachers were completely excluded from decision making beyond their own classrooms. The MO and the church made all of the decisions about the running of the school. While teachers were paid according to the district pay scale, Foundations teachers taught almost two hours more than MUSD teachers, and their school year was longer. They were also not part of the teachers' union.

Upon terminating their relationship with the BTEF, the SLC had significant levels of parental and teacher involvement in governance, though the school struggled to forge networks that would provide financial stability. Just months after the SLC began, tensions emerged about the role of the school's board of directors versus the BTEF. In a meeting to clarify the roles of the two groups, the CEO of the BTEF said that he imagined that the relationship between the two groups would evolve over three phases. These included (1) securing the charter approval, (2) preparing the school to start with funds and facility security, and finally, (3) operating the school.

The board, on the other hand, was unaware that the BTEF was not performing operational responsibilities all along. These included the paying of utility bills, getting insurance for the school and the board, and other basic responsibilities. In addition, payroll services for the staff and educational services for the students were not attended to. According notes from a meeting between the groups, the parties agreed that the SLC Board had fiduciary responsibility for the school: "It will operate independently from [BTEF], raise its own funds, provide strategic directions for [SLC], and approve budgets and major expenditures. [BTEF] will act as [SLC's] agent and operate the school day-to-day." Both parties would raise money from private and governmental sources on behalf of the school.

Eventually, the BTEF and the SLC's board settled upon an agreement that gave the BTEF operating responsibilities for two years unless renewed. The agreement stated that the chain of accountability flowed from the MUSD school board to the SLC board and finally, to the BTEF. The agreement stipulated that the BTEF would be responsible for assisting the SLC board on a number of activities.

Despite this agreement, there were still complaints about the quality and effectiveness of the BTEF on the agreed-upon tasks. Janet Nelson, a first-grade teacher who had been at the SLC from the beginning reported, "So they reneged on a lot of things. They weren't paying our bills on time. When I first started they were paying . . . we didn't think . . . we weren't sure we were going to get paid the first month, and the poor office manager never got a check on time, I mean, she would be like two or three months in the hole." The BTEF promised training and bonuses that the teachers never saw. For example, Nelson, who had been at the school from the beginning recalled that the BTEF's unfulfilled promises included trips to a warm, seaside resort town for a staff retreat, bonuses in excess of $1000, and teacher training and development.

Neal Smith, another first-grade teacher, confirmed many of Nelson's assertions. He too recalled late and absent paychecks, unanswered requests for help, and unpaid school utility bills. He commented, "especially as a teacher, I felt that we were self-serving, you know, we did everything." One task that the teachers undertook was sharing food services with a local elementary school. The teachers would pick up the food from that school's cafeteria.

The data about the (lack of) formal governance at the Foundations Charter School showed that authority and control at the school was located outside of it. It seemed to rest somewhere between the BTEF and the Vista Christian Church. Teachers had little control over school policy, but were told they were responsible for improving student learning.

Teachers reported that they had made repeated requests for representation on the school's board. Interestingly, many teachers said that they did not even understand what the board actually did, when they met, and whether teachers' concerns were even considered. Tayna Tharp, a veteran teacher at the school, said that when she asked to have some teacher concerns addressed, she was told that the principal would present the concerns to the board. Tharp, however, thought that the principal was not in classrooms enough to appreciate the teachers' issues. "But they didn't see our point, and I just can't understand why. And it actually, it got on my nerves. That really bugged me." During the school's first year, Tharp estimated that the board had met once. "So even if we had some sort of concern to take to the board, we couldn't. Who sits on this board, I could not tell you." This lack of clarity caused Tharp to mistrust the BTEF. She explained:

> They're the governing body or whatever. If you figure that you could actually trust them that would be one thing. But I personally don't trust them. I know at one point they were talking about they were going to have the district not do our paychecks anymore and they were going to take that over. I thought, well the minute they started that I was out of here, because I don't trust that. I need my check.

When Principal Damien tried to explain what the board did, it felt as if he was reaching, often speaking in hypothetical, conditional terms:

> I think the board would be the image of the school. I would portray the image, but if there was a problem I'm sure the board would let me know that those problems exist. The finances that come through the foundations would, I would say would be approved by the board because the board would be getting a lot of those, and then I would know exactly how much I have to spend, in addition to, I'm saying over and above the ADA and what the state would give us.

Damien's description of governing board duties and responsibilities suggested that these functions were opaque to him. While he described numerous examples of interaction with church officials, he did not have the same level of detail about the governance of the school. Office manager Wanda Cartwright observed that neither she, nor Damien had even seen the school's budget, and that she did not know how the principal could make decisions without that basic knowledge.

Teachers at the SLC struggled to answer basic questions about the role played by the BTEF. Just a year after the contract expired, teachers had trouble describing what the role of the BTEF had ever been. Their recollections were vague; many recalled that some BTEF representatives came around from time to time. Indeed, talking to teachers revealed that there was little direct effect on their classroom practice in terms of support. Michael Dasfuke could not recall any examples of the BTEF assisting him in his teaching. In fact, he indicated that he did not trust the group's motivation for being at the school in the first place. He remembered being concerned that the BTEF could decide one day that they wanted to close the school down, feeling no accountability to the community. He said, "I saw [the BTEF] as operating from a business perspective, that's what I noticed, I mean, it's the kind of people who wouldn't mind telling me that we don't have a job for you today." Another teacher, Janet Nelson, felt that the BTEF abdicated responsibility for ensuring that the teachers had materials to help them deliver the "world class education" promised in the SLC charter. She surveyed her classroom as she explained,

> They didn't provide the money for the furnishings; all these furnishings were donated by an outside source. The manipulatives, most of the manipulatives that we started with were also donated by an outside source. I mean, I guess there was money for pencils and paper, and those kinds of things, but there was no money for computers or furniture or anything like that. Most of these . . . all the things that you see, most of the things that you see in here . . . all the things really came some way, either donated or the school was able to buy them after the second and third year.

Mrs. Nelson continued, "The things that would assist me in doing my day-to-day operations, ok, did not come from them. And I know that a lot of other things have to be done but it's seemed like the priority was more on them getting credit for things rather than them actually doing the things they needed to do to make sure that we did achieve." She went on to comment that she was originally enamored of the idea that an outside organization would come in and provide support to the school, "you know, that would sponsor us, you know, until we could get on our feet and stuff."

## Community Empowerment

Community empowerment varied in each school, and revealed the complexity in defining what parties are included in "community." While there were parent councils at each school, parental participation on both of the schools' boards of directors was minimal; one parent served on each. On the other hand, both schools' boards of directors were comprised of members of the African American church, business, educational, and legal communities. Both boards had BTEF representatives serving as well.

At the SLC, powerful community networks were such that when the BTEF was found to be deficient, the charter school board let its partnership with the BTEF end, though the school struggled financially to stay afloat following the separation. The board's monitoring of some of the BTEF's practices provided them with the evidentiary grounds to end the partnership.

Randall Evans, a SLC board of director's member, argued that the issues for which the BTEF was responsible, namely the day-to-day management of the school, were badly neglected. He liked the promises of the BTEF to a "holographic carrot." He allowed, however, that the BTEF had served an absolutely critical role early on in the charter application process. The first item was that the BTEF provided the school with a $250,000 bond required by the LUSD to show that the school had sufficient start-up funds. The second item was that representatives from the BTEF assured the LUSD that the SLC had the backing of a "nine billion dollar [organization], so funding was absolutely no obstacle in anything that we'd like to do." With these assurances, the LUSD approved the charter. In retrospect, community leaders realized they had placed too much trust in the BTEF.

To underscore the failed partnership with the BTEF, Evans shared a parable by Rumi (Barks & Moyne, 1995). The parable tells the story of a traveler and his donkey. This traveler asks the servant of the home at which the traveler is to attend a party to care for the beloved donkey who had carried him on his long journey. He nags the servant to take special care with his prized animal, giving it rest, water, and the proper food. The servant replies irritably, reminding the traveler that he knows how to care for the animal properly, and encourages him to relax. Then, the servant goes off to recreate with his friends, completely neglecting the care of the donkey. Rumi concludes the parable with an admonition to those who have a prized possession:

> The [traveler] then lay down to sleep and had terrible dreams about his donkey, how it was being torn to pieces by a wolf, or falling helplessly into a ditch. And his dreaming was right! His donkey was being totally neglected, weak and gasping, without food or water all the nightlong. The servant had done nothing he said he would. There are such vicious and empty flatterers in your life. Do the careful, donkey-tending work. Don't trust that to anyone else. (Barks & Moyne, 1995, pp. 71–73)

Ultimately, the SLC board decided it would be best to simply let the contract expire without extending it. The teachers and parents agreed with the move, despite the difficulties that continued. According to Janet Nelson, the first-grade teacher, "I'm glad it's over . . . yeah, I'm glad they're gone, I'm glad." Neal Smith echoed this sentiment, saying, "we haven't missed a beat, so, you know, we've just been moving on just . . . it was like . . . severing ties with them hasn't hurt us at all." According to parent council president Ansa Evers, "It got to be a lot of conflicts 'cause we wanted to use a certain learning technique, they'd be no, you need to use this. And [we'd want to have] our teachers trained in one way, no you should be doing this." She continued "and so they basically . . . they want you to do what they want you to do and not what you want to do. So they was [sic] trying to take our goal and make it into their goal. And it just kept . . . it would be a conflict all the time, so . . . I mean, what was best for everybody . . . we did pretty good going out on our own and becoming independent."

In the aftermath of the BTEF, there was extensive involvement of teachers and parents in school-site decision-making. The board of directors met regularly, and meetings focused upon school policy. Parent meetings took place bimonthly, and were standing-room-only. The board of directors' president regularly attended parent and faculty meetings, and the climate was collaborative. The board left the development and implementation of local school issues to the teachers, principal, and parent council and all of these parties seemed to be meaningfully involved. At the board of directors' meetings, community members were in attendance, and their concerns were taken seriously. By most accounts, overall community involvement flourished in the aftermath of the BTEF.

The school district context proved important. The LUSD had learned from the experience of the SLC, and procedures had been enacted that caught the BTEF proposing questionable schools even as the relationship between the BTEF and the SLC had soured. The district prohibited the BTEF from operating charters in the LUSD. Comparatively, the MUSD did not provide close oversight. At Foundations, teachers and parents identified the church pastor, William Paulson, as head of the school. Paulson explained that Foundations Elementary Charter School was "a faith-based charter school," punctuating his words by pounding the palm of his hand softly on the table where we sat.

Paulson said that the BTEF had approached him about starting a school just like they had the SLC. Though he wanted his own Christian school, he recognized that many families could not pay tuition, thus he embraced the charter school idea. In a pamphlet distributed to the church community, Paulson described his vision for the church and the role the charter school would play in helping him realize his mission. Paulson hoped to build a new church facility, "that is equipped with the finest technology for communication of the presentation of the Gospel." In addition, Paulson planned to build a business complex and childcare center. Paulson estimated that construction costs would be approximately $10,000,000. Once the childcare center and business complex were built, the church would have revenues from these operations.

There was another important revenue stream. Paulson wrote, "The current rental income from [Foundations] will provide additional resources for the mortgage payment." The current church, once vacated, could then be used for charter school classrooms. The school's expansion would benefit the church, for as Paulson wrote, "The more classroom space we have, the more students we can accommodate, the more students we accommodate, the more boys and girls we prepare for adulthood. And last but not least, the more revenue we will generate through [Foundations] for the church." Paulson saw the charter school as a means to expand his ministry, in part through capital provided by the school, even as he sought to serve African American children.

The heavy involvement of the Vista Christian Church indicated that the accountability mechanisms of the district over its charter schools were weak —at least in terms of enforcing California statutes prohibiting public funds to go to religious schools. When asked how the district ensured that schools were not in violation of even these liberal guidelines, MUSD lawyer, Gerry Sanda admitted that no one in the district was really watching after the charter school began operating.

Consequently, the Foundations charter school community was largely comprised of students, parents, and staff who were affiliated with the Vista Christian Church. Many teachers complained that the ability of the church community to have a school that matched its values and served its congregants came at the expense of their own professional empowerment. School professionals did not have the opportunity to shape school policy, and many parents placed their trust in their pastor.

The principal, Shane Damien saw his own role as the one responsible for daily school operations. Yet, it seemed that most of his work involved negotiating with the church to make sure school and church functions did not conflict with one another. The school deferred use of the facility in the event of some church functions. One afternoon, a repast was held in the school's auditorium following a funeral service at the church; school activities normally held in the room were cancelled that day. On such days when church luncheons were held, any school uses of that space were cancelled or curtailed. It was unclear if the board had decided that the school would share with the church or if it was de facto policy. Wilma Sessions, a community member of the board of directors, complained that the board had only met once that she could recall, and commented that she could not discern who "owned" the school.

The transparency of records for Foundations was problematic. I was unable to obtain some documents that would normally be available, such as budgets, salary information, and minutes from board meetings, and Principal Damien did not have access to them, either. Thus, at Foundations, while the

church community was empowered to have a school, professional empowerment seemed to be lacking as a result, and the predominantly African
American, female teaching staff were disgruntled with their treatment by
the church.

## DISCUSSION AND CONCLUSIONS

These two cases reveal that the African American struggle for educational
empowerment endures even when school choice is afforded to parents in the
form of charter schools. Counter to the hopes of conservative and progressive
advocates of charter school reform, these two cases demonstrate that choice
alone is not a sufficient policy mechanism to generate the full empowerment
of African American teachers, school leaders, and parents. Management
organizations that bring top-down business models to the management of
public schools are not always in concert with the preferences of teachers and
community members.

Yet, charter schools have also provided many African American communities with the opportunity to create alternatives to traditional public schools.
Sustaining such schools as independently operated, however, continues to
be a struggle in the face of a growing preference from policy makers and phi-
lanthropies for franchises, or networks of charter schools. These models,
while sometimes boasting high achievement scores, have also been shown to
have high student attrition rates, and serve fewer special education students.

The potential for professional and community empowerment in the two
cases was most optimal when the schools had strong social networks to school
district administration, government officials, and the private sector. Policy
makers could facilitate the development of grassroots schools by targeting
them with resources, technical assistance, and capacity building. Comparatively, MOs hold that their school design is optimal when it is adhered to
without alterations (National Charter School Research Project, 2007). When
donors, MOs, and board members have the ability to withdraw support for
the school if their preferences are not executed, empowerment might not
extend to full participation in the governance of the school for teachers,
parents, and community members (Scott, 2009).

Certainly not all MO-charter school partnerships present the challenges
described in this chapter. They do serve as cautionary tales about the degree
to which the current, management organization model for charter school reform incorporates the leadership and voices of the African American communities they propose to serve. Indeed, the history of African American
education is replete with struggles—successful and not—for control and the
power to influence the governance, curriculum, and personnel choices of
the schools their children attend. In many ways, privatization challenges this
possibility, but the loss of power is not necessarily predetermined, nor is
schooling under public governance a panacea. As the SLC board of directors'
president said, quoting Rumi, African Americans must "do the careful,

donkey tending work" as they continually seek empowerment and quality schooling for their communities in an increasingly privatized public sector.

## NOTES

1. EMOs typically operate on a for-profit basis, and CMOs typically operate on a non-profit basis. EMOs can manage charter schools and traditional district schools while CMOs operate charter schools exclusively. There are also partner organizations that provide varying levels of management expertise that do not identify as EMOs or CMOs, and who work with charters and traditional public schools. I refer to the range of private management organizations in a generalized way: management organizations (MOs).

2. I do not advance a comparative argument about empowerment in traditional public schools or school districts. The history of African American schooling demonstrates that parents and communities have engaged in long struggles to have their voices, values, and concerns addressed by public and private school officials.

3. The names of schools, teachers, and MO are pseudonyms. Contact the author for additional information regarding the overall study context and methods.

## REFERENCES

Arons, S. (1989). Educational choice as a civil rights strategy. In N.E. Devins (Ed.), *Public values, private schools* (pp. 63–87). London: The Falmer Press.

Ascher, C., Echazarreta, J., Jacobowitz, R., McBride, Y., Troy, T., & Wamba, N. (2001). *Going charter: New models of support.* New York: Institute for Education and Social Policy, New York University.

Barks, C., & Moyne, J. (1995). *The essential Rumi.* San Francisco: Harper Collins.

Blackwell, K. (2007). School choice and civil rights. *Townhall.com.* Retrieved from http://townhall.com/columnists/KenBlackwell/2007/04/06/school_choice_and _civil_rights

Bolick, C. (1998). *Transformation: The promise and politics of empowerment.* Oakland: Institute for Contemporary Studies.

Bulkley, K. (2005). Losing voice? Educational management organizations and charter schools' educational programs. *Education and Urban Society, 37*(2), 204–234.

Chubb, J., & Moe, T. (1990). *Politics, markets, and America's schools.* Washington DC: The Brookings Institution.

Cramer, P., & Green, E. (2010). Joel Klein's bumby learning curve on the path to radical change. *Gotham Schools.* Retrieved from http://gothamschools. org/2010/11/10/joel-kleins-bumpy-learning-curve-on-the-path-to-radical -change/

Engel, M. (2000). *The struggle for control of public education: Market ideology vs. democratic values.* Philadelphia: Temple University Press.

Forman, J.J. (2005). The secret history of school choice: How progressives got there first. *The Georgetown Law Journal, 93,* 1287–1319.

Garcia, D.R., Barber, R.T., & Molnar, A. (2009). Profiting from public education: Education management organizations (EMOs) and student achievement. *Teachers College Record, 111*(5), 1352–1379.

Gill, B., Zimmer, R., Christman, J., & Blanc, S. (2007). *State takeover, school restructuring, private management, and student achievment in Philadelphia.* Santa Monica, CA: The RAND Corporation.

Handler, J.F. (1996). *Down from bureaucracy: The ambiguity of privatization and empowerment.* Princeton: Princeton University Press.

Lawyers Committee for Civil Rights under Law, National Association for the Advancement of Colored People (NAACP), NAACP Legal Defense and Educational Fund, I., National Council for Educating Black Children, National Urban League, Rainbow PUSH Coalition, & Schott Foundation for Public Education. (2010). *Framework for providing all students an opportunity to learn through reauthorization of the Elementary and Secondary Education Act.* Retrieved from: http://naacpldf.org/files/case_issue/Framework%20for%20Providing%20All%20Students%20an%20Opportunity%20to%20Learn%202.pdf

Murtadha, K., & Watts, D. M. (2005). Linking the struggle of education and social justice: historical perspectives of African American leadership in schools. *Education Administration Quarterly, 41*(4), 591–608.

National Charter School Research Project. (2007). *Quantity counts: The growth of charter school management organizations.* Seattle: Center on Reinventing Public Education, University of Washington.

Pedroni, T.C. (2007). *Market movements: African American involvement in school voucher reform.* New York Routledge.

Scott, J. (2009). The politics of venture philanthropy in charter school policy and advocacy. *Educational Policy, 23*(1), 106–136.

Scott, J., & DiMartino, C.C. (2010). Hybridized, franchised, duplicated, and replicated: Charter schools and management organizations. In C. Lubienski & P. Weitzel (Eds.), *Forum on the future of public education.* Cambridge: Harvard Education Press.

Scott, J., & Fruchter, N. (2009). Community resistance to school privatization: The case of New York City. In R. Fisher (Ed.), *The people shall rule: ACORN, community organizing, and the struggle for economic justice.* Nashville: Vanderbilt University Press.

Scott, J., & Holme, J.J. (2002). Public schools, private resources: The role of social networks in California charter school reform. In A.S. Wells (Ed.), *Where charter school policy fails: The problems of accountability and equity* (pp. 102–128). New York: Teachers College Press.

Shanker, A. (1988). Restructuring our schools. *Peabody Journal of Education, 65*(3), 88–99.

Smith, S. (2001). *The democratic potential of charter schools.* New York: Peter Lang.

Sullivan, K.E. (2000). *Let our children go.* Indianapolis: Progressive Press.

Tyack, D., & Cuban, L. (1995). *Tinkering toward utopia: A century of public school reform.* Cambridge: Harvard University Press.

Walker, V.S. (1996). *Their highest potential: An African American school community in the segregated south.* Chapel Hill: The University of North Carolina Press.

Wells, A.S., Grutzik, C., Carnochan, S., Slayton, J., & Vasudeva, A. (1999). Underlying policy assumptions of charter school reform: the multiple meanings of a movement. *Teachers College Record, 100*(3), 513–535.

# 14

. . . . . . . . . . . . . . . . . . . . . . . . . . . . . . . . . . . . . . . .

# Closed: Competition, Segregation, and the Black Student Experience in Charter Schools

*David R. Garcia and Monica L. Stigler*

## INTRODUCTION

Charter schools did not exist at the time *Visible Now* was originally published (Slaughter & Johnson, 1988). Today, charter schools are the most expansive form of school choice. While voucher plans have routinely stalled, charter schools have blossomed across the United States. As of 2009, a total of 4,662 charter schools operated in 40 states and enrolled 1.4 million students (Christensen, Meijer-Irons, & Lake, 2010). Despite their rapid growth, charter schools remain paradoxical. Charter schools have garnered bipartisan support, yet they are at the forefront of many contemporary school choice debates (Henig, 2008; Carnoy, Jacobsen, Mishel, & Rothstein, 2005). They remain polemic because the charter school concept casts a wide net that accommodates a host of strange bedfellows and these precarious arrangements reveal a number of latent contradictions in education policy.

The purpose of this chapter is to examine the Black student experience in charter schools. We frame the chapter via two different perspectives: (1) charter schools as quasi-private schools and (2) charter schools as community schools. We chose to juxtapose these two perspectives because they offer different interpretations on the segregation of Black students in charter schools and on the use of competition as an education reform strategy. After introducing the perspectives, we conduct a national analysis of charter school laws and Black student enrollments before turning our focus toward charter schools in the western United States, the region with the most competitive charter school environments. Finally, we detail the Black student experience in Arizona, a state with an aggressive charter school law and one of the most unregulated school choice environments in the United States.

## CHARTER SCHOOLS AS QUASI-PRIVATE SCHOOLS

Charter schools are autonomous public schools. They are exempt from many of the rules and regulations that govern district schools. They are granted more autonomy in exchange for increased accountability. Charter schools are held accountable through two primary mechanisms. First, they are accountable to the conditions of their contract or charter with a public authorizing body. Second, charter schools are accountable to parents through school choice. Charter schools are most controversial because, in some states, they can be operated by organizations or people from outside the district school system, which represents a fundamental shift in public schooling from government-operated schools to government-funded, privately-delivered schools (Lubienski, 2001).

When charter schools emerged in the 1990s, neither policy makers nor academics had experience with large-scale, decentralized public school choice. Charter schools were a new type of public school, a hybrid that fused together elements from both the public and private schools that preceded them. Thus, many regarded charters schools as a precursor to vouchers (McEwan, 2000). Opponents associated charter schools with privatization policies and warned of the encroachment of market-based reform into public education. The argument in favor of charter schools held that competition was beneficial to the improvement of the entire public school system (Hoxby, 1994) and that students would be better served by breaking the "exclusive franchise" held by traditional school districts (Kolderie, 1990). Policy makers expected parents to send their students to good schools, while poor quality schools, charter and district schools alike, would be forced to either improve or close.

The perception of charter schools as quasi-private entities reminded many that Blacks and other minorities have been historically underrepresented in school choice policies. Traditionally, White and advantaged parents have used school choice as a means of advancing their individual interests (Glass, 2008). For example, in the years immediately following *Brown v. Board of Education of Topeka, Kansas* southern school districts initiated "freedom of choice" plans, which were official school district policies that allowed White students to continue "choosing" to attend all-White schools. Freedom of choice plans subverted the U.S. Supreme Court's desegregation order and these choice plans were eventually outlawed in 1973 (Wells, 1993).

Likewise, charter schools can be viewed as institutionalized policies that ossify segregation rather than promote integration (Levy, 2010). Many critics contended that unrestricted school choice would resegregate public schools via White flight, leaving Black students stranded in district schools (Howe, Eisenhart, & Betebenner, 2002; Molnar, 1996; Hess & Leal, 2001; Cobb & Glass, 1999). Student enrollment in charter schools, however, has not materialized according to the prognostications of charter school opponents (Garcia, 2010). In many states, Black students are overrepresented in charter schools (Frankenberg & Lee, 2003; Frankenberg, Siegel-Hawley, & Wang, 2010) and there is a growing awareness of Black parents and students as agents in school choice, acting on their behalf as opposed to being acted upon (Pedroni, 2006).

## CHARTER SCHOOLS AS COMMUNITY SCHOOLS

The sprawling roots of the charter school movement are also fixed to other public school choice initiatives, such as community schools. In the 1970s, Black activists founded community schools out of frustration with failed desegregation policies. They demanded community control over their public schools, a mission shared by many contemporary charter schools that serve Black students (Stulberg, 2004). The community school perspective offers self-determination as a mechanism for educational reform where Black communities can leverage the autonomy afforded by charter school policies to build successful and culturally relevant educational opportunities (Murrell, 1999).

The perspective of charter schools as community schools reopens the debate on the goal of *Brown v. Board of Education of Topeka, Kansas* to reveal the tensions between desegregation and educational equality. If one interprets the goal of *Brown* as desegregation, then there is obvious concern for how charter schools exacerbate segregation by sanctioning the existence of predominantly Black charter schools. If one interprets *Brown* as advancing educational equality, then charter schools represent an opportunity for communities to establish educational alternatives in cases where district schools have failed to improve the quality of education for Black students (Stulberg, 2006). Black charter school parents may not react negatively to single-race charter schools if students are receiving a quality education (Yancey, 2004). For example, according to the director of a predominantly Black charter school in North Carolina, "I hear parents say: 'My kid is reading a year above grade level. I don't care whether he is sitting next to a White student or not' " (Schnaiberg, 1998, p. 22).

### Charter School Laws and Black Student Enrollment:
### A National Analysis

Charter schools share a common name but they are not all alike. Rather, each state's charter school law is unique and the characteristics of individual charter schools reflect the policies of the state in which they were created. In some states, charter schools are direct competitors to district schools with high levels of autonomy and reward structures that encourage competitive behaviors. In other states, charter schools are highly regulated, rendering them nearly indistinguishable from district schools. In addition, some states require charter schools to maintain a certain racial balance and other states require charter schools to target specific types of students. Both requirements influence the racial composition of the charter school student population. Finally, Black students and charter school student enrollments are unevenly distributed across the country. Some states have considerably higher concentrations of Black students and higher concentrations of charter school students than other states.

In this section, we examine state charter school laws along with the density of the Black population to unveil an insightful contradiction; the highest concentrations of U.S. Black students are not exposed to the ultra-competitive charter schools that have attracted the most controversy. Rather, the states with the highest concentrations of Black students are more likely to have the most regulated charter schools and charter school students are underrepresented relative to the nation.

We analyzed state charter school laws using the ranking developed by the Center for Education Reform (CER), a school choice advocacy organization (Center for Education Reform, 2010). The CER rankings classify strong state charter school laws as those with multiple authorizers and fewer regulations. We converted the 2010 CER state rankings into a 4-point grade scale, ranging from an A (4 points) for the strongest laws to an F (0 points) for the weakest. We then divided all 40 states with charter school laws (including Washington, D.C.) into four regions (Northeast, South, Midwest, and West) according to the U.S. Census definitions and separated out those states without a charter law (U.S. Census Bureau, 2010). Data from the National Center for Education Statistics was used to determine the total student population by race/ethnicity in each state. The total number of students enrolled in charter schools by state was obtained from CER. Finally, we calculated the Location Quotient (LQ) to compare the regional percent charter school student enrollment with the national percent charter school student enrollment. To interpret the LQ, values less than 1 indicate that the regional charter school student enrollment is underrepresented relative to the national percent and values greater than 1 indicate that the regional percent of charter student enrollment is overrepresented relative to the nation.

We found that the states with the weakest charter school laws have the highest concentrations of Black students and a low representation of charter school students. On average, Southern states have the weakest charter school laws (GPA = 1.69). Yet, in 2008, 24 percent of all students enrolled in public schools in the South region were Black (National Center for Education Statistics, 2008) and the LQ for the South was 0.8, indicating a lower percent of charter school students relative to the nation. For example, the charter school law in Mississippi, where one-half of all public school students are Black, was ranked as the weakest in the nation before it expired in 2009 and was not renewed by the state legislature (Center for Education Reform, 2010). The District of Columbia, where 83 percent of the student population is Black, is the notable exception in the South region for its aggressive charter school law (*A* grade) and the enrollment of more than 30,000 students in over 100 charter schools.

The states in the West region had the strongest charter school laws (GPA = 2.27) and charter school students were overrepresented relative to the nation (West LQ: 1.6). The western states, however, also have the lowest concentrations of Black student enrollment. California, with an *A* grade, and Arizona, with a *B* grade, have the most charter schools and the highest charter school student enrollments in the country. California has 860 charter schools and enrolls nearly 300,000 charter school students. Arizona, despite a student population that is about 1/6 the size of California, has 566 charter schools and an enrollment of 132,229 charter school students. While California and Arizona have aggressive charter school laws, these states have Black student populations of just 7.7 percent and 5.6 percent, respectively. Of the 11 states that constitute the West region, only Nevada has a Black student population over 10 percent (*B* grade and 11% Black student population).

## BLACK STUDENTS TEND TO SELF-SEGREGATE IN CHARTER SCHOOLS

Based on the history of school choice, the prognostications about charter schools held that they would further segregate public education through the exit of White students (i.e., White flight), leaving district schools with disproportionate numbers of minority students. We expand this narrowed perspective of segregation, where White students are the only group assumed to avail themselves of school choice options, to examine the school choice decisions of all individual ethnic/racial groups. The following analyses compare the school choice outcomes of both White and Black students along with Hispanic students, Arizona's largest minority group, as an additional reference.

The results are derived from tracking school attendance patterns using a statewide database of nearly 8 million Arizona student-level records for the years 1997–2004. The school attendance patterns allow for a comparison of the racial composition of the district schools that students exited in *year x* to the charter schools they entered in *year x+ 1*. We track the school attendance patterns for all students in elementary grades 2–8 and grade 9, the transition year between elementary and high school.

Segregation levels are measured using the Intergroup Exposure (IE) Index. The IE Index compares the degree of integration between two mutually exclusive groups—the reference and context group. The IE index is the weighted average proportion of students in the context group relative to students in the reference group. For interpretive purposes, the IE Index is converted to a percentage and described as "the average student in the reference group attends the same school as *y* percent of students in the context group." Both high and low values indicate homogenous conditions and low levels of integration (Archbald, 2000). For example, in an analysis in which White students are the reference group and Black students are the context group, a low value on the IE Index indicates a concentration of White

**Table 14.1**
**Average Intergroup Exposure Index by Racial/Ethnic Group, District Schools (Year x), 1997–2003**

| Reference Group | White | Black | Hispanic |
|---|---|---|---|
| White (Elem) | | 0.03 | 0.16 |
| White (HS) | | 0.03 | 0.16 |
| Black (Elem) | 0.21 | | 0.42 |
| Black (HS) | 0.32 | | 0.44 |
| Hispanic (Elem) | 0.18 | 0.07 | |
| Hispanic (HS) | 0.19 | 0.06 | |

students (reference group) and a high value indicates a concentration of Black students (context group).

In Arizona, Black students were largely segregated in district schools before entering a charter school. White students who left a district elementary school to attend a charter school from 1997–2003 attended with only 3 percent Black students and 16 percent Hispanic students, on average. The average Black student that left a district school attended with 21 percent White students in elementary schools and 32 percent White students before the high school transition (see Table 14.1). Black students also attended district schools with over 40 percent Hispanic students, on average, before entering a charter school.

Once students exercised school choice, they entered charter schools that were more racially segregated than the district schools they exited. Most importantly, in Arizona, the segregated conditions in charter schools are more attributable to Black students self-segregating in charter schools than White students leaving their minority peers behind. After exercising school choice, the average White student entered a charter school with exactly the same percentage of Black students as the district school they exited. In Arizona, there is evidence of White flight but the tendency was for White students to segregate from their Hispanic peers, rather than to separate from Black students. The average White elementary grade student was exposed to 6 percent less Hispanic students in charter schools than the district schools they exited (see Table 14.2).

Black students, on the other hand, exposed themselves to considerably fewer White students once they entered a charter school. The average Black elementary student was exposed to approximately 12 percent fewer White students in charter schools compared to the district schools they exited. In addition, Black elementary students also segregated themselves from their Hispanic peers. After exercising choice, the average Black elementary student attended a charter school with 19 percent fewer Hispanic students than the district school they exited.

**Table 14.2**
**Average Intergroup Exposure Index by Racial/Ethnic Group, Difference Between Charter Schools (Year x + 1) and District Schools (Year x), 1998–2004**

| Reference Group | White | Black | Hispanic |
|---|---|---|---|
| White (Elem) | | 0.00 | −0.06 |
| White (HS) | | 0.00 | −0.03 |
| Black (Elem) | −0.11 | | −0.19 |
| Black (HS) | −0.12 | | 0.04 |
| Hispanic (Elem) | −0.02 | 0.03 | |
| Hispanic (HS) | −0.04 | 0.01 | |

## SCHOOL CLOSURES AND THE THREAT TO CHARTER SCHOOLS AS COMMUNITY SCHOOLS

We began our inquiry by identifying the 10 Arizona charter schools with the highest percentages of Black students for both the 1998 and 2004 academic years (20 schools total) to chronicle the formative years of Arizona charter schools. Our goal was to provide a detailed account of charter schools that served predominantly Black student populations but our investigation took an unexpected turn. We were surprised to learn that 12 (60%) of these schools had closed their doors (see Table 14.3), an extremely high failure rate.

Charter school closures have a negative impact on communities, families, and students. Closures are traumatic and often heavily contested events (Hess, 2001). Parents and students are left with a sense of betrayal (Karanxha, 2009) and face several challenges as they adjust to a new school environment. Closures are particularly disruptive when they occur mid-year with little to no advance notice for parents.

From a competitive standpoint school closures can be seen as a positive by-product of market forces. In theory, competition filters out poor quality organizations. For many school choice proponents, a failing school is a welcome sign that indicates the end of the public school monopoly. From a community perspective, however, the boarded up doors of the local charter school symbolize an unfulfilled commitment.

In Arizona, charter schools close by either surrendering their charter voluntarily or the charter authorizer may cease operations by revoking the school's charter. Nationally, surrenders and revocations are rare events because charter authorizers often choose not to renew charter contracts in order to handle problem schools (Gau, 2006). In the remainder of this section, we chronicle the high-profile closure of Dove Learning Academy, a charter school that once served the Black community.

**Table 14.3**
**Operational Status of Charter Schools with Highest Black Student Enrollments (in 1998 and 2004)**

| School Name | Students | Percent Black | Year Opened | Status | Action |
|---|---|---|---|---|---|
| **1998** | | | | | |
| Teen Choice Leadership | 125 | 91.2 | 1995 | Closed | Surrendered |
| Future Development Education & Performing Arts Academy | 116 | 90.6 | 1996 | Closed | Revoked |
| ATOP Academy College Preparatory/East | 30 | 73.2 | 1995 | Closed | Revoked |
| ATOP Academy College Preparatory/West | 77 | 58.3 | 1995 | Closed | Revoked |
| Enterprise Academy | 22 | 40.0 | 1997 | Closed | Surrendered |
| Omega Academy | 27 | 19.4 | 1997 | Open | |
| Copper Canyon Academy | 11 | 17.2 | 1998 | Open | |
| Phoenix Advantage Charter School | 26 | 15.9 | 1996 | Open | |
| The Village | 11 | 15.3 | 1997 | Closed | Surrendered |
| Bennett Academy | 9 | 13.6 | 1995 | Open | |
| **2004** | | | | | |
| Ascending Roots School | 59 | 93.7 | 2003 | Closed | Revoked |
| Progressive Junior High School | 47 | 85.5 | 2002 | Closed | Revoked |
| Teen Choice Leadership | 85 | 75.9 | 1995 | Closed | Surrendered |
| SABIS International | 301 | 57.7 | 2001 | Open | |
| Enterprise Academy | 57 | 55.9 | 1997 | Closed | Surrendered |
| Dove Academy College Preparatory | 98 | 53.3 | 2002 | Closed | Revoked |
| Phoenix Academy Performing Arts | 49 | 34.8 | 1998 | Open | |
| C.I. Wilson Academy | 80 | 30.2 | 2001 | Closed | Surrendered |
| Cortez Park Charter Elementary | 50 | 17.1 | 2002 | Open | |
| Paradise Education Center | 50 | 6.8 | 2000 | Open | |

*Note:* Includes schools serving some combination of elementary grades K–8, some schools may serve high school grades as well.

One of the most high-profile charter school closings in Arizona was the revocation of Dove Learning Academy. In 2002, a former kindergarten instructor and public sector professional opened Dove Learning Academy. During its four years in operation, the school failed to comply with several state requirements including fingerprint and background checks, proper financial practices, and curriculum and instruction standards. The list of Dove Learning Academy's violations included:

1. Dove Learning Academy's athletic director provided direct and unsupervised instruction to students for at least two years before applying for a fingerprint clearance where his conviction for armed robbery was revealed.
2. The school was out of compliance with Generally Accepted Accounting Principles (GAAP). It maintained insufficient supporting documentation to account for $250,000 in checks and was delinquent in paying its vendors.
3. In 2005, Dove Learning Academy received an "underperforming" label from the AZ Learns system used to evaluate academic performance.
4. The school began serving students in 10th grade although it was legally permitted to provide instruction for grades K–9 only.

Dove Learning Academy's charter was revoked on March 31, 2006, but the school continued to operate through April. On April 18th, Arizona Charter Board staff members observed 30–40 students being dropped off at Dove Learning Academy and several other students arriving to the school by bus. The Arizona Charter Board expressed concern that the school was still in operation and inquired if Dove Learning Academy had sent a notification letter to parents about the revocation. A copy of the letter revealed that on April 3rd the school notified the parents that "Dove is no longer receiving public school funding ... the board's decision brings a financial hardship to the school and will force the school to adjust some of its programs ... We are still going through the appeal process and will continue serving your students through this transition period." The school did not acknowledge that it was ordered to cease operation and parents continued to bring their children to the school. Dove Learning Academy's closing made local headlines and contributed to a highly negative public perception of Arizona's charter school movement.

Although Dove Learning Academy was quite possibly an extreme case, other charter schools serving Black students whose charters were revoked had similar problems (see Table 14.3). For example, one school employed at least six persons without proper fingerprint clearance or criminal background checks; another school provided 156 fewer annual instructional hours than required by state law; and a third had serious building code violations with consequent repeated interruption of instructional services to students.

## CONCLUSION

The perspective of charter schools as quasi-private and community schools offers divergent viewpoints from which to understand two of the most contested aspects of charter schools: (1) competition and (2) segregation. The view of charter schools as quasi-private schools harkens a business model where charter schools are framed as competitors to district schools. In the business model, education reform is achieved through market movements as parents exercise their choice to exit their children from underperforming schools in search of the best educational environment possible. School closures are an inherent and important part of market realities because they signify an efficient market where the threat of student exit encourages all schools to improve the quality of education. Yet, we question the extent to which Black students nationally are exposed to the ultra-competitive charter schools that have generated the most controversy. In general, the states with the highest concentrations of Black students are home to more pedestrian charter school policies that are not intended to foster competition between schools. Rather, the most aggressive charter school policies are found in the western United States where only a small percentage of the student population is Black.

In a quasi-private school model, there is an underlying assumption that choice results in segregation. Historically, White and advantaged parents have used school choice to separate themselves from minority students, leaving Black students in poor quality district schools. Thus, academics have been most concerned about White flight. We encourage a more inclusive view that regards Black students and their parents as agents who affirmatively use school choice policies to their own interests, rather than being acted upon by the majority population (Pedroni, 2006). Our position is bolstered by evidence that at least some of the resegregation of public schools associated with school choice is the result of Black students self-segregating in charter schools rather than White students leaving their Black peers behind.

The perspective of charter schools as community schools offers a contrasting interpretation of segregation. Per the community model, charter schools are expected to reflect the values of the local community and the specific student population that the school has chosen to serve. Charter schools that serve the Black community are expected to enroll a high percentage of Black students. If one views the primary mandate of *Brown v. Board of Education of Topeka, Kansas* as the desegregation of public education, then the concentration of Black students in charter schools runs counter to civil rights advances. But the resegregation of public education via racially isolated charter schools forces us to reconsider who is leaving whom behind and to expand our frameworks for understanding school choice dynamics. If *Brown* is regarded as a mandate for educational equality, then the potential resegregation of public education associated with school choice is of less consequence, granted that segregated charter schools provide Black students with a quality education. There is mixed evidence that charter schools offer improved academic environments relative to district schools, which forebodes a pending debate on the merits of racially isolated charter schools.

Finally, from the community school perspective, self-determination and not competition, is the primary agent that drives educational improvement. In many cases, charter schools embody the hopes of the community as committed advocates leverage school choice to take charge of their children's education. Yet, charter schools remain agents of the state and, even in the most unrestricted environments, are required to abide by state laws. Here, the aspiration of charter schools as self-determined entities meets the administrative challenges of running a public organization. Charter schools often struggle with meeting state policy directives (Murrell, 1999) leading to school closures due to noncompliance issues. When charter schools carry the hopes of the local community, closures can be seen as a failure on behalf of the entire community and an unfortunate setback to meaningful progress.

## REFERENCES

Archbald, D.A. (2000). School choice and school stratification: Shortcomings of the stratification critique and recommendations for theory and research. *Educational Policy, 14*(2), 214–240.

Carnoy, M., Jacobsen, R., Mishel, L., & Rothstein, R. (2005). *The charter school dust-up: Examining the evidence on enrollment and achievement.* New York: Teachers College Press.

Center for Education Reform (2010). *"Race to the Top" for charter schools: Which state has what it takes to win.* Retrieved from http://charterschoolresearch.com/

Christensen, J., Meijer-Irons, J., & Lake, R.J. (2010). The charter landscape, 2004–2009. In R.J. Lake (Ed.), *Hopes, fears, & reality: A balanced look at American charter schools in 2009.* Bothell: University of Washington, National Charter School Research Project.

Cobb, C.D., & Glass, G.V. (1999). Ethnic segregation in Arizona charter schools [Electronic Version]. *Education Policy Analysis Archives, 7,* (39). Retrieved October 7, 2000 from http://epaa.asu.edu/epaa/v7n1/

Frankenberg, E., & Lee, C. (2003). Charter schools and race: A lost opportunity for integrated education. [Electronic Version]. *Education Policy Analysis Archives, 11,* (23). Retrieved October 17, 2004 from http://epaa.asu.edu/epaa/v11n32/

Frankenberg, E., Siegel-Hawley, G., & Wang, J. (2010). *Choice without equity: Charter school segregation and the need for civil rights standards.* Los Angeles, CA: The Civil Rights Project/Proyecto Derechos Civiles at UCLA; www.civilrightsproject.ucla.edu

Garcia, D.R. (2010). Charter schools challenge traditional notions of segregation. In C. Lubienski & P. Weitzel (Eds.), *The charter school experiment: Two decades of evidence and evolving expectations.* Cambridge, MA: Harvard Education Press.

Gau, R. (2006). *Trends in charter school authorizing.* Washington, DC: Thomas B. Fordham Institute.

Glass, G.V. (2008). *Fertilizers, pills & magnetic strips.* Charlotte, NC: Information Age Publishing.

Henig, J.R. (2008). *Spin cycle: How research is used in policy debates: The case of charter schools*. New York: Russell Sage Foundation.

Hess, F. (2001). "Whaddya mean you want to close my school?" The politics of regulatory accountability in charter schooling. *Education and Urban Society, 33*(2), 141–156.

Hess, F.M., & Leal, D.L. (2001). Quality, race, and the urban education marketplace. *Urban Affairs Review, 37*(2), 249–266.

Hoxby, C.M. (1994). *Does competition among public schools benefit students and taxpayers?* (NBER Working Papers 4979): National Bureau of Economic Research, Inc.

Howe, K., Eisenhart, M., & Betebenner, D. (2002). The price of public school choice. *Educational Leadership, 59*(7), 20–24.

Karanxha, Z. (2009). *When the dream turns into a nightmare: A case study of a closed charter school*. Paper presented at the 2009 AERA Annual Meeting.

Kolderie, T. (1990). *Beyond choice to new public schools: Withdrawing the exclusive franchise in public education*. Washington, DC: Progressive Policy Institute.

Lacireno-Paquet, N., Holyoke, T.T., Moser, M., & Henig, J.R. (2002). Creaming versus cropping: Charter school enrollment practices in response to market incentives. *Educational Evaluation and Policy Analysis, 24*(2), 145–158.

Levy, T. (2010). Charter schools legislation and the element of race. *The Western Journal of Black Studies, 34*(1), 43–52.

Lubienski, C. (2001). Redefining "public" education: Charter schools, common schools and the rhetoric of reform. *Teachers College Record, 103*(4), 634–666.

McEwan, P.J. (2000). The potential impact of large-scale voucher programs. *Review of Educational Research, 70*(2), 103–149.

Molnar, A. (1996). Charter schools: The smiling face of disinvestment. *Educational Leadership, 54*(2), 9–15.

Murrell, P.C. (1999). Chartering the village: The making of an African-centered charter school. *Urban Education, 33*(5), 565–583.

National Center for Education Statistics (2008). *The condition of education: Participation in education*. Retrieved August 10, 2010 from http://nces.ed.gov/programs/coe/2010/ section1/table-1er-2.asp

Pedroni, T.C. (2006). Acting neoliberal: Is Black support for vouchers a rejection of progressive educational values? *Educational Studies, 40*(3), 265–278.

Rapp, K.E., & Eckes, S.E. (2007). Dispelling the myth of "white flight:" An examination of minority enrollment in charter schools. *Educational Policy, 21*(4), 615–661.

Rofes, E., & Stulberg, L.M. (Eds.). (2004). *The emancipatory promise of charter schools: Towards a progressive politics of school choice*. Albany, NY: SUNY.

Schnaiberg, L. (1998, August 5). Predominantly Black charters focus of debate in N.C. *Education Week*, 22.

Slaughter, D.T., & Johnson, D.J. (1988). *Visible Now: Blacks in private schools*. Westport, CT: Greenwood Press.

Stulberg, L.M. (2006). School choice discourse and the legacy of Brown. *Journal of School Choice, 1*(1), 23–45.

U.S. Census Bureau, (2010). Census Bureau Regions and Divisions. Retrieved June 3, 2010 from http://www.census.gov/geo/www/us_regdiv.pdf

Wells, A.S. (1993). *Time to choose: America at the crossroads of school choice policy*. New York: Hill and Wang.

Yancey, P. (2004). Independent Black schools and the charter movement. In E. Rofes & L.M. Stulberg (Eds.), *The emancipatory promise of charter schools* (Chapter 5). Albany, NY: SUNY Press.

. . . . . . . . . . . . . . . . . . . . . . . . . . . . . . . . . . . . . . . .

# 15

# Commentary: "The Teachers' Unions Strike Back?" No Need to Wait for "Superman": Magnet Schools Have Brought Success to Urban Public School Students for Over 30 Years

## V.P. Franklin

Davis Guggenheim's highly promoted documentary film *Waiting for Superman* reminded me of D.W. Griffiths' classic silent film *Birth of a Nation*, released with much fanfare in 1915. Based on Thomas Dixon's novel and play *The Clansman*, the film portrayed the Reconstruction era after the Civil War as a period of "Negro rule" that ended only with the rise of the Ku Klux Klan. *Birth of a Nation* presented distorted and inaccurate images of Black politicians and their roles in southern legislatures during those years, and demonized African Americans and their desire for first-class citizenship rights. The film was a highly successful recruiting vehicle for the Klan whose membership reached new heights in the 1920s. Similarly, *Waiting for Superman* demonizes teachers' unions and seeks to recruit parents and school officials to the cause of the "charter school revolution."[1]

President Woodrow Wilson premiered *Birth of a Nation* in the White House, declaring it was "history written in lightening"; and recently President Barack Obama invited the five children profiled in *Waiting for Superman* to the Oval Office for a photo-op. Some might question this comparison pointing out that *Birth of a Nation* was not history, but pure fiction, and *Waiting for Superman* is a documentary based on real events and real people. But what the films have in common is that they demonize, intentionally or unintentionally, an entire group of people. In cities across the country, African Americans mounted mass protests at movie theaters showing *Birth of a Nation*, many times organized by the local NAACP chapters. Some members of teachers' unions have called for a boycott of *Waiting for Superman* as well, but few protests have been registered.

But just as W.E.B. Du Bois and other Black and White historians set to work producing fully documented studies addressing the lies and distortions in *Birth of a Nation*, educational historians and other researchers should be mounting research projects and organizing symposia challenging the thrust of the anti-union bias in *Waiting for Superman*. For example, although an answer is never provided in the film, the question that should be addressed is: Have unionized public school teachers in the past produced high levels of student engagement, parental involvement, and academic achievement in public schools similar to or better than that attributed to the Kipp Schools, the Harlem School Zone, Summit Academy, and Harlem Success profiled in *Waiting for Superman*? The answer is "yes," but in the film the narrator only mentioned once the high demand for the limited spaces in the public magnet schools.

For over 30 years, unionized public school teachers have created positive and successful educational environments in the thousands of magnet schools opened in cities across the country. Beginning in the 1970s, school districts under court order to desegregate, or voluntarily pursuing school desegregation but not interested in "forced busing" programs, turned to the opening of "magnet schools" to promote racial balance. The magnet schools sought to attract White students back into predominantly Black or minority public schools. The U.S. Office of Education through appropriations from the ESEA Title VII made funds available for the opening of magnet schools in Philadelphia, Minneapolis, Cincinnati, Denver, Houston, and hundreds of other urban school districts. Magnet schools were opened that specialized in the performing arts, music, science and technology, foreign languages, agricultural science, sports and athletics, business, engineering and technology, health careers, and many other areas.

In a *Teachers College Record* article in December 1978, entitled "Freedom Schooling," Ronald Batchelor and I called attention to the potential of the "magnet school model" to improve student engagement and academic achievement levels in urban public schools. We now have over 30 years of data, and in a recent survey of the magnet schools by Susan Eaton of the Charles Hamilton Houston Research Center at Harvard Law School, published in *The Nation* in June 2010, she reported that over the last several decades "the real track record of success" was with magnet schools. In states where comparisons were made in the academic achievement levels for Black and White, magnet and non-magnet students, researchers found that the African American and Latino students in magnet schools "made greater gains in math and reading than did their fellow students who stayed in the traditional urban school." And White students "attending magnets outdid their peers at traditional suburban (and generally much whiter) schools, too. The so-called achievement gap between white students and students of color tended to be smaller in magnet schools than it was in traditional schools in these states." Other articles have appeared recently[2] about the success of students enrolled in magnet schools announcing that they are "The Overlooked Model" and "The Forgotten Choice" in U.S. public education.

The teachers' unions need to respond to *Waiting to Superman* and other attempts at demonizing unionized public school teachers by pointing to the success of the magnet schools, and posit them as an alternative to the charter school model. At the same time, in the face of the increasing use of standardized test scores to evaluate students and teachers, even to the point of publishing teachers' names and their students' test scores in local newspapers, the teachers' unions should respond by calling for the support of "freedom schools" and "freedom schooling programs." These schools would be modeled after the magnet schools, but would utilize mastery learning techniques and approaches to instruct young people in the visual and performing arts, sports and athletics, peace and social justice, communications and the media, architecture, health careers, and other areas. When the goal is mastery of a set of skills and a body of knowledge, rather that scoring high on reading and math tests, educators in the arts, music, science and technology, health, legal, or engineering professions would be the ones to determine who is or is not a "good teacher." Freedom schooling programs, built upon the successful magnet school models, offer an alternative to both the traditional public schools and the charter schools focused primarily of improving student performance on standardized math and reading tests. The teachers' unions must challenge the idea that the only way to determine a "good teacher" is by his or her students' performance on standardized tests. I am sure that I am not the only educator who is considered a "good teacher," but has never given his students a multiple-choice or standardized test.

In the past, many students' educational careers, particularly students of color, have been derailed by the use and abuse of standardized test results; and given the increasing use of standardized test scores to evaluate teacher performance, for the first time in several decades, the interests of the teachers' unions and urban minority students coincide. The teachers' unions should be mobilizing their members and parents to challenge the expansion of the testing regime in public schools and put forward the "freedom schooling model" as an alternative approach to school reform, in which students and teachers would be evaluated for their mastery of a wide range of skills and fields of knowledge. There is no need to wait for "Superman"; over the last 30 years unionized public school teachers in hundreds of magnet schools have increased students' levels of engagement and academic achievement through innovative, alternative educational programs. The teachers' unions need to be emphasizing that historical reality.

## NOTES

1. This Commentary is based on the Constance E. Clayton Invitational Lecture delivered by the author at the Graduate School of Education, University of Pennsylvania, on October 6, 2010.

2. See, for example, Erica Frankenberg and Genevieve Siegel-Hawley, "An Overlooked Model" in *American School Board Journal* (November 2009), 34–35, www.asbj.com; and "The Forgotten Choice: Rethinking Magnet Schools in a Changing Landscape," The Civil Rights Project (Los Angeles: UCLA, 2009).

## REFERENCES

Batchelor, R. & Franklin, V.P. (1978, December) Freedom schooling: A new approach to federal-local cooperation in public education, *Teachers College Record*, 225–248.

Dillon, Naomi (2009, November). Moving out: Magnet schools hold great promise for districts. *American School Board Journal*, 32–33, www.asbj.com

Eaton, S. (2010, June) The pull of magnets. In Special Issue, "A New Vision of School Reform," *The Nation*, 30–31.

Frankenberg, Erica, & Siegel-Hawley, Genevieve (2009), The forgotten choice: Rethinking magnet schools in a changing landscape, *The Civil Rights Project*. Los Angeles: UCLA.

Frankenberg, Erica, & Siegel-Hawley, Genevieve (2009, November). An overlooked model. *American School Board Journal*, 34–35, www.asbj.com

Smrekar, Clair (1999). *School Choice in Urban America: Magnet Schools and the Pursuit of Equity*. New York: Teachers College Press.

# PART IV

· · · · · · · · · · · · · · · · · · · · · · · · · · · · · · · · · · · · · · ·

# Race and the Contemporary Education of African American Children: Theoretical and Policy Issues

After the election of the first Black president of the United States in 2008, news commentators stated we had entered into a post-racial society. While we do not know what is meant by "post-racial," we do know that there continues to be health disparities between racial groups in our country. We also know that youth of color continue to lag behind their White counterparts in various measures of academic achievement. Furthermore, our major cities—home to large populations of people of color—are facing economic crises that directly impact schools. These facts attest to the continuing need to have conversations about race on multiple levels and across contexts. By doing so, we can better understand how to promote the positive development of Black youth—particularly within schools.

The following authors offer cogent theoretical and policy perspectives on how Black youth navigate their schools and the impact of various factors on Black youth's educational outcomes. Part IV begins with an examination of a metaphorical space for the adaptive development of Black youth attending independent schools, continues with an exploration of how various types of schools relate to the academic achievement of Black youth and finally, delves into the impact of racial composition and school socioeconomic status on Black student achievement. Underlying chapters in this Part is a nuanced examination of the multiple ways that race matters in providing successful experiences for Black youth across educational settings.

. . . . . . . . . . . . . . . . . . . . . . . . . . . . . . . . . . . . . . . . . . . . .

# 16

# Enhancing the Schooling Experience of African American Students in Predominantly White Independent Schools: Conceptual and Strategic Considerations to Developing a Critical Third Space

*Robert Cooper*

## INTRODUCTION

Ensuring both excellence (quality schooling) and equity (access, participation, and benefit) in U.S. public education remains one of the greatest challenges of the twenty-first century. The inability of the U.S. K–12 educational system to meet this challenge is resulting in an unprecedented number of African American families pursuing educational opportunities for their children outside the conventional tax-free public and neighborhood school. With the proliferation of alternatives to traditional public schools, particularly charter schools, and the increasing access to a number of private/independent elite and parochial schools, African American families are exploring and choosing educational alternatives to educate the next generation of African American youth. Given the persistent educational gap in this country between African American students and their White counterparts (Darling-Hammond, 2004; Teranishi, Allen, & Solorzano 2004), prevailing wisdom in the African American community, particularly among the middle class who live in neighborhoods with failing public schools, suggests that student who want to be prepared for post-secondary educational opportunities must be educated outside their traditional neighborhood school. This type of thinking leads to a belief that every alternative to public education is a good one. However, this thinking fails to recognize two of the most important root causes of the systemic inequalities that drive the U.S. system and ultimately, shape the schooling opportunities, experiences, and success of African American students in schools: colorblindness and meritocracy (Guinier & Torres, 2002).

Decades of research highlight the wide variety of reasons attributed to why African American students consistently do less well in school than students of other races. Frequently cited reasons include disproportionate poverty levels (Baker, 1998), minority status (Lagerwey & Phillips, 2003; Martinez, DeGarmo, & Eddy, 2004), teen pregnancy (National Center for Health Statistics, 2001), discontinuity of social values between home and school (Boykin, 1986; Delpit, 1995), lack of social capital (Hao & Bronstead-Burns, 1998), lack of role models (Rouse, 1998), and school policies (Cabrera & Padilla, 2004; Donato, Menchaca, & Valencia, 1993). Despite the plethora of research on the multiplicity of factors that contribute to the persistent underachievement of African American students across varying types of schooling contexts, one of the most consistent factors related to this underachievement is race.

Many educational theorists who study the relationship between race and education have documented how race influences, both consciously and unconsciously, how students interact, respond, and speak to their teachers and fellow students, as well as how students access, navigate, and negotiate their schooling experience (Davis & Jordan, 1995; Gregory & Mosely, 2004; Cooper & Chizhik, 2004). Given the important role race plays in the schooling experience of African American students, this chapter hypothesizes how racialized school norms, policies, and practices affect the schooling experience of African American in predominantly White independent schools. While early research on African American students in independent schools primarily focused on the failures of these students to achieve at the same academic level as their White counterparts (Jencks et al. 1972), more recent scholarship has focused on factors that contribute to their success (Arrington, Hall & Stevenson, 2003; Ladson-Billings, 2000). Since the 1960s, many independent schools have enacted policies of nondiscrimination and have actively recruited minority students in efforts to create a more diverse student body on their campuses (Speede-Franklin, 1988). Consequently, the number of African American families considering and selecting independent school as a viable educational option has increased over the past four decades, thus making the issues of academic success of African American students attending independent schools of significant importance.

Despite the efforts of predominantly White independent schools to create learning environments that are supportive and welcoming to African American students, research suggests that these institutions, with their history of racial exclusion, are often places where African American students still find it difficult to fit in (Brookins, 1988; Zweigenhaft & Domhoff, 1991). Students report feeling alienated from the culture of the school and from their parents and friends (Cookson & Persell, 1991). Research also suggests that African American students at these institutions have weaker social relationships with their teachers than do their peers, and that this lack of connection has a negative impact on their motivation and overall academic performance (Datnow & Cooper, 2000; Arrington, Hall, & Stevenson 2003).

In light of these experiences for African American students, this chapter refines and broadens a theoretical concept that has the potential to enhance the schooling experience of students attending predominantly White independent schools. This concept, a Critical Third Space (CTS) (Cooper & Huh, 2008) is a metaphorical space focused on individual sense-making activity, where students begin to define who they are as intellectual beings and establish goals and aspirations for the future (Gutierrez, 2008). Building on my previous conceptual and empirical work on this topic, I elaborate on this theoretical concept to explore its utility within the independent school context. Regardless of the context, this metaphorical space is a space of empowerment and transformation. It is in this metaphorical space, I argue, where African American students learn to exert their individual agency and harness the social and political capital of their schooling environment to pursue their education and career goals. I draw on notions of stereotype threat and microaggression to illuminate the interconnectedness of the schooling experiences of African American youth across varying schooling contexts: independent schools, public schools, charter schools, etc.

To illustrate the transformative potential of this concept, I draw on empirical work from the UCLA EASE Project. The UCLA EASE Project is a multidisciplinary research collaborative which engages in research activities that promote greater equality of educational opportunities for urban youth. The primary purpose of the Project is to conduct and disseminate research that broadens our understanding of issues of equity and access in the K–16 education pipeline. From its inception in the fall of 2001, the work of the EASE Project has focused on identifying and better understanding the conditions needed in schools to improve educational outcomes so that more students have access to post-secondary opportunities. As part of the on-going work of the EASE Project, African American parents and students who have considered and/or enrolled in an a predominantly White independent school have participated in individual interviews and focus groups to discuss their educational experiences, as well as their educational aspirations and motivations. I use these data to illuminate the utility of a Critical Third Space, in increasing academic outcomes for African Americans students attending predominantly White independent schools.

### Developing a Critical Third Space from a Political Race Perspective: Conceptual Considerations

There are three important spheres of influence on the schooling experience and achievement of African American students: (1) the family/community, (2) peer networks and school norms, and (3) policies and practices (Cooper & Datnow, 2000; Cooper & Hu, 2008). Each sphere of influence has embedded within it a socialization process by which students come to understand and value the importance of success in school. Following the lead of several scholars who have written about the development of a third space (Bhabha, 1994; Gutierrez, Baquedano-Lopez, Alvarez, & Chiu, 1999; Gutierrez, 2008), I call the intersection and integration of the three spheres of influence the Critical Third Space. Whereas my use of the concept of the third space differs from other scholars who view the third space as a way to build bridges between the multiple worlds of students (Bhabha, 1994; Gutierrez, Baquedano-Lopez, Alvarez, & Chiu, 1999), I define Critical Third Space as the interaction and integration of the multiple worlds students navigate between during their adolescent development to be successful in their educational pursuits. It is in this space that students are socialized towards a reflective achievement ideology and a positive racial identity, which lead to both academic and social success in school (Cooper & Datnow, 2000). Reflective achievement ideology in this context refers to developing the attitudes, values, and practices that are consistent with school success in spite of the structural inequalities and acts of discrimination they might encounter in their schooling experience. For example, reflective achievement ideology involves students feeling intellectually equal to their peers and viewing education as an important component of their future life aspirations. Achievement ideology, mediated by behaviors like studying, participating in class discussions, and being involved in after-school activities, leads to better academic performance. Positive ethnic identity, on the other hand, refers to a student's ability to interact cross-culturally and embrace and be empowered by their racial history and experience.

The Critical Third Space is the place where students are empowered to be critical of institutional systems and institutions, wherein they are both products of and participants in. It is in this metaphorical space where African American students develop the aspirations, motivations, and resiliency to overcome the adversities that stand between them and their desired objectives. The Critical Third Space is important because it provides opportunities for success in school, while also giving voice to those often silenced because of their marginalization in this society (Moje, Ciechanowski, & Ellis, 2004).

Critical Third Space gives students voice through what Guinier and Torres (2002) have called "Political Race." Political Race is a framework that illustrates how the lived experience of race in the United States continues to serve an important function in the construction of individual selves as well as in the construction of social policy. Political Race, in essence, is an attempt to illuminate how race is linked to power and resource allocation. My use of Political Race in this context is an attempt to situate school norms, policies, and practices, particularly institutional beliefs and expectations within the broader discourse of race in this country and to illuminate how African American students are stigmatized by widespread beliefs regarding their racial group. The widespread beliefs that often stigmatize students affect their ability to negotiate educational goals, aspirations, and experiences, despite the educational context in which they attend school. Obviously, there are schooling contexts that are more receptive to cultivating the development of a Critical Third Space, but all contexts must first acknowledge the historical and cultural socialization process that stigmatize certain racial groups and privilege others.

The concept of Political Race possesses three major elements: (1) it has a diagnostic function; (2) it embraces an aspirational goal; and (3) it hopes to jumpstart an activist project. As a diagnostic tool, Political Race is used to determine how race influences institutional expectations and how those expectations get internalized by students. Within this diagnosis, the racial nature of the school illuminates how African American students are viewed and treated differently from their student counterparts. The diagnostic function of Political Race sets the foundation for the other two tenets which focus on understanding how changes can be implemented to improve the educational experiences of African American students, regardless of the educational context.

The Political Race framework is extended in this chapter by employing the concepts of stereotype threat and racial microaggressions to better understand how institutional norms and expectations are communicated to students and affect their academic performance, engagement, and aspirations. These two concepts, both of which focus on the affects of race and racism, are used to highlight how both subtle and overt forms of racial discrimination in the form of institutional norms and expectations can undermine the academic achievement and aspirations of African American students.

### Institutional Barriers in Predominantly White Independent Schools to Developing a Critical Third Space: Strategic Considerations

Contemporary scholars who study African American students have suggested that greater attention be paid to how students participate in the multiple and often conflicting and contradictory social systems that they must navigate through to be successful in their educational pursuits (Boykin, 1986; Stanton-Salazar, 1997). For many students, participation in multiple social systems and contexts is made easier by being introduced and exposed to people and ideas that are reflective of the diversity of society and not confined to the social norms of their family and immediate community. For many African American students, this means bringing issues of race, culture, and social class issues into the foreground of their individual and group identity. It means examining social systems, such as health care, the criminal justice system, and schools, with an eye on whom in society benefits from them and how these benefits are tied to inequalities associated with race, social class, language, gender, and other social categories (Rogers & Quartz, 2000). This is the work I contend takes place in the Critical Third Space. Unfortunately, for many African American students attending predominantly White independent schools, there are systemic norms and values that retard the development of the Critical Third Space.

Many educators acknowledge that different groups of students experience school differently, however, few are willing to publicly admit that the race of the student is a key factor in determining that experience. While many predominantly White independent schools are increasingly achieving racial sensitivity in their admission process, unfortunately, they also continue to strive for racial neutrality in their institutional culture and curriculum. Racial neutrality is defined as the deliberate avoidance of acknowledging the ways in which our culture has historically created structures, laws, and practices that privilege certain racial groups over others in this country (Chang, 2004). Racial neutrality fails to recognize the unequal power relationship between racial minorities and those of the dominant culture. Racial neutrality is sustained on independent school campuses through a variety of educational strategies, policies, and practices that are based on assumptions driven by a false sense of institutional meritocracy. Perhaps, one of the most significant assumptions pertaining to race neutrality that affects the schooling experience of African American students is that of racial colorblindness (Hytten & Warren, 2003; Guinier & Torres, 2005). Colorblindness is a complex ideology in which people are taught to ignore race and the existing power relationship that privileges the dominant ideology and culture in our society (Gordon, 2005). Colorblindness maintains that race does not exist in a meaningful way and posits that the benefits accrued to an individual are earned through individual merit rather than systemically conferred. It is a common occurrence for schools to celebrate diversity, while ignoring race.

In my work with Black students in independent schools, I discussed race in their school contexts. Natasha, a freshman at a predominantly White independent school just outside of Los Angeles, when asked about her experience with being a Black student at her school stated "We don't really talk about it. We have a diversity club on campus and we explore all the issues of difference . . . we don't really talk about race. We do have a club for African American girls on campus, but that's it." Further conversation with Natasha indicated that she felt that there was a push to empower the girls on campus, but no meaningful activities to facilitate positive racial identity development among students. Natasha did not report experiencing any overt acts of discrimination at her school, but felt there was no institutional support and leadership in educating the school community about the positive accomplishments and contributions of African American to the larger society. Natasha indicated none of the classes or school-wide assemblies dealt specifically with race. The result of this colorblind institutional approach to school climate, culture, and curricula, according to Natasha, has created a tension among and between African American students. This tension that has created a schism in the African American student population—a schism that forces students to "prove their blackness." Like much of the earlier research on independent schools, Natasha spoke about how the normal pressures of "fitting in" with peers are heightened in this environment. Common adolescent issues such as fashion, music, and relationships all take on greater importance for African American students in independent schools. Students struggle with questions of "acting White," and what that notion even means, if they adopt the culture and values of the institution (Cooper & Datnow, 2000).

Guinier and Torres (2002) suggest that when students are "raced Black," there is a predictable set of attitudes and behaviors that students are expected to exemplify. The struggle for African American students in the independent school setting is to not accept the expectations of others, but to be confident in their own self-identity, to be clear about who they are, and to be able to articulate their own future trajectory. Despite the tension that Natasha spoke about between the African American students on her campus, she was clear to acknowledge the strong social bond that the African American students shared on her campus and how that bond was critical to the academic performance and sense of identity and belonging of African American students.

Barbara, an 11th grader at an independent school 45 minutes north of Los Angeles, expressed similar sentiments as Natasha with regards to the issues of race at her school. When asked how being an African American student impacts her experience and academic performance, Barbara stated that the classes are so rigorous at her school that "race has nothing to do with academic performance . . . it is all about doing the work." Barbara, a recent transfer student to the school, repeatedly spoke about the rigorous academic demands placed upon the students and how it was the students who work hard that received the top grades. It was clear from speaking with Barbara, that as a new student, she had been socialized to accept the institutional meritocracy that permeated the school culture. Barbara's experience, which is very common for students attending an independent school according to my research, reinforces the idea that these school environments operate on the notion that student academic assessment (grades) is an accurate reflection of a student's intellectual capacity and effort.

I highlight the experiences of Natasha and Barbara not to suggest that institutional colorblindness and meritocracy exist exclusively in predominantly White independent schools, but rather to illustrate that the challenges that African American students face in their educational pursuit are similar and consistent across educational contexts. Research documents the fact that in many traditional school contexts for many African American students notions of colorblindness and meritocracy exist. The prevalence of this belief allows schools, and the educators who work in them, to perpetuate a deficit perspective about African American students; a perspective that has become normalized. The deficit perspective, which grew out of research in the 1960s (see Deutsch & Brown, 1964), focuses on perceived cultural, psychological, and/or mental deficiencies (Sleeter & Grant, 1994) and blames the student for his/her academic failure.

Such normative beliefs result in African American students being disproportionately placed in the least academically rigorous courses in the school and identified as having a disproportionate share of the discipline problems. These negative educational experiences often lead to feelings of isolation, alienation, inferiority, and a sense of defeat for African American students. The negative schooling outcomes experienced by African American students speak to the importance of the development of a Critical Third Space. It is in this space where students recognize, but not own, the negative normative expectations that are associated with being African American. Anthony, a father of a young man applying to an independent school stated that it is the low expectations that some public schools have for African American students that is driving him to consider an independent school: "My son is an excellent football player and we are looking to receive a scholarship for him to play at the school ... We are excited about this opportunity because the academic expectations are very different at the [independent] school." While the expectations at independent schools are different from many public schools serving African American students, this father does not acknowledge the fact that educators in independent schools, like all members of society, are limited by their experiences and guided by their assumptions (Cohen, Kepner, & Swanson, 1993). The values and beliefs that educators at the independent school bring to the schooling environment are the accumulation of their social interactions, family background, and formal and informal training and may be similar to the values and beliefs of the educators at his son's neighborhood school.

For so many African American students, race and racism continue to play an important role in how they navigate and are regarded in educational spaces (Ladson-Billings, 2000). This is often manifested in implicit and explicit expectations based on stereotyped behaviors and characteristics of their racial group. Although Natasha did not identify the tension between African American students on her campus as having its genesis in any racially motivated source, the work of scholars who have studied stereotype threat is helpful to our understanding of that tension. Bonilla-Silva (1997) posits that stereotypes originate from "(1) material realities or conditions endured by the group, (2) genuine ignorance about the group or (3) rigid distorted views on the group's physical, cultural or moral nature (p. 476)." These stereotypes range in type and relate to many aspects of a particular racial group, including intelligence, character, and appearance. Within the educational setting, these definitions provide an understanding of how the race of a student prompts teachers to make assumptions and act in accordance with such assumptions. Solorzano & Yosso (2001) contend that racial stereotypes affect African Americans, and all students of color, in the following ways:

(1) having low educational and occupational expectations for Students of Color; (2) placing Students of Color in separate school and, in some cases, separate classrooms within schools; (3) remediating or "dumbing down" the curriculum and pedagogy for Students of Color; and (4) expecting Students of Color to one day occupy certain types and levels of occupations. (p. 10)

Pierce's (1970) work suggests that racialized expectations and stereotypes regarding racial groups are communicated through subtle inferences known as "microaggressions." Pierce's insight informs the work of Solorzano, Ceja, and Yosso (2001) who studied the college experiences of African American students. Their study found that race and racism had a significant influence on African Americans students' experiences in college. Within academic spaces, students reported feeling frustrated and isolated as professors and fellow classmates held and inferred negative stereotypes about their academic capabilities. Many of the students indicated their academic experience and performance were adversely affected by their racialized treatment on campus.

The work of Steele and Aronson (1995) further explicate the effects of negative stereotypes. Specifically, they studied how stereotypes influence the performance of African American students' on high-stakes standardized tests that were believed to measure intelligence. When students were prompted to report their race, their test scores were significantly lower. They call this phenomenon "stereotype threat," is defined as

> a social-psychological predicament that can arise from widely known negative stereotypes about one's group ... the existence of such a stereotype means that anything one does or any of one's features that confirm to it make the stereotypes more plausible as a self-characterization in the eyes of others, and perhaps even in one's own eyes. We call this predicament stereotype threat and argue it is experienced, essentially, as a self-evaluative threat. (p. 797)

Schools play a critical role in socializing students to understand who they are and their role in society. Implicit in the development of a Critical Third Space for African American students is the idea that educators must create the conditions within schools for students to identify the metaphorical space that allows them to become critical of the systematic inequalities found in society in general and the cultural assumptions that drive school policy and practice at their school. Moreover, it is in the Critical Third Space where students develop the skills to use that information to inspire and motivate themselves to pursue their academic and career aspirations.

## CONCLUSION

Despite 50 years of advancements in intergroup relationships, improving the academic outcomes of African American students begins with an understanding the *social distribution of possibilities*, a term used to describe unequal distribution of opportunities to participate in different social and institutional contexts (Wellman, 1983; Stanton-Salazar, 1997). The vast majority of African American students in this country, by virtue of neighborhood school assignments, are systematically denied access to the types of people, experiences, skills, and funds of knowledge and discourse—or support networks—that middle-class non-African American students consistently depend upon to secure their successful and privileged participation in schooling processes in this country (Cooper & Jordan, 2003; Cooper & Chizic, 2004).

Although the historic *Brown v. Board of Education* decision of 1954 has legally ensured African American students equal access to educational opportunities as their non- African American peers receive, research suggest that African American students are still not provided the same educational experience even when attending the same schools or assigned to the same classroom as their non-African American peers (Cooper & Jordan, 2003). In this chapter, I laid out conceptual and strategic considerations for the development of the Critical Third Space; a metaphorical space of empowerment and transformation. It is in this space, I argue that African American students can develop the ability to overcome the challenges that are endemic to their educational experience. While in this chapter I argue the utility of this concept in the independent school context in general, this concept is also important to the enhancement of the schooling experience of African American students more broadly across the increasingly varied schooling contexts in which they are being educated. Drawing on political race theory and notions of stereotype threat and microaggression, I attempted to illuminate the schooling experiences of African American youth across varying schooling contexts with an emphasis on the independent school context. Regardless of the schooling environment of choice, there is a cultural socialization process that binds African American students together so that no matter what school they attend, the schooling experience in this country is far more similar than different.

## REFERENCES

Arrington, E. G., Hall, D. M., & Stevenson, H. C. (2003). The success of African American students in Independent Schools Project. *Independent School Magazine*, *62*(4), 11–21.

Baker, J. A. (1998). The social context of school satisfaction among urban, low-income African-American students. *School Psychology Quarterly*, *13*, 25–44. doi: 10.1521/scpq.17.2.109.20856

Bhabha, H. (1994). *The location of culture*. London: Routledge.

Bonilla-Silva, E. (1997). Rethinking racism: Toward a structural interpretation. *American Sociological Review*, *62*(3), 465–480. doi: 10.2307/209223

Boykin, A. W. (1986). The triple quandary and the schooling of Afro-American children. In U. Neisser (Ed.), *School achievement of minority children: New perspectives* (pp. 57–92). Hillsdale, NJ: Lawrence Erlbaum.

Brookins, G. (1988). Making the honor roll: A Black parent's perspective on private education. In D. Slaughter & D. Johnson (Eds.), *Visible Now: Blacks in private schools* (pp. 12–20). Westport, CN: Greenwood Press.

Cabrera, N. L., & Padilla, A.M. (2004). Entering and succeeding in the "Culture of College": The story of two Mexican heritage students. *Hispanic Journal of Behavioral Sciences*, *26*(2), 152–170. doi: 10.1177/0739986305283221

Chang, M. (2004). *Racial politics in an era of transnational citizenship*. Lanham, MD: Lexington Books.

Cohen, E., Kepner, D., & Swanson, P. (1993). Dismantling status hierarchies in heterogeneous classrooms. In J. Oakes (Ed.), *New educational communities: Schools and classrooms where a children can be*. Chicago: University of Chicago Press.

Cookson, P. W., & Persell, C. H. (1991). Race and class in America's elite boarding schools: African-Americans as the outsiders within. *Journal of Negro Education*, *60*(2), 219–228.

Cooper, R., & Chizhik, E. (2004). Talking about race in schools post brown: A public relations challenge. *Journal of School Public Relations, 25*(2), 203–219.

Cooper, R., & Datnow, A. (2000). African-American students' success in independent schools: A model of family, peer, community, and school influences. In M. Sanders, (Ed.), *Schooling students placed at risk: Research, policy, and practice in the education of poor and minority adolescents* (pp. 187–206). New Jersey: Erlbaum.

Cooper, R., & Huh, C. (2008). The role of schools in the development of a multicultural worldview. In J. Asamen, M. Ellis, & B. Gordon (Eds.), *Handbook of development, multiculturalism, and media* (pp. 143–164). Thousand Oaks, CA: Sage Publications.

Cooper, R., & Jordan, W. (2003) Cultural issues related to comprehensive high school reform. *Urban Education, 38*(4), 380–397. doi: 10.1177/0042085903038004003

Darling-Hammond, L. (2004). The color line in American education: Race, resources, and student achievement. *Du Bois Review, 1*(2), 213–246. doi: 10.1017/S1742058X04040019

Datnow, A., & Cooper, R. (2000). Creating a climate for diversity? The institutional response of predominately white independent schools to African-American students. In M. Sanders (Ed.), *Schooling students placed at risk: Research, policy, and practice in the education of poor and minority adolescents* (pp. 207–228). New Jersey; Erlbaum.

Davis, J. E., & Jordan, W. J. (1994). The effects of school context, structure, and experiences on African American males in middle and high school. *Journal of Negro Education, 63*(4), 570–587. doi: 10.2307/2967298

Delpit, L. (1995). *Other people's children: Cultural conflict in the classroom.* New York The New Press.

Deutsch, M., & Brown, B. (1964). Social influences in Negro–White intelligence differences. *Journal of Social Issues, 20*, 24–35. doi: 10.1111/j.1540-4560.1964.tb01698.x

Donato, R., Menchaca, M., & Valencia, R. R. (1993). Segregation, desegregation, and the integration of Chicano students: Problems and prospects. In R.R. Valencia (Ed.), *Chicano school failure and success: Research and policy agendas for the 1990's* (pp. 27–63). New York: Falmer Press.

Gordon, J, (2005). White on White: Researcher reflexivity and the logics of privilege in which schools undertaking reform. *Urban Review, 37*(4), 279–302. doi: 10.1234/12345678

Gregory, A., & Mosely, P. M. (2004). The discipline gap: Teachers' views on the over-representation of African American student in the discipline system. *Equity & Excellence in Education, 37*(1), 18–30.

Guinier, L., & Torres, G. (2002). *The miner's canary: Enlisting race, resisting power, transforming democracy.* Cambridge, Massachusetts: Harvard University Press.

Gutierrez, K.D. (2008). Developing a social critical literacy in the third space. *Reading Research Quarterly, 43*(2), 148–164. doi: 10.1598/RRQ.43.2.4

Gutierrez, K. D., Baquedano-Lopez, P., Alvarez, H., & Chiu, M. (1999). Building a culture of collaboration through hybrid language practices. *Theory Into Practice, 38*, 87–93. doi: 10.1353/tip.2004.0003

Hao, L., & Bonstead-Bruns, M. (1998). Parent–child differences in educational expectations and the academic achievement of immigrant and native students. *Sociology of Education, 71*(3), 175–198. doi: 10.2307/2673202

Hytten, K., & Warren, J. (2003). Engaging Whiteness: How racial power gets reified in education. *International Journal of Qualitative Studies in Education, 16*(1), 65–89.

Jencks, C., M. Smith, H. Acland, M. J. Bane, D. Cohen, H. Gintis, B. Heyns, & S. Michelson (1972). *Inequality: A reassessment of the effect of family and schooling in America*. New York: Basic Books.

Ladson-Billings, G. (2000). Fighting for our lives: Preparing teachers to teach African American students. *Journal of Teacher Education, 51*(3), 206–214.

Lagerwey, M.D., & Phillips, E. (2003). Voices from the pipeline: High school completion among rural Latinos. *Journal of Cultural Diversity, 10*, 42–49.

Martinez, C.R., DeGarmo, D.S., & Eddy, J.M. (2004). Promoting academic success among Latino youth. *Hispanic Journal of Behavioral Science, 26*, 128–151.

Moje, E.B., Ciechanowski, K.M., Kramer, K., Ellis, L., Carrillo, R., & Collazo, T. (2004). Working toward third space in content area literacy: An examination of everyday funds of knowledge and Discourse. Reading Research Quarterly, *39*(1), 38–70.

National Center of Health Statistics. (2001). New CDC report tracks trends in teen births from 1940–2000. Retrieved November 3, 2005 from: http://www.cdc.gov/nchs/releases/01facts/teenbirths.htm

Nespor, J. (1987). The role of beliefs in the practice of teaching. *Journal of Curriculum Studies, 19*, 317–328.

Pierce, C. M. (1970). Offensive mechanisms: The vehicle for microaggressions. In F.B. Barbour (Ed.), *The Black 70s* (pp. 265–282). Boston: Porter-Sargent.

Rogers, J., & Quartz, K. (2000, April). *Teaching for social justice: Framing the complexity and contradiction*. Paper presented at the annual meeting of the American Education Research Association, New Orleans, LA.

Rouse, K. G. (1998). Resilience from poverty and stress. *Human Development and Family Life Bulletin, 4*(1), 1–10.

Sleeter, C., &. Grant, C. (1994). *Making choices for multicultural education: Five approaches to race, class and gender*. New York, New York: Macmillan

Solórzano, D. G., & Yosso, T. J. (2001). From racial stereotyping and deficit discourse: Toward a critical race theory in teacher education. *Multicultural Education, 9*(1), 2–8.

Speede-Franklin, W. A. (1988). Ethnic diversity: patterns and implications of minorities in independent schools. In D.T. Slaughter & D. Johnson (Eds.), *Visible Now: Blacks in private school* (pp. 21–31). Westport, CT: Greenwich Press.

Stanton-Salazar, R. D. (1997). A social capital framework for understanding the socialization of racial minority children and youth. *Harvard Educational Review, 67*(1), 1–40.

Steele, C. M., & Aronson, J. (1995). Stereotype threat and the intellectual test performance of African Americans. *Journal of Personality and Social Psychology, 69*(5), 797–811.

Teranishi, R., Allen, W. R., & Solórzano, D.G. (2004). Opportunity at the crossroads: Racial inequality, school segregation, and higher education in California. *Teachers College Record, 106*(11), 2224–2245.

Wellman, B. (1983). Network analysis: Some basic principles. In R. Collins (Ed.), *Sociological theory*. San Francisco: Jossey-Bass (pp. 155–200).

Zweigenhaft, R., & Domhoff, G. (1991). *Blacks in White establishments*. New Haven, CT: Yale University Press.

· · · · · · · · · · · · · · · · · · · · · · · · · · · · · · · · · · · · · · · · · · ·

# 17

# The Changing Landscape: Enhancing the Public School Option for Black Youth

*Lara Perez-Felkner, E.C. Hedberg,*
*and Barbara Schneider*

## INTRODUCTION

Although school choice options have expanded throughout the United States, it remains unclear whether they have significantly changed the educational opportunity structures of the students attending them (Finn, Manno, & Vanourek, 2001; Renzulli & Roscigno, 2005). New public high school institutions including charters have been instituted to enhance Black academic performance and access to postsecondary school. The current analysis historically compares and contrasts Black youths' postsecondary enrollment with other racial and ethnic groups', focusing on the types of high schools that the students attended. The intent is to characterize the types of public institutions that have been particularly successful in enhancing Black high school students' access to postsecondary institutions.

While Black postsecondary attainment rates rose in the 1990s, the academic racial gap among Blacks and Whites widened. In 1990, 13 percent of Black, non-Hispanic young adults (aged 25–29 years old) completed a Bachelor's degree or higher compared to 26 percent of White non-Hispanic adults, (Current Population Survey, 2009a). By 2000, 18 percent of Black, non-Hispanic 25–29 year olds had completed a Bachelor's degree or higher in comparison to 34 percent of White, non-Hispanics (a difference of 16 percentage points); by 2009, the gap had increased further to a difference of over 18 percentage points (Current Population Survey, 2009a). This escalating racial inequality prompts questions about the secondary school experiences of U.S. youth from the late 1980s through the 2000s.

One hallmark of educational reform has been an increased emphasis on market-based solutions that provide opportunities for students and their families to choose the schools they will attend. While not an entirely new type of reform (public school choice options have been offered since the 1960s in the form of magnet schools, designed to address racial inequalities in education[1]), choice gained considerable momentum with the introduction of charter schools. Charter schools are granted autonomy through short-term contractual charters from school boards, state and local districts, or other public educational entities. This autonomy is designed to foster innovation aimed at improving students' outcomes (Bulkley & Fisler, 2003; Renzulli & Roscigno, 2005). Although not the case in all districts (Wells, Holme, Lopez, & Cooper, 2003), charter schools primarily enroll socioeconomically disadvantaged students who score low on their achievement tests, and experience similar or greater socioeconomic and academic disadvantages than their student peers (Hoxby, 2004; Rapp & Eckes, 2007). The admission process at charter schools usually occurs through a lottery system.

Charter schools are increasingly occupying a central role in school reform. By 2007–2008, 370,158 9th through 12th grade students were enrolled in charter schools. Over a quarter of these students (27%) were Black, non-Hispanic and 28 percent were Latino.[2] These numbers are likely to continue to increase as local and state-level investments in charter schools are expanding, due in part to incentives provided by initiatives such as the Race to the Top program and Promise Neighborhoods (U.S. Department of Education, 2010).

Recent studies report that charter schools improve the high school graduation and college matriculation rates of their students, compared to traditional public schools, particularly in certain states and cities (Booker, Sass, Gill, & Zimmer, 2008; Zimmer & Buddin, 2007). Overall however, evidence of charter schools' impact on student academic performance is mixed, especially for Black youth. In the past, more traditional privatization options such as Catholic schools and schools affiliated with the elite National Association for Independent Schools (NAIS), have shown similar results for Black students (Slaughter-Defoe & Johnson, 1988).[3] It is unclear whether these types of private schools will continue to show mixed results.

### Racial Differences in College Enrollment

Preparing minority students for entry to four-year colleges has been a major emphasis of school choice programs. The question becomes whether newer types of public schools are more successful in increasing Black postsecondary enrollment than traditional public schools. In the 1990s and 2000s, the movement toward "college for all" gained accelerated momentum. The proportion of 18- to 24-year-olds enrolled in college rose from 36 percent in 2000 to 41 percent in 2009 (Current Population Survey, 2009b). In fall 2010, 19.1 million students were expected to attend two-year and four-year postsecondary institutions in the United States, up from 15.3 million in fall 2000 (NCES, 2009). Of these, 12.1 million students were expected to attend public or private four-year institutions, 6.7 million were expected to attend public two-year colleges, and 0.3 million were expected to attend private two-year colleges (NCES, 2009). Much of this enrollment growth has been in the two-year college sector (see Rosenbaum, 2001). These institutions have been largely designed to provide a stepping stone to a four-year degree for students with limited resources (Rosenbaum, Deil-Amen, & Person, 2006), Research suggests however that youth with limited economic and social resources are less likely to benefit from the two-year system compared to students with more resources (Goldrick-Rab, 2006).

Some of the variation in postsecondary enrollments has been traced to differences in high school academic preparation. High schools have been shown to have different levels of academic emphasis, or press (Lee & Smith, 1999; Murphy, Weil, Hallinger, & Mitman, 1982). Schools high in academic press tend to place considerable emphasis on academic achievement and preparing students for college, encouraging rigorous coursework, school discipline, and College Board test-taking (Lee & Smith, 1999; Murphy et al., 1982). For example, advanced mathematics and science course taking has been found to be predictive of students' preparedness for college (Muller, Riegle-Crumb, Schiller, Wilkinson, & Frank, 2010; Schneider, Swanson, & Riegle-Crumb, 1998).

On the other hand, institutions high in academic press do not necessarily foster strong student attachment to their school (Phillips, 1997). Racial composition has been found to play a role in students' attachment to their schools such that schools with low proportions of underrepresented minority students have lower levels of attachment among members of those groups (Johnson, Crosnoe, & Elder, 2001). The social isolation associated with racial composition has been found to affect students long-term, for example, in the workplace years after high school (Stearns, 2010). Thus, schools' social contexts are important to consider when examining underrepresented minorities' pathways to college.

Student engagement in school is another factor that has been shown to affect students' postsecondary trajectories. Extensive research has associated student engagement in school (e.g., students' efforts on their math homework) with positive academic outcomes (Eccles, 2007; Fredricks, Blumenfeld, & Paris, 2004). A related concept, students' *attachment* to their schools, has also been associated with students' postsecondary enrollment (Hallinan, 2008). Attachment can be measured in regards to both behavior (e.g., participation in extracurricular activities) and affect (e.g., feelings about one's school) (Johnson, Crosnoe, & Elder, 2001).

Certainly part of gains in two-year college attendance can be credited to their lower costs in comparison to tuition at four-year institutions. It is important to look beyond costs. There are likely to be other factors operating within high schools that are associated with the growth of enrollment at two-year colleges among recent high school graduates. For Black students, it may be the case that two-year institutions are a more viable strategy for beginning a college education than seeking admission to a four-year college. This may be because of a lack of academic press, and social and emotional support in high school.

### Measuring a Decade of Change

Changes in school organization can be tracked using longitudinal data collected by the U.S. Department of Education's National Center for Education Statistics. Two of the most recent longitudinal secondary school studies, The National Educational Longitudinal Study of 1988 (NELS: 1988) and the Educational Longitudinal Study (ELS: 2002) were specifically designed to examine the process by which underrepresented youth move through the educational system toward, or away from, their postsecondary aspirations over time (Ingels et al., 2007). The 12 years separating NELS and ELS cohorts span an important decade of change in Black families' access to different types of high schools.[4] NELS and ELS data can be used to examine similar students over time and unpack the relationship between public school choice and postsecondary opportunities. By comparing cohorts, it is possible to explore whether the increased participation of Blacks in new public school contexts is improving their educational outcomes. These data can also be used to show how Black student postsecondary enrollments have changed.

Attempting to compare the association between postsecondary enrollment and high school preparation can be particularly difficult as there are quite a number of different types of public high schools. To be able to compare school types across the two longitudinal data sets, the following analysis divides these schools into five categories: (1) public schools of assignment, (2) assigned-choice hybrids, (3) public schools of choice, (4) Catholic or parochial schools, and (5) other private schools.[5]

We conducted a series of descriptive analyses that show increases in public high school enrollment.[6] This rise corresponds to the increasing availability of school choice in the public school sector. Residentially assigned (traditional) public schools enrolled 31 percent fewer sophomores in 2002 while alternative public school types made dramatic gains. These gains include increases in both existing choice types (e.g., magnets) and new choice types which did not exist in 1990 (e.g., charters). Public schools of choice more than doubled their enrollees, primarily reflecting increased enrollment in charter and magnet schools (16,188 and 94,140 in 2002, respectively). Assignment-choice combination schools (e.g., charter schools within traditional assigned public schools) increased their share of enrollees from 14 percent of the sample to 34 percent of the sample, rivaling the share of students enrolled in traditional public schools of assignment (46% of the sample). These changes were greater for Black sophomores who were enrolled in public schools over private schools in 2002 compared to 1990. Enrollments in public schools of choice also increased, with the largest increase seen in the Black population. This was also the case for Hispanics and Whites, although the increase for Whites was considerably smaller.

The increased enrollment of Black students in public schools does not correspond to general declines in private school enrollment. Rather, the two percent increase corresponds to a three percent decline in Blacks' participation in Catholic schools. In 1990, six percent of Black sophomores were enrolled in Catholic schools; this figure decreased to only three percent by 2002. Nonparochial private schools increased their enrollment across all groups during this interval however, increasing their share of Black enrollment between 1990 and 2002 from 1.1 percent to 2.1 percent.

### Differences by School Sector for Minority Youth

Given that more Blacks are attending public schools of choice, are their educational experiences different than they were a decade ago? Moreover, are they significantly different when compared to other racial and ethnic groups? In addressing this question, it is important to consider potential associations between different racial and ethnic groups' postsecondary transition outcomes and high school characteristics, family engagement, prior student academic experiences in high school, and student perceptions of school climate.

The pathway to college is complex and not always similar across racial and ethnic groups. Reporting information beyond enrollment patterns, Table 17.1 presents results for measures that examine Black adolescents' pro-academic behaviors, including the number of hours per week that students spend on extracurricular activities and mathematics homework, and the rigor of their mathematics and science coursework.

We also report students' perceptions of academic support from their teachers, based on student rankings of the degree to which they experience teacher-related high expectations, interest, praise, and support in the classroom. Student self-reports of peers' college expectations, interactions with other racial and ethnic groups, and safety concerns are also discussed.

Black youth in the ELS cohort completed higher levels of education than in the NELS cohort although they continued to lag behind their White and Asian peers. Slightly more Black youth did not complete high school. The proportion of Black youth enrolled in or completing two-year college degrees, two years after high school, remained stable between the 1990 and 2002 cohorts and statistically insignificant from that of their White and Asian peers.

Although White and Asian youth strongly increased their enrollment in four-year colleges during this period, the proportion of Black seniors on the path to a bachelors' degree rose only slightly. Overall, the postsecondary educational attainment pathways of Black youth improved, albeit modestly, in the 1990s and early 2000s. Schools of choice attended by Black students tend to be located in more urban and suburban districts, as compared to schools of

Table 17.1
Descriptive Characteristics of Black Subsample by School Type and Year in which Respondents Were in 10th Grade

| | Public School, Assigned | | Public, Assigned-choice Combined | | Public, School of Choice | | Catholic | | Other Private | |
|---|---|---|---|---|---|---|---|---|---|---|
| | 1990 | 2002 | 1990 | 2002 | 1990 | 2002 | 1990 | 2002 | 1990 | 2002 |
| | 62,611 | 52,207 | 13,238 | 41,235 | 9,103 | 21,843 | 5,918 | 3,761 | 1,080 | 2,515 |
| | $\bar{X}$ (SD) | $\bar{X}$ (SD) | $\bar{X}$ (SD) | $\bar{X}$ (SD) | $\bar{X}$ (SD) | $\bar{X}$ (SD) | $\bar{X}$ (SD) | $\bar{X}$ (SD) | $\bar{X}$ (SD) | $\bar{X}$ (SD) |
| **Background Characteristics[a]** | | | | | | | | | | |
| Female | 0.58 | 0.58 | 0.41 | 0.52 | 0.72 | 0.58 | 0.76 | 0.59 | 0.25* | 0.63 |
| | (0.49) | (0.50) | (0.50) | (0.50) | (0.45) | (0.50) | (0.43) | (0.50) | (0.44) | (0.49) |
| Male | 0.42 | 0.42 | 0.59 | 0.48 | 0.28 | 0.42 | 0.24 | 0.41 | 0.75* | 0.37 |
| | (0.49) | (0.50) | (0.50) | (0.50) | (0.45) | (0.50) | (0.43) | (0.50) | (0.44) | (0.49) |
| Socioeconomic status | −0.44 | −0.16 | −0.38 | −0.17 | −0.61 | 0.02 | −0.08* | 0.30*** | 0.59*** | −0.11 |
| | (0.74) | (0.68) | (0.80) | (0.69) | (0.79) | (0.74) | (0.55) | (0.63) | (0.43) | (0.73) |
| Overall academic ability | −0.28 | −0.44 | −0.23 | −0.55 | −0.26 | −0.23 | −0.24 | 0.05*** | 0.50*** | 0.11** |
| | (0.97) | (0.75) | (0.91) | (0.77) | (0.81) | (0.82) | (0.55) | (0.89) | (0.55) | (0.68) |
| College educational expectations | 4.83 | 5.28 | 4.88 | 5.49 | 4.77 | 5.56 | 5.56** | 6.05*** | 5.49 | 5.68 |
| | (1.49) | (1.29) | (1.29) | (1.13) | (1.46) | (1.18) | (1.22) | (0.89) | (0.95) | (0.98) |

(Continued)

Table 17.1 (Continued)

| | Public School, Assigned | | Public, Assigned-choice Combined | | Public, School of Choice | | Catholic | | Other Private | |
|---|---|---|---|---|---|---|---|---|---|---|
| | 1990 | 2002 | 1990 | 2002 | 1990 | 2002 | 1990 | 2002 | 1990 | 2002 |
| | 62,611 | 52,207 | 13,238 | 41,235 | 9,103 | 21,843 | 5,918 | 3,761 | 1,080 | 2,515 |
| | $\bar{X}$ (SD) | $\bar{X}$ (SD) | $\bar{X}$ (SD) | $\bar{X}$ (SD) | $\bar{X}$ (SD) | $\bar{X}$ (SD) | $\bar{X}$ (SD) | $\bar{X}$ (SD) | $\bar{X}$ (SD) | $\bar{X}$ (SD) |
| **Family Engagement**[b] | | | | | | | | | | |
| Parent expectations (10th) | 5.57 (1.35) | 5.17 (1.45) | 5.75 (1.24) | 5.33 (1.37) | 5.50 (1.49) | 5.47 (1.36) | 6.20* (0.92) | 5.68 (1.16) | 6.26 (0.48) | 5.75 (0.98) |
| **Student Academic Experiences in High School 9th through 12th** | | | | | | | | | | |
| Weekly hours spent on extracurricular activities | 1.74 (0.99) | 2.32 (1.23) | 1.93 (1.16) | 2.31 (1.25) | 1.50 (0.84) | 2.08 (1.17) | 1.74 (1.22) | 2.69 (1.26) | 2.77*** (0.67) | 2.52 (1.17) |
| Weekly math homework hours | 2.33 (1.46) | 3.33 (2.69) | 2.27 (1.31) | 3.20 (2.73) | 2.36 (1.69) | 3.36 (2.49) | 2.37 (1.65) | 3.11 (2.02) | 4.06*** (2.34) | 3.06 (1.55) |
| Math pipeline completion[c] | 3.08 (1.00) | 5.37 (1.35) | 2.74 (1.17) | 5.31 (1.23) | 3.85*** (1.51) | 5.61 (1.35) | 3.31 (1.07) | 5.99** (1.28) | 3.87* (0.39) | 5.98 (1.38) |

Table 17.1 (Continued)

| | Public School, Assigned | | Public, Assigned-choice Combined | | Public, School of Choice | | Catholic | | Other Private | |
|---|---|---|---|---|---|---|---|---|---|---|
| | 1990 | 2002 | 1990 | 2002 | 1990 | 2002 | 1990 | 2002 | 1990 | 2002 |
| | 62,611 | 52,207 | 13,238 | 41,235 | 9,103 | 21,843 | 5,918 | 3,761 | 1,080 | 2,515 |
| | $\bar{X}$ (SD) | $\bar{X}$ (SD) | $\bar{X}$ (SD) | $\bar{X}$ (SD) | $\bar{X}$ (SD) | $\bar{X}$ (SD) | $\bar{X}$ (SD) | $\bar{X}$ (SD) | $\bar{X}$ (SD) | $\bar{X}$ (SD) |
| Science pipeline completion[c] | 4.52 | 4.98 | 4.07* | 4.97 | 4.68 | 5.22 | 4.62 | 5.36 | 4.49 | 5.46 |
| | (1.14) | (1.02) | (1.00) | (1.01) | (1.00) | (1.00) | (1.52) | (1.11) | (0.79) | (1.20) |
| **Student Experience of School Climate 9th through 12th[d]** | | | | | | | | | | |
| Friends' plans to attend 4-year college | 3.41 | 3.42 | 3.20 | 3.31 | 3.38 | 3.62 | 3.93* | 3.92** | 3.48 | 3.78 |
| | (1.01) | (1.06) | (1.10) | (1.07) | (1.16) | (0.95) | (0.96) | (0.92) | (1.09) | (1.09) |
| Sense of community | 2.85 | 2.85 | 2.91 | 2.79 | 2.96 | 2.79 | 3.03 | 3.19* | 3.52** | 2.86 |
| | (0.80) | (0.77) | (0.83) | (0.82) | (0.67) | (0.70) | (0.76) | (0.69) | (0.79) | (0.72) |
| Students at school are friendly with other racial groups | 3.19 | 3.25 | 3.22 | 3.30 | 3.27 | 3.24 | 3.07 | 3.31 | 1.96*** | 3.34 |
| | (0.80) | (0.77) | (0.67) | (0.67) | (0.55) | (0.52) | (0.77) | (0.65) | (1.29) | (0.72) |
| Feel safe at school | 3.30 | 3.17 | 3.29 | 3.11 | 3.42 | 3.32 | 3.39 | 3.65*** | 3.90 | 3.63* |
| | (0.73) | (0.80) | (0.90) | (0.77) | (0.72) | (0.62) | (0.78) | (0.48) | (0.37) | (0.65) |

(*Continued*)

241

Table 17.1 (Continued)

| High School Characteristics[c] | Public School, Assigned 1990 $\bar{X}$ (SD) | Public School, Assigned 2002 $\bar{X}$ (SD) | Public, Assigned-choice Combined 1990 $\bar{X}$ (SD) | Public, Assigned-choice Combined 2002 $\bar{X}$ (SD) | Public, School of Choice 1990 $\bar{X}$ (SD) | Public, School of Choice 2002 $\bar{X}$ (SD) | Catholic 1990 $\bar{X}$ (SD) | Catholic 2002 $\bar{X}$ (SD) | Other Private 1990 $\bar{X}$ (SD) | Other Private 2002 $\bar{X}$ (SD) |
|---|---|---|---|---|---|---|---|---|---|---|
| | 62,611 | 52,207 | 13,238 | 41,235 | 9,103 | 21,843 | 5,918 | 3,761 | 1,080 | 2,515 |
| Urban | 0.28 | 0.23 | 0.54*** | 0.49*** | 0.73*** | 0.67*** | 0.97*** | 0.64*** | 0.10 | 0.51* |
| | (0.45) | (0.42) | (0.50) | (0.50) | (0.45) | (0.47) | (0.17) | (0.48) | (0.30) | (0.51) |
| Suburban | 0.35 | 0.59 | 0.18* | 0.43* | 0.03*** | 0.27*** | 0.03*** | 0.36** | 0.90*** | 0.15*** |
| | (0.48) | (0.49) | (0.39) | (0.50) | (0.17) | (0.45) | (0.17) | (0.48) | (0.30) | (0.36) |
| Rural | 0.37 | 0.18 | 0.28 | 0.09 | 0.24 | 0.05* | 0.00*** | 0.00*** | 0.00** | 0.35 |
| | (0.48) | (0.39) | (0.45) | (0.28) | (0.43) | (0.23) | (0.00) | (0.00) | (0.00) | (0.48) |
| % Minority | 46.44 | 55.36 | 62.01*** | 61.66 | 67.83*** | 68.61** | 52.02 | 43.10* | 25.22* | 24.61*** |
| | (29.47) | (28.90) | (33.84) | (26.12) | (28.18) | (24.90) | (39.04) | (35.05) | (18.31) | (19.13) |
| Plans to take SAT or ACT | 2.18 | 2.46 | 2.26 | 2.45 | 2.23 | 2.53 | 2.63*** | 2.83*** | 2.63*** | 2.77*** |
| | (0.35) | (0.24) | (0.39) | (0.23) | (0.48) | (0.32) | (0.37) | (0.19) | (0.18) | (0.21) |
| Student enrollment in 2-year college or university | 2.88 | 3.51 | 3.17* | 3.68 | 2.81 | 3.56 | 2.55 | 2.93*** | 1.44*** | 2.38*** |
| | (0.74) | (0.77) | (0.97) | (0.72) | (0.98) | (0.81) | (0.66) | (1.07) | (0.96) | (0.98) |

Table 17.1 (Continued)

| | Public School, Assigned 1990 (62,611) | Public School, Assigned 2002 (52,207) | Public, Assigned-choice Combined 1990 (13,238) | Public, Assigned-choice Combined 2002 (41,235) | Public, School of Choice 1990 (9,103) | Public, School of Choice 2002 (21,843) | Catholic 1990 (5,918) | Catholic 2002 (3,761) | Other Private 1990 (1,080) | Other Private 2002 (2,515) |
|---|---|---|---|---|---|---|---|---|---|---|
| | $\bar{X}$ (SD) | $\bar{X}$ (SD) | $\bar{X}$ (SD) | $\bar{X}$ (SD) | $\bar{X}$ (SD) | $\bar{X}$ (SD) | $\bar{X}$ (SD) | $\bar{X}$ (SD) | $\bar{X}$ (SD) | $\bar{X}$ (SD) |
| Student enrollment in 4-year college or university | 4.01 (0.87) | 4.17 (0.96) | 3.83 (0.95) | 4.02 (0.98) | 4.68*** (1.05) | 4.65*** (0.97) | 5.38*** (0.75) | 5.54*** (0.58) | 5.87*** (0.39) | 5.38*** (0.75) |
| **Transition Outcomes**[f] | | | | | | | | | | |
| Does not complete high school | 0.01 (0.09) | 0.05 (0.21) | 0.07** (0.26) | 0.02 (0.15) | 0.00 (0.00) | 0.00 (0.00) | 0.06 (0.24) | 0.00 (0.00) | 0.00 (0.00) | 0.00 (0.00) |
| High school graduate or GED | 0.24 (0.43) | 0.27 (0.45) | 0.21 (0.41) | 0.23 (0.42) | 0.30 (0.46) | 0.19 (0.39) | 0.03* (0.18) | 0.11 (0.32) | 0.00 (0.00) | 0.25 (0.44) |
| Attend 2-year college or university | 0.29 (0.45) | 0.31 (0.47) | 0.38 (0.49) | 0.30 (0.46) | 0.26 (0.44) | 0.22 (0.42) | 0.14 (0.35) | 0.08** (0.27) | 0.00 (0.00) | 0.10 (0.31) |

(Continued)

243

Table 17.1 (Continued)

| | Public School, Assigned | | Public, Assigned-choice Combined | | Public, School of Choice | | Catholic | | Other Private | |
|---|---|---|---|---|---|---|---|---|---|---|
| | 1990 | 2002 | 1990 | 2002 | 1990 | 2002 | 1990 | 2002 | 1990 | 2002 |
| | 62,611 | 52,207 | 13,238 | 41,235 | 9,103 | 21,843 | 5,918 | 3,761 | 1,080 | 2,515 |
| | $\bar{X}$ (SD) | $\bar{X}$ (SD) | $\bar{X}$ (SD) | $\bar{X}$ (SD) | $\bar{X}$ (SD) | $\bar{X}$ (SD) | $\bar{X}$ (SD) | $\bar{X}$ (SD) | $\bar{X}$ (SD) | $\bar{X}$ (SD) |
| Attend 4-year college or university | 0.47 | 0.44 | 0.34 | 0.53 | 0.44 | 0.61 | 0.77*** | 0.85*** | 1.00*** | 0.74* |
| | (0.50) | (0.50) | (0.48) | (0.50) | (0.50) | (0.49) | (0.42) | (0.36) | (0.00) | (0.45) |

*Note.* Data are weighted to population means. Significant differences were calculated using t-tests using White-Asian as the comparison group for each. We also evaluated differences in the following measures, found to be statistically insignificant: foreign-born status, family composition, number of siblings, parent volunteering, academic support from teachers, not feeling "put down" by classroom peers, and disruptions at school impede learning.

[a]Family composition was coded 1 for married or marriage-like relationships and 0 for all other nonmissing categories. SES and academic ability are constructed by NCES. SES is a standardized z-score ranging from −2.11 to 1.82 in 2002 and −2.97 to 2.56 in 1990. Academic ability is a standardized z-score ranging from −3.011 to 3.075 in 2002 and −1.589 to 3.425 in 1990. Students' educational expectations in the 10th grade are coded 1 (less than high school diploma) to 7 (doctorate).

[b]Parent expectations and volunteering were obtained from the 10th grade parent survey. Parent educational expectations are coded 1 (less than high school diploma) to 7 (doctorate).

[c]These measures were generated by NCES from the Transcript File. Math and science pipeline measures were also generated by NCES and range from 1 (no course in the subject) to 8 (most advanced courses) and 1 (no course in the subject) to 7 (most advanced courses), respectively.

[d]These measures pertain to students' 10th grade year, with the exception of friends' plans to attend a four-year college, which was assessed in the student 12th grade survey.

[e]SAT/ACT plans are derived by averaging 12th grade responses, aggregated to the school level and averaged within each school cluster, ranging continuously from 0 (not planning to take) to 2 (have taken). Percentage enrolled corresponds to administrator-reported proportions of high school graduates' postsecondary enrollments, coded by NCES from 1 (0%) to 6 (75–100%). Percent minority refers to the percent of non-White students. These variables were obtained from the school administrator surveys.

[f]The first four outcomes in this category are mutually exclusive. The variable "Does not complete high school" is a dummy: 0 (high school graduates) and 1 (those who did not receive a H.S. diploma, including GED recipients).

*$p < 0.05$, **$p < 0.01$, ***$p < 0.001$.

*Source*: U.S. Department of Education, National Center for Education Statistics. Educational Longitudinal Study of 2002 (ELS: 2002) and National Educational Longitudinal Study of 1988 (NELS: 1988).

assignment, with greater proportions of their students eligible for free- or reduced-price lunch, enrolled in dropout prevention programs, and significantly more being classified as non-White. Schools of choice have higher proportions of students who have taken or plan to take college entrance exams and significantly more graduates enrolling in four-year colleges or universities across all racial and ethnic groups.

Comparing public school types, for both cohorts, there are no significant differences in transition outcomes. Significant growth has occurred nationally in two-year college enrollment, with many of these schools targeted toward urban and lower-income populations. For Black youth enrolled in schools of assignment and assigned-choice combinations, there are no significant differences between sectors or study years, however. For schools of choice, the mean for attending a two-year college or university for those in the 2002 cohort (0.2) is not significantly lower than that for the assigned public school students (0.3).

With respect to four-year college enrollment or completion status two years after high school, there are no significant differences between sectors and study years for schools of assignment and assigned-choice combinations; differences are only significant in comparing assigned public schools to Catholic and other private schools. Schools of choice were less successful than the other public school sectors in the 1990 cohort. Twelve years later, schools of choice gained an advantage, gaining about 17 percentage points, suggesting a trend toward further improvement consistent with recent published findings on the positive effect of charter schools on college enrollment (e.g., Booker et al., 2008).

Looking at some of the likely predictors of postsecondary attendance, we find that Black sophomores' educational expectations rose between 1990 and 2002, along with their preparedness. On a scale from 1 to 7 in which 5 represents graduating from college, Black sophomores' expectations increased from 4.9 to 5.3 for the period between 1990 and 2002. Their parents' expectations for them decreased slightly during this period however, suggesting possible decreases in parents' ability to support their children's rising expectations.

Turning to their academic preparation for college, Black students' time spent on math homework rose in this twelve-year period, from 2.4 to 3.3 hours per week, reaching the weekly investment of White and Asian students. Further gains were made in advanced course taking in math and science, however the racial gap persisted. In 2002, despite completing an additional full math course and seven-tenths of a science course, Black sophomores remained over one-half of a course behind their White and Asian peers in math and one-third of a course behind them in science.

Regarding completion of advanced math and science coursework, in the ELS cohort, there is only slight variance between the three public categories: Blacks in choice settings complete an average of 5.6 math pipeline courses in comparison to 5.4 in schools of assignment and 6.0 in parochial and non-parochial private schools. In the same cohort, White and Asian students in schools of choice complete 6.1 math pipeline courses, compared to the 6.0 completed by their peers in assigned public schools. With the exception of the Hispanic subsample, there are no significant differences between schools of choice and assigned public schools on math coursework completed.

Public school youth are, on average, from significantly lower socioeconomic backgrounds than those in Catholic and other private schools, with slightly fewer siblings and a lower tendency to have married parents, a characteristic most pronounced for Black sophomores enrolled in public schools of choice. Based on standardized ability test scores taken in cohorts' baseline years, the academic ability of Black sophomores varies little between the three types of public schools; Blacks in stand-alone schools of choice score slightly higher in 2002 and it was insignificantly different from the mean for assigned public schools.

### Postsecondary Enrollment

While informative, the above descriptive findings do not take into account that students who attend public schools of choice may be quite different from students who do not, with a selection factor which accounts for their performance beyond the type of school they attended. To take such potential selection issues into account, we undertook another analysis. To adjust for factors that may be present but are not associated with any measures, a multinomial logistic regression analysis compares the postsecondary enrollment of youth who attended high schools of choice to that of their peers in other public school sectors.

To accomplish this, we fit a model to the data predicting the relative chances of a student attending a two-year college, compared to no college at all, and the chances of attending a four-year institution, compared to no college at all. We examined not only the direct effect of a student attending a school of choice, but also the propensity that a student attended a school of choice. An auxiliary logistic regression is employed to predict the chance that a student attended a high school of choice as a function of race, academic ability, gender, socioeconomic status, siblings, and family composition. We then calculated the predicted chances that a student would enter a school of choice. These estimated chances were entered into the model as covariates to estimate the true effect of being in a school of choice on college matriculation without having that effect confounded by other factors correlated with entering a school of choice, namely socioeconomic status and academic ability.

In our analyses of public school students reported in Table 17.2, we find no statistically significant benefit associated with attending a school of choice. While the strength of the observed association is stronger for the current cohort of students, the statistical uncertainty is too large for these patterns to be considered representative of the population. While these models

Table 17.2
Effect of High School Context in Sophomore Year on Public School Students' Postsecondary Enrollment Status, 1994 and 2006

| | 1994 | | | | | | 2006 | | | | | |
| | 2-year college | | | 4-year college | | | 2-year college | | | 4-year college | | |
| Characteristics | RRR sig | Slope | SE | RRR sig | Slope | SE | RRR sig | Slope | SE | RRR sig | Slope | SE |
|---|---|---|---|---|---|---|---|---|---|---|---|---|
| **School Sector (Sophomore Year)** | | | | | | | | | | | | |
| Propensity to be in a school of choice | 1.403* | 0.338 | 0.157 | 1.676** | 0.517 | 0.171 | 0.900 | −0.105 | 0.088 | 0.922 | −0.081 | 0.101 |
| **Background Characteristics** | | | | | | | | | | | | |
| Race | | | | | | | | | | | | |
| Black/African American | 0.059* | −2.827 | 1.323 | 0.017** | −4.066 | 1.409 | 2.741 | 1.008 | 0.892 | 3.512 | 1.256 | 1.037 |
| Hispanic/Latino | 0.254* | −1.370 | 0.689 | 0.103** | −2.273 | 0.735 | 2.563 | 0.941 | 0.859 | 2.122 | 0.752 | 1.020 |
| Number of siblings | 0.940* | −0.062 | 0.028 | 0.948 | −0.053 | 0.031 | 0.876*** | −0.132 | 0.035 | 0.915* | −0.089 | 0.040 |
| Socioeconomic status | 2.233*** | 0.803 | 0.216 | 4.805*** | 1.570 | 0.227 | 1.506* | 0.409 | 0.203 | 2.262*** | 0.816 | 0.227 |
| Baseline academic ability | 1.139 | 0.130 | 0.067 | 1.362*** | 0.309 | 0.067 | 1.210 | 0.191 | 0.121 | 1.861*** | 0.621 | 0.137 |
| College educational expectations | 1.176*** | 0.162 | 0.045 | 1.339*** | 0.292 | 0.048 | 1.224*** | 0.202 | 0.047 | 1.371*** | 0.315 | 0.053 |

*(Continued)*

Table 17.2 (Continued)

| Characteristics | 1994 | | | | | | 2006 | | | | | |
|---|---|---|---|---|---|---|---|---|---|---|---|---|
| | 2-year college | | | 4-year college | | | 2-year college | | | 4-year college | | |
| | RRR sig | Slope | SE | RRR sig | Slope | SE | RRR sig | Slope | SE | RRR sig | Slope | SE |
| **Family Engagement in College Preparation** | | | | | | | | | | | | |
| Parent expectations (10th) | 1.069 | 0.067 | 0.036 | 1.131** | 0.124 | 0.042 | 0.934 | −0.068 | 0.041 | 0.995 | −0.005 | 0.046 |
| Parent volunteering in school (10th) | 1.199 | 0.181 | 0.126 | 1.356* | 0.304 | 0.124 | 0.903 | −0.102 | 0.127 | 1.068 | 0.066 | 0.128 |
| **Student Academic Experiences in High School 9th through 12th** | | | | | | | | | | | | |
| Hours spent per week on extracurricular activities | 1.063 | 0.062 | 0.043 | 1.129** | 0.121 | 0.042 | 1.010 | 0.010 | 0.048 | 1.228*** | 0.205 | 0.047 |
| Math pipeline completion | 1.226*** | 0.204 | 0.052 | 1.584*** | 0.460 | 0.053 | 1.038 | 0.037 | 0.052 | 1.586*** | 0.461 | 0.053 |
| Science pipeline completion | 1.250*** | 0.224 | 0.051 | 1.541*** | 0.433 | 0.054 | 1.103 | 0.098 | 0.053 | 1.261*** | 0.232 | 0.055 |
| **Student Experience of School Climate 9th through 12th** | | | | | | | | | | | | |
| Friends' plans to attend 4-year college | 1.217*** | 0.197 | 0.046 | 1.553*** | 0.440 | 0.047 | 1.044 | 0.043 | 0.057 | 1.579*** | 0.457 | 0.063 |
| Sense of community | 0.854* | −0.158 | 0.064 | 0.912 | −0.092 | 0.065 | 0.890 | −0.116 | 0.077 | 0.928 | −0.074 | 0.081 |

Table 17.2 (Continued)

| | 1994 | | | | | | 2006 | | | | | |
| | 2-year college | | | 4-year college | | | 2-year college | | | 4-year college | | |
| Characteristics | RRR sig | Slope | SE | RRR sig | Slope | SE | RRR sig | Slope | SE | RRR sig | Slope | SE |
|---|---|---|---|---|---|---|---|---|---|---|---|---|
| **High School Characteristics** | | | | | | | | | | | | |
| % Minority | 1.005* | 0.005 | 0.002 | 1.002 | 0.002 | 0.002 | 0.999 | −0.001 | 0.003 | 1.000 | 0.000 | 0.003 |
| Plans to take SAT or ACT | 1.737*** | 0.552 | 0.153 | 1.620** | 0.482 | 0.149 | 1.078 | 0.075 | 0.213 | 1.584* | 0.460 | 0.222 |
| % enroll in 2-year college or university | 1.325*** | 0.282 | 0.054 | 0.931 | −0.071 | 0.054 | 1.504*** | 0.408 | 0.070 | 0.992 | −0.008 | 0.069 |
| % enroll in 4-year college or university | 0.951 | −0.050 | 0.057 | 1.131* | 0.123 | 0.056 | 0.979 | −0.022 | 0.058 | 1.210*** | 0.191 | 0.059 |
| Intercept | *** | −3.288 | 0.659 | *** | −4.336 | 0.700 | *** | −1.758 | 0.897 | *** | −7.078 | 0.954 |
| Pseudo R-square | 0.252 | | | | | | 0.215 | | | | | |
| Log Likelihood | −860122 | | | | | | −856794 | | | | | |
| N observations | 7183 | | | | | | 4038 | | | | | |

*Note.* Data are weighted to population means. Relative risk ratios, slopes, and standard errors are reported. Models also included the following, non-significant predictors: public school of choice, foreign-born status, family composition, weekly hours spent on math homework, academic support from teachers, not feeling "put down" by classroom peers, disruptions at school impede learning, school students are friendly with other racial groups, feel safe at school, and urbanicity.

*p < 0.05, **p < 0.01, ***p < 0.001.

*Source:* U.S. Department of Education, National Center for Education Statistics, National Longitudinal Study of 1988 (NELS: 1988) and Educational Longitudinal Study of 2002 (ELS: 2002).

include a predictor of the propensity to attend a school of choice as a function of race, socioeconomic status, and family composition, auxiliary models (not reported) that do not include this predictor still show no effect for schools of choice. The propensity predictor, however, was a significant predictor for the earlier NELS cohort.

Our most interesting finding concerns the decreasing effects of race, socioeconomic status, and parent behaviors on matriculation. Race had a significant negative impact on matriculation, holding all factors constant, in the NELS cohort. Yet, we found no effects of race, all else being equal, in the ELS cohort. Furthermore, the effect of socioeconomic status has decreased dramatically. In the earlier NELS cohort, each standard deviation increase on the socioeconomic scale produced a 123.3 percent increase in the odds of matriculation into a two-year institution and a 580.5 percent increase in the odds of matriculation into a four-year institution. Comparing these results to the later ELS cohort results, we see that the effect of socioeconomic status has been cut nearly in half for matriculation into a two-year or four-year institutions. A student's socioeconomic status still matters for matriculation, but now only half as much. Finally, we see a decrease in the effectiveness of parental behaviors. Parental expectations and volunteering behavior were predictive of matriculation into a four-year institution in the earlier NELS cohort, but not in the ELS cohort.

While parental indicators appear to have lost efficacy between the cohorts represented by NELS and ELS, indicators of student ability and behavior have remained. A student's number of hours spent on extracurricular activities was a predictor of four-year matriculation in both cohorts. The effect of math and science pipeline course taking was also stable in predicting four-year institution matriculation. Moreover, the effect of these indicators is quite strong. In both cohorts, math pipelines were associated with an over 50 percent increase in the chance of matriculation into four-year institutions. While the effect of science pipelines was reduced between cohorts, the effect was still very strong. Most importantly, however, was the increase in the effect of baseline academic ability. In the earlier NELS cohort, each standard deviation increase in baseline academic ability led to a 36 percent increase in the odds of matriculation into four-year institutions. This effect increased to an 86 percent improvement in the odds of matriculation by the later ELS cohort.

While there have been many changes to the pattern of effects between the cohorts in NELS and ELS, the effect of peer behaviors appears to have remained stable. The effect of friends' plans to attend a four-year institution remained almost the same between cohorts, with each increase in the scale associated with over a 50 percent increase in the odds of four-year matriculation. We see the same effect for the percent of students who plan to take the ACT or SAT tests. Finally, the effects of recent graduates attending a two-year institution on respondents' two-year institution matriculation, and recent graduates attending a four-year institution on four-year institution matriculation, were also stable between cohorts.

Based on the results presented here, we find four major trends in college matriculation between the cohorts represented in NELS and ELS. First, the impact of race and socioeconomic status indicators has decreased over time. Second, there is also some evidence that the impact of both student characteristics and behavior have increased. However, in the third major trend we identified, the effects of peer groups and expectations have remained stable. Finally, our models have less of an ability to predict matriculation into two-year institutions as they did for past cohorts. In many instances, such as math and science pipeline predictors, or peer behaviors, items that had predictive power for two-year institution matriculation in the earlier NELS cohort were no longer significant in the later ELS cohort.

## DISCUSSION

Black enrollment in schools of choice has more than doubled between 1990 and 2002. Although the student populations of choice schools (magnets, charters, and other schools of choice) attended by Black youth are proportionally more socioeconomically disadvantaged than other school types, more of their graduates enroll in two-year and four-year institutions. After accounting for the propensity to select into a school of choice, however, enrollment in a school of choice bears little effect on youths' postsecondary educational enrollment two years after high school. Aside from their academic ability, aspirations, and socioeconomic status, the only factors that significantly predict four-year college enrollment are peers and coursework, specifically, students friends' plans to go to a four-year college and students' completion of advanced science and math coursework. Although college-going peer networks and advanced course taking fit the purpose of schools of choice, the results presented in Table 17.1 show that they are not significantly more likely to be found in schools of choice than in traditional public schools.

Moreover, the results of our multivariate analysis show a democratization of college access. So many students are enrolling in two-year institutions that our models have little predictive power. In addition, we have seen the effects of typical status predictors—race, socioeconomic status, parental behaviors—decrease dramatically. Concurrent with these changes, we have also documented that the ability of students to influence their matriculation has remained through their academic ability, extracurricular activities, and class-taking behaviors. Each of these trends paints a clear picture that external influences on matriculation are losing strength while student-centered influences remain. In short, students are in more control of their destiny than before.

These findings are consistent with other national and local studies of the efficacy of schools of choice on educational attainment in the early 2000s.

More recent studies suggest that some charter schools are highly effective at improving the high school graduation and college enrollment of their graduates, for example, those in Chicago and Florida (Booker et al., 2008). Although school choice options for underrepresented minority youth have widely expanded, Black youth attending these schools do not report the attributes—such as, a college-going culture—most associated with academically successful schools. It may be the case that in particular districts, such as New York, choice schools may show more positive postsecondary matriculation rates. On average, students enrolled in schools of choice do not have significantly better chances of entering four-year colleges than their peers in more traditional public schools, based on this national longitudinal study.

## ACKNOWLEDGMENT

This material is based upon work supported by the National Science Foundation under Grant No. 0815295. Any opinions, findings, and conclusions or recommendations expressed in this material are those of the authors and do not necessarily reflect the views of the National Science Foundation.

## NOTES

1. First opening in the 1960s, magnet schools have been employed in school desegregation initiatives, to recruit White families to send their children to urban public schools and to provide "better" schools for inner-city youth (Metz, 2003). Supported by state and local educational entities, these schools were designated "magnets" because they drew students from across districts to individual schools. Magnet schools tend to employ selective enrollment procedures to generate their student populations, most of which are based on academic performance or some other criteria-based entry (e.g. audition, interview), creating a particularly talented student body.

2. Authors' calculations using the 2007–08 school year Common Core of Data database for elementary and secondary public schools.

3. Vouchers for private school access have been proposed as a viable option for equality of opportunity in education, first proposed in the 1960s (see Friedman, 1962). During the 1980s and 1990s, this discourse gave rise to increased options for new and existing forms of public school choice (Kahlenberg, 2003; Peterson & Campbell, 2001).

4. NELS: 1988 respondents were high school sophomores in 1990; ELS: 2002 respondents were high school sophomores in 2002.

5. Investigating the NCES coding of school types by school administrators of students at schools with the same school ID, we determined that sufficient "schools within schools" existed and were not reliably documented as such (e.g. schools for which 40% of cases were coded "magnet" and 60% were coded "assigned"). We recoded these schools as hybrid assigned-choice schools; such multiple codings of individual schools did not occur systematically for other school types in these datasets.

6. This information is available in a table, by request to the authors. Additional tables reporting supplementary analyses of Hispanic and White and Asian subsamples, referenced in the text, are also available by request.

# REFERENCES

Booker, K., Sass, T.R., Gill, B., & Zimmer, R. (2008). *Going beyond test scores: Evaluating charter school impact on educational attainment in Chicago and Florida. RAND Education Working Paper*. Retrieved from http://www.rand.org/pubs/working_papers/2008/RAND_WR610.pdf

Bulkley, K., & Fisler, J. (2003). A decade of charter schools: From theory to practice. *Educational Policy, 17*(3), 317–342.

Current Population Survey (CPS). (2009a). *Current Population Survey March 1970 through March 2009*. Washington, D.C.: U.S. Census Bureau. Retrieved from http://nces.ed.gov/programs/digest/d09/tables/dt09_008.asp.

Current Population Survey (CPS). (2009b). *Enrollment rates of 18- to 24-year-olds in degree-granting institutions, by type of institution and sex and race/ethnicity of student: 1967 through 2008*. U.S. Census Bureau. Retrieved from http://nces.ed.gov/programs/digest/d09/tables/dt09_204.asp.

Eccles, J.S. (2007). Families, schools, and developing achievement-related motivations and engagement. In J.E. Grusec & P.D. Hastings (Eds.), *Handbook of socialization: Theory and research* (pp. 665–691). New York: Guilford Press.

Finn, C.E., Manno, B.V., & Vanourek, G. (2001). "Charter Schools: Taking Stock." In P.E. Peterson & D.E. Campbell (Eds.), *Charters, couchers, and public education* (pp. 19–42). Washington, D.C.: Brookings Institution Press.

Fredricks, J.A., Blumenfeld, P.C., & Paris, A.H. (2004). School engagement: Potential of the concept, state of the evidence. *Review of Educational Research, 74*(1), 59–109.

Friedman, M. (1962). *Capitalism and freedom* (2002 ed.). Chicago: University of Chicago Press.

Goldrick-Rab, S. (2006). Following their every move: An investigation of social class differences in college pathways. *Sociology of Education, 79*(1), 61.

Hallinan, M.T. (2008). Teacher influences on students' attachment to school. *Sociology of Education, 81*, 271–283.

Hoxby, C.M. (September, 2004). *A Straightforward Comparison of Charter Schools and Regular Public Schools in the United States. SBER Working Paper*. Cambridge, MA: National Bureau of Economic Research.

Ingels, S.J., Pratt, D.J., Wilson, D., Burns, L.J., Currivan, D., Rogers, J.E., et al. (2007). *Educational Longitudinal Study of 2002 (ELS: 2002): Base-Year to Second Follow-Up Data File Documentation* (NCES 2008-347). In U.S. Department of Education (Ed.). Washington, D.C.: National Center for Education Statistics.

Johnson, M.K., Crosnoe, R., & Elder, G.H., Jr. (2001). Students attachment and academic engagement: The role of race and ethnicity. *Sociology of Education, 74*(4), 318–340.

Kahlenberg, R.D. (Ed.). (2003). *Public school choice vs. private school vouchers*. New York: Century Foundation Press.

Lee, V.E., & Smith, J.B. (1999). Social support and achievement for young adolescents in Chicago: The role of school academic press. *American Educational Research Journal, 36*(4), 907–945.

Metz, M.H. (2003). *Different by design: The context and character of three magnet schools.* New York: Teachers College Press.

Muller, C., Riegle-Crumb, C., Schiller, K.S., Wilkinson, L., & Frank, K.A. (2010). Race and academic achievement in racially diverse high schools: Opportunity and stratification. *Teachers College Record, 112*(4), 4–5.

Murphy, J. F., Weil, M., Hallinger, P., & Mitman, A. (1982). Academic press: Translating high expectations into school policies and classroom practices. *Educational Leadership, 40*(3), 22.

National Center for Education Statistics (NCES). (2009). *"Fall Enrollment Survey" (IPEDS-EF:92–99), and Spring 2001 through Spring 2007; and Enrollment in Degree-Granting Institutions Model, 1980–2006.* U.S. Department of Education.

Peterson, P.E., & Campbell, D.E. (Eds.). (2001). *Charters, vouchers, and public education.* Washington, D.C.: Brookings Institution Press.

Phillips, M. (1997). What makes schools effective? A comparison of the relationships of communitarian climate and academic climate to mathematics achievement and attendance during middle school. *American Educational Research Journal, 34* (4), 633–662.

Rapp, K.E., & Eckes, S.E. (2007). Dispelling the myth of "White Flight": An examination of minority enrollment in charter schools. *Educational Policy, 21*(4), 615–661.

Renzulli, L.A., & Roscigno, V.J. (2005). Charter school policy, implementation, and diffusion across the United States. *Sociology of Education, 78*(4), 344–365.

Rosenbaum, J.E. (2001). *Beyond college for all: Career paths for the forgotten half.* New York: Russell Sage Foundation.

Rosenbaum, J.E., Deil-Amen, R., & Person, A.E. (2006). *After admission: From college access to college success.* New York: Russell Sage Foundation.

Schneider, B., Swanson, C.B., & Riegle-Crumb, C. (1998). Opportunities for learning: Course sequences and positional advantages. *Social Psychology of Education, 2*(1), 25–53.

Slaughter-Defoe, D.T., & Johnson, D.J. (1988). *Visible Now: Blacks in private schools.* Westport, CT: Greenwood Press.

Stearns, E. (2010). Long-term correlates of high school racial composition: Perpetuation theory reexamined. *Teachers College Record, 112*(6), 1654–1678.

U.S. Department of Education. (2010). *Budget of the United States Government, Fiscal Year 2011* Washington, DC: Office of Management and Budget. Retrieved from http://www.whitehouse.gov/omb/budget/fy2011/assets/education.pdf

Wells, A.S., Holme, J.J., Lopez, A., & Cooper, C.W. (2003). Charter schools and racial and social class segregation: Yet another sorting machine? In R. D. Kahlenberg (Ed.), *Public school choice vs. private school vouchers.* New York: Century Foundation Press.

Zimmer, R., & Buddin, R. (2007). Getting inside the black box: Examining how the operation of charter schools affects performance. *Peabody Journal of Education, 82*(2), 231–273.

# 18

. . . . . . . . . . . . . . . . . . . . . . . . . . . . . . . . . . . . . . . . . . .

# Where Should African American Parents Send Their Children to School? Disentangling Schools' Racial Composition from Students' Financial Resources

*Jelani Mandara, Inez Moore, Scott Richman, and Fatima Varner*

## INTRODUCTION

More than fifty five years after the *Brown v. Board of Education of Topeka, Kansas* ruling (1954), U.S. school children continue to face severe inequities in the quality of education they receive. Consequently, African American children lag behind their European American counterparts on most indicators of achievement. These trends force most African American parents to wrestle with unique and often very difficult choices regarding the education of their children. Unlike European American parents, African American parents cannot assume that a school is an appropriate place for their children simply because it boasts high overall test scores. This is often not an indicator of how well the African American students at the school perform. Furthermore, most African American parents do not want their children to be socially isolated or singled out, so they are also very concerned about the proportion of African Americans at the school and in the local community. However, children tend to perform better at schools with higher SES peers, presumably because those schools tend to have better facilities, more experienced teachers, more AP courses, and more academically oriented extracurricular activities. Given that most of the schools with higher SES students are also primarily European American and are located in primarily White neighborhoods, this creates a conundrum for those African American parents who want their children to have a great education, but who are also concerned with their children being exposed to other African American children.

Their choice is further compounded by the increasing racial resegregation of public schools. Ultimately then, many African American parents feel they must choose based on either the racial composition or the SES of the students at a school.

Current research does not offer African American parents much help with their decisions, because the SES of students and racial dynamics of schools are so confounded. The purpose of this chapter was to disentangle the effects of a school's racial composition and SES on the achievement of African American students. Using school report card data from all Illinois 5th and 11th grades, we examined the unique and interactive effects of school-level racial composition and student SES on African American students test scores. The ultimate goal was to help African American parents make more informed choices about the type of school their children should attend.

### School Racial Composition and Academic Achievement

Most researchers support the assumption that students' achievement is heavily dependent on the social contexts which they identify and operate within. This assumption becomes apparent with the persistent finding that African American students in predominately African American schools, on average, perform lower on achievement tests than African American students in predominantly European American schools (Bankston & Caldas, 2000, 2001; Brooks-Gunn, Klebanov, Smith, Duncan, & Lee, 2003; Coleman et al., 1966; Jencks & Phillips, 1999; Lee, 2004; Mickelson, 2001). In 1954, *Brown v. Board of Education* case brought the primary educational problem that plagued African American families to the political arena. Met with extreme opposition and marked by revolutionary outcomes, the court ultimately concluded that school segregation was unequal and therefore unconstitutional. The *Brown v. Board of Education* decision was marked by fervent attempts to integrate schools through enforced busing, desegregation mandates, and reassignment plans (Ipka, 2003; Mickelson, 2001). Though successful at launch, a majority of the desegregation policies once so zealously defended have currently been abandoned due to disinterested political parties and constituents (Ipka, 2003; Mickelson, 2001; Rumberger & Palardy, 2005). Consequently, many U.S. schools have experienced the process of segregation, desegregation, and finally resegregation.

In the midst of a resegregated school culture, many researchers have examined the degree to which the racial composition of schools influences academic achievement (Bankston & Caldas, 2000; Goldsmith, 2004; Ipka, 2003; Mickelson, 2001; Rumberger & Palardy, 2005; Wong & Nicotera, 2004). These researchers generally agree with early studies such as the *Coleman Report* (Coleman, 1968), which argued that the greater the proportion of minority students in a school, the less well African American students tend to perform. For instance, Mickelson (2001) found that the greater time spent in a segregated African American elementary school predicted lower grades and test scores in high school for African American students. Another study found that African American children in integrated schools made significantly greater gains in reading during the summer months than those in primarily African American schools (Entwisle & Alexander, 1994). Caldas and Bankston (1998) used data from over 40,000 students in Louisiana and found that high proportions of African American students in a school is negatively related to African American student achievement, regardless of their family's SES. Thus, they argued that the current trend towards resegregation will have detrimental effects on African American achievement. This conclusion implies that African American parents with the means should send their children to primarily European American schools.

However, the answers to the schooling choices most African American parents face are much more complicated. For one reason, many studies did not find such benefits for African American children in integrated or primarily European American schools compared to those in primarily African American schools. In fact, a reanalysis of the *Coleman Report* data suggested that the benefits of integration for African American children are questionable (Jencks & Mayer, 1990). One early study of 2,150 African American high school students from the early 1970s found that southern African American students graduating from predominantly European American high schools were less likely to attend and graduate from college than those from primarily African American high schools in the South (Crain & Mahard, 1978). Furthermore, the test scores of southern African American students were not related to the school racial composition. An evaluation of Milwaukee's desegregation efforts concluded that the effects were slight and statistically insignificant (Mitchell, 1989). In a more recent study, Goldsmith (2004) used the National Education Longitudinal data and found that Latinos' and African American's beliefs are more optimistic and more pro-school in primarily non-European American schools, especially when these schools also employ many minority teachers. Thus, these studies suggest that parents also have to think about the atmosphere of the school regarding integration, and not just whether there is an abundance of European Americans at a school.

### The Current Study

Although many important and policy relevant findings have been uncovered in the prior studies, they have yet to adequately disentangle the effects of schools' racial compositions from their peers' economic backgrounds. For instance, Mickelson (2001) interviewed high school teachers and found that many students who were placed in advanced, college-preparatory tracks had a higher quality and consistent parental involvement than students who were placed in lower tracks. Specifically, many principals confessed that many of the students labeled as gifted or advanced were, in fact, more politically equipped with parental support rather than actual "gifted ability."

Subsequently, a disproportionate number of European American students fill advanced placement classrooms and college preparatory tracks. Thus, at primarily European American schools, African American students may be more likely to face overt race-based tracking and lower teacher expectations than at primarily African American schools.

Since schools with a high proportion of poorer African Americans tend to have the fewest educational resources (Mickelson, 2001), we would not expect them to perform very well overall at those schools either. Therefore, we would expect African American students to perform their best at primarily African American schools that also have a higher proportion of middle and upper SES students. Not only would those students likely be less exposed to overt race-based tracking and teacher expectations, since someone at the school has to be in the higher tracks and AP courses, the correlation between race and achievement would not be as apparent for them. This would then likely reduce the other social pressures that even higher SES African American students at primarily European American schools are burdened with, such as those related to stereotype threat (Steele, 1997) or the negative peer pressure for achieving related to the "acting White" phenomenon (Fordham & Ogbu, 1986). Given the importance of school resources on all students' achievement, and that those from lower SES backgrounds tend to attend the lowest resourced schools, we also expected African American students who go to school with primarily lower SES students of any background to perform poorly. To test these hypotheses, we collected school level student SES, racial demographics, and African American student achievement test score data from the annual school report cards of all available 5th and 11th grade schools in Illinois. This state was chosen because it not only has readily available report card data, but because it also has a very large and economically diverse population of African Americans who reside in a variety of different communities.

## METHOD

### Participants

The sample included 748 public elementary and 235 high schools in Illinois during the 2006–2007 school year. Only the schools with complete demographic data and performance scores for African American students were used in the sample. The elementary schools averaged 501 students overall, 58 percent of which were African American. The high schools averaged 1,657 students and were 39 percent African American.

### Measures

#### *Reading and Mathematics Achievement*

The 2007 Illinois State Achievement Test (ISAT) and Prairie State Achievement Examination (PSAE) were the instruments used by the state to measure reading and math performance in 5th and 11th grade, respectively. Both exams are administered in the spring by trained staff. The ISAT included 51 reading items ($\alpha = .89$) and 65 mathematics items ($\alpha = .93$) (Illinois State Board of Education Division of Assessment, 2007). The PSAE included 33 reading items ($\alpha = .80$) and 33 mathematics items ($\alpha = .90$) (ACT and the Illinois State Board of Education, 2007). Scores are presented on the school report cards as grouped performance categories. For the current study, we calculated the percentage of African American students at each school who at least met state standards in reading and math.

### School Racial Composition

To assess the degree to which a school is primarily African American, primarily European American, or balanced, we subtracted the percent of European American students from the percentage of African American students at each school. Thus, a score of 0 represents an equal percentage of European American and African American students enrolled at a school. The larger the positive values, the higher the percentage African American students at the school. The larger the negative values, the higher the percentage of European American students at the school. Although there are several schools with large Hispanic student bodies, very few African Americans attended such schools in Illinois.

### School Economic Profile (SEP)

This measure is the percentage of non low-income students enrolled at a school. In Illinois, low-income is defined as being eligible for the Federal Free/Reduced-Cost Lunch Program.

## RESULTS

The descriptive statics and zero-order correlations among the study variables for the 5th and 11th grade samples are presented in Table 18.1. As can be seen, the racial composition of schools is very strongly correlated with the SEP in both grades. The fewer African Americans at a school, the higher the SEP tended to be. As typically found, the fewer African Americans at a school and especially the higher the SEP, the better the average African American students tended to perform on the reading and math tests. The students in the 5th grade were more likely to be in racially segregated schools, while the high schools tended to be more diverse. Also of note is the finding that although the average reading and math test passage rates for African American students in the 5th grade were only 46 percent and 62 percent, they dramatically dropped to only 29 percent and 21 percent by the 11th grade.

To test the main hypotheses of the study, hierarchical regression analyses were conducted for math and reading scores for each grade separately. Racial

**Table 18.1**
**Descriptive Statistics for School Demographic Variables by Grade**

| Variables | 5th Grade Mean | 11th Grade Mean | Race Comp. | SEP | Reading | Math |
|---|---|---|---|---|---|---|
| Race Comp. | 37% | −1% | – | −.74 | −.32 | −.38 |
| SEP | 70% | 51% | −.81 | – | .52 | .50 |
| Reading | 46% | 29% | −.27 | .40 | – | .77 |
| Math | 62% | 21% | −.38 | .49 | .88 | – |

*Note*: Race Comp. = School Racial Composition; SEP = School Economic Profile. $N = 748$ elementary schools and 235 high schools. Correlations for 5th grade are displayed above the diagonal and the 11th grade correlations are below the diagonal. All correlations are significant at $p < .01$.

composition and SEP were entered in the first model and the interaction term was entered in the second model. These results were strong and very similar for both grades (see Table 18.2). In the 5th grade, racial composition and SEP each had significant main effects on reading scores, but only SEP had a significant main effect on math scores. The main effects of SEP were also much stronger than the racial composition main effects. However, for both reading and math scores, there was a strong and significant interaction between racial composition and SEP. Over 50 percent of the variance in reading and math passage rates were explained by the two main effects and racial composition and SEP interaction.

To decompose the interactions, the post hoc probing techniques described by Holmbeck (2002), were used. The results were very similar for both reading and math scores. Figures 18.1 and 18.2 illustrate the plots for reading and

**Table 18.2**
**Regressions of Percentage of Students Meeting State Performance Standards on School Demographic Factors by Grade and Subject Area**

|  | 5th Grade | | | | 11th Grade | | | |
|---|---|---|---|---|---|---|---|---|
|  | Reading | | Math | | Reading | | Math | |
| Racial Comp. | −.05** | −.05** | −.01 | .00 | −.04 | −.05* | −.01 | −.02 |
| SEP | .40** | .45** | .39** | .39** | .27** | .27** | .26** | .26** |
| Racial Comp. X SEP |  | −.17** |  | −.23** |  | −.16* |  | −.16* |
| $R^2$ | .53 | .54 | .50 | .53 | .42 | .44 | .49 | .51 |

*Note:* Race Comp. = School Racial Composition; SEP = School Economic Profile. $N = 748$ elementary schools and 235 high schools. $^{**}p < .01$, $^{*}p < .05$.

**Figure 18.1**
**Percent of 5th Grade African American Students Meeting Expectations in Reading by SEP and School Racial Composition**

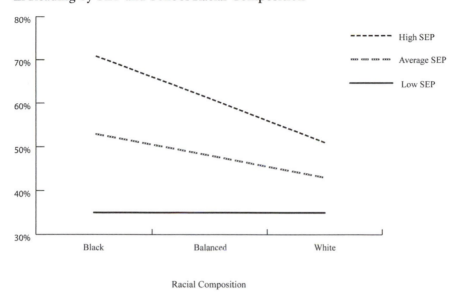

**Figure 18.2**
**Percent of 5th Grade African American Students Meeting Expectations in Math by SEP and School Racial Composition**

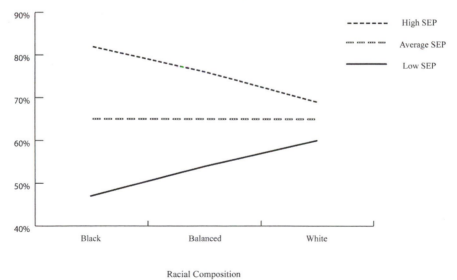

math scores separately. As predicted, those African American students at schools with higher SEP but primarily African American racial composition were significantly more likely to pass the reading and math tests than those at primarily African American and average or low SEP schools. They were also more likely to pass than those at primarily European American and higher, average or lower SEP schools. Also, African American students were least likely to pass in the lowest SEP schools, but especially the lower SEP and primarily African American schools for math. However, very interestingly, SEP did not matter in the primarily European American schools. Their passage rates were very similar in high, average, and lower SEP European American schools for reading and math.

The same analyses were conducted for the 11th grade reading and math passage rates. As can be seen in Table 18.2, the main effects of racial composition were not significant for either reading or math passage rates. Although somewhat smaller than in the 5th grades, the main effects of SEP were still strong and significant in the 11th grade for both reading and math passage rates. Virtually identical to the 5th grade results, the interactions between racial composition and SEP were also strong and significant for both passage rates. The amount of variance explained was still around 50 percent for math, but only about 44 percent for reading scores.

As with the 5th grade scores, post hoc probing techniques were used and the results revealed the same pattern for reading and math scores. Figures 18.3 and 18.4 illustrate the plot for reading and math passage rates. Once again, those African American students at primarily African American but higher SEP schools were significantly more likely to pass both tests than those African American students at any other type of school. Although the average 11th grade math passage rate for African American students was only 21 percent overall, roughly 40 percent of those at the higher SEP but primarily African American schools passed the test. Their passage rates were only about 25 percent at the higher SEP but primarily European American schools. The rates were similar but slightly higher in reading. Also, as with the 5th grade scores, they scored their lowest in the poor primarily African American schools, and SEP did not predict their passage rates in the primarily European American schools.

## DISCUSSION

The purpose of this study was to use empirical data to help African American parents make a more informed decision about the type of schools they should send their children. Prior studies could not make sound recommendations because they did not adequately disentangle the effects of schools' racial compositions from their economic profiles. This study assessed the unique and interactive effects of both demographic factors. We argued that students would perform better in higher SES and primarily African American schools

**Figure 18.3**
**Percent of 11th Grade African American Students Meeting Expectations in Reading by SEP and School Racial Composition**

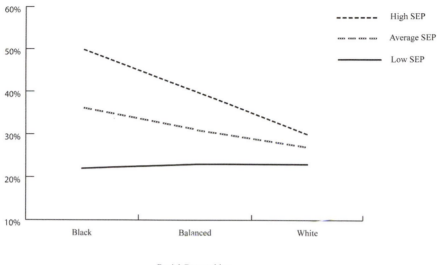

**Figure 18.4**
**Percent of 11th Grade African American Students Meeting Expectations in Math by SEP and School Racial Composition**

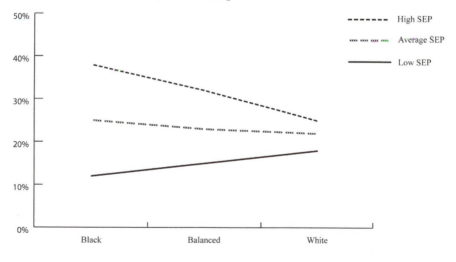

because they would be less likely to face race-based discrimination in tracking and teacher expectations, as well as be less likely to be burdened by social pressures such as stereotype threat or the "acting White" phenomenon. However, unlike in the schools with high proportions of poorer African American students, those African Americans at the schools with more middle and higher SES African American students would have access to the educational resources they need. As predicted, we found that those African American students who attended school with primarily middle and higher SES African American students performed better than African American students at all other schools. This finding was strong and consistent for both math and reading in elementary and even later in high school. We also found that they scored the lowest in schools with primarily lower SES African American students.

Clearly, the main difference between those African American students at schools with primarily poor African Americans and the ones with primarily non-poor African Americans are the resources available to them. The higher SES students tend to live in districts with more educational resources. In fact, the SES of the average student at the school seems to be a stronger predictor of achievement than even the SES of a student's own family. For instance, Rumberger and Palardy (2005) recently found that poor African American students in higher SES schools scored higher on achievement tests than higher SES African American students at low SES schools. The specific mediators of school level SES seem to be greater parental involvement and teacher quality (Mickelson, 2001) and more advanced courses (Byrnes, 2003) at the higher SES schools. For instance, Mickelson (2001) found that poor and segregated African American schools had significantly fewer resources than other schools in the same district. Teachers at poor segregated African American schools in the district were more likely to be pre-service teachers, non-tenured, non-certified, and without a Master's degree. The schools with high percentages of non-poor African Americans probably do not have as many educational resources as the schools with high proportions of upper SES European American students, but they are undoubtedly better equipped than the schools most poor African Americans have to attend.

What is most interesting about the results of the current study is that even though African American students at the schools with primarily higher SES European American students had access to the best school resources, they still performed significantly worse than African American students at schools with primarily higher SES African American students. In fact, the African American students at the schools with higher SES European American students performed about the same as those at the schools with poor European Americans and even those at the schools with average SES African Americans. Thus, it is not just the schools' racial composition or their students' economic profile that matter, but an interactive combination of both. As we discussed previously, this is likely due to those African American students at schools with primarily higher SES European Americans experiencing much greater race-based tracking and expectations, as well as more social pressures to not achieve.

Another interesting finding was that as strong as the effects of SEP were overall, and have been in every prior study, it did not matter for African American students at the primarily European American schools. We predicted that African American students at schools with primarily lower SES European American students would perform significantly worse than those going to schools with wealthier European American students. However, the African American students scored about the same in primarily lower SES and higher SES European American schools. One likely reason is that unlike the schools with large percentages of lower SES African American students, schools with primarily lower SES European American students still have ample educational resources. Prior research has suggested this to be the case (Borman & Overman, 2001).

This study is obviously not without limitations. For one, it is still just correlational and cross sectional. It is possible that those specific African American students at the higher SES primarily African American schools would have performed the best on the achievement tests regardless of the racial composition or the SEP of their school. Given all the research in this area, that is doubtful, but still possible. Since no randomized trial can be performed, the best available evidence would probably be to observe changes in school climate, as a function of changing racial composition, documenting African American academic performance during the process.

Probably the most significant limitation of the current study is that there are a small number of schools in Illinois (or any state) which are primarily African American and have few students from lower SES backgrounds. Thus, the estimates are based on only a few data points. For example, we briefly examined the demographic characteristics of various schools around the country and found that the few schools with high percentages of African Americans and low poverty rates tended to be relegated to the suburbs of primarily African American cities such as Atlanta, Washington DC, and the South Side of Chicago. If there were more schools with that profile, it is possible that the results would be different.

There are important implications we can cautiously draw from this study. Obviously, African American parents need to be concerned about the resources of schools, such as the abundance of AP courses, the educational level of the teachers, and the extracurricular activities. However, they should also know that African American children seem to perform their best when they are surrounded by non-poor African American children, and not wealthy European American children. It could be, as we argue, that those schools are less racist, have higher academic expectations of them, a higher percentage of African American teachers, and have ample educational resources. It could also be that other factors in the children's neighborhoods or homes complement the schools they attend. Whatever future educational researchers discover about such schools, we believe it is appropriate to suggest to parents of African American children that, to the degree possible, they should try to enroll their individual children in schools with high percentages of non-poor African American students.

# REFERENCES

ACT and the Illinois State Board of Education (2007). *Prairie State Achievement Examination Technical Manual 2007*. Springfield, IL: Illinois State Board of Education.

Bankston, C.L., & Caldas, S.J. (2000). White enrollment in non-public school, public school racial composition, and student performance. *The Sociological Quarterly*, *41*, 539–550.

Borman, G.D., & Overman, L.T. (2004). Academic resilience in mathematics among poor and minority students. *The Elementary School Journal, 104* (3), 177–195.

Brooks-Gunn, J., Klebanov, P.K., Smith, J., Duncan, G.J., & Lee, K. (2003). The Black–White test score gap in young children, contribution of test and family characteristics. *Applied Developmental Science*, 7, 239–252.

Byrnes, J.P. (2003). Factors predictive of mathematics achievement in White, Black, and Hispanic 12th graders. *Journal of Educational Psychology*, *95*, 316–326.

Caldas, S.J., & Bankston, C. (2001). Effect of school population socioeconomic status on individual academic achievement. *The Journal of Educational Research*, *90*, 269–277

Coleman, J.S., Campbell, E.Q., Hobson, C.J., McPartland, J., Mood, A.M., Weinfeld, F.D., & York, R.L. (1966). *Equality of educational opportunity*. Washington, D.C.: U.S. Government Printing Office.

Crain, R.L., & Mahard, R.E. (1978). School racial composition and black college attendance and achievement test performance. *Sociology of Education*, *51*, 81–101.

Entwisle, D.R., & Alexander, K.L. (1994). Winter setback: The racial composition of schools and learning to read. *American Sociological Review*, *59*, 446–460.

Fordham, S., & Ogbu, J.U. (1986). Black students' school success: Coping with the "burden of 'acting white.' " *The Urban Review*, *18*, 176–206.

Goldsmith, P.A. (2004). Schools' racial mix, students' optimism, and the Black–White and Latino–White achievement gaps. *Sociology of Education*, 77, 121–147.

Holmbeck, G.N. (2002). Post-hoc probing of significant moderational and mediational effects in studies of pediatric populations. *Journal of Pediatric Psychology*, 27, 87–96.

Illinois State Board of Education Division of Assessment. (2007). *Illinois standards achievement test 2007 technical manual*. Springfield, IL: Illinois State Board of Education.

Ipka, V.W. (2003). At risk children in resegregated schools: an analysis of the achievement gap. *Journal of Instructional Psychology*, *30*, 294–304.

Jencks, C., & Mayer, S.E. (1990). The social consequences of growing up in a poor neighborhood: A review. In M. McGeary & L. Lynn (Eds.), *Inner city poverty in the United States*. Washington, DC: National Academy Press

Jencks, C., & Phillips, M. (1998). *The Black–White test score gap*. Washington DC: The Brookings Institute.

Lee, J. (2004). Multiple facets of inequity in racial and ethnic achievement gaps. *Peabody Journal of Education*, *79*, 51–73.

Mickelson, R.A. (2001). The effects of segregation on African American high school seniors' academic achievement. *Journal of Negro Education*, *68*, 566–587.

Mitchell, G.A. (1989). An evaluation of state-financed school integration in metropolitan Milwaukee. *Wisconsin Policy Research Institute Report*, *2*(5), 1–118.

Rothstein, R. (2004). *Class and schools: Using social, economic, and educational reform to close the Black-White achievement gap*. Washington DC: Economic Policy Institute.

Rumberger, R. & Palardy, G. (2005). Does segregation still matter? The impact of student composition on academic achievement in high school. *Teachers College Record*, *107*, 1999–2045.

Steele, C. (1997). A threat in the air: How stereotypes shape intellectual identity and performance. *American Psychologist*, *52*, 613–629.

Wong, K.K., & Nicotera, A. C. (2004). Brown v. board of education and the Coleman report: social science research and the debate on educational equality. *Peabody Journal of Education*, *79*, 122–135.

· · · · · · · · · · · · · · · · · · · · · · · · · · · · · · · · · · · · · · · · · ·

# 19

# Visible Now? Black Educational Choices for the Few, the Desperate, and the Far Between

*Howard C. Stevenson, Diana T. Slaughter-Defoe,*
*Edith G. Arrington,*
*and Deborah J. Johnson*

"If I don't get him out of this public school, I am going to lose him. I know I am." Two weeks prior to submitting the final draft of this volume to the publisher, one of the editors received a frantic telephone message from an African American mother of an 8-year-old boy asking for financial assistance to get him out of his current predominantly White public school and into a racially diverse private school. "I have no choice but to leave him in the school and he is not advancing." The mother was desperate in her request after reading the research of two of the authors on the emotional experiences of Black students in predominantly White schools. Her worry for her and her child's emotional well-being was clear. "There are no choices . . . I can't take it. He can't take it. He is being stifled emotionally, psychologically, and intellectually." Her desperation was evident in her voice and her tearful request to participate in any research studies we might be conducting to help offset the cost of her child's tuition in a better school.

In our opinion, this is not an extreme response. Given the problems facing Black parents who look for better schooling, we argue that for one's precious children, the consequences of poor schooling are dire enough to remortgage a home, move to live in with relatives in a better school district, or simply home school. There is no question that this mother's problem can be looked at from very different vantage points. Still, the question this mother deals with daily and reminds educational researchers, professionals, and policy-makers to address immediately is, "What do we do for Black students who have few to no educational options?" In this volume, educational researchers have provided qualitative and quantitative research to ultimately address her question, by first examining the consequences of the educational choices presently being made by similarly-, or better-situated Black parents for their children and families.

## COMMITMENT TO THE QUEST FOR EDUCATIONAL EQUITY

The plethora of school reform approaches over the last two decades have all centered on a theme of commitment to equity and egalitarianism. These noble efforts represent no small feat given the suffering that people of color, and African Americans, in particular, have endured within the context of schooling before and since the *Brown v. Board of Education* decision. Most everyone involved with alternative schooling for Black students has hopes and dreams for educational access and empowerment. The contributors to this volume have applied both macro-level and micro-level reasoning to the question of educational choice. Some believe in a universal equity and their school reform research and programmatic efforts are developed accordingly (e.g., Perez-Feltner et al.). Others believe that these ideals are actualized only through microscopic investigations at the level of individuals as they cope with how these ideals do not work within schooling contexts (e.g., C. Wilson Cooper; Mandara et al.).

Our guiding light in compiling this work has been Slaughter and Johnson's 1988 classic volume on independent and parochial schooling, *Visible Now: Blacks in private schools*. Their effort to illuminate the voices of students and parents as they navigated through independent and private schools directs us now as we attempt to clarify educational choice in an age of school reform turmoil. Prior to this volume, perhaps no collected work since *Visible Now* has captured the experiences of Black students and families so broadly. Notwithstanding that the fight for who defines educational quality and choice has become furious since 1988, we should not forget nor make invisible the voices of the recipients or "consumers" of these schooling services.

Schooling has represented the most powerful vehicle toward successful social mobility and full U.S. citizenship for all Americans, as much as it has been the site of racial chaos. Still, the educational equity focus on "all of us" may have resulted in the failure to address the unique schooling struggles of the "few of us" who are different by race and class (and demographic changes indicate that the "few of us" are not actually that few in number). As such, the school reform initiatives to date have been reluctant to focus on subgroups of racialized students and families who differentially experience school environments as less safe, less hopeful, less flexible, less sensitive to cultural diversity or racial literacy, and less competent at teaching students to attain successful social mobility.

In this volume, we found that having multiple educational options outside of public schooling seemed like a pipe-dream for many African American families until the last decade. These options have proven to be significant in a small number of situations, false in some instances and in others, not as substantive as promised. Still, the stress and hope for a better education and life for one's children are deeply held and this yearning seeps through low and high resourced Black communities across the nation. The recent jailing of an African American mother, Kelly Williams-Bolar (Meyer, 2011), for using an alternate address in Akron, Ohio so that her children might enroll and attend a better school in a high academically performing school district, is one example of the desperate impact of both stress and hope on students and families wanting better educational opportunities. Paradoxically, the incident also affirms the depth of struggle entertained by parents who, though marginalized and devalued themselves by society, are nonetheless determined to provide the best for the children.

This volume's interest in the alternatives to public schooling is important because there are many gaps in educational opportunities for Black families, who often rely on luck as much as access. When we consider school choice for Black families, this volume has highlighted that various theoretical, political, legal, and economic contexts may result in vastly different definitions of "choice." Garcia and Stigler, for example, make it clear that the definition of charter schools depends on state laws that vary significantly across the country. For some of the authors in this volume, educational choice is defined by the presence of and access to charter or independent schooling (e.g., Carlson). For others, choice is a dream that is more or less possible after considering the multiple contextual, racial, and legal barriers that block the presence of or access to alternative school choices (e.g., Franklin).

Some authors assert that school choice for Blacks and minorities cannot be understood outside of the self-interests and political maneuvering of Whites seeking to make life better for their children. As such, a critical race theoretical frame, while not specified by any author in understanding the school choice dilemmas of Black parents and students, argues that serious study of this topic implicates entrenched racial politics. As such, Black parents may be holding a promissory note that guarantees the free expression of angst rather than the procurement of quality alternative education. This frames the debate on educational choice by suggesting that Black families hold a "bracketed freedom" in choosing alternative schooling for their children unless they can access larger power sources to rise above the racial politics inherent in U.S. public and private education (see Huerta et al.).

### The Challenges of "Quality Education" for African American Students

In this volume, we find that having access to quality public, charter, or private schooling is a more deeply layered challenge than simply the presence of alternative schooling. The emotional challenges for Black students of surviving, excelling, and graduating from these various schooling environments are no small matter (e.g., Stevenson, Arrington, Brown, Kuriloff et al., Johnson et al.). Quality is open to dispute as well, but there are some fairly clear conclusions that we can draw from this work, using charter schools as an example, given their greatly expanded presence in the academic lives of African American students since *Visible Now* was published in 1988 by Slaughter and Johnson.

One conclusion is that research on charter schools, in general, has neither been proven nor disproven as a solution for Black students' underachievement, brokered access to educational equity, or greater parental voice and empowerment (Huerta et al.; Scott). The quality of research on how Black families navigate the multiple and limited school choice options for their children is mediocre (Lundy-Wagner & Turner). This volume has attempted to raise relevant questions and provide a structure for that research to develop and grow. Still, criticism remains about the lack of rigor as well as the limited culturally relevant framing of educational equity questions for Black students. While charter schooling represents an increasingly frequent educational choice alternative, most studies find them lacking in providing improved quality education. This increase in the frequency of charter schools without the educational improvement benefit has characteristics of "bait-and-switch" and may reflect a more insidious and systemic exclusion of Black students from mainstream academic achievement. "The more, the better" would not be an appropriate theme for the growth of charter schools servicing an increasingly higher percentage of Black students in the United States.

Yet, there is some evidence that Black students in charter schools are making gains equal to and better than their public school counterparts (Lundy-Wagner & Turner). Limited comparison data on public versus private schooling is available to isolate the elements that are central to these gains and more research is necessary. In some cases, public schooling is faring as well as independent and charter schooling with respect to academic outcomes and extracurricular activities. It appears that when parents have choices, they feel better about their children having the opportunity to actualize the dream of success and financial stability that these choices offer.

Several chapters in this volume propose that future research appreciates these multiple yet limited educational choice options. Unfortunately, for low resourced Black families who are forced to take advantage of the least successful school choice options, their aspirations of future social mobility is "bracketed" as well as their freedom. African American parents' hopes and dreams for their children are like any other parents' hopes and dreams. But, if their choices amount to no more than relief from their children's educational potential falling into the hands of the worst schools (schools that foreshadow a "school to prison" pipeline), rather than into the hands of the best schooling, their dreams will not be realized. In fact, it could be argued that in the case of school closings and legal barriers to the creation of charter schools in some states, educational choices for Black students are decreasing by virtue of a Darwinian attrition process. The poorest families get to choose from the least effective school options, which fight furiously and unsuccessfully to procure the best resources and thus die in the fight to improve public education. So many Black families are left where they started. The loss of educational choice is an untold and invisible story that Black families experience without prediction. From these chapters, we have also learned that what is good for market forces may not be what is empowering for the Black community of families.

### Racial Conflict and Educational Choice

Throughout this volume, authors debate the politics of racial hierarchy as a static reality despite novel educational reform efforts and how these efforts can often collide with the promise of racial inclusivity. As such, school leadership matters in clarifying this tension. Through historical framing, Shange and Slaughter-Defoe highlight the subtle ways independent school administrators lead in the age of multiculturalism politics. Black educational choice is defined through the administrator's lens and leadership approach toward population diversity. While Oak Lawn Academy had numerical diversity, the head of school eschewed cultural diversity (mostly as a numerical reality) and voice as an irrelevant byproduct of maintaining a commitment to conservative elitist intellectual values. Conversely, Roman School's head was viscerally and consciously engaged to fight educational racism. By doing so, he shifted the educational excellence bar from an ecumenical understanding of educational equity to one where the trees are as or more important in defining the forest. That is, the majority of students ("all of us") benefit only if the negative experiences of Black and other students of color ("few of us") are addressed, their rejection reduced, and their assimilation rendered less necessary.

Many Black students' academic motivation and intellectual curiosity is reduced once they get access to the educational opportunity that results from their parents' choosing the best schools. Kuriloff and colleagues assert that despite the equal academic achievement abilities that Black students share with all students upon entry to independent schools, the achievement disparities begin after entry. Their work highlights social and contextual factors that inhibit student academic achievement through emotional burdens. Focusing the lens on the "few" continues as Arrington, Stevenson, Brown, Johnson, and Cooper use research tools that target the "both–and" racialized experiences of students and parents. Key to their focus rests on Slaughter-Defoe's earlier proclamation of schools as "contexts of socialization." That is, since schools racially socialize whether or not they consciously admit to it, direct research methods and analyses on racial coping are necessary. Even when Black families choose independent schooling to escape the safety and/or academic concerns of public schooling, they must still face challenges to their racial identities, challenges to which educational leadership ought be sensitive. The "capital" associated with parental race/class is nicely discussed in Rana et al., who present a context in which Black immigrant youth are parented by well-meaning and somewhat more privileged White foster parents. Black students and Black parents are often left to make meaning of the school's racial amnesia, denial, and illiteracy about the multiple socialization processes. Through their voices, Black students reveal that it is both academically enriching and psychologically jarring to be one of the few in a predominantly White and highly economically resourced school. Racial stress presents itself as a particular contextual insult that if addressed is a coping triumph, but if not, may become a coping failure.

Balancing the hassles and the uplifts of predominantly White independent schools is also racially stressful for parents who directly and vicariously witness their children's growth and regression of academic and racial identities, in the face of "subliminal" racial socialization. Racial counter-socialization or the direct teaching and reappraising of racial stress coping may be a better way to help parents and students understand the choices they have available to them—what Cooper calls that Critical Third Space. Sharing of one's racial struggles was a useful strategy to uncover both parent and student fears of becoming successful survivors of independent schooling. Within the research interviews and focus groups, the safety for students and parents to talk openly about their frustration with and resolution of the school's racial politics can call schools to greater accountability in developing diversity mission policies and practices that are fluid rather than static or symbolic. It so happens that the racially discriminatory experiences perceived and experienced by both students and parents can redefine what "choice" means. If schools can create safe spaces to listen to and "hear" these voices of pain and promise, ingredients for racially literate schooling environments may recast the view of these schools as, "predominantly White, but."

## FUTURE CONSIDERATIONS

Partly due to limited space, time, and knowledge of the topics, we did not address other relevant areas of school choice, such as home schooling and African-centered or culturally responsive schooling. Though on the rise, less than one percent of Black children are home-schooled, and a number of historically significant African-centered schools (e.g., Chicago's Institute for Positive Education) have reinvented themselves as charters. Nonetheless, the growing development of home-schooling among African American families, and of African-centered and culturally responsive charter schooling are important areas of study for future volumes on this topic. This latter group was not well established within the current charter movement but as they grow, their worth may prove to be the missing element in explaining whether charter schooling for Black students marries cultural affirmation to academic achievement. Commentators (Franklin, Carlson) observe that other earlier successful initiatives are frequently abandoned in the wake of new political hegemonies. Therefore, political and economic power also continues to be required, coupled with the intense scrutiny and monitoring of all educational reform initiatives by future cadres of scholars who firmly refuse to "believe it until they see it."

Our collective goal in this volume has primarily been to keep visible the experiences of Black parents and students as they navigate private, charter (public) schooling, and public schooling generally, in this new century. These voices are daily at risk of extinction and deserve hearing at macro- and micro-systemic levels. The contributors to this volume have found that parent and student voices on the educational quality issue are sometimes heard through strong assertions, fearful whispers and yes, even in desperate pleadings, but not without political power. Voice alone is not enough to keep visible the unique educational experiences of Black parents and students. Future research should consider mixed method strategies that integrate systemic, cultural, political, economic, and individual factors that explain academic and resource investment gaps for Black families. Non-public schooling cannot tout or rest on its "alternative" identity status unless it acts to remedy distal and proximal racial politics for the "few" as a central equity issue for all students. Until the least resourced family among us receives the best schooling experience that is considerate of their background, lens, desperation, and potential and leads to concrete academic achievement, educational choice will remain an unfulfilled option.

## REFERENCE

Meyer, E. (2011, January 5). Unusual trial ready to begin in student residency debate. *Beacon Journal*, http://www.ohio.com/news/112920979.html

# About the Editors and Contributors

## Editors

**Dr. DIANA T. SLAUGHTER-DEFOE** is the Constance E. Clayton Professor Emerita in Urban Education in the Graduate School of Education at the University of Pennsylvania. With Dr. Deborah J. Johnson, in 1988 she edited *Visible Now: Blacks in private schools*, published by Greenwood Press.

**Dr. HOWARD C. STEVENSON** is Associate Professor of Education and former chair of the Applied Psychology and Human Development Division in the Graduate School of Education at the University of Pennsylvania. His research interests include the development of theory, measurement, and interventions on racial/ethnic socialization as a mediator of racial stress for youth and families.

**Dr. EDITH G. ARRINGTON** is a Licensed Psychologist whose research, consultation and writing interests focus on diversity, race and development across contexts. She is currently a Project Manager at the OMG Center for Collaborative Learning in Philadelphia, PA.

**Dr. DEBORAH J. JOHNSON** is Professor of Human Development and Family Studies at Michigan State University. She has published on parental socialization and African American child outcomes and she was co-editor of a special section on "Excavating Culture" and ethnic/racial socialization in the journal *Cultural Diversity and Ethnic Minority Psychology*. She has also coauthored publications with Diana Slaughter-Defoe.

## Contributors

**Ms. MEETA BANERJEE** is a Doctoral candidate in the Ecological-Community Psychology program at Michigan State University. With Dr. Deborah Johnson, she has published an article titled "Ethnic socialization and parental involvement: Predictors of cognitive performance in African American children" in the *Journal of Youth and Adolescence*.

**Dr. JAMES A. BANKS** holds the Kerry and Linda Killinger Endowed Chair in Diversity Studies and is Founding Director of the Center for Multicultural Education at the University of Washington, Seattle. Professor Banks is a member of the National Academy of Education and is a past President of the American Educational Research Association (AERA) and of the National Council for the Social Studies (NCSS). His most recent book is *Routledge International Companion to Multicultural Education*. He is editing the *Encyclopedia of Diversity in Education* (4 volumes) that will be published by Sage in 2012.

**Ms. LAURA V. BATES** is a Research Associate with University Outreach and Engagement at Michigan State University. As research manager for the longitudinal study of resilience and adaptation among Sudanese refugee youth, she is co-author of a number of publications based on the research.

**Dr. ENORA BROWN** is Associate Professor in the Department of Educational Policy Studies and Research in the School of Education at DePaul University. Her publications include: *The Critical Middle School Reader* (2005), and articles and chapters in critical studies in human development, adolescent and teacher identity, and educational policy and youth development, with an emphasis on race and social class.

**Dr. KAREN G. CARLSON** is Assistant Professor and Chair of Educational Administration Programs at Dominican University in River Forest, IL. She is a retired school superintendent, having served in educational leadership positions including associate superintendent and principal of two awarding-winning urban schools, and presently consults nationwide with school districts.

**Dr. ROBERT COOPER** is Associate Professor in the Urban Schooling Division at the UCLA Graduate School of Education and Information Studies. He writes extensively on issues of educational equity and urban school policy and leadership.

**Mr. CHAD D'ENTREMONT** is the Director of Research and Policy at Strategies for Children, Inc. He is also Doctoral candidate in the Politics and Education program at Teachers College, Columbia University; his research focuses on how ideology shapes education policy, with specific attention paid to school choice and the privatization of educational services.

**Dr. V.P. FRANKLIN** is the Presidential Chair and Distinguished Professor of History and Education, at the University of California, Riverside. He also serves as the Editor of *The Journal of African American History* (formerly *The Journal of Negro History*).

**Dr. BRUCE FULLER** is Professor of Education and Public Policy at the University of California, Berkeley. His work focuses on how decentralized organizations might deliver on their promise of lifting children and families, and building from local cultural strengths; he is author of *Standardized Childhood* (Stanford), *Inside Charter Schools* (Harvard), and *Government Confronts Culture* (Taylor & Francis).

**Dr. DAVID R. GARCIA** is Associate Professor in the Mary Lou Fulton Teachers College at Arizona State University. His research has appeared in numerous journals including *Teachers College Record, Educational Policy*, and the *Journal of School Choice;* and he is presently co-editor of two academic journals, *Education Policy Analysis Archives* and *Review of Research in Education*.

**Ms. RACHEL GARVER** is a Doctoral student in Urban Education in the department of Teaching and Learning at New York University. She also serves as a Graduate Assistant for Research and Evaluation at the Metropolitan Center for Urban Education.

**Mr. E.C. HEDBERG** is a Research Scientist at NORC at the University of Chicago. His current research focuses on using state data systems to better understand design effects for education experiments.

**Dr. LUIS A. HUERTA** is Associate Professor of Education and Public Policy at Teachers College-Columbia University. His research and scholarship focus on school choice reforms (including charter schools, homeschooling, tuition tax credits and vouchers) and school finance policy; recent scholarship is published in *Educational Policy, Journal of Education Finance*, and the *Peabody Journal of Education*.

**Dr. PETER KURILOFF** is Professor in the Foundations and Practices of Education at the University of Pennsylvania's Graduate School of Education and Research Director of the Center for the Study of Boys' and Girls' Lives (www.csbgl.org). His research interests lie in studying the effects of schooling and gender (at the intersection of race, class, and ethnicity) on the wellbeing of children.

**Dr. VALERIE C. LUNDY-WAGNER** is Assistant Professor and Faculty Fellow of Higher and Postsecondary Education at New York University in the Steinhardt School for Culture, Education, and Human Development. Her research focuses on the relationship of ethnicity/race, gender, and socioeconomic status as they pertain to degree completion overall, in the STEM fields, and at historically Black colleges and universities.

**Dr. JELANI MANDARA** is Associate Professor of Human Development and Social Policy, School of Education and Social Policy, at Northwestern University. He studies how family dynamics and other contextual factors influence African American child development.

**Ms. INEZ MOORE** is a Master's student in Education Administration and Policy at Howard University, Washington, DC.

**Mr. MICHAEL J. MYERS II** is the Special Assistant to the President of award-winning Paul Quinn College in Dallas, Texas. He is the author of a forthcoming chapter entitled, "Setting an Example: The Philanthropic Contributions of Alpha Phi Alpha Fraternity, Incorporated."

**Ms. LYNETTE PARKER** is a Doctoral candidate in the Policy, Organizations, Measurement and Evaluation Program at the University of California Berkeley.

**Dr. LARA PEREZ-FELKNER** is a Postdoctoral Fellow at NORC at the University of Chicago. Her research examines the social context of schools in relation to college and career track outcomes, with a particular focus on underrepresented minorities and gender.

**Dr. DESIREE B. QIN** is Assistant Professor of Human Development and Family Studies at Michigan State University. Her research focuses on understanding how immigration, culture, gender, and ecological contexts impact adolescent development.

**Ms. MEENAL RANA** is a Doctoral candidate in the department of Human Development and Family Studies, Michigan State University. She was collaborator and research assistant for the study of resilience and adaptation among Sudanese refugee youth.

**Mr. SCOTT RICHMAN** is a Doctoral candidate in Human Development and Social Policy at Northwestern University. He studies determinants of parenting behaviors and ethnic and gender disparities in achievement and social outcomes.

**Mr. ANDREW SALTARELLI** is a Doctoral candidate in the College of Education at Michigan State University. He was a research assistant for the longitudinal study of resilience and adaptation among Sudanese refugee youth.

**Dr. BARBARA SCHNEIDER** is the John A. Hannah Chair and University Distinguished Professor in the College of Education and Department of Sociology at Michigan State University. Author of 13 books and numerous articles, her research focuses on the social context of schools, families, and work.

**Dr. JANELLE T. SCOTT** is Assistant Professor in the Graduate School of Education and African American Studies Department at the University of California at Berkeley. She is the editor of *School Choice and Diversity: What the Evidence Says* (2005, Teachers College Press).

**Ms. SAVANNAH SHANGE** is a Doctoral student and Fontaine Fellow pursuing a joint degree in Africana Studies and Education at the University of Pennsylvania. Continuing research interests in racialization, her dissertation research focuses on the impact of gentrification and neoliberal dispossession on working-class communities of color in San Francisco.

**Ms. AMANDA C. SOTO** is a Research Associate with the Center for the Study of Boys' and Girls' Lives in Philadelphia, Pennsylvania and has been an instructor at the University of Pennsylvania. Through CSBGL, she has participated in several studies exploring student achievement and structural issues in independent schools.

**Ms. MONICA L. STIGLER** is a Doctoral student in the Educational Leadership and Policy Studies program at the Mary Lou Fulton Teachers College at Arizona State University.

**Dr. FATIMA VARNER** is a Postdoctoral Research Fellow with the Center for the Study of Black Youth in Context at the University of Michigan. She studies the influence of family processes on African American adolescents' academic achievement and mental health.

**Dr. HERBERT M. TURNER III** is President and Principal Scientist at ANALYTICA, Inc., and Adjunct Assistant Professor at the PENN Graduate School of Education.

**Dr. CAMILLE M. WILSON** is Associate Professor in the Department of Educational Leadership and Cultural Foundations at the University of North Carolina at Greensboro. Her research and teaching focus on school-family relations, transformative leadership, and equity-oriented reform that integrates critical, culturally relevant, and gendered perspectives.

# Index

**DATE DUE**

Demco

**Property of
Baker College
of Allen Park**